D0268501

Developments in West European Politics 2

Developments titles available from Palgrave

Laura Cram, Desmond Dinan and Neill Nugent (eds)
DEVELOPMENTS IN THE EUROPEAN UNION

Patrick Dunleavy, Andrew Gamble, Richard Heffernan, Ian Holliday
and Gillian Peele (eds)
DEVELOPMENTS IN BRITISH POLITICS 6
(Revised Edition)

Alain Guyomarch, Peter A. Hall, Jack Hayward and Howard Machin
(eds)
DEVELOPMENTS IN FRENCH POLITICS 2

Gillian Peele, Christopher Bailey, Bruce Cain and B. Guy Peters (eds)
DEVELOPMENTS IN AMERICAN POLITICS 4

Paul Heywood, Erik Jones and Martin Rhodes (eds)
DEVELOPMENTS IN WEST EUROPEAN POLITICS 2

Gordon Smith, William E. Paterson and Stephen Padgett (eds)
DEVELOPMENTS IN GERMAN POLITICS 2

Stephen White, Judy Batt and Paul Lewis (eds)
DEVELOPMENTS IN CENTRAL AND EAST EUROPEAN
POLITICS 2

Stephen White, Alex Pravda and Zvi Gitelman (eds)
DEVELOPMENTS IN RUSSIAN POLITICS 5

Of related interest

Ian Holliday, Andrew Gamble and Geraint Parry (eds)
FUNDAMENTALS IN BRITISH POLITICS

If you have any comments or suggestions regarding the above or
other possible *Developments* titles, please write to Steven Kennedy,
Publishing Director, Palgrave, Houndmills, Basingstoke RG21 6XS,
UK, or e-mail s.kennedy@palgrave.com

Developments in West European Politics 2

edited by

Paul Heywood

Erik Jones

and

Martin Rhodes

palgrave

First published 2002 by
PALGRAVE
Houndmills, Basingstoke, Hampshire RG21 6XS and
175 Fifth Avenue, New York, N.Y. 10010
Companies and representatives throughout the world

PALGRAVE is the new global academic imprint of
St. Martin's Press LLC Scholarly and Reference Division and
Palgrave Publishers Ltd (formerly Macmillan Press Ltd).

ISBN 0–333–92868–7 hardback
ISBN 0–333–92869–5 paperback

This new book is designed as a direct replacement for *Developments in
West European Politics*, edited by Martin Rhodes, Paul Heywood and
Vincent Wright (1997)

This book is printed on paper suitable for recycling and
made from fully managed and sustained forest sources.

A catalogue record for this book is available
from the British Library.

Library of Congress Cataloging-in-Publication Data

Developments in West European politics.—2nd ed./edited by Paul Heywood,
Erik Jones, Martin Rhodes.
      p.cm.
   Includes bibliographical references and index.
   ISBN 0–333–92868–7—ISBN 0–333–92869–5 (pbk.)
   1. European federation. 2. Europe—Economic integration. 3. Europe—
Politics and government—1989– 4. Europe, Western—Politics and
government—1989– I. Heywood, Paul. II. Jones, Erik. III. Rhodes, Martin,
1956 Feb. 23–
   JN15.D47 2002
   940.55'9—dc21   2002017001

10   9   8   7   6   5   4   3   2
11   10   09   08   07   06   05   04   03

Printed and bound in Great Britain by
Creative Print & Design (Wales), Ebbw Vale

*This volume is dedicated to the memory of
Vincent Wright*

Contents

List of Tables

Preface and Acknowledgements

A lot has changed in West European politics since this volume's prede-cessor appeared in 1997. Indeed, at times the pace of change has been staggering. During the months in which we put *Developments in West European Politics 2* (*DWEP 2*) together, our contributors have had to deal with the rapid deepening and widening of the European Union (including the ups and downs of the European single currency, the euro). They have confronted the re-emergence of popular protest both against the traditional evils of racism and inequality – as in some of the north-ern cities of England – and against the more novel issues surrounding 'globalization' – as in Gothenburg or Prague. They have witnessed the roller coaster performance of the so-called dot.com economy, the upsurge of concern over immigration and xenophobia, the continuing and accelerating transformation of European welfare states, the precip-itous and alarming decline in voter engagement, the further rise of fundamentalism (both religious and otherwise), and the traumatic events of 11 September 2001 as well as their aftermath.

Within the context of these developments, our understanding of West European politics has changed as well. The principal issues remain much the same – integration, globalization, security, participation, extremism, environmentalism, corruption, and so forth. However, our perspectives on these issues have adapted to encompass not only news-worthy events but also new insights, new scholarship, new actors, and new institutions. The challenge, therefore, has been to develop a frame-work within which our analysis could be comprehensive and yet still comprehensible, and through which we could focus on developments in West European politics without allowing ourselves to be driven simply to reflect on the 'news' as it happens (or has happened).

Our response has been to emphasize continuity as well as change. Hence, in many respects, our contributors stand on the shoulders of those who participated in the first volume called *Developments in West European Politics*. More specifically, we as editors have drawn inspiration from the scholarship and fellowship of the late Vincent Wright, to whose memory this volume is dedicated. However, apart from two of the editors, all of the contributors to *DWEP 2* are new. And while some of the themes remain the same, all of the analysis is new as well. In this sense, *DWEP 2* does not revise the claims made in its predecessor. Rather, it builds on that previous volume just as it builds on the scholarship and analysis that has been published both before and since *Developments in West European Politics* appeared in 1997. *DWEP 2* is as new as the developments it encompasses.

As editors, we would like to express our thanks to all of our contributors for their patience and understanding during the long production process. Of course a part of that gratitude should spill over onto the corps of doctoral students both at Nottingham (particularly Mette Jolly and Siobhan Daly) and at the European University Institute who helped us to track down incomplete bibliographic references and related source material. We would also like to thank Steven Kennedy and Cecily Wilson at Palgrave for their help in shepherding us through the numerous drafts and revisions. Finally, we should acknowledge the institutional support provided by the University of Nottingham and the European University Institute, without which this undertaking would never have been possible.

Paul Heywood
Erik Jones
Martin Rhodes

Acknowledgements

The initial analysis for Chapter 5, 'Participation and Voting', was carried out at the ZA-EUROLAB at the Zentralarchiv (ZA) für Empirische Sozialforschung an der Universität Köln with support from the European Community (Access to Research Infrastructure Action of the Improving Human Potential Programme). The author is grateful to the Director of the ZA, Ekkehard Mochmann, for the invitation and the use of facilities. Particular thanks are also due to the staff of the EUROLAB within the ZA: Reiner Mauer, Ingvill C. Mochmann and Wolfgang Zenk-Möltgen for their help and support.

For Chapter 7, 'Extremist Movements', the author thanks Uwe Backes (TU Dresden), Roger Eatwell (University of Bath), Adam Lent (Sheffield University), Neil Macmaster (University of East Anglia), and the editors for their valuable comments on earlier drafts.

Notes on the Contributors

David Broughton is Senior Lecturer in Politics, School of European Studies, University of Cardiff.

Giovanna Campani is Senior Lecturer, Inter-cultural Education, Faculty of Education Sciences, University of Florence.

Neil Carter is Senior Lecturer in Politics, Department of Politics, University of York.

Michelle Cini is Senior Lecturer in Politics and Jean Monnet Lecturer in European Community Studies, Department of Politics, University of Bristol.

Rainer Eising is a Research Fellow, Institute for Political Science, University of Hagen.

Paul Heywood is Sir Francis Hill Professor of European Politics, School of Politics, University of Nottingham.

Erik Jones is Reader in Political Science and Jean Monnet Chair in European Integration, University of Nottingham.

Christian Joppke is Professor of Sociology, Department of Political and Social Sciences, European University Institute.

Michael Keating is Professor of Regional Studies, Department of Political and Social Sciences, European University Institute.

David Levy is Controller Public Policy, British Broadcasting Corporation.

Cas Mudde is Lecturer in Politics, Department of Politics, University of Edinburgh. (From July 2002, Lecturer in Politics, University of Antwerp-UFSIA.)

Véronique Pujas is CNRS–CIDSP Research Fellow, Institute for Political Studies, University of Grenoble.

Martin Rhodes is Professor of European Public Policy, Department of Political and Social Sciences, European University Institute.

Thomas Risse is Professor of International Politics, Department of Political and Social Science, Free University of Berlin.

Helene Sjursen is a Senior Researcher, Advanced Research on the Europeanization of the Nation-State (ARENA), University of Oslo.

Paul Webb is Professor of Politics, School of Social Sciences, University of Sussex.

Europe

KEY:
Azer.	Azerbaijan
Bos.	Bosnia
K.	Kosovo
L.	Liechtenstein
Ma.	Macedonia
Mo.	Monte-Negro
Rus. Fed.	Russian Federation

ICELAND

NORWAY
Oslo

Stockholm
SWEDEN

NORTH
SEA

Dublin
IRELAND
GREAT
BRITAIN

DENMARK
Copenhagen

London
Amsterdam
NETHERLANDS
Berlin
GERMANY

Brussels
BELGIUM

ATLANTIC OCEAN

Paris
LUXEMBOURG

Prague
CZECH REP.

FRANCE

Berne
SWITZERLAND
L.
Vienna
AUSTRIA

BAY OF
BISCAY

Ljubljana
SLOVENIA
Zagreb
CROATIA

ANDORRA
MONACO

Bos.
Sarajevo

PORTUGAL
Lisbon
Madrid
SPAIN

ITALY
Rome

CORSICA

BALLEARIC IS.
SARDINIA

MEDITERRANEAN SEA

SICILY

MOROCCO

MALTA

TUNISIA

Introduction: West European States Confront the Challenge of a New Millennium

PAUL HEYWOOD, ERIK JONES AND MARTIN RHODES

In the post-Cold War era, when the political constants which defined the world order throughout the second half of the twentieth century have been undermined, even our most basic points of reference are subject to challenge. One key issue which confronts any analyst of 'developments in West European politics' is to identify what we understand by the term 'Western Europe'. The Cold War provided a simple dividing line according to political ideology and economic organization, but that no longer holds. What was once the German Democratic Republic has been re-united with the former 'West' Germany, whilst countries like Hungary and the Czech Republic now exhibit many of the characteristics we have traditionally associated with the non-communist 'west European' states.

A logical step might be to use the European Union (EU) as a proxy for 'Western Europe'. However, even though none of the former Eastern Bloc countries have yet become members, the EU is not a good synonym: the capitals of Austria and Finland, which are both EU member states, are farther to the East than the capitals of Croatia and the Czech Republic, both of which are still hoping to join. And other 'western' states, such as Switzerland and Norway, are not members of the EU. Nor does language provide much help. Austrian German is too far to the East, whilst Finnish – with its distant links to Hungarian, Turkish and Korean – is too far to the West. Religion also falls short as an indicator. Most countries in Europe (from west to east) contain significant non-Christian minorities, whilst Catholic Poland is farther to the East than the predominantly Islamic Albania – and indeed Armenia has a claim to be the world's first Christian country.

If defining the notion of 'Western Europe' presents particular challenges, then deciding what the idea of 'politics' might encompass within such an area poses even greater difficulties. This is not the place for a philosophical discussion of the meaning of the term 'politics' – but, nonetheless, choices have to be made about its scope and referents in the context of analysing recent developments. Thus, should we focus on elections, or on what happens between polling dates? Should politics be

1

seen as being about aspirations or about realities? Should the focus be local, regional, transnational or supranational? Where does politics end and security or economics begin? How can they be disentangled and, indeed, does it even make sense any longer to distinguish between politics, security and economics? More to the point, what can be seen as not being politics?

Such critical reflection may seem somewhat ironic given that Western Europe provided the paradigm for the organization of modern politics, in the shape of the nation-state. The Peace of Westphalia in 1648 marked the end of the Holy Roman Empire and the establishment of the modern state, constructed around the concept of territorial sovereignty. The French Revolution of 1789, which gave rise to the idea of sovereignty resting with the people, marked the decline of the dynastic empires of the West and further underlined the centrality of the nation-state as the organizing principle for modern politics. Indeed, during the nineteenth century, nation-states steadily conquered the globe with their fusion of territorial and popular sovereignty. And in the twentieth century, the nation-state sparked three global conflicts – two hot though brief, and one cold but enduring. What the nation-state will accomplish in the twenty-first century remains to be seen. What remains clear, amidst the confusion that characterizes the post-Cold War global order, is that the nation-state continues to represent a potent force in West European politics.

The twin context of global uncertainty combined with institutional resilience forms the backdrop to this second iteration of *Developments in West European Politics*. As in the first volume, our starting point is the recognition that Western Europe is experiencing a period of accelerating change. Much of this change is confusing, much of its impact is contingent, and many of its implications are complex – hence, the uncertainty. However, it is important to recognize that not everything is uncertain. Despite the rapid pace of change – in areas ranging from ideology to international economic organization, from civic participation to trust in government, from global security to perceptions of risk – there are some aspects of political organization which appear to remain constant. The challenge for analysis, therefore, is to identify what the constants are and what they may tell us about the developments with which this volume is concerned.

The chapters which follow are organized into four parts which frame our analysis of developments in West European politics around the continuing centrality of the nation-state. Our working assumption is that the nation-state remains the central edifice through which political organization is structured, and that as such it changes only slowly. Therefore the focus in this volume is on how states in Western Europe have been affected by the myriad changes which have taken place in the context within which they operate. We start by examining the relationship between the state and Europe, before turning to a series of further questions about the state: does it still command the loyalty of its citizens; do its institutions deliver on popular demands; can it respond to new challenges? Many of the responses provided by the contributors to this volume focus on specific contexts. Thus, individual chapters analyse developments in relationships between, for instance, the state and the European Union or the state and society, or else developments in particular problem areas such as security, the environment or organized crime.

One central point which emerges clearly is that, although the nation-state itself remains essentially unchanged in terms of representing a specific combination of territorial organization and popular sovereignty, the capacities and competences of individual states have changed significantly over time. For example, France and Germany have not lost their physical or cultural identity, yet neither state any longer controls its own currency, both are subject to a raft of commitments made in international and European law, both are obliged to compete – or at least enable their firms to compete – in increasingly integrated European and world markets regulated according to international agreements, and both must seek to represent their political, commercial and diplomatic interests in a variety of international and supranational fora. Thus, whilst at one level the nation-state remains the same, it is clear also that at other levels the state has changed. Taken together, the chapters in this volume seek to analyse and explain these continuities and changes.

Globalization, integration, and the nation-state in Europe

The challenges confronting the European nation-state stem in large part from changes in the world economy. Since the Second World War, the international trade in goods, services and capital has become a vital part of daily commerce in all advanced industrial societies, whether they are small or large. Correspondingly, the ideal of national self-sufficiency has become ever more unrealistic. Nation-states depend upon one another in a complex division of labour that surely brings traditional conceptions of territorial sovereignty into question. Meanwhile, the revolution in information technology and manufacturing practice has liberated firms from the constraint of geography and – in many senses, but not all – from the grasp of state regulatory authority. The point here is not that states can no longer control firms, but rather that the nature and extent of that control are changing. The change involved is primarily one of scale and dimension, rather than fact. Indeed, it could be argued that 'globalizing' trends simply reinforce the argument developed by Lindblom (1977) that business enjoys a structurally entrenched position of privilege in capitalist societies, but one which has become increasingly extended to an international arena. Hence whether or not 'globalization' is the bugbear of the modern state, what is undeniable is that Europe's nation-states must adapt to economic changes if they are to survive, and that such adaptation will continue to take place mainly in the regulatory environment within which their economies operate.

Within this increasingly globalized world, one of the most contested issues in contemporary Europe is EU integration. The very meaning, scope and implications of integration are subject to intense debate. For the so-called Eurosceptics, an increasingly vociferous force in many EU states, Europe is the apotheosis of the state in crisis. The introduction of the single currency is but a stepping stone towards the creation of a federal 'super-state', which will result in nation-states not only losing their sovereignty, but also their very identity. For the so-called Euro-optimists, Europe is the necessary response to globalization and represents a rescue of the nation-state. Indeed, the logic of the EU's development demands ever-greater integration, which is seen as essential to underpin its future effectiveness as new members join. However, as Erik Jones demonstrates in his opening chapter, there is not only uncertainty within the EU over its future direction, but also seemingly contradictory trends according to the policy area in question. Critically, decision-making within the European Union remains subject to the constraints of majority voting – albeit, in many cases, qualified majority voting (QMV). On a host of different issues, running from economic and monetary union (EMU), through common foreign and security policy (CFSP), to justice and home affairs, institutional reform and the key issue of enlargement, the reality of decision-making within the EU is one that shows little evidence of trends towards centralization or federalization. Instead, nation-states retain considerable capacity for autonomy and, indeed, obstruction – witness the increasing number of 'opt-outs' demanded to accommodate special cases (for instance, the UK and Ireland on the Schengen Acquis; Denmark and the UK on the Maastricht Treaty; Finland on energy liberalization). Thus, in our assessment of the relationship between the European Union and the nation-state, and how it has evolved over recent years, we should be aware that the EU remains multilayered and that its basic structures are distinctly 'unfederal' – in spite of the growing competence of supranational authorities.

In looking at the nature of the European economy, and in particular at the nature of the changing relationships between market integration, currency union and Europe's social polity, Martin Rhodes illustrates a number of complex, subtle and – again – apparently contradictory changes. Nonetheless, the central message that emerges from Rhodes' chapter is that the nation-state remains the key player in all the major areas of concern over economic policy within Europe, especially in regard to control of the social welfare system – in spite of growing importance of the European policy context. In practice, it does appear to be the case that there is a new polity in the making with a shift towards a less rigid structure of 'network governance' in a number of policy fields, characterized by flexible and multilevel arrangements. However, as is also suggested in the chapter by Jones, several of these developments have little to do with any form of federalization and there remains considerable uncertainty about future directions in the balance and mix between nation-states on the one hand, and any wider conception of Europe or the European Union on the other.

Economic globalization is not the only major challenge to which states must adapt; the conditions for war and peace have changed as well. And when we turn to the question of security, traditionally one of the primordial concerns of any nation-state, Helene Sjursen argues that there have been some significant developments in the post-Cold War era. Whilst European nation-states still think in terms of 'the state' or the group of states with which they are associated as representing one dimension of their security interests, they are also increasingly starting to view the world in terms of non-territorial threats, and to link security issues more directly to international rules and norms. The attacks launched on the United States of America on 11 September 2001, with their profound implications for security in Western Europe too, provide a graphic example of how conventional notions of territorial security are having to be revised. The 'state' as such is certainly not being removed from the equation, but its position is nonetheless becoming more relative within a broader, and ever-more complex, international context. Different states in Europe have rethought to different degrees their position *vis-à-vis* their neighbours and *vis-à-vis* the international security environment – as clearly demonstrated by Sjursen in the cases of France, Germany and Norway. One conclusion which emerges is that national idiosyncrasies ensure that European security issues are still perceived differently in different national contexts. It was ever thus, but it does mean that although European states must develop new understandings of their security interests, and in spite of the provisions for the Common Foreign and Security Policy (CFSP) established at Maastricht and Amsterdam, there is no single 'European' view which is likely to render national viewpoints redundant – in spite of the pronouncements made by EU leaders in the immediate aftermath of the 11 September attack.

Legitimacy

If nation-states retain their central importance in providing the organizational framework of politics in Western Europe, they nonetheless face an increasing number of challenges to their ability to carry out their traditional roles. It has often been observed that in democratic states there is a close, even mutually interdependent, relationship between legitimacy and effectiveness. However, as we have seen, states have been confronted by a range of new challenges in the context of global uncertainty. Their citizens naturally look to states to provide meaning and order to such uncertainties, yet when states fail to deliver – as they almost inevitably must – their legitimacy may be called into question, in turn giving rise to more challenges.

One of the most pressing challenges in contemporary Western Europe concerns the question of identity: to what extent has the development of the European Union given rise to a new 'European' identity, or do collective identities remain firmly anchored within nation-states? If the latter, as many believe, then the process of European integration can be seen as a threat not just to sovereignty and policy autonomy, but also to the very coherence of national identity. It is perhaps unsurprising, therefore, that there has been a rise in the political salience of sub-national identities, partly in reaction to globalization and European integration. However, Thomas Risse argues in his chapter against essentialist understandings of identity, which see them rooted to some form of ethnic core, and instead uses the metaphors of 'layer cake' and 'marble cake' to suggest that citizens are able to maintain multiple identities. European identity, in Risse's understanding, is intimately related to national experiences: indeed, national identity and European identity are in some cases, such as Germany or Italy, so interconnected that they cannot be easily separated. In other cases, such as Britain, Europe remains 'other'. Thus, after forty years of adjustment to the growing reality of a European quasi-polity, both elite and public identification with the European project differs markedly from one state to another. Ultimately, such variations are likely to endure no matter how much Europe moves in the direction of a supranational state. The real issue of concern is therefore the extent to which elites and publics throughout Europe develop their own national (or sub-national) versions of 'European' identity in a benign or hostile manner.

By definition, representative democracies rely on civic participation.

In contemporary Western Europe this has usually been organized through elections in which voters express support for political parties. However, one of the major concerns in several European states has been an apparent growing disillusionment on the part of voters with the entire political process – reflected in declining levels of participation (especially in second-order elections), falling levels of party membership and a more general decline in associational activity. Susan Pharr and Robert Putnam (2000) have spoken of 'disaffected democracies', in which citizens increasingly express frustration with governments' incapacity to perform effectively and deliver on promises. Some of the contextual reasons for such institutional incapacity have been outlined above, but the chapters by David Broughton and Paul Webb suggest that their impact on the process of politics in Western Europe should not be exaggerated. As Webb demonstrates, there is significant stability in Europe's party systems, which have exhibited little essential change over the last quarter century or so and remain dominated by centripetal and moderate forms of multipartyism. However, party systems have been fragmented in part, though not very significantly, by various cleavage structures which have emerged or reemerged in recent years, including racial tensions, a revival of centre–periphery conflicts and the issue of European integration.

Broughton's analysis of participation and voting indicates that there is in fact considerable stability in voter turnout in European states, as well as evidence of realism among European publics over what they can reasonably expect from politicians. Thus, the analyses by both Webb and Broughton would seem to refute the idea that any sea change has occurred or is occurring in the European political scene. But the question of Europe does pose real challenges, not least because of the uncertainties over its future direction: whilst it does not seem to figure as a core issue in regard to politics 'on the ground', and clearly seems to exercise voters much less than it does politicians, elites in nation-states are increasingly finding that the reality of European integration significantly alters the ways in which they can construct and pursue their interests.

Indeed, as Broughton acknowledges, there is clear dissatisfaction with political elites in Western Europe and various new forms of mobilization are partly substituting for a decline in the perceived relevance of traditional forms and channels of participation. This theme is also taken up in Cas Mudde's chapter on extremist movements in Europe. Like Broughton and Webb, Mudde confirms that mainstream parties have essentially remained stable, and that in general the EU has not become a divisive issue in most European polities. However, he does point out ways in which the EU and other factors have influenced the rise of 'new' extremism – most notably territorial extremism which seeks to use the 'threat' of EU integration to advance the claims of regional independence from 'moribund' and irrelevant nation-states. Of particular concern is the emergence of an ethnic extremism within territorial expressions of discontent, which marries elements of the old-style isolationist extreme left with the anti-cosmopolitanism of the extreme right. Whilst territorial extremism plays more easily into the hands of the extreme right, there may be an emerging cleavage in which elites operating increasingly within an international context are opposed by domestic groups who remain localized and suspicious of global developments in all their forms – but most obviously immigration. So far, such groups have remained on the fringes of mainstream politics, but there are signs in several European states – for instance, Austria and Italy – that they can tap into a more populist strand within the electorate.

Effectiveness

As indicated above, the capacity of states to command the loyalty of their citizens is closely correlated to their ability to deliver on popular demands. Politicians, of course, seek to play a key role in shaping popular demands through structuring the parameters of the political agenda. Thus, whilst political party commitments and manifestoes are in part responsive to citizens' interests, they are also in part attempts to establish the terms of reference for political activity. All modern political parties in West European democracies arguably find themselves caught in a catch-22: if they are honest with their electorates about the real constraints on their autonomy and activities they would be obliged to so scale down their electoral commitments as to render themselves unelectable on the grounds that they would do nothing if actually elected. On the other hand, by making promises about fundamental reform which are unlikely to be realizable in practice, they lay themselves more obviously open to the charge that they have failed to deliver once in office. Of course, the extent to which governments really can make a difference varies significantly according to policy area, and is a matter of academic dispute. But there is growing evidence that the increasing internationalization of economies, together with European integration, has constrained the capacity of governments within Europe to design and implement autonomous economic policies. By the same token, it is usually – though certainly not always – on the basis of their reputation for competence in managing the economy that governments are judged by electorates.

In his chapter on executive capacity, Paul Heywood argues that in response to such constraints, the main identifiable common trend across European polities has been a shift from government to governance. This has involved a ceding of central responsibilities upwards, downwards and sideways, to the point where in a complex and multilevel policy environment regulation and coordination have become the principal concern of governments, rather than control. This does not mean that in the domestic arena governments no longer seek to take control, but rather that they seek to do this more directly in a smaller number of areas than in the past, and in a manner which seeks to maximize credibility whilst minimizing costs. In large part, this trend towards more control over less has been driven by the overload of the 1970s, when the expansion of states – most notably in terms of the their responsibility for large sections of the economy – led to governments being held responsible for everything, both in administrative and in electoral terms. The key to understanding the willingness of governments to delegate significant powers to other agencies lies in their desire to stake a claim to efficiency through offering credibility.

Rainer Eising and Michelle Cini follow on from Heywood in their chapter, in which they underline the complexity of political change in contemporary Europe. They examine modes of governance in Europe, with particular reference to the organization of interests, and analyse how these are changing in the face of market or functional pressures, ideological transformation and trends towards Europeanization. In practice, the reconfiguration of interest organization and activity within Europe has not demonstrated any clear logic of convergence across countries or particular sectors, whilst forms of adaptation even within similar systems of governance can actually be quite diverse. The Europeanization of interest-group activity, on the other hand, reveals that greater pluralism is not necessarily the result of a transfer of the focus of lobbying to the less structured 'networked' European sphere of policy-making.

For all the organizational and institutional adaptation taking place within European states, the effectiveness of government and the health of democracy ultimately depend on the extent to which citizens are prepared to trust the political and administrative class. One of the main threats to trust has been the emergence over the last decade of major corruption-related scandals throughout most European democracies. In their analysis, Paul Heywood, Véronique Pujas and Martin Rhodes argue that whilst political corruption represents a significant challenge to governments in many European states, it is one which remains poorly understood, and has been frequently obfuscated by notions of an uncorrupt Protestant north versus a corrupt Catholic south. Recent large-scale scandals in both France and Germany have given the lie to such simplistic analyses. Instead, Heywood, Pujas and Rhodes identify two key developments: first, changes in the nature of governance as well as the rising financial cost of the political process have increased the incentives and opportunities for corruption in all countries, particularly within political parties; second, 'corrupt' behaviour has been uncovered and redefined as illicit by non-state actors, notably the press and the judiciary, as the cosy informal networks and bargains which underpinned government during the Cold War have broken down over the last ten to fifteen years. Political space, which used to be the virtual preserve of parties, has become increasingly contested – and the political class finds itself competing with those very elements in the press and the judiciary upon which it previously depended. The direct challenge to traditional parties by figures such as Silvio Berlusconi and Antonio di Pietro in Italy, Pedro J. Ramírez and Baltazar Garzón in Spain, Joerg Haider in Austria, and the growing political influence of corporations such as Rupert Murdoch's News International, underline the declining capacity of politicians to structure and control political space. However, rather than just representing a challenge to democracy, scandal should also be seen as evidence that democracy is working. Activities which may damage the 'democratic transcript' are being revealed, confronted and sometimes even prevented.

The problems posed by public apathy, ideological extremism, private interests and corruption all work to undermine the traditional pathways to political authority. Elections, legislatures, executives and agencies throughout Europe are to a greater or lesser extent suffering from a sense of malaise. One response has been the rise of new forms of political authority. Some of these work toward stability. Indeed, investigating magistrates have taken centre stage in a number of European states through their attempts to enforce (and sometimes even to create) the rule of law. In Italy, for example, the magistrates and the judiciary emerged during the 1990s as a necessary corrective for the abuses of the ruling classes. The result was a profound change in the structure of Italian politics. In France, Spain and the UK, for instance – and, indeed, in the European Union – the courts have played a less dramatic though no less significant role in resolving disputes – particularly in areas concerning the ethics of 'life and death' issues, such as reproductive technology, as well as in more general questions relating to the respective competence of different levels of government. Similarly, at both national and European levels, citizen access and recourse to the courts to contest government decisions or to assert and defend their rights has grown significantly in recent years. This judicialization of domestic politics does not play a major role in the analyses presented in this volume into the adaptation of Europe's nation-states, but it should not be regarded as playing a trivial role either.

A far more dramatic form of political contestation which has assumed increased salience in recent years concerns the location of sovereignty. As Michael Keating's chapter shows, a complex picture has emerged of changing relations between subnational, national and supranational levels of governance, in which sovereignty has become a permanently contested notion. Whilst such contestation is hardly new in Western Europe, what has changed is that 'regionalism' has become simultaneously an economic, political and institutional phenomenon which can no longer be contained within any one of these three dimensions. One of the key challenges facing states in Western Europe is what to do when people who share the same territory no longer wish to share the same political or economic resources, and mobilize to achieve their ends. 'Europeanization' has in turn contributed to the mobilization of regional actors through the creation of new levels of political authority and policy-making. Whilst such developments should not be seen as setting in stone a new multilevel hierarchy, it is likely that Europe will continue to see a proliferation of different types of territory with different forms and capacities. These may be strengthened in a European Union made up of greater internal territorial diversity, particularly as new member states join, with an extension of joint decision-making power between different levels of authority. The risk, however, is that struggles over sovereignty and competences will pull Europe's states in an increasingly centrifugal direction, thereby undermining the capacity of either the EU or individual states in Europe to govern effectively.

Resilience

States in Europe of course also face a host of other, sometimes more immediate challenges. The extent to which they are expected and able to develop appropriate responses to these challenges may provide some indicators as to the continued coherence of the nation-state as the principal locus of political organization. One of the most important of the challenges currently facing all states is environmental change, a key threat which is analysed in Neil Carter's chapter. Carter argues that, in practice, governments and the EU are incapable of responding to the environmental challenge, owing to the opposition of traditional clienteles, the problems of dealing with powerful industry lobbies and the fragmentation of the European Commission. The picture Carter presents is therefore one of state incapacity, or at least of how a pressing public-goods set of issues has failed to elicit an adequate set of government responses across EU authorities and the member states. Nonetheless, even if it is accepted that governments in Europe have not demonstrated the capacity to develop genuine environmental governance, Carter points out that any way forward will require greater institutionalization of environmental concerns by using state mechanisms to coordinate with environmental groups, to educate the public more effectively and to nurture a sense of 'ecological citizenship'. If states are failing in this enterprise, they nonetheless remain the only realistic prospect for progress.

In his discussion of the information society, David Levy also focuses on the issue of what the state is capable of in a contemporary world of powerful cross-border actors and the technologies they propagate as well as the power they pursue. This is an area in which nations have tried to defend their own cultural and/or industrial policy objectives but in which also the convergent and increasingly cross-border nature of the technologies involved have created a regulatory deficit at the national level and influenced a shift of regulatory capacity from member states to the EU itself. In this area probably more than many others, the state has been 'hollowed out' and the pattern of development – both in technological and regulatory terms – is ever-more European. Broadcasting remains the most nationally-based of the policy areas, but the information society more generally is something that is being developed 'beyond' traditional nation-bound authorities and cultures.

Of course not all challenges are technological and some are distinctly human. By the same token, not all responses are necessarily centred on the institutions of the state. In his chapter on European immigration policies, Christian Joppke outlines how EU member states have tried to pass the buck on immigration control not just to higher (supranational) levels, but also to lower (regional) levels – but without actually resolving any of the major tensions that exist between these levels of authority or between the ambitions of stemming and soliciting migrants. In practice, the focus of European-level policies is almost exclusively on stemming the flow of migrants, and the dispute during 2001 between France and the UK over responsibility for asylum-seekers attempting to access the UK illegally via the Channel Tunnel provides a clear example of the inability of Europe collectively to control its borders both in fact and as a policy issue. What Joppke's analysis suggests overall is that Europe is not yet succeeding in developing consistent national or supranational policies in the area of immigration. The likely prospect is that immigration politics will become increasingly contentious and, whilst Joppke does not make this argument, the potential to fuel a rise in racist politics is an alarming reality, which presents European states with yet one further challenge.

Human challenges are also the subject of the final chapter, by Giovanna Campani, which discusses the globalization of crime as a critical threat to democracies and the standards they traditionally try to uphold. Global crime networks have benefited from the erosion of the rule of law in many former communist countries as well as from less restricted global flows of capital, which in turn have enhanced the fluidity with which criminals are able to launder their proceeds, therefore shifting their centres of activity around the world. Such developments require new political structures to tackle them and Campani highlights how the Europeanization of police and security issues can be seen as a functional – if not yet adequate – response to these issues. Migration and the poor integration of migrants in Western European societies feeds into the problem of the internationalization of crime, which is closely linked to the alarming rise in the trafficking of women for sexual exploitation. In common with the other chapters in this section on challenges to the state, Campani underlines the imperative need for states to cooperate by building stronger linkages, strengthening civic awareness, and developing formal structures through which to confront the threats they face.

The state of the state and the primacy of politics

The problem of organized crime brings us back to the central importance of political organization and the continuing centrality of the state in politics. Clearly the state is not alone in its function of structuring collective action, whether in Western Europe or elsewhere. The state may not always be effective. It may struggle to retain its popular legitimacy, and it may rely increasingly upon other institutional arrangements whether above states, between them or within them. Nevertheless, the unique combination of territorial and popular sovereignty that constitutes the West European state remains an important bulwark for security, for stability, for innovation and for self-expression. As such, the state remains central to the politics of Western Europe not just by intention but also by design. Our analysis suggests that West Europeans remain committed to the development of the state as an essential basis for the development of West European politics.

Such analysis does not, however, address the problematic status of 'Western Europe' or, indeed, of the 'West'. Paradoxically, while any notion of the state remains firmly rooted in geography, notions of 'Western Europe' appear ready to dissolve in ever-more ephemeral conceptions of culture and identity. Beneath this paradox lies the reality of social construction and not some immutable law of politics. The state remains because it remains useful in purely functional terms. By contrast, Western Europe develops according to the affinities of its beholders. As a result, future analysts of developments in West European politics will face an even greater challenge in defining the boundaries of their subject.

PART I

The State and Europe

Chapter 1

Europe at the Crossroads

ERIK JONES

No discussion of 'the state of the state' in Western Europe can avoid the topic of European integration. Is the European Union (EU) rescuing the state or is it replacing the national state with a European one? Should we continue to talk about a European state system or should we rather embrace conceptions of multilevel governance? Does it make sense to distinguish between domestic politics and international relations, or is everything in Europe now 'Euro-mestic'? These are all questions about obsolescence. They point to the possible demise of the nation-state, the state system, and even the conception of stateness. They are also questions about innovation. If not the state, then what? Unfortunately, the answers are hesitant, contingent, open-ended. We can speculate about where European integration is headed and what it implies, but we cannot know.

The temptation is to reject such uncertainty and to embrace speculation as fact. If we are not sure about the general direction of European integration, then it could be argued that we should take cues from the major European projects and extrapolate from there. More important, the claim could be that we should use such extrapolations as the basis for public debate. Hence, for example, Oxford political theorist Larry Siedentop (2000) contends that because monetary union represents the centralization of political control over monetary policy at the European level, the European Union must be moving in a federal direction. That being the case, Siedentop goes on to claim that it is time for Europeans to begin discussing just what sort of federal system – if any – they would like to embrace.

Siedentop's line of reasoning may provide a strong provocation for debating how things should be in Europe. However it is a weak basis for understanding how things actually are. Uncertainty is not an obstacle for analysis; it is a starting point. The ambiguous nature of European integration forms an essential backdrop against which to examine the various challenges to and changes in state capacity and state-society relations. The transformation of the European integration is at least part (but not parcel) of the transformation of European governance

(Peterson and Bomberg, 2000). If we replace the ambiguity in the nature of integration with an asserted certainty, then we are sure to misapprehend developments in West European politics.

The purpose of this chapter is to analyse the ambiguity of European integration during the period from 1997 to 2001. My argument is that such ambiguity is ubiquitous. None of the major policy developments in Europe over the five year period provides a clear indication of the direction of progress. Correspondingly, none provides a clear indictment of the European state system or of the nation-state. Rather, the process of European integration moves in different directions in different areas at different times and for different reasons. We cannot be sure what all this motion actually means; but we can recognize that this lack of certainty is an important feature in its own right.

The argument is made in six sections. The first provides an overview of developments through the lens of European Council summits. The second focuses on macroeconomic policies and monetary union. The third examines foreign and security policy. The fourth considers justice and home affairs. The fifth turns to institutional reform and enlargement. The sixth section concludes.

Summits and subjects

The European Council is the driving force behind the process of European integration. Meeting 'at least twice a year', the European Council brings together the President of the European Commission and the heads of state and government of the EU member states in order to 'provide the [European] Union with the necessary impetus for its development . . . [and to] define the general political guidelines thereof' (Treaty on European Union [TEU], Article 4). That said, these meetings usually last only two days and include a range of informal gatherings, state dinners and photo calls. Thus while the record of European Council summits provides a concise overview of the progress of European integration, the actions and attentions of any one European Council summit cannot embrace the whole of the Union.

If the objective is to get a sense of where integration is headed, it is not enough to read the results of only one summit; rather, it is necessary to take the meetings of the European Council in groups. Table 1.1 provides an overview of the activities of the European Council during a period that extends from the Amsterdam summit in June 1997 to the Gothenburg summit in June 2001. The table lists the major initiatives taken by the European Council in the four principal areas of development: economic and monetary union (EMU); common foreign and security policy (CFSP);

justice and home affairs (JHA); and institutional reform and enlargement. This is not a complete record of European Council actions because it excludes both the monitoring of ongoing reforms and decisions taken with respect to specific initiatives under the common foreign and security policy (such as declarations on Kosovo or on the Middle East). As constructed, the table focuses more on the progress of European integration than on the pattern of European governance.

The Amsterdam summit is a good starting point for analysing integration because the treaty revisions agreed at that summit entailed an important change not only in the scope of activity across the four major areas, but also in the pattern of European Council summits and European Council involvement. Before Amsterdam, the European Council met twice a year in June and December – with the exception being a March 1996 meeting in Turin to launch the process of treaty negotiations, or intergovernmental conference (IGC), that culminated at Amsterdam. These twice-yearly meetings coincided with the end of six-month-long presidencies of the Council of Ministers held by particular member states and provided the member state acting as president the opportunity to showcase the achievements of its presidency. After the Amsterdam negotiations, the European Council began to meet an average of three times annually. The general summits continued to take place in June and December. However, the activities of the European Council included a number of 'special' summits held either in October/November or in March. These special summits were not meant to showcase progress in general, but rather to focus attention on specific initiatives such as employment (Luxembourg), EU finances (Berlin), justice and home affairs (Tampere), and the coordination of economic policy reform (Lisbon).

The Nice, Stockholm and Gothenburg summits represent a good stopping point because they suggest a further change both in the patterns of integration and in the activities of the European Council. As will be elaborated in the penultimate section of this chapter, the treaty reforms negotiated at Nice – while not as substantial as those at Amsterdam – point to a change in the interaction between member states and the Union. The Stockholm summit is the first regularized March meeting of the European Council with the purpose of monitoring economic performance as well as the coordination of economic policy reform. And the Gothenburg summit may turn out to be among the last European Council summits to be held within the member state that holds the rotating presidency in the Council of Ministers.

This last point requires explanation. The Gothenburg summit was the first meeting of the European Council to confront violent public demonstrations. These demonstrations emerged from a growing pattern of

Table 1.1 *Summits and subjects*

European Council Summit venue (date)	Economic and Monetary Union	Common Foreign and Security	Justice, and Home Affairs Policy	Institutional Reform and Enlargement
Amsterdam (16–17 June 1997)	• Stability and growth pact • Resolution on growth and employment		• Action Plan on the fight against organized crime	• Amsterdam Treaty • Agenda 2000 (anticipated)
• *Amsterdam Treaty*	• Title on employment • Final preparations for EMU	• Strengthen CFSP through European Council • Designation of Secretary General of the Council of Ministers as High Representative of CFSP • Declaration on enhanced cooperation between the European Union and the Western European Union	• Strengthen cooperation in justice and policing • Harmonize treatment of asylum seekers and refugees • Strengthen cooperation in civil matters • Protocol integrating the Schengen *acquis* into the framework of the European Union	• Amend decision-making procedures • Provisions on closer cooperation • Protocol on the institutions with the prospect of enlargement of the European Union
Luxembourg (20–1 November 1997)*	• Active promotion of employment (Luxembourg Process)			
Luxembourg (12–13 December 1997)	• Resolution on economic policy coordination in EMU			• Launch of enlargement process (set for March 1998)
Cardiff (15–16 June 1998)	• Active market reform (Cardiff Process)			
Vienna (11–12 December 1998)	• External representation of EMU • Acknowledgment of Euro-11 Group	• Note of Franco-British declaration at Saint-Malo (4 December)	• Action Plan on freedom, justice and security	

Summit (date)			
Berlin* (24–5 March 1999)			• Budget reform in light of Agenda 2000 • Appointment of Commission President (Romano Prodi) • Call for new Intergovernmental Conference (IGC) • Call for more inclusive enlargement process
Cologne (3–4 June 1999)	• Resolution on the European employment pact • Macroeconomic dialogue (Cologne Process)	• Appointment of High Representative (Javier Solana) • Declaration on strengthening capacity to undertake 'Petersberg tasks' • Common strategy on Russia	• Decision to draw up a 'Charter of Fundamental Rights of the European Union'
Tampere* (15–16 October 1999)			• Common asylum and migration policy • Enhanced legal transparency • Fight against organized crime • Appointment of commission on Charter of Fundamental Rights
Helsinki (10–11 December 1999)	• Agreement on 60 000 person rapid deployment force • Call to strengthen crisis management capability		• Change to more inclusive enlargement process (principle of differentiation) • Agenda for IGC
Lisbon (23–4 March 2000)*	• Adoption of 'open method of coordination' (Lisbon Strategy) • Call for regular economic summits		

European Council Summit venue (date)	Economic and Monetary Union	Common Foreign and Security	Justice, and Home Affairs Policy	Institutional Reform and Enlargement
Feira (19–20 June 2000)				• Focus on preparations for IGC
Nice (7–9 December 2000)	• Statement on European social agenda • Resolution on precautionary principle		• Proclamation of Charter of Fundamental Rights (but deferred consideration of legal force)	• Adoption of Nice Treaty
• Nice Treaty		• Statement that Treaty ratification is not a precondition for implementation of those measures agreed at and before Helsinki	• Procedure to identify and make recommendations to Member States in danger of contravening fundamental rights • Protocol on the statute of the Court of Justice	• Council voting weights and procedures • Members of the European Commission • Members of European Parliament • Use of qualified majority voting • Protocol on enlargement • Provisions for enhanced cooperation
Stockholm (23–4 March 2001)	• Focus on economic performance and structural reform (Broad Economic Policy Guidelines)			
Gothenburg (15–16 June 2001)	• Add environmental sustainability to Lisbon strategy	• Call for European security and defense policy (ESDP)		• Call to prepare for enlargement by the end of 2002

Note: * indicates a special summit. The March summits became regularized starting with the Stockholm European Council.

popular protest at international summits that stretched back to 1999 and through meetings of the International Monetary Fund (IMF) in Prague and of the World Trade Organization (WTO) in Seattle. However, the ferocity of the violence caught both the EU heads of state and government and the Swedish police by surprise. The result was a public-relations nightmare that has fostered the widespread belief that the European Council will establish a permanent venue in Brussels for the future.

The Gothenburg summit is also useful because it highlights the fact that the European Council is reactive as well as proactive. Events that take place before or when the summits are held can have an influence on the content of the decisions or initiatives that are taken. This reactive behaviour is evident in several of the entries to the table. Consider the following consecutive examples: the December 1998 Vienna European Council took note of Anglo-French calls for enhanced European security cooperation at St Malo; the March 1999 Berlin European Council appointed Romano Prodi as President of the European Commission in response to the sudden resignation of Jacques Santer; and the June 1999 Cologne European Council called for a more inclusive enlargement process in the aftermath of NATO's involvement in Kosovo. The reactive nature of the Council is also evident in the extraordinary summit held in Gent in October 2001 to discuss the implications of the September 11 terrorist attack on the World Trade Centre in New York. The point here is not to suggest that the European Council is purely reactive. Rather it is to accept that the European Council is not alone in providing impetus to the process of European integration.

Finally, the Gothenburg summit underscores the potential gap between the activities of the European Council and the evolution of popular opinion. When the heads of state and government of the European Union convened in Gothenburg, they faced not only a throng of protestors but also the Irish veto of the Nice Treaty in a popular referendum held only days before. Rightly or wrongly, the violence that surrounded the summit could be put aside as the misguided actions of a small group of fanatics. The Irish rejection of the Nice Treaty could not. And attempts by European Commission President Romano Prodi to downplay the significance of the Irish referendum only served to reinforce perceptions of the division between elite actions in the European Council and popular attitudes within the member states.

Recognition of this gap is important because just as the European Council does not have a monopoly on the impetus given to European integration, it also does not have sole power over which initiatives succeed and which do not. The simple fact that the European Council takes a decision does not mean that the decision will be acted upon or that the actions will be accepted as legitimate. This limitation is also evident elsewhere. The Irish referendum was not the only setback faced by the European Council after Amsterdam. Conflicts between the member states have proven problematic as well – and with ambiguous results. Such conflict was evident throughout the year 2000. During the Portuguese presidency, the conflict centred on the presence of the right-wing Freedom Party in the Austrian government. During the French presidency, it centred on the relative balance of power between smaller and larger member states. In both cases, the result was to slow down the process of decision-making within the European Council, to restrict the areas for negotiated compromise, and to defer tough decisions. Even taking European Council summits in a group, it is not always possible to determine where European integration is headed.

Economic and monetary union

Still it could be argued that the direction of integration in specific areas is more transparent than the broad patterns of European Council activity. Economic and monetary union (EMU), for example, constitutes a clear case of centralizing authority at the European level. With the irrevocable fixing of bilateral exchange rates among participating countries (May 1998), the constitution of a European Central Bank (ECB – June 1998), and the transfer of monetary policy authority from national to European institutions (January 1999), there can be little doubt but that EMU represents a fundamental change in state competence and state capacity.

That said, the monetary institutions of EMU make up only one half of the story. They are the 'monetary' in the economic and monetary union, but not the 'economic'. Moreover, the structure and functioning of these monetary institutions had already been agreed at the December 1991 European Council summit in Maastricht. During the preparations for the 1996–97 intergovernmental conference, voices in both the member states and the European Commission were adamant that these monetary provisions should *not* form part of the negotiations over treaty revisions (cf. Ludlow, Barre and Ersbøll 1995, pp. 86–95, 124). To the extent to which the European Council was willing to discuss monetary arrangements after Maastricht, the focus for discussion has centred resolutely on the implementation of past agreements and not on the generation of new initiatives. The European Council played an important role in ensuring that monetary integration did take place after Amsterdam; however, it played very little role in determining how that monetary integration would look or what it would mean.

The economic side of EMU was the focus for European Council activity at and after the Amsterdam summit. Returning to the first column of Table 1.1, the initiatives launched at Amsterdam centred on two European Council resolutions – on the 'Stability and Growth Pact' and on 'Growth and Employment' – and one major revision to the Treaty Establishing the European Community (TEC) – the addition of a chapter on employment. The Stability and Growth Pact commits member states to balance their fiscal accounts over the medium term. The Resolution on Growth and Employment commits them to develop the economic pillar of EMU in order, 'among other objectives, [to] bring more jobs within the reach of the citizens of Europe' (European Council, 1997: Annex p. 10). And the chapter on employment commits them to 'work towards developing a coordinated strategy' (TEC, Article 125).

These economic commitments are centralized insofar as they emanate from agreements taken in the European Council. However, they are decentralized in that each places the onus for action onto the member states and even on the subnational level. Borrowing from the language of the Resolution on Growth and Employment: 'The European Council calls upon all the social and economic agents, including the national, regional and local authorities and the social partners, to face fully their responsibilities within their respective sphere of activity' (European Council, 1997: Annex p. 10).

The decentralized nature of the economic side of EMU developed into two different forms of policy coordination, one closed and one open. The closed policy coordination concerns macroeconomic or fiscal measures and is bounded by rules, norms and collective compliance. The open policy coordination concerns market structural reforms and centres on benchmarks, targets and shared best-practice. Closed policy coordination places greater emphasis on the responsibilities of the member states. Open policy coordination places greater emphasis on the possibilities for member-state achievement. Crucially, however, the member states are more important in either form of coordination than are the boundaries and possibilities that constitute the difference between being closed or open.

The closed form of macroeconomic policy coordination emerges from the Growth and Stability Pact as well as the underlying treaty-based procedures for multilateral surveillance and for excessive deficits which the Pact reinforces. The boundaries include not only the agreement to achieve medium-term fiscal balance, but also the responsibility to ensure that the macroeconomic policies of any one member state do not cause adverse effects in any other, and the obligation to respect the political independence of European monetary authorities. The European Council reiterated the importance of these boundaries repeatedly: in its Luxembourg resolution on economic policy coordination in EMU; in its Vienna discussions on external representation and on the composition of an informal Euro-11 group within the Council of Economic and Finance Ministers; and in its Lisbon decision to hold regular economic summits during the Spring.

Despite the wealth of repetition, however, the effectiveness of the rules rests more on member-state compliance than on European Council (or other EU) enforcement. The central instrument for this closed form of policy coordination is the set of annual broad economic policy guidelines (BEPGs) adopted by the Council of Ministers and discussed in European Council. These guidelines contain both an assessment of the general economic performance of the EU and specific recommendations for each member state to follow in the interests of policy coordination. However, should the member state in question choose not to follow the guidelines there is little that the European Council or Council of Ministers can do. For example, the Irish government ignored a recommendation in the BEPGs for the year 2000 that called for an increase in the surplus on Irish fiscal accounts. In response, the Council of Ministers issued a public reprimand during the early months of 2001, which had a big impact in the press (at least among those who read about such things). Having acknowledged the public humiliation, however, the Irish government effectively chose to ignore that reprimand as well.

The open method of coordination in market structural reform policies emerges from the Amsterdam resolution on growth and employment and from the chapter on employment in the TEC. However, where the closed coordination of macroeconomic policies could build upon treaty-based procedures for multilateral surveillance and excessive deficits, the open coordination of market structural reforms had to develop procedures of its own. Those procedures emerged as 'processes' started by the special Luxembourg summit on employment, the Cardiff summit and the Cologne summit:

- the Luxembourg process calls upon member states to engage in active measures to create employment;
- the Cardiff process calls for coordinated reform of labour and product markets; and,
- the Cologne process calls for macroeconomic dialogue between economic policy-makers, monetary authorities and the social partners – meaning representatives of industry and labour.

In turn, it was the Lisbon summit that brought these processes together in the open method of coordination. The principles underwriting the open method relate more closely to self-help than to self-discipline. The member states are responsible for establishing benchmarks for achievement, setting targets, undertaking reforms and evaluating their own and each-other's success. The process includes a healthy dose of competition and moral suasion, but it does not include an institutionalized mechanism for enforced compliance. Open coordination is centrally orchestrated but individually applied.

The summits after Lisbon have added to the scope of policy coordination without fundamentally changing the procedures. Moreover, the bulk of activity has been on the more decentralized, open method for coordination. Reference to the European social agenda at Nice and to environmental sustainability at both Nice and Gothenburg serve to broaden the foundations for the economic side of EMU without adding to the centralization implied by having a single European monetary authority. Thus even if we accept that the monetary union negotiated at Maastricht in 1991 was a centralizing force, we should concede that the economic union elaborated at and after the 1997 Amsterdam summit is more ambivalent.

Common foreign and security policy (CFSP)

The change in the pattern of integration between the Maastricht's Europe and Amsterdam's Europe is reversed in the area of foreign and security policy. Where the Maastricht Treaty provisions for CFSP are relatively decentralized, the Amsterdam Treaty provisions are relatively centralized. And where developments after Maastricht centred on the elaboration of agreement where possible, developments after Amsterdam have focused on the facilitation of agreement where necessary. This change in emphasis is evident throughout the revisions to the chapter on CFSP, but can be seen particularly in the expanded role of the European Council, the creation of a High Representative for the common foreign and security policy, and appropriation of capabilities belonging to the West European Union (WEU).

The European Council has a more prominent role in constructing the common foreign and security policy than in any other policy area. Instead of simply providing impetus for further integration, 'the European Council shall define the principles of an general guidelines for the common foreign and security policy' (TEU, Article 13, para. 1). This language appears in both the Maastricht and Amsterdam Treaties. However, the Amsterdam Treaty extends the role of the European Council to include both 'matters with defence implications' and the authority to decide on 'strategies to be implemented by the Union in areas where the Member States have important interests in common' (TEU, Article 13, paras 1 and 2).

The Amsterdam Treaty also provides the European Council with a coherent means to represent the CFSP to the outside world. The designation of the Secretary General of the Council of Ministers 'to exercise the function of High Representative for the common foreign and security policy' (TEU, Article 18, para. 3) helps to overcome the problems that arise as a result of the six-monthly rotation in the presidency of the Council of Ministers and therefore also in the European Council. Thus, while technically the representative of the European Union remains the head of state or government of whichever member state holds the Council presidency, for practical purposes the European Council can rely on the High Representative to act as the visible face of the Union from one presidency to the next.

Armed with specific responsibilities and aided by a High Representative, the European Council and the Council of Ministers nevertheless lack the capability to act decisively in foreign and security affairs. The Maastricht Treaty provided little institutional support for the analysis of issues of potential concern or for the design, implementation and monitoring of foreign and security policies, the Maatricht Treaty 'requests' assistance from the West European Union in security matters and provides for a 'Political Committee' to 'monitor the international situation . . . [and] the implementation of policies', but that is all. By contrast, the Amsterdam Treaty retains the Political Committee and opens up 'the possibility of the integration of the WEU into the Union' with a view to developing the capabilities to undertake 'humanitarian and rescue tasks, peace-keeping tasks, and tasks of combat forces in crisis management, including peacemaking' (TEU, Article 17, paras 1 and 2). This list of tasks constitutes the core of WEU activities as outlined in the 1992 Petersberg declaration on 'strengthening the WEU's operational role' by the West European Union Council of Ministers (WEU, 1992). Nevertheless, the Amsterdam Council was undecided over what should be the precise relationship between the EU and the WEU.

The evolution of changes since Amsterdam has been progressive. For example, the pattern for common strategies under the CFSP was set at the 1999 European Council summit in Cologne with the declaration of a joint strategy on Russia. The 19-page document annexed to the Presidency Conclusions covers the gamut of relations from economics to security and at a level of detail that contrasted strongly with the record of joint actions after Maastricht (Mahncke, 2001, pp. 238–9). The progressive evolution is also evident in the June 1999 appointment of Javier Solana as the first High Representative for the CFSP. Solana not only brought with him the credibility he had earned while stewarding the NATO alliance through the conflict in Kosovo, he also brought the tacit recognition of the United States government that had acceded to his appointment as NATO Secretary General in the first place.

Evidence of progress is most stark in relations between the European Union and the WEU. The original negotiations at Amsterdam stalled as a result of a conflict between France and the United Kingdom; the French government was eager to incorporate the WEU into the European Union while the United Kingdom was not. This deadlock persisted until the Autumn of 1998. Meeting at an informal gathering of the European Council at Porschach, Austria, the British Prime Minister, Tony Blair, indicated his country's willingness to change its position on European security. This change in British policy was followed in December 1998 by a joint Anglo-French declaration that 'the Union must have the capacity for autonomous action, backed up by credible military forces, the means to decide to use them and a readiness to do so, in order to respond to international crises' (WEU, 1998). In turn, this St Malo Declaration, acknowledged at the December 1998 Vienna Council, provided the impetus for a rapid change in relations between the WEU and the EU (Shearer, 2000).

During the Autumn of 1999, Javier Solana was named Secretary General of the WEU in addition to his responsibilities as High Representative for the CFSP. Soon thereafter, the Helsinki European Council summit agreed to the creation of a 60 000 strong rapid- deployment force for use in the undertaking of those 'Petersberg tasks' set down in the Amsterdam Treaty and which lay at the heart of WEU competence. The Helsinki Council also called for the creation of an independent capacity for crisis management and response to issues of both a military and a civilian nature. These developments were then fleshed out at a November 2000 'capabilities commitment conference' and incorporated into the treaty reforms agreed at the December 2000 European Council summit at Nice. By the end of 2000, the EU had successfully incorporated virtually all of the operational functions of the West European Union.

The development of the European Union's common foreign and security policy was more rapid and more coherent after the Treaty of Amsterdam than it was after the Treaty of Maastricht. Nevertheless, the progress of development remains ambiguous when cast against the background of state capacity. The Amsterdam revisions expand the scope of CFSP but they also reinforce the cooperative and intergovernmental nature of the policy area (Mahncke, 2001). Europe's new common foreign and security policy is relatively centralized but it is not supranational. The grant of authority to the European Council displaces responsibility that would otherwise fall on the Council of Ministers. The High Representative is drawn from the Council and not the Commission. In both cases, the less supranational alternative was selected despite institutional pressures from both the Council and the Commission to have things the other way around.

The CFSP is not only cooperative and intergovernmental, it is also limited in scope. Those elements of the WEU that have been absorbed by the European Union are intended to complement and not to replace member-state obligations to the North Atlantic Treaty Organization (NATO). Borrowing from the draft presidency report on European security and defence policy that was submitted to the Nice European Council summit: 'This does not involve the creation of a European army. The commitment of national resources by Member States to such [Petersberg] operations will be based on their sovereign decisions' (European Council, 2000a, p. 1). This division of responsibilities was immediately evident after 11 September 2001. While the NATO member states chose to invoke Article 5 of the North Atlantic Treaty and to act on the premise that an attack on one country (the United States) is an attack on the alliance as a whole, the European Union opted for a more supportive and yet less bellicose role. Rather than focusing on the projection of force abroad, the EU centred its attention on ensuring security at home. Hence, while it is clear that the climate for CFSP has changed importantly in the transition from Maastricht's Europe to Amsterdam's Europe, it is not at all clear what that change implies for the future.

Justice and home affairs

Integration in the area of justice and home affairs is driven by two over-lapping forces: the unintended consequences of integration in other areas, and the judicialization of governance (Stone Sweet, 1999, 2000). The unintended consequences of integration include problems such as the impact of relaxing internal border controls on organized crime, terrorism and illegal immigration, or the difficulty of ensuring the legal protection of workers who are free to move from one country to the next. Unintended consequences also include such opportunities as the sharing of information (or police intelligence) across jurisdictions, the harmonization of administrative procedures, and the establishment of basic principles for civil protection. Integration in the area of justice and home affairs represents an attempt to solve the problems or take advantage of the possibilities.

Still unintended consequences constitute only part of the motivation.

The other part derives from the judicialization of governance – which is to say, from the general movement towards the establishment of rules, norms and procedures for the resolution of disputes between different groups in society. Where there is conflict, there is also the motivation to institutionalize the solution to a particular dispute or to establish mechanisms for dispute resolution. The provisions relating to justice and home affairs in the Treaty on European Union include both types of arrangements. For example, the provisions on police and judicial cooperation in criminal matters (TEU, Title VI) include passages delineating actions to be taken at the national, transnational and European levels as well as passages outlining the role of the European Court of Justice in adjudicating conflicts of meaning and jurisdiction.

The unintended consequences of integration and the judicialization of governance are mutually reinforcing. The problems and possibilities that arise from integration do not have the same importance across member states or across groups within member states. Germany is much more exposed to illegal immigration than Ireland, for example, and Swedish nationals have stronger civil protection than do the British. In this way, efforts to address the unintended consequences of integration constitute at least potential sources of conflict, whether between member states or between parties within and across the member states. By the same token, the process of integration in the area of justice and home affairs gives rise to unintended consequences all its own. More to the point, the procedures established for dispute resolution can have the consequence of constructing norms or rules that can change the basis for future adjudication and thus either provoke conflict or create the opportunity for conflict resolution. In Germany, for example, the establishment of common rules for asylum across Europe have helped to overturn longstanding attitudes towards the status of political refugees and towards relations between countries within the European Union and those outside.

In the overlap between unintended consequences and the judicialization of governance, it is easy to imagine the emergence of an ever-tighter and reinforcing network of European norms, rules and procedures. However, such imaginings overlook the possibility that conflicts will only find resolution in the disestablishment of European rules or procedures – the norm being that member state or individual preferences be unencumbered by action at the European level. This norm is expressed in the provisions for cooperation in criminal matters (TEU, Title VI) and the provisions on visas, asylum, immigration and so forth (TEC, Title IV). It manifests both as the blanket assertion that 'this Title shall not affect the exercise of responsibilities incumbent upon Member States with regard to the maintenance of law and order and the safeguarding of internal security' (TEC, Article 64; TEU, Article 33) and, more subtly, in the numerous avenues for exemption, derogation or contestation of action.

Given the possibility that the unintended consequences of integration can be disintegrative, it becomes much more difficult to make generalizations about the level at which problems will be addressed, opportunities will be availed to, or disputes will be resolved. As a result, the pattern of integration in justice and home affairs since Amsterdam reveals a high degree of idiosyncrasy. The focus for action lies on particular problems and not on policy areas or institutions *per se*. Both the Amsterdam action plan on the fight against organized crime and the Vienna action plan on freedom, justice and security contain a wide range of measures without any overarching framework (Monar, 2001). The development of general principles is piecemeal and contested (Smith and Wallace, 2001), and, given the opportunity to establish a charter of fundamental rights for the European Union, the Nice European Council could agree only on the issuance of a 'proclamation' while at the same time deferring consideration as to its legal force.

The conflict that erupted between February and September 2000 over the inclusion of the far-right Freedom Party in the Austrian government illustrates the challenges involved in establishing the European Union as 'an area of freedom, security and justice' (TEC, Article 61). The dispute centred on two factors: whether member states can legitimately include in their governing coalitions those political parties that are on record as advocating extremist views whatever the level of electoral support for such parties; and whether (and how) the member states of the EU can sanction one of their own number for threatening to violate the fundamental values of the Union. The result on both counts was muddled. Austria suffered seven months of diplomatic isolation only to force an end to the deadlock by threatening to hold a referendum on popular support for European integration that would be sure to inflame domestic Euroscepticism. Meanwhile the EU member states became divided between those who viewed the sanctions on Austria as justified and those who expressed concern that a larger member state would never be treated so harshly. Rather than establishing the importance of fundamental principles, the conflict with Austria appeared to underscore the inequality between member states. The treaty amendments negotiated at Nice include a procedure for action when there is 'a clear risk of a serious breach by a Member State of the [fundamental] principles' (European Council, 2000b, Article 7, para. 1) of the Union and yet it is unclear when such a procedure would ever be invoked.

Institutional reform and enlargement

The conflict between the rest of the European Union and Austria also underscored the complex relationship between the process of reforming the institutions of the European Union and the process of enlarging the EU to the countries of Central and Eastern Europe. On the one hand, the xenophobic sentiments expressed by members of the Freedom Party are completely inimical to the solidarity explicit in the enlargement project: the Central and East European countries *are* European. On the other hand, maintaining a collaborative relationship with the Austrian government is essential for the success of institutional reforms that are themselves prerequisite for enlargement: The institutions of the EU must be reformed if they are not to collapse under the weight of numbers, and the process of institutional reform requires unanimous support of existing member states.

The tension between unanimity and solidarity lies at the heart of the relationship between institutional reform and enlargement. For the two projects to succeed, all member states must agree to make sacrifices in the common interest and in the interest of others. On the surface, this challenge sounds wholly unsuited to an intergovernmental arrangement between sovereign member states. The jealous representatives of the national interest may be willing to pool sovereignty as part of some 'European Rescue of the Nation-State', but they are unlikely to engage willingly in an act of collective self-sacrifice.

The point to note, however, is that the challenges of institutional reform and enlargement exist beyond the relationship between these two processes. Institutional reform was necessary before enlargement and would be required even if enlargement were not to take place. By the same token, enlargement is attractive for reasons that have little to do with the institutions of the European Union. Indeed, the relationship between institutional reform and enlargement constrains – and does not warrant or justify – both activities.

The need for institutional reform in the European Union was evident in the early 1990s during the Austrian and Nordic enlargement. The concern at the time centred on three elements: the weighting of votes in the Council of Ministers, the number of Commissioners, and the use of qualified majority voting. The argument was that institutions designed for six countries – and progressively adapted to 12 – could not function with 16 or more. Decision-making would slow down, policy implementation would become unduly fragmented, and the Union as a whole would lose direction. Hence, even though Norway ultimately voted not to join the Union, the consensus was that something would have to be done to streamline the process of European governance. The intergovernmental conference which started at Turin in March 1996 and culminated 15 months later in Amsterdam was originally intended to tackle the problem of institutional reform (Ludlow *et al.*, 1995).

The Amsterdam European Council failed to reform the institutions of the Union. Instead, the 'protocol on the institutions with the prospect of enlargement . . .' suggests only that the problem be deferred until the number of countries joining the Union equals the number of additional Commissioners held by the larger member states – which is to say, five. In this way, the accession of Central and East European countries is a political and not a mechanical cause for the reform of EU institutions. Although the impact of increasing numbers is real, the trigger for reform is arbitrary. As if to make this clear, when the European Council revisited the question of institutional reform at the Nice summit in 2000, the 'protocol on the enlargement of the European Union' raised the trigger for reform of the Commission to 27 member states in total – in other words, from five new entrants to 12 (European Council, 2000b, Annex 1, Article 4).

The change in the trigger for institutional reform has less to do with the problem of EU decision-making than with the status of the enlargement process. When the Amsterdam Council met in 1997, the likelihood was that the first wave of enlargement would include only five countries and would take some time to bring about. When the Nice Council met in 2000, the likelihood was that enlargement would encompass 12 countries and could begin within only a few years' time. By the Gothenburg summit, the European Council was willing to pronounce the goal that the Union should be ready to begin accepting new members by as early as 2003. The point to note is that while progress on institutional reform has been slow, the pace of enlargement has been fast and accelerating.

The rapid pace of enlargement reflects the threat of political instability in Central and Eastern Europe. During the Amsterdam summit, this threat was perceived as marginal; hence the Agenda 2000 proposal for adapting the finances of the Union to the enlargement process foresaw a careful separation of candidate countries into those who could make the adjustment relatively easily and those who could not. The first group would receive limited support for a relatively rapid accession. The second group would receive considerably less support for a much slower set of negotiations. This was the enlargement process anticipated at the Luxembourg European Council and inaugurated in March 1998.

The budget negotiations at the March 1999 European Council summit in Berlin revealed the extent to which even this cautious approach to enlargement raised difficulties for existing member states. The willingness of net contributors to Union coffers to finance generous support to Central and Eastern Europe was as limited as the willingness of net recipients to see their current benefits diminish. As a consequence, the budgetary negotiations were not only tense, but the results were tightly constrained and inflexible (Jones, 2000).

NATO involvement in Kosovo took place between the Berlin summit in March and the Cologne summit in June 1999. As a result, the European Council began to consider the merits of a more inclusive enlargement. The reasoning was that the cost of continued instability is likely to far outweigh the cost of a more rapid accession of Central and East European countries to the EU. Hence, if the prospect of enlargement can belay instability in Central and Eastern Europe, then the process of enlargement should be made more inclusive (Cecchini *et al.*, 2001). This change in the pattern of enlargement was adopted at the December 1999 Helsinki summit with the result that countries now negotiate at their own pace rather than in slow and fast groups. And, as each of the European Councils meeting after Helsinki have noted, the pace is fast and accelerating.

The contrast between the slow pace of institutional reform and the fast pace of enlargement was evident at the December 2000 European Council summit in Nice. Moreover, the tension between unanimity and solidarity remained unresolved. Although the French presidency did succeed in generating a set of reforms for EU institutions, these reforms were only partial, contested and even inequitable. Virtually no-one considered the Nice summit more than a minimal success (Jones, 2001), and with the Irish veto of the Nice Treaty in June 2001, even that grudging concession was called into question.

Conclusions

The European Union is integrating, but it is unclear what that means. It is progressing, but it is unclear towards what. And it is developing, but it is unclear how. What is clear is that Western Europe faces a number of challenges for the future. Such challenges relate not only to the tension between institutional reform and enlargement, but also to the evolution of mechanisms and norms for the resolution of disputes between member states. The European Union must wrestle with its own attempts to assert its interests in world affairs and it must accommodate a wide range of divergent economic structures and concerns. Finally, it must ensure that the European Council does not move too far away from popular support or democratic legitimation. The complexity of such challenges is immense. The first step to analysing developments in West European politics is to accept this reality.

The conclusion is that it is better to analyse European integration piecemeal than to extrapolate from parts of the integration process in order to anticipate the progression of the whole. The grand alternatives for Europe's continental organization are worthy of public debate, but they should not be allowed to displace a careful consideration of the problems faced by European governments and by the institutions of the EU. Indeed the same point applies to consideration of the 'state of the state'. And it is this concern for the particularity of challenges to governance which informs the underlying structure for the rest of this volume.

Chapter 2

Globalization, EMU and Welfare State Futures

MARTIN RHODES

The emerging polity of the European Union (EU), the evolution of governance at the intersection of the EU and its member states, the capacity of Europe to defend the core policies (and core beliefs) of its so-called social model, and the ongoing transformation of national decision-making systems have all become the focus of growing academic interest over recent years. Gradually there has been a shift away from an earlier obsession with the strains of 'negative' versus 'positive' integration and the dangers of social dumping or social devaluation, towards an understanding that economic and monetary union (EMU), the single market and 'globalization' would in reality have much less dramatic consequences for Europe's social and economic fabric – and that some of these might even be welfare-enhancing. Welfare state problems generated by changing demographics, the 'growth-to-limits' in social security budgets and persistent long-term unemployment could even be resolved, in this more optimistic view, as part of a multilayered, but coordinated, pan-European project for the 'European social model'. This, in essence, as discussed in the final section of this chapter, is what recent innovations in EU policy-making have been all about.

This new appreciation that a multilevel social and labour market regime in Europe might be both effective for economic adjustment under EMU as well as normatively acceptable to Europeans, raises a number of critical questions about state antonomy under new external constraints. The prevailing wisdom is that these constraints are tightening both in terms of formal institutions (the EU and EMU) and market forces (for example, globalization). I argue instead that considerable autonomy remains, despite these constraints, and that there is correspondingly considerable scope for welfare state diversity as well. For sure welfare states need to change (for many reasons, most of them intrinsic to domestic welfare systems and how they function); and 'Europe', it is true, is assuming a greater role and influence. But none of these developments should read as implying the 'end of the welfare state', 'welfare state convergence' or even, in most cases 'less welfare'. On most measures, most European welfare states are larger and more generous today than they have ever been before; and given the right combination of policy reforms, there is no reason why that state of affairs cannot be sustained. Moreover, far from there having been a unidirectional and negative EU–EMU-globalization impact on welfare states, as this chapter shows, national forms of socio-economic governance have changed over the last decade in ways that cushion and accommodate the transformation of the European economy. In this sense, welfare states are 'productive' for, not incompatible with, economic growth and development. Innovations in national governance systems, spanning wages and the labour market, the adjustment of social protection systems and general budgetary policy have not only critically facilitated this process, but have also in many respects helped lay the ground for subsequent developments at higher levels of EU policy coordination. But in the process, the varying capacities for adjustment of European welfare states has also been exposed, as have their particular strengths and weaknesses as systems of social protection and inclusion. Welfare 'sustainability', in response primarily to internal pressures, but within a changing and perhaps more constraining international environment, has become the core issue for European countries.

The first section of this chapter briefly summarizes the recent policy debate on these issues. We then look at the nature of the so-called 'global imperatives', including economic internationalization and European integration, before considering how welfare states and wage bargaining systems in Europe may be affected by (and affect) these developments. The final section speculates about the future of a multilevel system of governance for the 'European social model'. In this way, the present chapter builds upon the one preceding – by starting with developments in the European Union and pushing consideration both outward toward more global imperatives and inward toward the welfare state.

The debate: Europeanization and national welfare systems

Much of the debate on the supposed 'social deficit' of the EU has mirrored many of the misplaced assumptions concerning the EU's 'democratic deficit'. Many observers (both Euro-pessimists and Europhiles) made an automatic equation between the creation of a Europe-wide market under the single market programme, the destruction of national social compacts and the separation of the individual from national social citizenship. In this view there was a big disequilibrium: the creation of a pan-European market which would destroy national welfare states in the absence of a parallel European welfare state and industrial relations system. A similar set of arguments pointed out that national systems of parliamentary representation were being marginalized by the transfer of key aspects of decision-making to the Council of Ministers, and that the next obvious steps were the creation of a European parliament with full powers and the transfer of still more decision-making powers to Brussels. In the worst nightmares of Europhobes the destruction of national democratic systems would then be complete.

But most analysts of European democracy were aware of the fact that the democratic 'deficit' was due less to the failure to create a European government with all the parallel requisites of a national state, than because of the poor articulation between levels of democratic representation and the difficulties of creating a workable link between the European parliament, the Council of Ministers and the European Commission. The creation of an 'imperfect democracy' at the European level has not deprived national parliamentary systems of their democratic essence, but rather added an additional level to the multilevel European polity. Only recently, though, has there emerged a similar acceptance that in the realm of social and labour-market policy the problem might lie less in the absence of a 'European industrial relations system' or a 'European social constitution' (though there are still those committed to their creation), than in the ways in which multiple levels of decision-making (which had emerged over time) were articulated.

Until a recently, the following assumptions were commonplace (if not universal) amongst 'experts' (see Rhodes, 2001a):

- national bargaining systems were collapsing as firms (empowered by the new mobility of capital) broke with long-standing wage negotiating systems and social compacts;
- corporatism was also breaking down as market integration (and more generally 'globalization') induced a shift in the policy preferences of capital and labour, creating new cross-class coalitions in the exposed and sheltered sectors of economies;
- that EMU convergence and globalization would have a disciplinary 'neo-liberal' impact which would lead to welfare retrenchment and a collapse of social solidarity, compounded by the rapidly shifting geography of industrial location under the single market;
- and that as national systems of social citizenship were eroded, the problems of putting in place a European social welfare system would lead instead to a convergence on residual, 'neo-liberal' social security systems.

Of course, it was always unlikely that institutionally embedded industrial relations systems and the historical accretion of social security entitlements and programmes could be unravelled rapidly by changes in the external environment. Many have subsequently set about correcting this assumption by elaborating the reasons why change cannot occur in this way, with much recent investment in theories of 'path dependence'. Among those who realized this, a large number – especially economists – posited a rather different set of problems: that it was precisely the political problems of reform in complex, multiple veto-point European polities that would trigger EMU's eventual demise. Nightmare scenarios of collapse due to the impact of asymmetric or symmetric external shocks have pervaded the literature.

More recently, driven more by events, it should be said, rather than by a new set of theoretical insights into how a multilevel socio-economic system might function effectively, a new set of analyses has appeared which centres on innovations in coordination across the EU. These span the recent Cologne, Cardiff, Luxembourg and Lisbon processes which focus, respectively, on macro-economic policies, structural policies, employment and the 'knowledge economy' (see Chapter 1). As discussed below, these processes have been accompanied by the emergence of new forms and forums of policy-making which link the supranational, national and sub-national levels of the EU polity.

Even those who had been dismissive of the import of EU intervention in the social and employment sphere in the past (such as Teague, 2001) are now prepared to allow for the fact that the multiplication of tiers and spheres of Euro-activity might be producing scope for a new type of deliberative democracy. The neo-liberal market might not triumph after all; the absence of a European 'social constitution' or Euro-industrial relations system might not matter if national welfare and labour relations systems could be preserved with the help of European 'steering'; and rather than a separation of economic citizenship from the nation-state (without its replacement by a fully-fledged European alternative), citizenship – both social and economic – might now be 'nested' and protected at various levels of the Euro polity (Faist, 2000).

At the same time, as also discussed below, the process of EMU convergence has itself wrought important changes across European governance systems that may help sustain rather than destroy them – especially in the area of budgetary and wages policy, the two most critical areas of action for EMU entry in line with inflation and deficit criteria. Central to this process of innovation has been the emergence – across Europe – of different types of national 'social pact', or their functional equivalents, as a means of stabilizing macro-economic management and of reforming social and employment systems.

The critical questions are, however, first whether these innovations are sufficient to deal with the more general pressures from the global and increasingly integrated European economies; second whether national welfare systems have sufficient domestic adjustment capacity; and third how effectively that capacity can be connected with and enhanced by a pan-European strategy.

Globalization and economic integration

It has often been argued that globalization, the creation of EMU (especially the 'austerity' related to EMU's debt and deficit convergence criteria) and life under EMU's Stability and Growth Pact will disrupt the difficult and fragile compromises that underpin EU-country social contracts (see Rhodes, 2001b, for a survey and critique of the arguments). External pressures (trade and tax competition, the enhanced influenced of actors in liberated international financial markets) were set to unravel Europe's existing regulatory structures. Although there is no way of knowing exactly what will happen in the future, we can suggest that this scenario is much less probable than many have claimed, and that such forces are unlikely to be the most important subversive influences on the European social order. European welfare states remain large, expensive and highly redistributive and their systems of labour market protection both generous and extensive. Nevertheless, many studies of 'globalization' convey a quite different picture. Thus, in a recent and otherwise cautious study, Scholte (2000, pp. 224, 240) argued that 'globalization has promoted what critics have decried as a "race to the bottom" of labour conditions [*sic*]', while 'the huge expansion of globally mobile capital . . . has constrained states to abandon many of their redistributive policies.'

In fact, for Europe, there is no evidence for either of these claims. The facts are these: First, there is no necessary correlation between welfare-state size/redistribution and the competitiveness of a country's companies in export markets. The costs paid by firms and workers for welfare are often compensated for by high rates of productivity. Second, there has been no EU equivalent of the US 'Delaware effect' whereby the permissive corporate regulatory regime of the State of Delaware attracts a disproportionate share of large company incorporation and has arguably eroded standards of corporate regulation (Barnard, 2000). Nor is there evidence that the 'growing power of multinationals' or the capacity of firms to redeploy their activities across borders is unravelling traditional employment protection systems. It is true that in the perpetual struggle between capital and labour over labour-market regulation the 'threat of relocation' has sometimes been used to raise the stakes. But analyses of transnational investment patterns provide no support for the argument that multinationals are exploiting the differences in labour-market standards and regulatory institutions between Europe's diverse welfare regimes (Traxler and Woitech, 2000).

Third, nor is there evidence for 'social devaluation'. A recent cross-national study of social dumping in the OECD concluded that rather than a 'race to the bottom', social spending in most countries has been increasing at a faster rate than economic growth (Alber and Standing, 2000). In Europe, spending in all countries increased as a proportion of GDP in the 1990s, although that growth was increasingly constrained in the biggest welfare spenders – as, for example, in Finland and the Netherlands (Rhodes, 2001b). A cursory glance at social spending figures actually show a 'race to the top', with Portugal, for example, expanding the scale of its welfare state substantially rather than consolidating its status as a low-cost jurisdiction. In employment conditions, permanent contracts remain dominant (and highly regulated by collective agreements and statute), and although there has been a spread of new contract forms (short-term, part-time work) in Europe, countries with high levels of social protection have also extended that protection to these 'new' forms of work.

Fourth, tax competition in the EU, a supposedly major factor in the 'downward' convergence of welfare states, has failed to operate as predicted. As the European Commission (2000e, p. 67) demonstrates, there is no evidence that tax competition has reduced the tax burden on capital 'which has remained broadly stable over the past three decades'. While increased capital mobility in theory places downward pressures on tax rates, such pressures are countered by the fact that investors take many other factors into account when making investment decisions. At the same time, the high degree of complexity in modern economies makes it difficult for states to act 'rationally' in calculating the real gains of engaging in a competitive cost game (Dehejia and Genschel, 1999), while a growing welfare bill means that revenue must be found somewhere. Thus, tax systems are regularly reformed, but tax bases and total revenue have been sustained. In order to comply with EMU deficit constraints, many countries actually raised a range of taxes that they will now have to battle to reduce.

Finally, as for the globalization of finance, the power of financial actors to move money around the globe has generally not impacted upon the large European welfare states just because they are large. There is some evidence that once deficits and debts exceed a certain level (10 per cent and 100 per cent of GDP respectively), European governments have lost 'credibility' with the markets which have then downgraded their international debt ratings. But this is not some kind of 'neo-liberal' reflex action or punishment; rather it is an indicator that those countries have lost control of their budgets. The best evidence we have suggests that financial-market actors are much less concerned with the nature and size of welfare states – or in the composition of their funding and spending – than is generally supposed. For example, while bond-market participants may have concerns about certain macro-economic trends (such as the movement towards or away from certain levels of debt and 'risk'), they 'don't care about the micro-management of the economy' (Mosely, 2000, pp. 748–9).

If the 'globalization' threat has been exaggerated, what about EMU? For many observers, monetary integration is just one more nail in the coffin of the traditional welfare state. They argue that:

- the adoption of a single currency means a binding commitment to low budget deficits and debts, and therefore welfare states must suffer;
- that since under EMU countries can no longer devalue to improve competitiveness, they will shift the burden of adjustment to the labour market, forcing down wages and employment protection;
- that if to this is added the more competitive economy that a single currency will also promote, then EMU will have a 'neo-liberal disciplinary' effect eroding what is left of the distinctive Keynesian welfare-state tradition.

Although intuitively correct, these are actually difficult arguments to sustain. EMU is often linked with globalization as a reinforcing framework, driving neo-liberalism forward and embedding its deregulatory norms in the European economies. Although the Werner Committee first set out a plan for monetary union in 1970, the fact that EMU succeeded only some 25 years later is usually explained by the dramatic surge in short-term capital movements in the late 1970s (which triggered the launch of the EMS – a precursor of EMU – in 1978), or by the spread of neo-liberal ideas and 'sound money' ideology in the 1980s (McNamara, 1998).

But there are alternative explanations, including that which is partly responsible for the support of social democratic parties for EMU – the inability of governments to control domestic distributive conflict, especially in the wake of the oil-price shocks of the 1970s. The effect was to change the minds of European social democrats about how best to achieve wage and price stability, while also converting Europe's central bankers from the soft Keynesians they once were to hard-currency advocates. There are also alternatives to the assumption that EMU reinforces the effects of globalization. To the extent that EMU reduces the exchange-rate exposure of European countries, it should moderate rather than accentuate the impact of 'global' forces.

What about 'neo-liberal discipline'? If the shift to independent (of government) central banks and then to the independent European Central bank under EMU exercises a disciplinary effect on distributive conflict in the labour market, and has turned Europe from a zone of inflationary instability to one of price stability, then a major problem that had plagued the continent since the oil shocks of the 1970s has been solved. There is no reason why the incomes policies that helped European countries make that transition should 'impoverish' workers. A new balance between inflation control and growth has now to be reestablished, but that is not excluded under the Stability and Growth Pact that now regulates the EMU-country economies. Nor does the Stability and Growth Pact exclude high spending on welfare states; it simply ensures that such expenditure is covered by revenue, and that distributional conflict is not offset and absorbed by expanding public debt.

In reality, 'getting in shape for EMU' did nothing to prevent even the most debt-ridden and poorly managed European economies from reducing their deficits and debts while also boosting spending on social and employment policy. Higher taxes, privatization and lower interest payments, facilitated by falling interest rates, on smaller national debts, all allowed welfare states to keep on growing. Spending trends at constant prices for the EU15 show that over the period 1990–97, total benefits increased by nearly 20 per cent – and the most heavily indebted states (Italy and Belgium) increased real social spending by 16–18 per cent while also qualifying for EMU. Studies of benefit generosity and replacement rates show remarkable stability across the EMU convergence decade (Allan and Scruggs, 2000; Boeri, 2000). In other words, these welfare states did not become less generous. In pensions, only the most generous systems reduced entitlements slightly, while the less generous increased them. As for social assistance transfers, there has been a 'race to the top', with all systems becoming more generous. There is not much that is 'neo-liberal' about all this – a cause for celebration on the Left, evidence of European welfare state sclerosis for the Right.

Indeed, this evidence has led many economists to make the opposite argument to that made by many political scientists: that welfare states and labour markets in Europe are so immutable and rigid that, rather than EMU destroying welfare states, welfare states will destroy EMU. There are several key arguments here:

- that the very weak mobility of labour amongst the member states, due in part to the attachment of workers to national social systems, will impede adjustment to external shocks, increasing employment imbalances;
- that the presence of different legal systems, cultures, and social and political structures within EMU will mean that the impact of external shocks will also be uneven or asymmetric given varying national capacities for adjustment;
- and that the absence of a federal system of social security or other mechanisms of cross-national solidarity will produce growing distributive conflict across divergent social systems.

One response to these fears is simply to say that we just do not yet know whether, say, the uneven capacity of European countries to respond to the oil price shock in the 1970s would be repeated – and exacerbated – under EMU. What we do know, however, is that EMU will limit the exchange rate and inflationary chaos that could ensue from such a shock. Already the first was evident in the much reduced impact of the turbulence in currency markets imparted by the Asia Crisis in 1997–98 compared with previous such crises. More importantly, we also know that each of these claims either exaggerates the danger or underplays the innovations already made in the 1990s in systems of budgetary management and social-conflict resolution.

To take the issue of labour mobility first, much hinges on whether EMU fosters greater regional specialization or greater diversity. If greater diversification occurs, then the low responsiveness of European migration to regional disparities in per capita income and unemployment rates will be much less of a problem. What we know already from the best evidence available is that specialization patterns have changed very little in the last couple of decades (Bentivogli and Pagano, 1999; Middelfart-Knarvit *et al.*, 2000). If the creation of the single market has not generated major adjustments of this type, then the impact of EMU may not be as great as sometimes feared.

But there are other worries. De Grauwe and Skudelny (1999) fear that differences in social conflicts and bureaucratic inefficiency will lead to different effects on economic growth after the same terms of trade shock. Others (such as Martin, 1998, p. 20) argue that EMU is likely to generate a more general collapse of traditional mechanisms of wage solidarity, and a 'deflationary vicious circle of labour cost dumping, or competitive internal depreciations.' However, the pessimists should be reassured by the knowledge that adjustment mechanisms to counter such problems have already been strengthened in the last decade, while the process of ongoing integration will create others.

Thus, the 1990s have seen many states develop both greater fiscal decision-making capacity as well as new means of conflict resolution. Italy, Portugal and Belgium are 'vulnerable' cases of systems whose adjustment to EMU inflation and budgetary criteria were heavily assisted by a combination of such reforms. These strengthened the power of finance ministers, put new methods for coordinating national fiscal systems in place, and launched concerted incomes and social reform strategies. Policy effectiveness and capacities for channelling and defusing social conflict have both been improved. Optimistic economists (such as Artis and Zhang, 1999) also stress that greater synchronization of the business cycle across Europe will also reduce the likelihood that EMU will generate unsustainable disturbances to the socio-economic fabric of the continent. In light of these changes, arguments that EMU will fall apart without a harmonization of welfare systems, or the creation of a strong system of pan-European social transfers (that is a new, federal, social constitution), lose much of their force.

But none of this is to argue that welfare reform is unnecessary under EMU and the single market, or that the adjustment capacities of national welfare states are not a potent issue. It is and they are.

Welfare states and labour markets: performance and adjustment

To a large extent, concern about the fate of European welfare under globalization and EMU has been misplaced. The main problems currently confronting European welfare systems come from within rather than without. This is not to say that external pressures are irrelevant, but they should be considered alongside the much more critical issue of the sustainability of Europe's welfare states, dependent on the control of social security budgets whose costs (requiring high levels of taxation and social security contributions) are driven by a combination of demand- and supply-side factors:

- demographics (ageing, with profound implications for pensions, elderly care and health services);
- health technology (the availability and demand for ever-more sophisticated cures and treatments);
- and, in the 'Continental' and Southern countries, low levels of labour market participation (limiting the scale of the tax and contribution base and boosting passive benefit spending).

How well are welfare states and labour markets responding to these challenges? As the rich literature on 'welfare models' has shown

(Esping-Andersen, 1990, 1999; Scharpf and Schmidt, 2000a,b; Ebbinghaus and Manow, 2001), the reform agendas and adjustment capacities of Europe's diverse welfare regimes (Anglo-Saxon, Scandinavian, Continental and Southern) are shaped by different performances, 'problem constellations' and developmental logics. (The following discussion derives from Ferrera, Hemerijck and Rhodes, 2000.)

Welfare states

Employment performance – a key indicator of successful welfare state adjustment – varies enormously across Europe. Employment-to-population ratios (in 2000) range from 53 per cent in Italy to 76 per cent in Denmark; and unemployment from 2.4 per cent in Luxembourg to 14 per cent in Spain). But there is a general trend: countries with employment rates below the average (Germany, Belgium, France, Spain and Italy) are welfare states of the Continental or the Southern type. Their strong reliance on payroll taxes to finance social security drives up non-wage labour costs; and all have modest levels of public and private employment. Not all of these welfare states are stuck in an 'inactivity trap' (the Netherlands and Portugal have performed much better), but generally these countries are caught in a vicious circle of 'welfare without work'.

The Scandinavian countries of Denmark and Sweden do best: they lead in female, public and overall employment and suffer least from long-term and youth unemployment, and use early retirement much less than their Continental counterparts. They also do best in terms of welfare generosity and distributive performance. They are the proof that high rates of employment and large, expensive welfare states can successfully coexist. Even after the turbulent 1980s and 1990s (when they all experienced a crisis of rising unemployment and budgetary imbalances), they continue to be the most generous welfare states with very high levels of spending, especially on social services. The Continental welfare states remain at intermediate levels of generosity and spend less on social services (while also suffering from higher unemployment). The liberal Anglo-Saxon and the Southern welfare states are lean in both social spending and public services.

In terms of distribution, the Anglo-Saxon countries display not only high levels of wage dispersion, but also relatively high poverty rates and inequitable income distribution. The Continental welfare states again have a medium distribution performance, but the Southern welfare states, with average levels of wage dispersion, reveal strong disparities in income distribution and poverty. This has nothing to do with globalization: it is a consequence of their pension-heavy and 'insider'-biased welfare systems and the absence of adequate safety nets for young people, single mothers and the long-term unemployed. Although belonging to the continental cluster, Belgium, Germany and the Netherlands perform well along all three dimensions, coming close to the Nordic welfare states in terms of distributive outcomes.

None of this diversity, in terms of 'welfare effort' (the scale of spending) or distributive outcomes, is necessarily threatened by globalization or EMU, in part because, as already argued above, those effects (both actual and potential) have tended to be exaggerated. But each regime cluster suffers from specific problems that may also indicate problems of adjustment, including their general sustainability (the extent to which welfare entitlements, present and future, can be met), their adaptability (to greater competition and the emergence of 'post-industrial' employment) and their susceptibility to social conflict.

Despite their large size and high costs, Scandinavian welfare states are well-equipped to adjust to the new risks and needs associated with ageing societies and post-industrial employment. Basic income guarantees provide a safeguard against poverty and exclusion, as well as spells out of work and broken careers. Extensive, quality social services cater for the caring needs of families (such as for the young and the elderly), allowing high rates of female employment. High rates of employment also ease present and future financial strains on pension systems. These countries invest more than most in education and labour-market training (a crucial policy for more knowledge-intensive economies), but the high tax wedge, low wage dispersion and high minimum wages do impede private service-sector job-creation. Correcting this may require that traditional norms of universalism and egalitarianism in wages and job protection are relaxed.

Although the 'liberal' UK welfare state has no problem in creating private service-sector jobs, or in long-term pensions liabilities (due to a break in the link between state pensions and earnings in the 1980s), it faces serious problems on other fronts. New Labour is fighting against poverty and social exclusion through an increase in minimum guarantees, tax reforms and the introduction of new targeted programmes, while the underperforming health system is being strengthened and investment in human-capital policies increased to upgrade skills. Education expenditure was just below the EU average in the mid-1990s, but support for labour-market training was very modest. Government spending, however, has been heavily constrained by the unpopularity of higher taxes; and public services – including the economically critical transport system – continue to languish, falling behind the standards of most other European countries.

If Scandinavia has a 'flexibility' problem and the UK has mainly a 'security' problem, the Continental countries face a fight on both fronts. A major priority is strengthening their relatively solid education and training systems behind their high-skill systems of production. But this will not generate new and high levels of employment. As argued by various authors (Esping-Andersen, 1999; Scharpf, 2000b), the most promising solution is an expansion of services, producing higher female employment rates. But the social insurance logic of these systems and low levels of labour-market flexibility are ill-suited to such post-industrial developments, tending to price lower-end private services out of the market. In addition, these countries are finding it hard to make their pensions systems sustainable, given adverse demographic change and generous formulae for calculating benefits.

The Southern welfare states are fighting on all fronts. They are very generous in one area – social insurance pensions, which are proving very hard to reform – but weak in most others, including education, training and support for families. A major priority is an improvement of the basic safety net (the floor of tax-financed benefits) which is important for combatting poverty and exclusion as well as for cushioning the costs of economic change, for unemployment rates remain high and persistent, especially among the young. Spain and Portugal have made important steps in this direction, but certain key elements (such as a national minimum income guarantee) are still missing in Italy and Greece. They also require an expansion of the service sector, which might encourage more employment (especially for women) and reinvigorate fertility which is now amongst the lowest in the world. But given marked territorial disparities and the size of the underground economy, the promotion of this new welfare mix is no easy task in the South.

Labour markets

Perhaps the most critical issue for the future is how reforms in these welfare-state systems – which span social security systems and the labour market – can be achieved in the absence of widespread social conflict. For introducing changes in pensions, social benefits and employment protection inevitably comes up against vested interests committed to the status quo. The link with labour costs is a critical one here, for under EMU not only may competitive pressures be stronger, but rising social contributions can also lead to inflation-stoking wage claims. One of the key effects we can attribute to EMU is the vital connection that now exists between concerted welfare reform and wage bargaining.

Both neo-liberal theory and many of the forecasts set out by political scientists for the 1990s involved a decentralization and fragmentation of wage bargaining along Anglo-American lines. Social conflict in these circumstances might have been expected to increase. In fact, despite the usual skirmishing between employers and trade unions, there has been remarkable stability in patterns of wage bargaining across Europe. In some cases, existing systems have been strengthened while also being linked into the incomes policy and welfare reform components of broader social pacts.

We can explain this by the presence of both centralizing and decentralizing forces in domestic economies, but which are clearly linked to external developments. New mechanisms for social conflict management have developed to deal with the external constraint of Maastricht convergence criteria as well as the resolution of ongoing 'flexibility struggles' over acceptable levels of labour-market regulation. For as mentioned above, in addition to its impact on budgetary policy, EMU and the creation of the single market have placed new pressures on wage–cost competition and made competitive devaluation impossible. Meanwhile, employers in all systems are searching for greater flexibility in terms of contracts and pay.

But contrary to widespread expectations, they have also been reluctant to dismantle systems of wage coordination where unions retain important bargaining power. Because even if this power was reduced by high levels of unemployment in the 1980s and 1990s, demand for skilled labour in key sectors remained. In many countries it became clear that realizing flexibility reform strategies would be easier if the unions were on side to help. Furthermore, cost-competitiveness and monetary stability – as well as 'credibility' with international financial markets – do not place a premium on deregulated labour markets; for they require a means of preventing wage drift and the emergence of new inflationary pressures. This has led most governments to put in place new incomes policy arrangements – a critical component of many new national bargains on broader issues of welfare reform.

The potential for conflict among these contradictory pressures is considerable. But under the EMU convergence constraint even those countries least likely to achieve an incomes policy deal and so remove inflation from the labour market did so and were able to qualify. This process was assisted by the interaction of a number of different policy innovations within existing industrial relations systems. Sustaining wage coordination and the generalization of productivity-linked bargaining played a critical role – and will continue to do so now EMU is in place.

Four main types of wage coordination exist in Europe, elements of which overlap and interact in particular systems (derived from Traxler, 1999, and Schulten and Stueckler, 2000):

- inter-associational coordination by national cross-sectoral organizations (Belgium, Finland and Ireland have stronger forms of such coordination, while Germany has a non-binding central recommendation);
- intra-associational coordination between the peak employer and union organizations (Denmark, Finland, Germany, Ireland, Netherlands, Spain and Sweden, with a weaker form of peak level information exchange in Germany);
- pattern bargaining – that is, coordination by a sectoral trend-setter (evident in Austria, Denmark, Finland, Germany, the Netherlands and Norway);
- state imposed coordination via a legal pay indexation or a reference point in a statutory minimum wage (either set by national-legal agreements as in Belgium and Greece or by law as in the Netherlands, Portugal, Spain and the UK).

Rather than the predicted collapse of these systems on the lines of a decentralized, Anglo-American model, the major changes in recent years have been in Sweden (a major shift from intersectoral to sectoral bargaining in the early 1990s); in the Netherlands (a simultaneous decentralization and centralization, depending on the sector); and in Spain (where company agreements have declined in importance in favour of sectoral settlements). The UK is an outlier in the radical degree of change involved in the shift from sectoral to company bargaining in the 1980s and 1990s.

Rather than collapse, the general tendency has been to reinforce commitments to existing structures, alongside new links made in many countries between incomes policies and broader social pacts. Furthermore, analysts of EMU and wage bargaining argue that the flexible forms of coordinated bargaining that exist in most European countries should be further strengthened (Iversen, 1999; Traxler, 1999). This is because they provide for an effective response by unions to inflation signals from the bank, and also the possibility that wage moderation will facilitate a more accommodating monetary policy.

Their social pact extensions are also proving vital for introducing the necessary adjustments to welfare systems (in tax and contribution structures, pension liabilities, labour market reform and so forth) discussed above. Denmark, Finland, Greece, Ireland, Italy, Norway and Portugal have all either attempted or achieved national tripartite deals, some of which (Ireland, Portugal, Italy and Finland) have assumed the form of ongoing, quasi-institutionalized pacts. Others (Belgium, Netherlands and Sweden) have relied more on cross-sectoral bipartite agreements, although the Netherlands has also seen that system of agreements linked to the negotiation of more general welfare reforms.

The southern countries have relied greatly on tripartite or bipartite solutions to bring inflation rates into line with the Maastricht criteria, and three – Spain, Italy, Greece – have witnessed considerable changes to the articulation of bargaining levels in the process. Italy in particular has made major advances in welfare reform since the mid-1980s in the framework of its national social pact.

The larger countries of the Continental cluster – France and Germany – have done less well in putting new national strategies for welfare and the labour market in place. In the case of France, the absence of a national pact should not detract from the importance of social partner agreement in any major area of social security reform. In firms, there is a vigorous dialogue on employment reforms linked to the 35-hour week. But the failure to institutionalize a 1997 Wage and Employment Conference has deprived France of the benefits of a more centralized mechanism for wage bargaining. In Germany, an implicit social pact in the early 1990s helped facilitate the unification process and, more recently, the negotiation of a national employment policy has achieved some, albeit limited, success. But in contrast to France, Germany remains a highly coordinated economy, a key pillar of which has been continued employer commitment to a sectoral bargaining system for wages and an employer-led training system. The fact remains that a national agreement on social and employment policy reform – the Bündnis für Arbeit, or pact for employment – has proven very difficult to achieve.

Multilevel governance in EMU

This chapter began by discussing the linkages being forged between the different levels of Europe's systems of socio-economic governance. These now form the embryonic, multi-tiered architecture for the future adjustment of European welfare states and labour markets. This final section considers what is being done, and has still to be done, to make this work.

The key word for the Euro future is 'coordination'. For if EMU is to function well, if inflation and budget deficits are not to undermine the Stability and Growth Pact, and if there truly is to be a process of welfare and labour market reform steered and shaped by new linkages between European decision-making forums and national member states, then coordination in national-level economies must also be sustained. And in particular, if asymmetric external shocks are to be avoided, then the capacity for adjustment of countries with the least well-developed mechanisms for conflict resolution, budgetary management and reform implementation must also be improved.

If symmetric (that is pan-European) cost or demand shocks are also to be avoided, then there is also a critical need for European monetary and fiscal policy making to be anchored, once again, in responsive and stable national systems of social and economic governance. In other words, if EMU is to function effectively, if there is to be an effective coordination of monetary and fiscal policy across the EU, and if – as proponents of the 'European social model' also hope – Euro-wide mechanisms for welfare adjustment are also to be effective, then the following must also be achieved at the national level:

- systems of wage bargaining that can contain income dispersion and inflation, while also accommodating pressures for wage flexibility;
- systems of consensus creation on welfare reform priorities, which can accommodate new policy interdependencies and new groups claiming access to decision making;
- and budgetary systems that can contain and orient spending by sub-national authorities.

Although much ink has been spilt on the issue of globalization, the real issues therefore pertain to the internal operations of EMU and the sustainability of efficient and equitable systems of national governance under its aegis. Although many analysts of globalization are convinced that the nation state is being 'hollowed out', and in the absence of 'supra-state frameworks' to fill the 'regulatory gaps' (e.g. Scholte, 2000, p. 241), in Europe, the 'functional' demands of economic integration are for stronger institutions within the nation-state, alongside parallel innovations at the supra-state level.

Regarding the latter, a 'European social dimension' is already in existence. Over the years, a loosely-structured regime of pan-European rules and policy-making has been put in place, with:

- important substantive elements (in the form of Community legislation and European Court of Justice [ECJ] case law);
- procedural rules and innovations (especially with the expansion of qualified majority voting and the social partnership provisions of the Maastricht Treaty);
- and methods of enforcement (strengthened by Maastricht's empowerment of the ECJ to fine dilatory member states).

The result has been the creation of a multi-tiered policy system and a transition from sovereign to semi-sovereign welfare states, with key elements of European policy (on freedom of movement, employment protection and gender equality) implemented across the member states (Leibfried and Pierson, 2000).

But since the late 1990s there have been initiatives to create a new role for the EU in coordinating (rather than 'harmonizing') welfare systems and linking macroeconomic management with social and employment policies. There have yet to emerge any explicit mechanisms for coordinating wage-bargaining at the EU level (despite some minor cross-border developments in the metals sector). But there has been much speculation about how it might be achieved. Together, these developments begin to give empirical force to the notion of multilevel, or multi-layered governance as both a way of interpreting the evolution of the Euro-polity (see Marks, Hooghe and Blank, 1996), and as a new method for steering an increasingly complex and integrated EU economy.

In effect, several tiers of governance are beginning to mesh together. Regarding pan-European welfare coordination, an attempt is now being made to build on the so-called 'Luxembourg process' that for the last few years has been monitoring employment performance via National Action Plans. Since the EU's Lisbon Summit of Spring 2000, this process, now writ large for social systems more generally, has been dubbed an 'open method of coordination', with the aim of:

- fixing guidelines for social policy, combined with specific timetables for achieving short-, medium- and long-term goals;
- establishing quantitative and qualitative indicators and benchmarks tailored to the needs of different member states and sectors;
- translating European guidelines into national and regional policies by setting targets and measures; and
- using periodic monitoring, evaluation and peer reviews to promote 'mutual learning'.

These are all 'soft' mechanisms to promote reform in ways that are more flexible and more adapted to Europe's diverse social systems than standard EU policy instruments like directives. The first concrete steps to enhance pan-European coordination in welfare policy reform have been taken in social protection and pensions. In social protection, the extent to which work-activation measures are provided as an integral part of minimum income schemes will receive close attention; while in pensions there will be a stress on 'active ageing' – extending the retirement age – alongside an examination of the implications of second and third-tier pensions.

In terms of coordination across policy areas, since the Lisbon Summit in Spring 2000, social protection is being linked much more closely than in the past with employment and macro-economic policies. The European Council now meets every spring to address economic and social questions. Member states have to prepare each year a document illustrating their own social policy agenda, with indicators and targets; and this, it is hoped, will contribute to greater continuity and coherence in Council deliberations. This builds on the Cologne process that addresses the issue of policy interdependencies within EMU. It specifically promotes relations between European employer and union representatives, the Commission, ministers of finance and employment, the European Central Bank and governors of national central banks, focusing on the interconnections between wages, monetary, budgetary and fiscal policies (Goetschy, 2000).

Coordination is also the key word in wage bargaining under EMU, given Europe's highly uneven and differentiated system of industrial relations discussed above. Following Dolvik (2000, pp. 45–6) the best-case solution would be one in which cross-sectoral bargaining is sustained within countries, as cross-national bargaining within sectors (initially the metal industry, airlines and so forth) gradually begins to emerge. This could operate across levels, and be functionally compatible with the macro-economic requirements of EMU by 'conditioning (upstream) national participation in European coordination and transposing (downstream) European margins and parameters into national systems in accordance with different national and sectoral conditions'.

The eventual outcomes of this actual and anticipated process of institutional engineering are impossible to predict. But to return to the question posed at the beginning of this chapter – whether national adjustment capacities can be connected with and enhanced by a pan-European strategy – the answer is that, through a complex process of institutional innovation at both levels, that connection is being made. The project is underway. If national welfare systems can be made sustainable via supranational steering linked to subsidiary national bargains, then it is also possible that the new macroeconomic regime installed under EMU will enhance the welfare of Europe's citizens. Resolving the problem of the 'democratic deficit' could also be assisted; for the involvement of the representatives of capital and labour alongside their elected counterparts at the interlinked levels of the EU policy process, can only contribute to the 'deliberative' quality of Euro democracy.

Chapter 3

Reorganizing Security in Europe

HELENE SJURSEN

How do national states in Western Europe confront the challenges of security in a new millennium? What are the implications for states' capacity to defend themselves against a variety of potential external threats in the context of ever-more porous borders? These questions burst onto television screens across the globe with the tragic images of the September 11, 2001, terrorist attack on the World Trade Centre in New York. Nevertheless, questions about the changing nature of national security had already been around for quite some time, and their salience for consideration of the continuing relevance of the national state is nowhere more pressing than in Western Europe.

This chapter starts from the premise that the changes in European security primarily challenge the legitimacy basis of security policies of European states rather than their capacity to defend their citizens. It is in other words the very basis on which security policy is formulated that is at stake. In order to clarify this it is necessary to define security and identify the various changes to the security agenda in Europe. This will be done in the first section of the chapter. The second section looks more closely at what these changes have meant for the security policy of West European states, and in the third section the significance of the changes and possible future developments in European security are discussed.

Continuity and change in the European security agenda

The end of the Cold War constituted an important challenge to prevailing security and defence policies and perceptions of security in Western Europe. The challenge was not only to redefine the types of threats that Western Europe would have to contend with and to identify the best instruments to respond to such threats. In fact, the most important challenge was to the very basis on which European security policy was developed. Which interests, values and principles should be promoted and protected? Or to put it differently, the normative dimension to security policy became more visible.

According to Arnold Wolfers (1952, p. 484) security should be understood as the absence of threats to acquired values. Expanding on this, David Baldwin considers security to be a situation in which there is 'a low probability of damage to acquired values' (Baldwin, 1997, p. 13). Such a definition is, however, only a starting point; further specification is required in order for the concept to be helpful in empirical studies. We might start by asking whose security it is we are talking about. Furthermore, one might ask what values it is that should be defended? These are essentially questions of qualities and standards. Ultimately, they point to the issue of what kind of society we want to live in (and thus wish to protect). However, as the responses to the questions of 'whose security' and 'which values' have often been taken as a given, at least in studies of international relations, the fact that the security issue has a normative dimension has often been neglected. In international relations the state (usually assumed to be a coherent nation-state) has almost automatically been considered the 'referent object' of security (Buzan, 1991). As for the values to be defended, these have also been taken for granted: ultimately it is the territorial integrity and political independence of the state that is to be protected. Finally, security from what? Again, the answer was a state. Other states have usually been considered as the principal threat to territorial integrity and political independence.

These specifications to the concept of security are closely linked to a particular model of the international system – the Westphalian model (Held, 1993, p. 29). The political compromise that underlies this model is centred on a geographic basis for political organization, in which the principles of sovereignty, territorial integrity and non-intervention are key. Furthermore, due to the assumption of anarchy in the international system, striving for security is the ultimate concern of the foreign policies of states according to this model. There is no superior authority that can 'lay down the law' from a more independent or objective position than the individual states. The international system is, in other words, seen to be in a 'state of nature'. In such a system, politics is a struggle for power where each state must look after its interests as best it can and with all available means. Questions of values or of morality are considered to have little or no place in such a system: they belong to domestic politics.

During the Cold War the security and defence policies of West European states were to a large extent considered to rely on a logic such as the one outlined above. Perhaps the clearest example of this is French security and defence policy. The French security doctrine received its most coherent formulation with the election of Charles de Gaulle as president of the Fifth Republic in 1958. It was maintained by his predecessors and thus remained the basis for French security policy until the early 1990s. De Gaulle organized French security and defence policy around the principle of political autonomy. He was convinced that France needed an independent defence capacity in order to ensure this autonomy and to allow France to maximize her national interests. There was no doubt, in other words, about the referent object of security or of the values to be defended in this case. France even withdrew from the military integration in NATO in 1966 and developed an independent nuclear capacity for the same reasons of national autonomy. These initiatives have often been understood as an expression of anti-Americanism, but although this may be part of the explanation, French security and defence policy cannot be properly understood without taking into account these basic premises upon which it was built. At the heart of French security and defence policy was the nation-state, and it was this idea that gave legitimacy to French policy (Sauder, 1999). Remaining within NATO, other West European states seemed more pragmatic with regard to the question of autonomy. Still, their security and defence policies were organized around the same principle of territorial defence. As a traditional military alliance, membership in NATO was for a majority of these states seen as an efficient means to obtain this security objective.

The end of the Cold War constituted an important challenge to such perceptions of security in Western Europe. With the collapse of the Warsaw Pact, the perceived threat on which much of West European security and defence policies had been built since the end of the Second World War disappeared almost overnight. It now seemed increasingly unrealistic to suggest that West European states' security was challenged by an 'enemy state'. Moving away from the emphasis on defending the territory of the nation-state from an external military threat, discussions on security and defence policy increasingly began to focus on so-called non-territorial threats and to refer to an 'enlarged' security concept. These non-territorial threats were considered to take the form of terrorism, drug-trafficking, nuclear waste and also ethnic conflict that might spread beyond a particular state-territory. It was also argued more often that economic and social imbalances, environmental problems and humanitarian disasters were as important or perhaps even more important security risks than the threat of external military invasion.

Thus, the way in which the definition of security was specified started to change. In response to the question of 'security for whom?' it was no longer self-evident that the answer was the state. Increasingly, the focus turned from the state to the individual as the 'referent object' of security.

And as to the values to be defended, these were no longer only the territorial integrity of the state. In fact in several instances this integrity was challenged in the name of principles of human rights. As a result of these changes a debate also developed about the legitimacy of the use of military means outside the territory of the nation-state, with the aim of protecting international norms and rules.

The changes to the specifications of security should not, however, be seen as the exclusive result of the end of the Cold War; they must be understood in the context of broader changes in the European system of states. Also, these 'alternative approaches' to security were not new with the end of the Cold War. They constituted the basis on which for example the Helsinki process (now the Organization for Security and Cooperation in Europe [OSCE]) was launched in the early 1970s. However, it was only with the end of the Cold War that these ideas gained a wider acceptance.

A principal consequence of these broader changes to the international system is that the privileged status of the state is challenged, and with these challenges to the state the very basis upon which security policy has been built is also questioned. It is possible to note three conditions that illustrate the internal and external challenges to the state. Firstly, the emergence of new issues at the level of the international political agenda in Europe. Following from this, the conventional hierarchy of policy issues that gives priority to security and defence issues also seems to be abandoned. The second condition is the emergence of new transnational, supranational, economic and political and security actors in addition to the state, at the European level. What many of these actors have in common is that they do not have a territorial base and that they act without reference to a specific national interest. These various groupings may, to varying degrees, seek to defend their interests through European institutions outside the nation-state. The third condition is the strengthening of a normative and legal dimension in the international system. In a complex international system characterized by interdependence, order is the result of a network of agreements and international institutions and not exclusively of a balance of power. Such networks of international institutions cover a wide spectre of themes from environmental issues and human rights to defence issues. As a consequence, norms and rules at the international level do increasingly influence state behaviour and set standards for appropriate behaviour both between states and within states.

These challenges to the state constitute an opportunity to (re-) open the questions of the basis on which security policy should be formulated. When the referent object of security – the nation-state – is no longer taken as a given, the legitimacy of a security policy that relies exclusively on 'national security' is also jeopardized. Hence, the question of the basis on which we should develop European security policy – which interests, values, norms should be promoted and protected – comes to the fore. The normative dimension to security policy becomes visible.

It must, however, be added that although most agree that European security is changing, there is considerable uncertainty in assessments of the extent of change to the specifications of security as well in the evaluation of the implications of such a change. As the sudden shock of the World Trade Centre attacks has made clear, a sense of security or insecurity is subjective to a large extent. An important question thus becomes the direction in which policy-makers choose to take the issue. There does, however, seem to be a general agreement that security policy in Western Europe now holds three dimensions. The first is the traditional conception of security and defence policy where the purpose is to defend the territory of a nation-state or a group of states from a clearly identified external military threat. The second dimension considers the idea of mutual interdependence between states, so that national security is seen to depend on overall international stability and respect for international norms. With this dimension the focus in security and defence policy thus shifts towards non-territorial security threats. Sources of insecurity are often considered linked to issues such as ethnic conflicts, international crime and terrorism rather than to other states. In turn this leads to a discussion of the legitimacy of using military means in situations which are not concerned with defending national territory. The third dimension points to social and economic imbalances, humanitarian crises and environmental disasters as larger security challenges than military threats. Despite the immediate aftermath of September 11, 2001, the tendency in the European security agenda has been to move away from the first dimension of territorial defence and towards the third dimension of an enlarged security concept.

To what extent and in what ways have these changes in the European security agenda affected the basis on which West European nation-states develop their security and defence policies? In discussing this question the focus here will be on the first and second dimensions of security and defence policy outlined above. The third dimension is dealt with elsewhere in this volume.

Coping with change: the weight of national idiosyncrasies

Most West European states have sought to adapt to the changes in their security environment. The overall tendency has been to concentrate on

two things: first a refocus towards the ability to conduct crisis management operations and peacekeeping missions outside the national territory and a move away from territorial defence. This has also led to a
reduction in subsidies to the armed forces. Indeed much of the discussion on security policy in Western Europe was a discussion about how
to reallocate resources from security and defence to other policy arenas.
Second, there has been increased emphasis on international coordination and multilateral responses to security. Underlying these changes is
the assumption that security in one part of Europe depends on security
in Europe as a whole and that European security policy exists not only
to ensure stable relations between states, but also to protect certain
principles, such as the respect for democracy and human rights, that are
considered to be constitutive of West European states. Thus, a certain
change in the legitimacy basis for security and defence policy is visible.

Despite this seeming overall convergence in the interpretation of the
new security environment, national adaptations have taken different
paths. Some states started reforming their policies early in the 1990s,
others did not start this process until the end of the decade. Likewise,
the domestic political reactions to change have varied in the different
European states. These differences highlight the importance of institutional patterns, long-established norms and role conceptions for the
formulation of national security policy. Security policy is not formulated
from a *tabula rasa*; certain issues are taken as given from the outset and
constitute the premises on which policy choices are made. This also
means that the general principles on which there seems to be agreement
have taken on a different meaning in different national cultural/political
contexts. To challenge the political 'givens' is not always simple. In
order to illustrate the different paths to adaptation we will look at two
large states in Europe's core – France and Germany – and one small
state in Europe's periphery – Norway.

France: the end to exceptionalism?

As we have already noted the aim of national independence was central
to French security and defence policy. France was also a strong supporter
of separate European security and defence cooperation. Such cooperation
should, however, take the form of cooperation amongst nation-states.
European cooperation was thus seen and presented as an instrument for
French influence and French autonomy rather than as an initiative taken
for the common good. This has also meant that historically:

> Pressure from Paris in favour of the creation of some sort of European
> Security and Defence Identity (ESDI), sustained and imperative

though it has tended to be, has not always been complemented by any
actual Europeanisation of French defence policy and planning.
(Howorth, 1997, p. 23)

With the end of the Cold War one can observe several modifications
to the strong emphasis on autonomy and territorial defence in French
security policy. Some indicators of such change, such as the establishment of the Franco-German brigade, are found in the period before the
end of the Cold War. However, the speed and scope of change intensified and widened in the 1990s. According to Lisbeth Aggestam, changes
have taken place along three dimensions: to the concept of security; to
the approaches to institutional security cooperation; and to perceptions
of France's role in the European security system (Aggestam, 2000). A
key element of change was the publication of the White Book on
defence in 1994. A new military programme law (LPM) followed the
White Book in which a major review of French defence policy was
outlined for the period 1995–2000. After Jacques Chirac's election to
the Presidency in 1995 the changes were speeded up, amongst other
things, through a new LPM for 1997–2000 that replaced the one from
1994 (Howorth, 1997). The changes introduced through these reform
packages were important. They included, for example, the abolition of
conscription and the decision to rely on a professional army. The
changes did not provoke much protest in French public opinion or
amongst French political and military elites, which can perhaps in part
be understood in light of the experiences of the role of French military
in the process of decolonization in France.

If we look specifically at Aggestam's first dimension, the concept of
security, France has moved away from traditional notions of territorial
defence and national autonomy as well as a particular emphasis on the
military dimensions of defence and towards emphasizing interdependence amongst states as an important condition for security. France was
also, together with the United States, amongst the first Western states to
call for a change in the strategic doctrine of NATO, which would allow
NATO to take responsibility for crisis management and peace enforcement operations in addition to territorial defence (Howorth, 1997, pp.
25–6). This move towards the idea that European states must share
responsibility for security and towards a stronger emphasis on security
as a collective responsibility contrasts sharply with earlier years' emphasis on national autonomy. The change is, however, not complete:
France's nuclear policy has only been subject to minor adjustments. The
changes to the second dimension pointed to by Aggestam, approaches
to institutional security cooperation, follow logically from the changes
to the conception of security. The most tangible change here is probably

the announcement by Foreign Minister Hervé de Charette in 1995 that France would rejoin Nato's military committee; although, again, the break with the past must not be overemphasized: In fact, in times of East–West crisis all the presidents of the Fifth Republic – including de Gaulle – supported NATO and the United States. The decision to move closer to NATO was preceded by a number of small steps such as French participation in the Gulf War as a member of the Western coalition, as well as French participation in operations in the former Yugoslavia under NATO command (Le Gloannec, 1997). Several key factors in addition to the changing conceptions of security help explain this change in French policy. Among them are domestic political concerns such as the economic burden of developing European defence capabilities outside NATO for a French economy struggling in the mid-1990s with the effects of the Maastricht criteria for economic and monetary union (EMU). France continued, however, to be strongly in favour of an independent European security capacity. The return to NATO can thus be seen as an indicator of a changed attitude to multilateral security arrangements rather than as a departure from the French emphasis on the need to develop a security and defence capacity for the EU.

This leads us to Aggestam's last dimension: the perception of France in the European security system. At the core of France's European strategy is the relationship with Germany. It is also here that the multilateralization of French security policy is most clearly demonstrated, for example through the Franco-German brigade. At the same time, the relationship with Germany indicates that defence and security issues continue to be sensitive issues amongst European states. This was demonstrated by the initial German reaction to the unilateral French decision to abandon conscription and to change its strategic concept. This decision was made without prior Franco-German consultations. According to Le Gloannec (1997): 'Reactions in Germany to this reform project were bitter, particularly on the part of the defence ministry and the ministry of foreign affairs.' Such tensions were rapidly defused yet they underline the continued sensitivity of defence and security issues amongst West European states.

French aims within European defence concentrate on ensuring that France will be able to fulfill the obligations entailed in the so-called Petersberg tasks, which include humanitarian and rescue tasks, peacekeeping and crisis-management. These are not linked exclusively to French national interests. In fact, Aggestam sees a change towards '. . . an emphasis on Europe as an ethical and responsible power'. Thus, the emphasis on the need to maximize national interests seems to have been, if not abandoned altogether, then at least modified by an emphasis on the universal principles and the rights of individuals under a collective security regime. This is illustrated by the following statement by French President Jacques Chirac:

> So a Europe which is more ethical, which places at the heart of everything it does respect for a number of principles which, in the case of France, underpins a republican code of ethics, and, as far as the whole of Europe is concerned, constitute a shared code of ethics. (Aggestam, 2000, p. 75)

A radical transformation has taken place in French security and defence policy. The legitimacy of this policy was initially based on the ability to protect its citizens from external foreign invasion through the means of a strong and independent military force, but during the 1990s there was a move towards a conception in which security was increasingly seen as a collective issue and where multilateralism constituted a key element in the national approach to security. Interestingly, these changes have taken place without strong domestic protest.

Germany: towards normalization?

Contrary to the French case, multilateralism was the key to German security policy also during the Cold War. Thus, one should perhaps expect that the changes brought by the end of the Cold War would have been easy to deal with for Germany. This is only partly true. While multilateralism was easy, the logical corollary of collective security, namely German participation in 'out-of-area' operations, was a difficult issue.

The security and defence policy of the Federal Republic of Germany (FRG) – to the extent that the FRG can be said to have had an independent defence policy – was strongly influenced by the memory of Nazi Germany. This gave a particular weight in German politics to the principle that the use of force was considered illegitimate for any other reason than for the defence of national territory. The strong reservations against the engagement of German troops for any kind of operation outside national territory were also codified in the FRG's constitution. A further precaution against Germany's militaristic past was generalized conscription. The army was to remain under civilian control and the conscripts '. . . took no oath of obedience in the traditional sense and retained rights of individual conscience not tolerated in the American, British, or French armed forces' (Hodge, 1999a, p. 182). Finally, the Federal Republic's autonomy in military affairs was restricted externally through the Paris agreements. These made it unrealistic to envisage the engagement of West German troops outside the national territory from a legal and not only from a moral perspective.

With the end of the Cold War, the formal restrictions on Germany's security and defence policy were removed. The so-called 'Two-plus-Four' treaty lifted the international legal restrictions on Germany's sovereignty. The German Defence White Paper published in 1994 opened up the possibility of German participation in 'out-of-area' operations. Later the same year, the German constitutional court also gave an interpretation of the Basic Law which indicated that German troops could take part in combat under the umbrella of multilateral security organizations (Bohnen, 1997). Overall, however, the White Paper kept to the German tradition of emphasizing the 'civilian' dimension to security and underlined that the most important security goal of Germany was to maintain peace. The security strategy developed to support this aim was primarily diplomatic, focusing on economic integration, inclusive security institutions and disarmament (Hodge, 1999a, p. 190). As such, it echoed the overall changes in the European security agenda.

The element of continuity in Germany's security policy lies in the continued emphasis on multilateralism. According to the 'principles of participation' outlined by Klaus Kinkel, German Foreign Minster in 1994: 'Germany will never undertake peace missions alone' (Bohnen, 1997, p. 54). German security policy was already during the Cold War deeply integrated in multilateral units in NATO. The national German army was in itself relatively small and ill-equipped to function independently of NATO. Close integration in Western institutional frameworks had been a deliberate policy choice made by German Chancellor Konrad Adenauer after the end of the Second World War. Divided in two and not being allowed an independent defence capacity, the FRG became dependent on its Western allies on security and defence issues. However, it was equally important that membership in Western multilateral institutions allowed the FRG to operate internationally without being suspected of renewed German hegemonic ambitions (Rummel, 1996). It follows from this that the Federal Republic had been supportive of increased security cooperation inside the EU. Nonetheless, due to concern about the consequences that this might have for NATO, it was less enthusiastic on this issue than France. Although the multilateral approach in German security policy could be seen as externally imposed, it seemed to have been assimilated into or redefined as a German tradition and there was no question of abandoning this after reunification.

Despite the lifting of all the formal restrictions on the engagement of German troops in out-of-area operations and peacekeeping missions the reservations against such activities were strong inside Germany. The debate opened with the Gulf War during which German military troops did not participate although Germany contributed financially to the Western operation. The social democrats (SPD) and the greens argued strongly against German participation in military operations outside the national territory. Referring to German history, they considered Germany to have a particular obligation to show 'self-restraint' and act as a peaceful state. Nonetheless, the Gulf War was the last operation with explicit German non-participation. The UN operation in Cambodia was the first to have a German troop contingent – consisting in a field hospital. After this Germany took part in operations in Somalia, Bosnia and Kosovo (Takle, 2000). Germany's reluctance to take part in out-of-area operations came to a complete end with the participation in NATO's Kosovo operation. For the first time German armed forces took part in so-called peacemaking operations and not only peacekeeping operations. Nonetheless it remains a contested issue in German domestic politics.

As a state whose tradition since the end of the Second World War has been commitment to multilateralism, peaceful conflict resolution and emphasis on non-military means – in particular economic means – in security policy, a fully sovereign and reunified Germany was in many ways ahead of its West European colleagues in terms of adapting to the new security environment. However, the 'normalization' of Germany also meant facing difficult choices about the degree of political and military involvement in international affairs, and this became traumatic for both public authorities and citizens at large. The justification for the change that emerged towards the end of the 1990s in Germany's security posture was in many ways similar to that provided by France. The focus shifted from concerns about the German historical legacy towards an argument about Germany's responsibility to contribute to uphold respect for human rights and democracy also outside its own borders (Takle, 2000).

Norway: stuck in the past?

At first sight one would expect Norway to embrace the changes to European security policies after the end of the Cold War unreservedly. Throughout the Cold War, Norway supported the idea of an enlarged security concept and spoke for a policy of conciliation rather than confrontation in East–West relations. Norway also champions 'soft security', sees itself as a 'pioneer in peace', and takes an active part in peacekeeping operations similar to those planned for in the Petersberg tasks of the European Union and in the new strategic concept of NATO. However, rather than embracing the changes to European security,

Norway ardently resisted any change both to the content of Western security policy and to its institutional arrangements throughout the 1990s.

Norway was one of the last countries to accept the change in NATO's strategic concept in 1991. Furthermore, while most of Norway's allies started to redefine their military structure in response to the changes in the strategic environment with the end of the Cold War, Norway maintained its strategic doctrine from the Cold War, focusing on the risk of an external invasion in the north of Norway. And during the period before the NATO summit in Washington in April 1999, Norway consistently worked to protect Article 5 tasks from being put on an equal footing with the new security tasks within NATO. Here, the Norwegian perspective corresponded to that of many European states, but the Norwegian objectives were slightly different. While the other West European states seemed concerned chiefly about ensuring some control over American use of NATO for non-Article 5 missions, Norway's concern was that giving equal status to Article 5 and non-Article 5 operations would weaken NATO's defence guarantee to Norway.

Two elements of change did become identifiable towards the end of the 1990s. The first was an increasing public debate about Norway's defence strategy. The second was the publication of a report to Parliament in June 1999 that confirmed the need for reforms in Norwegian defence in order to make it possible for Norway to take part in international crisis management, as well as the establishment of two parallel defence studies that analysed Norway's defence priorities (St. meld nr 38, 1998–99). This second change came about as a result of changes in NATO and the EU/WEU, which were described by civil servants as constituting a 'constant pressure on Norway's defence concept'; they were not the result of change in Norway's perception of its own security situation (Sjursen, 2000).

It could, of course, be argued that the Norwegian reluctance to change was the result of the country's particular geographical or strategic position. As a small state bordering on Russia, Norway is exposed to security threats that other West European states do not face. However, with the end of the Cold War the security context changed. Although the border with Russia was still there, the challenges it posed to Norway were much more in line with those entailed in an enlarged security concept. The strategy of territorial defence did not offer an efficient response to these 'new' security challenges. A further pragmatic argument for the reluctance to change would focus on the economic benefits that Norway has had from NATO's traditional focus on the northern regions. Throughout the Cold War, Norway received NATO funding for the development of its infrastructure. These funds were used chiefly for investment in military projects but did at the same time lead to economic gains for the civilian economy. In the 1990s these subsidies from NATO were reduced substantially. The justification for the subsidies was the importance of Norway's position at the northern flank of NATO. Thus the reductions are a result of the reduced emphasis on collective defence and on a northern threat to NATO. Hence, one could perceive Norway's insistence on the continuation of NATO's 'old' strategy as motivated not only by Norwegian security interests but also by economic interests. Nonetheless, these economic arguments, although they probably contributed to the difficulty in changing Norwegian security and defence strategy, can hardly be presented as the sole cause of the slow changes in Norwegian defence policy.

Rather, the Norwegian example highlights the importance of institutional patterns, long-established norms and role conceptions for the formulation of national security policy. Norwegian security policy is heavily entrenched in deep-seated identity and world-views, and particularly important is the conception of Norway as a country that is different from its European allies – as a small and particularly peaceful nation that has had to withstand the assault of great powers in Europe (Sjursen, 2000).

Due largely to national idiosyncrasies, the changes in the European security agenda have been given a different meaning in different national settings. They have also challenged different dimensions in the security policies of West European nation-states. As a general rule, however, the emphasis on an 'enlarged' security concept and in particular on crisis management and 'out-of-area' operations has increased.

This change in conception is further confirmed by looking to other West European states than the ones mentioned here. In Britain a thorough review of British defence policy (the British Strategic Defence Review, SDR) was published in 1998. The review is described as setting '. . . the seal on the ending of the Cold War, finally giving up the 50-year belief that the centre of Britain's security concerns was the risk of war in Europe' (Rogers, 1998). In Italy, efforts have also been made to reform and reorient security and defence policy along such lines (Andreatta and Hill 1997, 73–4).

Interestingly, in the case of Britain changes seem to have been most important at the operational level and less important at the more conceptual level, in other words with regard to Britain's role in European and international security. This observation would strengthen the institutionalist account of the emergence of a new security paradigm. As Chuter (1997) shows, the British concept of defence has traditionally differed from the conceptions of its European allies. It was in many ways already closer to the conception of defence that gained predominance in the 1990s: the German and Italian conception of 'citizens in uniform' did not, for example, exist in Britain. Furthermore, most of the wars that Britain has fought have been fought outside its national territory. These differences, which were also reflected in the physical organization of British defence, probably meant that at the operational level Britain's security and defence policy was more disposed to the changes of the post-Cold War era. This was not so at the conceptual level: in fact, the role of Britain and of British defence and security policy in an increasingly interdependent world does not appear to have been revised in parallel with Britain's defence capabilities (Howorth, 2000).

Italy, on the other hand, experienced more difficulties in reorganizing its defence. The difficulties in Italy's case stem from a domestic political system characterized by bureaucratic politics and 'sub-rational logrolling among political factions' (Andreatta and Hill, 1997, p. 67). It must be added that in comparison with Britain the structure and organization of Italy's defence were less disposed to the changes of the end of the Cold War. However, Italy appeared perfectly at ease with the increased emphasis on multilateralization of security and defence policy. Political debate on the role and purpose of security and defence policy has been limited in both countries, but this is particularly surprising in the case of Italy. Due to its geographic location it is one of the European states that has concrete experiences with the 'new' European security environment. And in a longer term perspective it is also located 'potentially on the frontier of a new arc of crisis' (Andreatta and Hill, 1997, p. 67).

What is the significance of this change for the future development of European security? Are we observing a qualitative change in the European security agenda or are the fundamentals of European security still the same?

The collective European security agenda: future developments

It is a truism to observe that if 'security' is placed above everything else, fundamental principles of democracy and respect for human rights can easily be jeopardized. As we know, reference to the primacy of security has, and still is, used as a means to repress dissent. This means that introducing an enlarged security concept as we now see it in Western Europe could be a mixed blessing. Turning new issues such as immigration into questions of security is obviously problematic; such initiatives can easily spill over into other dimensions of domestic politics such as treatment of minorities, asylum and immigration policies. The net result might be to create internal enemies and have these replace external enemies. Likewise, abandoning or relaxing the principle of sovereign equality of states and of non-intervention in favour of intervention could lead to the revenge of might over right.

Are there concrete examples of such tendencies in Europe? The implications of September 11 are still too early to call. Nevertheless, even before the 'war on terrorism' was announced, it has been suggested that the EU's aim of developing 'an area of freedom, security and justice' represents serious risks of impeding on the individual liberties of the citizens of Europe (Monar, 2000). It may also lead to the creation of a fortress Europe and thus to higher insecurity for non-citizens of third countries through strict asylum and immigration policies as well as visa regimes. These individuals may also be subject to unequal treatment within the EU. Furthermore, it has been suggested that the arguments used to justify European integration more generally also rely to an unreasonably large extent on a security argument. It is in other words implied that the security argument is deliberately used to ensure the success of a political process favoured by those in power. Political and economic issues are redefined in terms of security in order to underline their urgency or their particular importance. Hence, Ole Waever has suggested that the process of domesticating security in Europe is being used as an instrument to construct a European political identity with the EU at its core. He argues that 'Europe' is built 'through a peculiar security argument. Europe's past of wars and divisions is held up as the other to be negated, and on this basis it is argued that "Europe" can only be if we avoid renewed fragmentation' (Waever, 1996). Such observations suggest that it should be an aim in itself to avoid, as far as possible the definition of issues as security issues.

However, returning to a 'narrow' definition of security is not enough. Or to put it differently, it is not only the enlarged security concept or the domestication of security that is the potential problem. What matters is the basis on which security policy is developed and the purposes that security policies are supposed to fulfil both domestically and internationally. Or to return to our initial questions, what matters is 'whose security' and 'security for what values'? We have suggested that what is taking place in Europe is a change in how West European nation-states respond to these questions. The nation-state has become woven into a complex network of dependency with other nation-states as well as transnational actors and supranational institutions. As a consequence of this, it is not only the capacity of the sovereign state to be autonomous that is challenged, but the privileged status of the state – institutionalized through the principle of sovereign equality – that is at stake. This means that the traditional role of security policy as a policy that aims to uphold the principle of external sovereignty also comes into question.

If we consider political processes exclusively as processes of competition for power, and actors as interested only in maximizing self-interest, the interpretation would nonetheless be that there are few 'real' changes to security in Europe and that an emphasis on an enlarged security concept only reflects a change of strategy by the 'real' powers in Europe. If we instead define politics as a system with rights and duties that place additional requirements on actors than simply the one of satisfying self-interest, the interpretation could be different. Here one would underline the role of laws, principles and processes of deliberation within an institutionalized system. Such a model of politics relies on a conception of rationality where actors are seen as rational when they are able to justify and explain their actions, and not only when they seek to maximize their own interests. A further important assumption for this perspective is that actors are not just self-interested but reasonable (Eriksen and Weigård, 1999). This is indeed a condition for the functioning of liberal democracy, where citizens are expected to be able to distinguish between different forms of justification for policy-choices and to assess which are acceptable and which are not. The question then is whether or not such a definition of politics as a system with rights and duties is suitable also at the international level in Europe.

The potential for such developments seems stronger today than previously because of the high degree of institutionalization at the supranational level. Traditionally, international law was not seen as an instrument that should protect individuals from abuses of power, but as an instrument that would guarantee the sovereign control of the state over a specific territory. With the strengthening of the United Nations, the principles of human rights have gained more force in international politics in general. However, unless these principles become positive legal rights it is difficult to avoid the suspicion that they only reflect the self-interest of the most powerful:

> Things look different when human rights not only come into play as a moral orientation for one's own political activity, but as rights which have to be implemented in a legal sense. Human rights possess the structural attributes of subjective rights which, irrespective of their purely moral content, by nature are dependent on attaining positive validity within a system of compulsory law. (Habermas, 1999, p. 270)

A move in this direction is particularly visible in Europe (Eriksen and Fossum, 2000). European states have, through the EU but also through the Council of Europe, moved further than most states in terms of establishing international organizations that demand a commitment beyond the traditional conceptions of intergovernmental cooperation between sovereign states: The EU has developed a common legal system with a higher status than national law. The expectation of legitimization of political choices *vis à vis* 'the other' is therefore particularly strong in the European context. National choices are more visible at the international level, and in addition national choices concern other states and their citizens directly. There are now agents outside the nation-state that can sanction illegitimate abuses of power and that citizens can appeal to if national decisions seem unacceptable. This is visible both in the EU's Charter of Fundamental Rights and in the European Convention on Human Rights developed in the context of the Council of Europe. Hence human rights are not just moral categories, but also becoming positive legal rights in Europe. It is expected of European states today that they respect human rights and basic civil and political rights (Zürn, 2000). In such a context security policy increasingly becomes an instrument to uphold the law rather than an instrument to defend self-interest in a system of anarchy. Respect for democracy and human rights become conditions for security.

Conclusions

There is general agreement amongst West European states that security and defence policies should be reformed in order to respond to and take advantage of the changes that have occurred in Europe in the aftermath of the Cold War, and now more so than ever. During the Cold War the security policies of West European nation-states were primarily based on what David Held has defined as pragmatic considerations (Held, 1987, p. 182); bipolarity and the need for a balance of power between NATO and the Warsaw Pact was taken as a given. This situation was not necessarily considered satisfactory from an ideal normative perspective, however it was accepted as inevitable. Indeed the assumption was that the situation could not be any different. With the combined effects of the end of the Cold War and the increased influence of supranational institutions, the political context is changed. With the constraints of block-to-block competition gone, Europe can and does to a large extent pursue a security policy that relies on something else than only national interest.

However, these elements of change are accompanied by elements of continuity. The chapter has shown that efforts to form new policies are countered not only by vested interests but also by established norms and institutional patterns. We have also seen in this chapter that, due to national idiosyncrasies, attempts to reform national security and defence policies have taken different paths in different states. Furthermore, these efforts have led to different reactions and different consequences in different European states.

PART II

Legitimacy: Do States Command the Loyalty of Their Citizens

Chapter 4

Nationalism and Collective Identities: Europe versus the Nation-State?

THOMAS RISSE

It is often claimed that collective identities continue to firmly reside with the nation-state and that, therefore, the prospects of building an 'ever-closer' European Union are doomed. But I argue in this chapter that it is wrong to see 'European' identity as compared to national, regional or local loyalties in a zero-sum fashion as either/or propositions. Individuals hold multiple identities and, thus, can identify with Florence, Tuscany, Italy and Europe or with Munich, Bavaria, Germany and Europe without having to face conflicts of loyalties. Which of these identities becomes salient or important in a given moment depends on the context in which people act. My Europeanness might become particularly salient when I travel in North America or Southeast Asia, while my Germanness might be important when I live in Italy, and so forth.

It follows that there is good news and bad news regarding the possibility of a common European identity. The good news is that pessimistic arguments about the impossibility of a European collective identity are exaggerated. References to a common Europeanness, common history, heritage and culture are embedded in various nation-state (or subnational) identities. It is virtually impossible to describe what it means to be German, Italian or French without some reference to a common European experience (this might also hold true for regional or even local identities). The European integration process has further reinforced such references and has made them more salient, as European policies become more significant in the daily lives of the citizens. In other words, there is more space for Europe in the various collective identities than is commonly assumed.

The bad news is that there is enormous variation among different countries (and within countries), ranging from, say, 'Englishness' in Britain whereby 'Europe' still constitutes the 'other', to strong identification with Europe in Italy as a way to overcome the problems of the

77

Italian polity. Moreover, 'Europe' probably means different things to different people. It is unclear whether European Germans and European Italians mean the same when they identify with a common European heritage. Even worse, we know from psychological studies that intolerance among social groups increases, the more group members transfer their own values to some higher-level community identify with it. In other words, the more Germans identify with Europe, but the more their visions of 'Europe' look more or less Germanic, the less tolerance they might feel for, say, Italians. In sum, an alleged European identity could have adverse consequences for peoples' respect for cultural, political and economic diversity in Europe.

This chapter proceeds in the following steps. I start with a brief overview on findings from mass survey data on questions of European identity. A more theoretical section follows discussing various ways to think about the notion of 'collective identities' in an effort to clarify what multiple identities mean for the question of European identity. I then report findings from research on identity-related discourses of political elites in Britain, France and Germany over the past fifty years. The chapter concludes with some thoughts on the meaning of these and other findings for the prospects of a European polity.

A European identity? Evidence from mass survey data

For the past decade, the Eurobarometer and other surveys have included questions on European identity in their regular mass public-opinion surveys in all member states of the European Union (EU). While we need to interpret these data with some scepticism as to their validity, they give some first and preliminary indications about trends in mass public opinion (see also Duchesne and Frognier, 1995). Table 4.1 contains the data on identity-related questions from the fall 1999 survey for selected EU member states (Eurobarometer 2000).

What can we conclude from these data? First, a majority of citizens across the EU member states seems to identify with Europe, at least to some degree and mostly in conjunction with their national identity. This would seem to disconfirm the notion that there is no European identity and that EU citizens in general have no positive feelings about Europe. Yet, the variation among member states is pretty high, as roughly two-thirds of Italians and Spanish identify with Europe as compared to only about one-third of the British.

Second, and on average, many more people feel some degree of national pride than identify with Europe, and the variation in national pride among European citizens is also less pronounced, ranging from

Table 4.1 Public opinion on Europe, October–November 1999, selected countries

Country/percentage of respondents	European identity (A)	European culture (B)	Support for EU (C)	Benefit from EU (D)	National pride (E)
European Union (15)	52	38	51	46	83
Italy	71	42	60	50	84
Spain	63	34	64	61	86
France	59	36	48	46	85
Belgium	57	35	54	50	73
Germany	49	43	47	37	67
Portugal	46	47	68	77	91
Ireland	45	30	82	88	96
Greece	41	49	59	70	97
United Kingdom	30	28	29	29	94

Note: (A) Respondents answering the question 'in the near future do you see yourself as . . .?' with 'European only'; 'European and (nationality)', or '(nationality) and European'; (B) respondents agreeing 'completely' or 'slightly' with the statement 'there is a cultural identity shared by all Europeans'; (C) respondents answering the question 'generally speaking, do you think that (our country's) membership of the European Union is . . .?' with 'a good thing'; (D) respondents answering the question 'taking everything into consideration, would you say that (our country) has on balance benefited or not from being a member of the European Union' with 'benefitted'; (E) respondents answering the question 'would you say that you are very proud, fairly proud, not at all proud to be (nationality)?' with 'very proud' or 'fairly proud'.
Source: Eurobarometer.

slightly more than two-thirds in Germany and Belgium to almost everybody in the UK, Ireland and Greece. However, national pride and European feelings do not appear to be contradictions in many parts of Europe. Most Italians express national pride (84 per cent), but they also identify with Europe (71 per cent). In the UK, however, the difference between the two number is 64 points. This suggests that feelings of national pride resonate in very different ways with feelings of European identity across the EU member states. European and English identity might represent a contradiction in Britain, while Europeanness and Italianness might well go together.

Third, and surprisingly, more Europeans have positive feelings about Europe than express support for the view that there is common European cultural identity (52 per cent versus 38 per cent on average among the EU15). But the variation among the citizens of the member states is, once again, enormous. Many more people in Italy, Spain, France and Belgium identify somewhat with Europe than believe in a common European culture. Interestingly enough, more Greeks see a common European culture than identify with Europe. About as many people in Germany, Portugal and Ireland, but also in the UK, identify with Europe and see a common European culture. This suggests that Europeans hold different views regarding both their own Europeanness and the existence of a common European identity. Even those who identify with Europe might not believe in a European common culture.

Fourth, as many European citizens identify somewhat with Europe as support European integration, if we look at the overall number of the EU15. Yet, support levels for European integration and European identity (or lack of both) only reach similar numbers among British, German, Belgian and Spanish citizens. Thirty-seven per cent more Irish and 22 per cent more Portugiese support European integration than identify with Europe, while relatively more French (11 per cent) express some European identity than support European integration. This means again that diffuse support for the European polity and European identity only go together in some member states. In general, one should not confuse feelings of European identity with support for EU membership, or vice versa.

Indeed, support for EU membership seems to be related to the expected benefits from this membership. In this case, the variation among member states is rather modest. Only in Germany and Italy do 10 per cent more people support EU membership than believe in the benefits of EU membership. Greece and Portugal are the outliers in the opposite direction; more citizens believe they profit from EU membership than actually support it.

Yet, the perceived utility of EU membership and identification with

Europe do not seem to be related, judging from these numbers. While the Irish overwhelmingly believe in the benefits of EU membership, they only show a very modest degree of European identity. In contrast, many more Italians (71 per cent) feel European than believe that they profit from EU membership (50 per cent). For Germany and France, the difference between the two attitudes are 12 and 13 points, respectively. These data disconfirm an interpretation of identity formation according to which the more people benefit from European integration, the more they tend to identify with Europe. This is precisely what early neo-functionalist theory thought about the ways in which European integration would lead to a common European identity (see for example Haas, 1958, p. 16). Mass opinion data seem to falsify this idea. Portuguese, Greek or Irish citizens do not show particularly high levels of identification with Europe, even though they agree that they profit enormously from EU membership.

In sum, these and other public-opinion data disconfirm part of the conventional wisdom about European identity, namely that the material benefits from EU membership drive identification processes, that the overall level of positive feelings about Europe among EU citizens is rather low, or that one cannot be proud of one's country and identify with Europe. Yet, even a superficial look at these data also shows the enormous variation across EU member states when it comes to questions of identity. As a result, survey data can only provide a first glance at the problem and we need to look much deeper in order to understand the dynamics of European identity and how it relates to national and other identities. But before proceeding further, we need some clarifications on the very concept of 'collective identity'.

How can we think about a European identity?

Essentialist concepts of collective identities take cultural variables such as membership in ethnic groups as a given which then develop into national identities during the process of nation-building. If the causal connection between 'culture' and 'identity' is a one-way street, however, there is not much one can do about this and supranational or postnationalist identities are impossible. Collective identities will firmly rest with the nation-state as the historically most successful connection between territory and people. French will remain French, while British remain British, and Germans remain Germans. 'Euro-pessimists' challenge the prospects for further European integration on precisely these grounds. They argue that a European polity is impossible because there is no European people, no common European history or common myths on which collective European identity could be built (see Kielmansegg, 1996; Smith, 1992).

This mode of reasoning leads to a 'zero-sum model' of collective identity; identification with one social group comes at the expense of identifying with other groups. Europeanness either will or will not gradually replace national, subnational or other identities relating to territorial spaces. As the data quoted above show, people do not seem to perceive it that way. Moreover, the theoretical foundations of such a concept are flawed. It is problematic to assume that individuals have only some limited space available for identifying with collectivities, and that the more you identify with Europe the less you can feel loyalty for your nation-state, your region or your locality.

Therefore, most scholars working on collective identities today embrace versions of social constructivist reasoning. From this perspective, the connection between cultural variables such as ethnic belongings or religious or ideological affiliations, on the one hand, and collective identities, on the other, is more historically contingent, tenuous and subject to constructions and reconstructions. Accordingly, social identities contain, first, ideas describing and categorizing an individual's membership in a social group including emotional, affective and evaluative components. Groups of individuals perceive that they have something in common on the basis of which they form an 'imagined community' (Anderson, 1991). Common Europeanness, for example, could constitute such a community. Second, this commonness is accentuated by a sense of difference with regard to other communities. Individuals frequently tend to view the group with which they identify in a more positive way than the 'out-group'. This does not mean, however, that the perceived differences between the 'in-group' and the 'out-group' are necessarily based on value judgements and that the 'other' is usually looked down at. But a sense of collective European identity is always accompanied by the need to differentiate 'Europeans' from 'others', be it Soviet communism during the Cold War, Islamic fundamentalism, or Anglo-American *laissez-faire* capitalism.

Third, national identities construct the 'imagined communities' of – mostly territorially defined – nation-states and are, therefore, closely linked to ideas about sovereignty and statehood. National identities often contain visions of just political and social orders. Fourth, social identities are context-bound (Oakes *et al.*, 1994, 100; Giesen, p. 1999). This means that different components of national identities are invoked depending on the policy area in question. Moreover, it also suggests that the more salient a social situation becomes for people, the more people identify with the respective social group (or strongly reject it). This leads to the proposition that levels of identification with or conscious rejection of Europe should increase, the more important the EU becomes in peoples' lives. Fifth, collective identities change the more gradually, the more they are incorporated in institutions, myths and symbols, as well as cultural understandings (Fiske and Taylor, 1984; Oakes *et al.*, 1994). This should be particularly relevant for collective identities pertaining to the nation-state which usually take quite some time and effort to construct and are then embedded in institutions and a country's political culture. As a result, we should expect that collective identification with Europe or the nation-state changes rather slowly.

Last but not least, individuals can feel loyalty to several social groups with which they identify. Women, for example, may feel a high degree of gender identity and a strong attachment to their region or their nation-state. In other words, individuals hold multiple identities, as the above data on European and national identities confirm. Two ways of conceptualizing multiple identities can be distinguished. According to a layer-cake model, identities are layered on several levels and we can differentiate among layers of collective identification from, say, local to regional, national and supranational identities. Local identities would then be invoked when people interact with other local communities, and so on. A Florentine citizen identifies with her local community when confronted with the Milanese, while her Tuscan identity might be invoked when dealing with a Sicilian (or even a Bavarian), and so on. A German travelling to France will feel her Germanic roots, while she might feel European when dealing with Americans.

A more complicated model of multiple identification is the marble-cake idea. Accordingly, the various identity components blend into each other, they can be nested or enmeshed. For example, since Tuscan history and culture cannot be separated from the broader European history and culture, Tuscans would not be able to even describe their distinctiveness without alluding to some European roots. Post-Second World War German identity has evolved into a European identity as a means of overcoming the country's nationalist and militarist past; as a result, Germanness and Europeanness are firmly enmeshed and cannot be separated easily.

Two conclusions follow. First, there might be much more Europeanness enshrined in national cultures and, hence, a much stronger collective European identity than is usually assumed. This identification process might encompass a much longer – and probably also more contested – history than the forty years of European integration. Second, however, it becomes very unclear whether Greeks, Italians, French or Germans mean the same when they talk about their 'Europeanness'. The French notion of 'mission civilisatrice', for example, might translate into a European civilizing mission these days; but

Germans would probably not feel very comfortable when confronted with such an interpretation of Europeanness. Again, insights from social psychological research suggest that increasing European identities among Italians, Germans and French might actually lead to less positive evaluations of Italians, Germans and French *vis-à-vis* each other. If people simply transfer the positive values and identity components of their in-group to a larger collectivity, the stronger they might distance themselves from out-groups belonging to the lower-level category (Mummenday and Wenzel, 1999). If Germans strongly identify with Europe, but 'Europe' is simply Germany writ large, the social distance they feel to Italy might actually increase.

In sum, then, the marble-cake concept claims, on the one hand, that there is much more Europeanness embedded in national, regional or other collective identities than is usually assumed. On the other hand, the meaning of 'Europe' might differ profoundly in the various national, subnational and other contexts. We can then reformulate the question of European identity into one of whether the different meanings of Europe show some overlap and whether there are common understandings of Europeanness, even though their historical and cultural embeddedness differs profoundly. To provide an example: Athenians might relate their understanding of European democracy to ancient Greece. French Europeanness also encompasses liberal values, but they are related to a Europeanized version of French enlightenment and republicanism values.

In the following, I use the marble-cake concept of collective identities to explore how Europeanization has influenced nation-state identities in France, Germany and the United Kingdom over the last fifty years (see also Marcussen *et al.*, 1999; Risse 2000; Risse *et al.*, 1999). I concentrate empirically on discourses among political elites, in particular the major political parties of the three countries.

Europe as Britain's 'other'

Probably the most remarkable feature of British elite attitudes towards European integration is their stability and lack of change. The fundamental orientations toward the European Community have remained essentially the same since the end of the Second World War, and have survived the ups and downs in British policies toward the EC/EU. More than twenty years after entry into the European Community, Britain is still regarded as 'of rather than in' Europe; it remains the 'awkward partner' and 'semi-detached' from Europe (Bailey, 1983; George, 1994). This general attitude has not changed since the 1950s:

Where do we stand? We are not members of the European Defence Community, nor do we intend to be merged in a Federal European system. We feel we have a special relation to both. This can be expressed by prepositions, by the preposition 'with' but not 'of' – we are with them, but not of them. We have our own Commonwealth and Empire. (Churchill, 1953)

British attitudes towards the European project reflect collectively-held beliefs about British, particularly English identity, since 'Britishness' has been identified with 'Englishness' throughout most of the post-Second World War era. There is still a feeling of 'them' versus 'us' between Britain and the continent which is reflected in the public-opinion polls quoted above. 'Europe' continues to be identified with the continent and perceived as 'the other' in contrast to Englishness. The social construction of 'Englishness' as the core of British nation-state identity comprises meanings attached to institutions, historical memory and symbols. Each of these components are hard to reconcile with a vision of European political order beyond intergovernmentalism, and it is not surprising that parts of English nation-state identity are often viewed as potentially threatened by European integration. Institutions such as the Parliament and the Crown form important elements of a collective nation-state identity, and the identity-related meanings attached to these institutions centre around a peculiar understanding of national sovereignty. The Crown symbolizes 'external sovereignty' in terms of independence from Rome and the Pope as well as from the European continent since 1066. Parliamentary or 'internal' sovereignty represents a most important constitutional principle relating to a 700-year-old parliamentary tradition and hard-fought victories over the King.

English sovereignty is, thus, directly linked to myths about a continuous history of liberal and democratic evolution and 'free-born Englishmen'. British objections against transferring sovereignty to European supranational institutions are usually justified on grounds of lacking democratic – meaning parliamentary – accountability. Identity-related understandings of Parliamentary sovereignty are directly linked to the prevailing visions of a European order comprising independent nation-states. Statements show a remarkable continuity of British attitudes towards the European Union and related identity constructions from the 1950s (and earlier) until today. In sum, British nation-state identity seems to be hardly affected by European integration, and 'Europe' is still largely constructed as the, albeit friendly, 'other'. While the British case is one of non-adaptation to the European Union, German nation-state identity transformed towards Europe before the integration process could have left its mark. In other words, Britain is a case of strong incompatibility between Europe and the nation-state, while Europe resonates well with contemporary German nation-state identity.

One's own past as Europe's 'other': the case of Germany

The German case is one of thorough and profound reconstruction of nation-state identity following the catastrophe of the Second World War. Thomas Mann's dictum that 'we do not want a German Europe, but a European Germany' quickly became the mantra of the postwar (West) German elites. Since the 1950s, a fundamental consensus has emerged among the political elites and has been shared by public opinion that European integration is in Germany's vital interest (see Katzenstein, 1997; Banchoff, 1999a).

After 1945, the Christian Democratic Party (CDU) immediately embraced European integration as the alternative to the nationalism of the past. As Ernst Haas put it, 'in leading circles of the CDU, the triptych of self-conscious anti-Nazism, Christian values, and dedication to European unity as a means of redemption for past German sins has played a crucial ideological role' (Haas, 1958, p. 127). Christianity, democracy and – later on – social market economy became the three pillars on which a collective European identity was to be based. It was sharply distinguished from both the German nationalist and militarist past and – during the late 1940s and early 1950s – from Soviet communism and Marxism. In other words, Germany's own past as well as communism constituted the 'others' in this identity construction.

But throughout the early 1950s there was no elite consensus on German nation-state identity. The Social Democrats (SPD) were the main opposition party to Adenauer's policies at the time. In the interwar period the SPD had been the first major German party to embrace the concept of a 'United States of Europe' in its 1925 Heidelberg programme, but when the party was forced into exile during the Nazi period the leadership fully embraced the notion of a democratic European federation which would almost naturally become a Socialist order. Europe, Germany, democracy and socialism were perceived as identical. The SPD's first postwar leader, Kurt Schumacher, a survivor of Nazi concentration camps, argued vigorously against the politics of Western integration, since it foreclosed the prospects of rapid reunification of the two Germanies (Paterson, 1974). Schumacher denounced the Council of Europe and the European Coal and Steel Community

(ECSC) as 'un-European', as 'mini-Europe', as conservative-clericalist and capitalist. At the same time, the SPD was at great pains to argue that it did not oppose European integration as such, just this particular version.

Two major election defeats later (1953 and 1957), the SPD changed course, thoroughly reforming their domestic and foreign policy programme. With regard to the latter, they revisited the 1925 Heidelberg programme and became staunch supporters of European integration. The changes culminated in the 1959 Godesberg programme.

From the 1960s on, a federalist consensus ('United States of Europe') prevailed among the German political elites comprising the main parties from the center-right to the center-left. This consensus outlasted the changes in government from the CDU to the SPD in 1969, from the SPD to the CDU in 1982, and the recent coalition between the SPD and the Green Party in 1998. Even more significant, German unification did not result in a reconsideration of German European policies. With the unexpected end of the East–West conflict and regained German sovereignty, a broad range of foreign policy opportunities emerged creating a situation in which the German elites could have redefined their national interests. But Germany did not reconsider its fundamental foreign policy orientations, since Germany's commitment to European integration had long outlived the context in which it had originally emerged (Banchoff, 1999a; Katzenstein, 1997). In the aftermath of unification, the German government accelerated rather than slowed down its support for further progress in European integration. German support for a single currency and for a European political union was perfectly in line with long-standing attitudes towards integration and the country's European nation-state identity.

This German federalist consensus went hand in hand with a peculiar identity construction in the aftermath of the Second World War. The German notion of what constitutes the 'other', the non-European, is related to European and German nationalist history. German nationalism came to be viewed as authoritarian, militaristic and anti-Semitic. Germany's nationalist and militarist past constituted the 'other' in the process of 'post-national' identity formation whereby Europeanness replaces traditional notions of nation-state identity. All federal governments from Konrad Adenauer onwards were determined to render the European unification process irreversible because they were convinced that the concept of a unified Europe was the most effective assurance against the renaissance of nationalism and disastrous conflicts. Nowadays, a 'good German' equals a 'good European' supporting a united Europe. 'Europe' in this identity construction stands for a stable peace order overcoming the continent's bloody past, for democracy and human rights (in contrast to European – and German – autocratic history), as well as for a social market economy including the welfare state (in contrast to both Soviet communism and Anglo-Saxon *laissez-faire* capitalism).

In sum, and in contrast to Great Britain, the German case is one of comprehensive transformation of post-Second World War nation-state identity. German Europeanness as a particular identity construction was contested throughout the 1950s, but became consensual afterwards. The European integration process did not create this identity, rather it reinforced and stabilized it by demonstrating that Germany can prosper economically and regain political clout in Europe through a policy of 'self-binding' in European institutions. German Euro-patriotism deeply affected elite perceptions of the country's national interests and attitudes towards European integration. This Euro-patriotism remained stable despite various challenges which might otherwise have led to changes in instrumental interests.

Europe as France writ large

In contrast to Britain and Germany, attitudes towards Europe shared by the French political elites underwent considerable changes over time. Policy-makers of the Third Republic such as Aristide Briand and Eduard Herriot were among the first who embraced a federalist vision of 'les États Unis d'Europe' during the interwar period. However, their visions did not become consensual within their own parties until after the Second World War.

During the 1950s and in conjunction with the first efforts towards European integration, a national debate took place which concerned French identity and basic political orientations in the postwar era. The Second World War and the German occupation served as traumatic experiences as a result of which French nation-state identity became deeply problematic and contested. Many controversies centred around how to deal with Germany as the most significant French 'other' at the time. Supporters of European integration argued in favour of creating supranational institutions in order to contain German power once and for all, while opponents favoured traditional balance-of-power strategies to deal with the German problem. The policy prescriptions correlated with the nation-state identity constructions prevailing in the respective parties at the time. There was no consensus among the French political elites about European integration as a solution for the German problem. The defeat of the treaty on the European Defence Community in the French National Assembly in 1954 showed the deep divisions among the political elites.

The next 'critical juncture' for French nation-state identity was the war in Algeria and the ongoing crisis of the Fourth Republic. When the Fifth Republic came into being in 1958, its founding father, President Charles de Gaulle, reconstructed French nation-state identity and managed to reunite a deeply divided nation around a common vision of the French in the world. De Gaulle's identity construction related to historical myths of Frenchness and combined them in a unique way. As the leader of the French resistance during the Second World War, he overcame the trauma of the Vichy regime and related to understandings of the French nation-state which combined a specific meaning of sovereignty with the values of enlightenment and democracy (Furet *et al.*, 1988; Nicolet, 1982; Saint-Etienne, 1992). The notion of sovereignty – understood as national independence from outside interference together with a sense of uniqueness (grandeur) – was used to build a bridge between post-revolutionary Republican France and the pre-revolutionary monarchy. The understanding of the French l'état-nation connoted the identity of the nation and democracy as well as the identity of French society with the Republic. Finally, de Gaulle reintroduced the notion of French exceptionalism and uniqueness in terms of a civilizing mission for the world (*mission civilisatrice*) destined to spread the universal values of enlightenment and of the French revolution. None of these nation-state identity constructions were particularly new, but de Gaulle combined them in a special way and managed to use them in order to legitimize the political institutions of the Fifth Republic.

Of course, these understandings were hard to reconcile with federalist visions of European order. Rather, '*l'Europe des nations*' (Europe of nation-states) became the battle-cry during de Gaulle's presidency. But the specific Gaullist nation-state identity construction only remained consensual among the political elites for about another ten years after de Gaulle's resignation. Beginning in the late 1970s, Europeanization gradually transformed French nation-state identity among the elites in conjunction with two critical junctures – the failure of President Mitterrand's economic policies in the early 1980s and the end of the Cold War in the late 1980s (Flynn, 1995).

When Mitterrand and the Socialist Party (PS) came into power in 1981, they initially embarked upon a project of creating democratic socialism in France based on leftist Keynesianism. This project bitterly failed when the adverse reactions of the capital markets hit the French economy which in turn led to a severe loss of electoral support for Mitterrand's policies. In 1983, Mitterrand had practically no choice other than changing course dramatically if he wanted to remain in power. This political change led to a deep crisis within the Socialist Party which then gradually abandoned the Socialist project and moved towards ideas once derisively labelled 'Social Democratic'. The PS's move towards Europe included an effort to reconstruct French nation-state identity. The French Socialists started highlighting the common European historical and cultural heritage, arguing increasingly that the French future was to be found in Europe. The French left started embracing the notion of a 'European France', extending the vision of the French *mission civilisatrice* towards Europe writ large. The peculiar historical and cultural legacies of France were transferred from the 'first nation-state' in Europe to the continent as a whole, because all European states were seen as children of enlightenment, democracy and Republicanism. This identity construction uses traditional understandings of Frenchness and the French nation-state and extends them to Europe. In contrast to English identity constructions where Europe is still the 'other', this understanding incorporates Europe into one's own collective nation-state identity and its understandings about sovereignty and political order. French identity is transformed but only to the degree that ideas about Europe can be incorporated into and resonate with previous visions of the state. This change pretty much corresponds to the marble-cake model of collective identity discussed above.

Similar changes in the prevailing visions of European order and reconstructions of French nation-state identity took place on the French right, albeit later. The heir of Charles de Gaulle's visions, the Rassemblement pour la République (RPR), provides another example of the French political elite changing course. The end of the Cold War was the decisive moment constituting another 'critical juncture' and crisis experience for French identity. When the Berlin wall came down, Germany united and the post-Cold War European security order was constructed, France – la grande nation – remained largely on the sidelines. The political debates surrounding the referendum on the Maastricht treaties in 1992 represented identity-related discourses about the new role of France in Europe and the world after the end of the Cold War. As in the 1950s, fear of German power dominated the debates. Supporters of Maastricht and EMU, particularly on the French right, argued in favour of a 'binding' strategy, while opponents supported a return to traditional balance of power politics. This time, supporters of European integration prevailed in all major parties.

In sum, the majority of the French political elite gradually incorporated Europe in notions of French distinctiveness and started identifying the future of France as a nation-state with European order. But a distinct minority across the political spectrum sticks to the old Gaullist concepts of French 'grandeur' and 'independence'. It remains to be seen, though, to what extent the identification with a 'Europe' that looks like France is actually compatible with a European integration process containing strong federal features which are different from the French state.

Conclusions

Empirical research indicates that nation-state identities are sticky and only slowly subject to change. In the case of the UK, Englishness is still defined in contrast to Europeanness whereby 'Europe' constitutes the 'other' of nation-state identity. Almost twenty years of EC/EU membership do not seem to have made much difference. In contrast, the German case is one of thorough reconstruction of nation-state identity in the post-Second World War period. Once German Europeanness became consensual among the political elites in the early 1960s, this nation-state identity has remained stable ever since. But German Europeanness preceded rather than followed progress in European integration. European integration made a difference in the French case in terms of transforming Gaullist nation-state identity, and since the 1980s the French elites from the center-right to the center-left have started identifying with European rather than strictly French distinctiveness.

How can these different developments be explained? In line with the marble-cake model of collective identities, new ideas about political order and identity constructions have to resonate with the notions embedded in collective nation-state identities. Classic British notions of political order, for example, emphasize parliamentary democracy and external sovereignty which is why only intergovernmentalist versions of European political order resonate with internal and external sovereignty. In the French case, state-centred republicanism – the duty to promote values such as brotherhood, freedom, equality and human rights, in short 'civilisation' – constitutes a continuous element in the French discourse about political order. Therefore, any European idea which resonates with French exceptionalism and which does not violate the state-centred concept of republicanism can legitimately be promoted in France, including a European rather than solely French exceptionalism. In Germany, concepts of a social market economy, democracy and political federalism were central elements in the discourse of German exiled elites during the war and among the entire political class after the Second World War. Ideas about European political order which resonated with these concepts were, therefore, considered legitimate in the German political debate. In addition, militarism and Nazism had thoroughly discredited a nationalist notion of Germany. Europe provided an alternative identity construction and, thus, a way out.

But how can we explain changes in collective identities pertaining to Europe? Perceived crises situations – 'critical junctures' – together with perceived instrumental interests seem to account for these transformations. In the Federal Republic of Germany, the SPD reached their critical juncture in the mid- to late 1950s when members of the party leadership realized that Kurt Schumacher's vision of 'Europe as a third force' was no longer a viable option given the realities of the European Coal and Steel Community (ECSC), the Treaty of Rome, and of two severe federal election defeats in a row. At the same time, the modern Western concept of European identity resonated well with the domestic programme of the party reformers who supported liberal democracy, market economy and the welfare state while giving up more far-reaching Socialist visions. The desire to gain political power facilitated the ideological change of the Social Democrats' party programme and their thorough reconstruction of German nation-state identity.

In the French case, it was only a question of time before the French-Gaullist nation-state identity would become incompatible with the Europeanization process and the overall French support for it. While German Europeanness and European integration went hand in hand, the gap between a French nationalist nation-state identity and the reality of European integration widened over time. When President Mitterrand's economic policies bumped up against the European monetary system in 1982–83, he opted for Europe to remain in power, but then set in motion a process which the German Social Democrats had experienced 25 years earlier – the parallel Social Democratization and adjustment to Europe in the French elites' nation-state identity. By the end of the decade, Frenchness and Europeanness had been reconciled among the French centre-left. The French Gaullists underwent a similar process after the end of the Cold War when they gradually realized that French exceptionalism and its *mission civilisatrice* could only be preserved within a European identity construction. Thus, French Europeanness became consensual among a majority of the political elites from the centre-right to the centre-left during the early 1990s.

In sum, more than forty years of European integration had different effects on the collective nation-state identities in the three countries. Supranationalism remains largely incompatible with deeply entrenched notions of Englishness and concepts of British sovereignty. In contrast, the emergence of a European polity reinforced and strengthened German postwar Europeanness. Finally, Europeanization gradually contributed to changing the French nation-state identity; Frenchness and Europeanness are no longer incompatible. But one should not overlook that this research pertained exclusively to the level of political elites; it is not at all clear whether the findings also apply to the level of the mass public. The opinion-poll data reported above are largely inconclusive with regard to this question.

In conclusion, however, we need to ask whether the gradual emergence of collective European identities, albeit in 'national colours', actually matters. Does 'identity' as a rather elusive concept actually explain anything with regard to European integration? Frankly, the answer is ambiguous. On the one hand, there is no immediate connection between the level of elite identification with Europe and national policies toward the EU in general. For example, there seems to be little correlation between European identities among elites and the degree of compliance with EU law. Britain has among the best compliance records with EU law and regulations, while France has the second worst. Or take Italy – there are few EU member states where people, both elites and masses, seem to identify more with Europe; yet Italy has the among the worst compliance records among the member states.

Does this mean that identification is completely irrelevant when it comes to actual policies toward the EU? Are we studying some epiphenomenon? On the other hand, one should not throw out the baby with the bathwater. Identification with Europe seems to matter most when it comes to treaty-making decisions, two examples being:

- The debate which the German Foreign Minister, Joschka Fischer, triggered in the summer of 2000 on the finalité politique of European integration pretty much followed national lines, and the national responses to Fischer largely correlated with the identity constructions prevailing in the various countries. Germans continued to embrace a federalist vision, French policy-makers remained more reluctant, and British officials rejected it outright.
- Policies toward the euro in the UK, France and Germany cannot be explained on the basis of economic or geostrategic interests alone, but have to be understood in the context of identity politics (see Risse *et al.*, 1999 for details). Germans embraced the single currency from the beginning, even though the economic benefits of giving up their cherished deutschmark appear far from clear. In contrast, the British official 'wait-and-see' attitude might actually hurt the British economy, but is very much in line with prevailing identity constructions.

In sum, identities matter and identity politics are one way in which European elites relate to their larger public. But two caveats need to be kept in mind: first, we still know surprisingly little of how fifty years of European integration have affected collective identities. Second, identity politics are only one among many factors influencing European policies and general attitudes towards European integration.

Chapter 5

Participation and Voting

DAVID BROUGHTON

For many political theorists, the main justifications of liberal democratic political systems are inextricably rooted in assumptions of government by the people and government for the people. These aims are supposed to be fulfilled by means of a variety of procedures of accountability, crucially regular and free elections at different levels of the political system. Mass participation via election turnout is seen as providing a vital contribution to ensuring that the political elite remains responsive to the wishes of the electorate based on the active participation of a critical citizenry in the political process. This will ensure that decisions taken in the name of the people broadly reflect the wishes of the people. In the absence of such sustained civic engagement, the fear has always been that political apathy at the bottom will most likely lead to authoritarian and arrogant attitudes at the top.

However, Scharpf (1999) has recently argued that European governments need to rely much more on output-oriented democracy (government for the people) rather than input-oriented democracy (government by the people) since there are legitimacy problems at both national government and European Union levels rendering the latter increasingly unworkable. This has been brought about by the loss of the problem-solving capacities of national governments via the dual and interrelated processes of economic globalization and European integration. Increasingly, the policies of national governments are being constrained by external forces beyond their control and the transfer of powers away from national governments (to both below and above national level) further limit the room for manoeuvre. The task for national governments in terms of shaping public opinion is to ensure that this increasing interdependency is not experienced as a 'delegitimating disappointment' (Scharpf, 2000a, p. 120).

In addition to specific involvement in the political process, different aspects of political participation are seen as being a 'good thing' since they generate overall support for the whole democratic system, ensuring the existence of a reservoir of goodwill. This can be called upon to combat the 'bad times' of economic recession, for example, and it

94

permits the system to take blows and criticism from perceived 'performance deficits' but not to collapse. Many of these ideas are derived from the seminal work of David Easton (1979), particularly the valuable distinction between 'specific' support and 'diffuse' support for the democratic system as a whole.

Recent developments in terms of voter turnout figures and perceived waves of inchoate dissatisfaction amongst the voters of Western Europe have given rise to increasing doubts about the ability of politicians to meet the changing demands of their electorates and to ensure that 'performance deficits' are effectively confronted. The data, however, are not straightforward to interpret, particularly in a cross-national context. In the 1990s, overall voter turnout does appear to be declining in most West European countries compared to previous decades since 1945, but it is not a uniform trend across the whole continent. It is more a case of 'trendless fluctuation' than a linear development, with substantial cross-national variations.

The type of election does, however, appear to be significant in terms of turnout. National elections still attract good turnouts, whilst by-elections, local, regional and European Parliament elections, along with referendums on various themes, are much more unpredictable with regard to rates of participation. Three other factors have been cited as potential influences on the level of election turnout: the type of electoral system in operation, whether compulsory voting is employed and the degree of 'competitiveness' of the election.

The IDEA study of voter turnout (IDEA, 1999) concluded that all three of these potential influences had some impact. The single transferable vote (STV) electoral system in operation in Ireland and Malta tends to produce high turnouts, particularly in the latter (see Tables 5.1 and 5.2 below), but other types of proportional representation electoral systems do not consistently achieve the same level. Compulsory voting in some form exists in Belgium, Greece, Italy and Luxembourg, although the enforcement of these rules and laws varies widely, making it difficult to draw any firm conclusions about their impact. Countries with compulsory voting do tend to have high turnout levels but not dramatically higher than those countries without any compulsion such as Denmark. The IDEA report also concluded that there was a clear link between the 'competitiveness' of the election and the level of voter turnout, meaning elections where the result is uncertain and likely to be close. In this context, the appeals of the parties may resonate more strongly with the voters and encourage more of them to turn out to vote. This may help to account for the rise in turnout in Germany in 1998, the fall in turnout in the United Kingdom in 1997, and the further steep decline in voter turnout in the United Kingdom in 2001.

For some people, a declining turnout at elections should not be regarded as a problem. They assert that this development is in fact a sign of satisfaction on the part of voters, not dissatisfaction. There is a broad 'culture of contentment'. No longer are elections seen as fundamental conflicts over basic issues of civil and political rights through which ordinary people can be mobilized and engaged. Instead, elections are increasingly dominated by obscure technocratic debates over the fine details of public policy for which the vast majority of people have neither time nor interest. There is therefore no 'crisis of disengagement' but simply a rational development of civil society towards relying upon a generalized, overall trust of political elites rather than a reliance on frequent individual participation as the principal means of holding politicians to account.

Critics of this thesis point to the roots of this development being firmly embedded in negative changes in the mass-media treatment of serious politics, producing an increasing number of 'information deficits', despite the easy accessibility of vast amounts of data from new electronic sources. Such critics spy a trend towards a lazy cynicism on the part of the media, leading to ill-formed, critical mass perceptions of politicians as being out-of-touch, untrustworthy and incompetent. For such critics, it is impossible both to be ignorant and free, harking back to classical theories concerning the place and responsibilities of the ordinary voter in a democratic political system.

For some, this development towards a lack of involvement of ordinary people in the political process amounts to a crisis of popular democracy, demonstrated by survey-based analysis of 'diffuse angst', a failure of the mobilisation capacities of political parties as shown by the decline in emotional attachment to parties and party membership, and an overall sense of weariness, disbelief and widespread cynicism about politics and politicians. This overall mood is best summed up by the widely used German word, *politikverdrossenheit*.

This chapter will set out recent trends in participation and voting in Western Europe to consider whether there is indeed a 'crisis of disengagement', using data from election turnouts and survey responses testing attitudes to politicians and wider political society. The first task is to examine what has been happening in national election turnout in Western Europe since the initial consolidation of the post-1945 democratic political systems.

Electoral turnouts since the Second World War

Table 5.1 sets out the average turnout figures at national elections by decade for 19 West European countries (the current countries of the

Table 5.1   *Average voter turnout since 1945*

Country/percent	1950s	1960s	1970s	1980s	1990s*
Austria	95.3	93.8	92.3	91.6	83.8
Belgium	93.1	91.3	93.0	93.9	91.5
Denmark	81.8	87.3	88.4	86.7	85.0
Finland	76.5	85.1	78.2	73.9	67.4
France	80.0	76.6	76.5	71.9	68.5
Germany	86.9	87.1	90.9	87.3	79.9
Greece	n/a	n/a	80.4	83.5	78.1
Ireland	74.3	74.2	76.5	72.9	67.3
Italy	93.8	92.9	92.3	89.0	84.5
Luxembourg	91.9	89.6	89.5	88.1	87.4
Netherlands	95.4	95.0	83.5	83.5	76.0
Portugal	n/a	n/a	87.5	78.0	65.2
Spain	n/a	n/a	72.6	73.4	74.6
Sweden	78.7	86.4	90.4	89.1	85.4
United Kingdom	80.3	76.6	75.0	74.1	69.6
Norway	78.8	82.8	81.6	83.1	76.3
Switzerland	69.0	64.2	52.3	48.2	43.8
Malta	78.1	90.3	94.0	95.4	96.2
Iceland	90.8	91.3	90.4	89.4	86.4
*Average**	*85.0*	*86.7*	*85.2*	*83.6*	*79.1*

Notes: * includes 2000–1; ** excludes Switzerland.
Source: International Institute for Democracy and Electoral Assistance (IDEA).

European Union along with Norway, Switzerland, Malta and Iceland), and there is also an overall average figure for the countries taken together (except Switzerland) in order to test for a broad trend over time. Switzerland was omitted from the average turnout figure as it appears to be a stark 'outlier' in terms of the degree to which its turnout has declined over time. In addition, the reliance on local direct democracy in Switzerland rather than national parties to make major policy decisions sets it apart from the other countries. Data for Greece, Portugal and Spain are only given for the time period that their elections were openly democratic in nature and duly comparable.

The table entries are the percentage turnouts produced by dividing the figure for registered voters by the total vote. This decision means that ineligible members of the population such as non-citizens are excluded but it also means that people are omitted who are in fact eligible, but who are not on the registration list. This seems acceptable in

Western Europe with generally high levels of voter registration, even given potential problems in terms of a declining level of registration over time. In the United Kingdom, for example, eligible voters 'disappeared' from the lists allegedly to avoid paying the poll tax in the early 1990s. This decision concerning the use of data on registered voters would be much more problematic if the United States was included in the study with its wholly voluntary registration process and the various differences between the individual states in terms of the laws of registration which have also changed over time.

Finally, we will deal with national elections producing national governments in this chapter rather than Presidential, sub-and supranational elections and referendums for ease of data and contextual comparability.

The first point to note from Table 5.1 is that average turnout across the chosen countries has indeed fallen over time, although not by much. The pattern is marked by the initial consolidation in turnout in the 1950s, the slight average increase in the 1960s, followed by a slight decline between the 1960s and the 1970s, another slight decline in the average figure in the 1980s, followed by a more noticeable decline of 4 per cent on average between the 1980s and 2001.

However, the overall average figures need to be 'unpacked' in more detail. For example, in Denmark, turnout is actually higher in the 1990s compared to the 1950s and it appears to have only suffered small declines in Sweden, Norway and Iceland too since the 1960s. Is there something different about the Scandinavian countries in that their turnout figures appear not to reflect the decline in turnout elsewhere in Western Europe? A further complication is that Finland would not appear to be 'typically Scandinavian' in this particular sense in that its turnout figure has fallen in a manner similar to other countries outside the Scandinavian group.

Most other countries have seen turnout declines such as Austria, the Netherlands, and Portugal, although none of them have seen the collapse in national turnout in Switzerland mentioned above (down by more than 25 per cent between the 1950s and the 1990s). Of these countries, the clearest decline is seen in the case of the Netherlands, whose turnout peaked in the 1950s at an average of 95.4 per cent but in the elections of the 1990s this figure fell to an average of 76 per cent.

Wattenberg (2000, p. 72) also notes the relative consistency in turnout in most of the Scandinavian countries and attributes this particular development to political parties in those countries continuing to strongly mobilize their respective voters to turn out. The decline of party loyalty and party identification in other countries has resulted in less reliance on parties providing cues as to how to translate opinions into voting choices. The decline in ideological differences between the major parties also reduces the starkness of the choice facing voters. The decline in long-standing party cleavages has led directly to a smaller percentage of the population being mobilized. A good example of this is in the Netherlands where three separate religious parties (two Protestant and one Catholic) joined together to form the Christian Democratic Appeal (CDA) in 1980. This resulted from the declining hold of the respective parties on their particular religious sub-cultures (Ten Napel, 1999).

Having broadly considered the changes in turnout rates in the post-war decades, we now want to look specifically at the two most recent national elections in our 19 countries.

Trends in political participation in the 1990s

Table 5.2 sets out the turnout figures for the last two national elections in our 19 West European countries in order to provide the most recent

Table 5.2 *Voting turnout at the last two national elections*

Country	Last election		Previous election		Change*
	Date	*Per cent*	*Date*	*Per cent*	
Austria	03/10/99	80.4	17/12/95	86.0	−5.6
Belgium	13/06/99	90.6	21/05/95	91.1	−0.5
Denmark	20/11/01	87.0	11/03/98	85.9	+1.1
Finland	21/03/99	65.3	19/03/95	68.6	−3.3
France	01/06/97	68.0	28/03/93	68.9	−0.9
Germany	27/09/98	83.0	16/10/94	79.0	+4.0
Greece	09/04/00	75.0	22/09/96	76.3	−1.3
Ireland	06/06/97	66.1	25/11/92	68.5	−2.4
Italy	13/05/01	81.4	21/04/96	82.9	−1.5
Luxembourg	13/06/99	86.5	12/06/94	88.3	−1.8
Netherlands	06/05/98	73.2	03/05/94	78.7	−5.5
Portugal	10/10/99	61.0	01/10/95	66.3	−5.3
Spain	12/03/00	68.7	03/03/96	78.1	−9.4
Sweden	20/09/98	81.4	18/09/94	88.1	−6.7
United Kingdom	07/06/01	59.4	01/05/97	71.5	−12.1
Norway	10/09/01	75.0	15/09/97	78.0	−3.0
Switzerland	24/10/99	43.2	22/10/95	42.2	+1.0
Malta	05/09/98	95.4	26/10/96	97.2	−1.8
Iceland	08/05/99	84.1	08/04/95	87.4	−3.3

Note: * Change is: (turnout at the last election) − (turnout at the previous election).
Source: International Institute for Democracy and Electoral Assistance (IDEA).

data for further comparative analysis. The table also notes the percentage change in turnout between the last two elections for each country.

We can see that in 16 of the 19 countries in the table, turnout fell compared to the immediately previous national election. In only four countries did turnout rise. The overall average turnout for the period 1992–96 was 78.6 per cent; for the latter half of the decade between 1997–2001 the average turnout was 75.8 per cent. It would seem, therefore, that turnout is indeed declining across the continent. However, we need to examine the data in more detail before drawing any conclusions about overall developments.

Some of the declines (and indeed two of the increases) in turnout are very small and could therefore represent specific and contingent 'blips' in turnout which will be reversed at the first national election of the new century. In addition, it is possible to reverse a declining turnout, as shown by Germany between 1994–98 when the turnout for elections to the Bundestag further recovered from the 'blip' of 1990 when the country was still grappling with the initial momentous consequences of unification earlier that year. In the past, Germany has recorded consistently high turnouts at postwar national elections, reaching a peak of 91 per cent in both 1972 and 1976, remarkable in a country without compulsory voting.

The six countries in the table (Austria, the Netherlands, Portugal, Spain, Sweden and the United Kingdom) which did suffer a noticeable decline in turnout between the last two national elections could provide us with clues to more general developments in turnout rates. On most usual criteria, however, this is a very 'mixed' group of countries.

For example, the decline in turnout in Portugal and Spain might be encouragingly related to their increasing democratic 'normality' after dictatorship in which both countries are seen more and more as being full members, not just of the European Union but of the European democratic mainstream. The main problem facing the Netherlands and Sweden is more likely to be related to maintaining their comfortable economic health and adapting their tried and tested political systems to the new challenges of globalization than any fears about the basic underpinnings of their societies. The decline in turnout in the United Kingdom in 1997 (to its lowest level since 1935) may well have been a reflection of an election result long assumed and discounted before polling day and an incisive reflection of the state of the incumbent Conservative government. Similar concerns about low turnout were frequently voiced in the run-up to the 2001 election in the UK and often for the same reasons, with the difference that the Conservatives were now in opposition.

However, in Austria the decline in turnout may much more be a reflection of disenchantment with the 'carve-up' of Austrian politics for so long by the Social Democrats and the Austrian People's Party in a series of long-lasting grand coalitions. Growing electoral support for the populist appeal of the Freedom Party under Jörg Haider has been another consequence. It is therefore in Austria that the system seems to be under some pressure from a grumbling and disenchanted electorate, all too ready and willing to voice its complaints about the actions of self-interested and unresponsive political elites.

Important questions of accountability, legitimacy, political trust and the potential for the opening of a 'democratic deficit' at national level (as well as at EU level) could, however, be profitably examined in other countries as well. For this, we need to consider survey responses to relevant questions drawn from the twice-yearly Eurobarometer surveys of the European Commission and those of the International Social Survey Programme (ISSP).

In order to gain some insight into mass attitudes towards political systems and the actions of politicians, a number of different questions have been employed in these surveys. Two main areas have been repeatedly examined. Firstly, the extent of overall satisfaction with democracy in the countries of the European Union has been measured, and, secondly, the amount of agreement with a set of statements which test attitudes towards politicians, the role of elections and the perceptions of the influence which ordinary citizens are able to exert on politics.

Satisfaction with democracy in EU countries

The first step is to look at changes over the most recent decade in the satisfaction of the European Union electorate with the way in which democracy works in their respective countries. Substantial and unidirectional changes over time in the direction of less satisfaction would provide evidence of increasing disenchantment with the workings of the different national political systems. Table 5.3 contains the responses to the same question asked in the Eurobarometer surveys at four time-points between 1991–2000 (for earlier results from 1973–93 derived from the same question, see Andeweg 1996, pp. 148–9). The question was: 'on the whole, are you very satisfied, fairly satisfied, not very satisfied or not at all satisfied with the way democracy works in (our country)?'

The table contains some interesting results. We should note in particular the consistently low level of satisfaction with democracy in Italy, and yet Italy has a consistently high rate of electoral turnout. There is some confusion in different sources over whether Italy has a 'compulsory' system of voting, given that it is based on strong social norms

Table 5.3 *Satisfaction with the functioning of democracy in EU member states*

Country/percentage of respondents*	October–November 1991		June–July 1994		October–November 1997		April–May 2000	
	Very + Fairly	Not Very + Not at All	Very + Fairly	Not Very + Not at All	Very + Fairly	Not Very + Not at All	Very + Fairly	Not Very + Not at All
Austria	n/a	n/a	n/a	n/a	55	39	56	38
Belgium	53	42	53	43	29	66	60	37
Denmark	73	26	78	21	77	22	79	21
Finland	n/a	n/a	n/a	n/a	50	48	64	32
France	43	53	47	49	48	49	60	35
Germany	61	36	52	46	45	52	54	43
Greece	34	62	32	66	38	60	53	46
Ireland	57	37	65	28	70	21	70	19
Italy	20	78	19	77	30	67	36	62
Luxembourg	77	16	72	20	70	23	74	20
Netherlands	63	34	65	34	71	27	80	18
Portugal	75	21	55	40	39	54	50	45
Spain	57	39	29	67	55	40	75	23
Sweden	n/a	n/a	n/a	n/a	56	40	63	34
United Kingdom	60	34	45	45	64	25	56	31
*Average***	50	46	44	52	49	47	57	39

Note: * Percentages will not total to 100 because 'don't know' or 'no reply' responses are excluded. ** Average is population-weighted.
Source: Eurobarometer.

rather than potential legal sanctions as in Belgium. The value of tracking change over time can be clearly demonstrated in the case of Belgium, where there was a collapse in satisfaction with Belgian democracy between 1994–97, with a strong recovery in 2000. This is unsurprising given the revelations surrounding the Dutroux child murder case and the very public failure of both the police and the overall judicial systems in 1996 (van Outrive, 1998). Consistently high levels of satisfaction with the workings of democracy are present in Denmark, Luxembourg, the Netherlands and Ireland, whilst more changeable responses are recorded in Germany, Spain and the United Kingdom.

In Germany, the data in the table were aggregated from separate West and East German samples, with the West German people usually being much more satisfied with German democracy than their East German counterparts. One specific reason for this is the differing interpretations of 'democracy' in the West and the East of Germany derived from different ideological cultures. Based on a variety of survey evidence, this is particularly clear in terms of choosing between freedom and equality, along with attitudes towards the value of indirect, representative democratic institutions as opposed to the desirability of involving citizens directly in the political process via referendums (Rohrschneider, 1999).

The strong dissatisfaction in Spain in the mid-1990s is likely to be linked to the corruption scandals that enveloped the last years of the PSOE in national power up until 1996. The United Kingdom sample includes a separate sample for Northern Ireland, whose respondents were clearly and consistently much less satisfied with the workings of democracy than those on the British mainland as the struggle for some kind of sustainable peace settlement in the province continued to prove elusive.

There are a number of critics of this particular Eurobarometer question who claim that it is not clear what this question is actually measuring (Holmberg, 1999). It is certainly possible that respondents are actually thinking of immediate policy concerns and making short-term evaluations of the present government's performance (either positively or negatively) rather than answering a more general question about 'democracy'. Democracy as the best political system available is largely unquestioned in most of the European Union. The respondents are therefore likely to be thinking much more about regime performance than fundamental democratic principles.

The 'satisfaction' question is useful for our purposes though as a general indication of satisfaction with democracy, particularly because it has been asked regularly over time, thus permitting us to track change. It is nevertheless important to supplement such general data with more precise questions that break down the overarching theme of 'satisfaction with democracy' into some of its key dimensions. We attempt this in the next two tables (5.4 and 5.5) when we consider the responses of European voters to a range of statements dealing with such themes as corruption amongst politicians and the perceived extent of citizen influence on politics.

Attitudes towards political society in Europe

Table 5.4 contains the responses to six statements drawn from a Eurobarometer survey in 1997 that attempt to tap attitudes to political society. We can analyse the data in terms of a rough 'pessimism/optimism' index that shows that the Danish respondents are the most optimistic based on the results to five of the six questions. Unlike the respondents in most other EU countries, the majority of Danes do not agree that corruption amongst politicians is increasing or that there is nothing that can be done to change things in Danish society. They are, however, more pessimistic about changing things in the world around them.

The French share a similar hope to the Danes about the possibility of changing society, whilst retaining a strong scepticism about corruption amongst politicians and the relative positions of the rich and poor in French society. The Italian respondents were similar to the French in their responses: strongly agreeing on the position of the rich and poor, but nevertheless optimistic that things could be changed in Italian society. The Luxembourgers were happier with the provision of public services than their counterparts in the rest of the European Union, and the Dutch were happier than most with the way their government, public bodies and public services operated. The Swedes were the most optimistic about their ability to change things in society.

We then considered (Table 5.5) data drawn from the International Social Survey Programme of 1996 that unfortunately only contained data from eight EU member states. On this occasion, the differences between the countries in terms of the four statements cited were not so striking as in Table 5.4 above. Few respondents thought that the average citizen had much influence on politics (a percentage range of 12 to 31 per cent agreed), whilst, with the exception of Dutch and French respondents, a majority of voters thought that even the best politicians did not have much impact. The Dutch and the Irish strongly retain their faith in the value of elections as a means of getting governments to pay attention to key issues, although there was strong support for this sentiment in each of the eight countries. Few respondents in any of the countries however thought that elected representatives tried to keep their promises once elected. This was particularly low in Italy (with only 11

Table 5.4   Attitudes toward society, March–April 1997

Country/ percentage agreement among respondents	Corruption among politicians is increasing	The way government and public bodies work is getting worse	I have little control over what is happening in the world around me	Public services look less and less after the interests of people like me	The rich are getting richer and the poor get poorer	There is nothing one can do to change things in our society
Austria	73	68	68	65	88	42
Belgium	96	91	85	81	94	51
Denmark	34	56	74	50	52	22
Finland	69	60	85	57	87	49
France	87	76	83	63	91	28
Germany	90	85	87	80	95	53
Greece	86	84	73	80	91	44
Ireland	87	73	82	68	88	46
Italy	71	77	87	74	86	24
Luxembourg	66	51	72	44	78	16
Netherlands	47	57	71	50	79	17
Portugal	84	77	45	74	88	33
Spain	70	61	71	68	84	47
Sweden	78	79	32	65	94	16
United Kingdom	84	82	89	76	87	47
Average*	75	72	74	66	85	35

Note: * Average is not population-weighted.
Source: Eurobarometer.

Table 5.5 *Attitudes toward politics, 1996*

Country/percentage agreement among respondents	The average citizen has considerable influence on politics	Even the best politician cannot have much impact because of the way government works	Elections are a good way of making governments pay attention to the important political issues facing our country	The people we elect as MPs try to keep the promises they have made during the election
France	31	43	59	20
Germany	16	56	65	18
Ireland	30	62	79	30
Italy	25	51	59	11
Netherlands	18	39	84	29
Spain	27	54	70	16
Sweden	12	54	71	15
United Kingdom	14	50	72	24
Average*	22	51	70	20

Note: * Average is not population-weighted.
Source: ISSP.

per cent agreeing), with the Dutch and the Irish again leading the pack of 'optimists'.

We can conclude from the data contained in Tables 5.4 and 5.5 that many European voters perceive that corruption amongst politicians is increasing, that the processes of government and public bodies are getting worse, that public services are not serving their interests, the rich in society are getting richer and the poor poorer, that the average citizen does not have much influence on politics, that even good politicians are constrained in terms of the impact they can have and that few respondents expect that promises made by politicians will be kept in office. Yet, many respondents believe that they can change things in their respective societies and that elections retain their importance as a means of holding a government to account for its actions.

These ideas feed into the wider debate concerning the links between civic engagement, social capital and social trust. Social capital refers to the networks and norms of civil society that enable society and its citizens to perform more 'productively' in terms of community institutions, reciprocity and mutual trust. There appears to be no direct link between a person's degree of social trust and their confidence in government. However, social trust does indirectly affect levels of political confidence mediated through the performance of representative institutions. This conclusion is derived from the work of Putnam (1993) and Newton and Norris (2000).

In this context, and given these attitudinal results, the relatively small decline in voter turnout noted in Table 5.2 above in the 1990s could be regarded instead as a considerable success rather than a failure. The results also suggest that European voters are clear eyed in terms of their expectations of what politicians can and do achieve and that the strong cross-national faith in the value of elections as an effective means of accountability remains largely undiminished.

The overall attitudinal picture is certain, however, to be subtly shaded and nuanced both by specific attitude and country. We would need to ask exactly the same questions again at one more point in time at least to gain further insight into the structure of these particular attitudes and to see whether they changed over time in reaction to particular events or personalities in particular countries. We can nevertheless still consider the main explanations offered to account for these attitudes towards politicians and the political process.

The main explanations

Norris (1999, pp. 21–5) uses three categories of explanation (political, institutional and cultural) to account for why there appears to be less civic engagement, including voter participation, than in the past:

- *Political: the failure of government performance?*   This category is based on the belief that relative expectations of government and its performance have changed. The changing role of the state in society from the 1980s onwards, with less emphasis on 'big' government, has interacted with perceptions of economic failure to engender a more distant relationship between the citizen and the state in terms of trust and the willingness to participate politically.
- *Institutional: the failure of constitutional design?*   This category focuses upon the perception of a widening of the gap between citizens and the state, with the role of political parties, interest groups and public opinion all undergoing considerable change. The major problem is seen to be the lack of accountability of those in power, with elections increasingly unable to be major influences on the direction of public policy in an era of low incumbency turnover. The 1998 federal election in Germany, for example, resulted in the first complete change of government in the 14 national elections of the postwar period, with previous changes of government having been implemented by changes in coalition partners. In addition, semi-permanent coalitions in some countries are rarely subject to serious electoral sanction (such as in Austria as mentioned earlier) and professionalism from politicians has received much greater emphasis. They are thus much more easily able to ensure their own political survival.
- *Cultural: modernization and changing values?*   This category centres on changes in values, a development often summarized as 'post-materialism' and is derived from the work of Inglehart (1977). With the growth in higher education, a more critical citizenry has arisen, one looking for greater participation in decision-making processes and being more and more willing to develop new forms of political participation outside the confines of traditional parties and interest groups. Such people are also interested in promoting 'new issues' such as the environment and increasing opportunities for women. There is now less support for traditional forms of authority and less respect for hierarchical and authoritarian values. This has come about through generational change, producing the perception that 'direct action', such as recent street protests taking place in and around major summit meetings in Seattle (World Trade Organization), Genoa (the 'Group of Eight' leading industrial nations), and Gothenburg (European Council) is an option equally as valid as working within channels of protest mediated by conventional liberal democratic institutions and mechanisms. The rise of Green parties in many West European countries is often regarded as being a direct consequence of this pressure for 'alternative' politics.

These three categories are certainly useful in setting out the key general arenas capable of providing underpinning explanations as to why traditionally structured political participation might decline. It is also important to note that the three explanatory categories above inevitably interact and overlap with one another. Value-change, generational shifts in outlook, growing cognitive abilities, along with subtly shifting socialization patterns and influential concrete experiences all gradually accumulate. They are then both reflected and refracted via the specific institutional context within which the political process is conducted. It is to that rapidly changing context that we now turn.

The changing institutional context of political participation

We saw earlier in Table 5.4 that few European electors had much faith in their ability to control what is happening in the world around them. For many, the increasing economic and political interdependences between countries as one result of European integration and the overall process of globalization render the individual voter a fringe spectator rather than an active participant in most political decision-making. Classical democratic theory was predicated on the existence and preeminence of the nation-state; today, this fundamental assumption is increasingly threadbare and outdated. The traditional national democratic institutions founded on this assumption have not yet succeeded in democratizing supra-national representative institutions such as the European Parliament.

Simultaneously, there has been a decline in the ideological input to mass politics. The political control of the Right in many countries throughout the 1980s produced a reaction from their successors that mainly implicitly but sometimes also explicitly accepted many of the policies which had been implemented during that particular decade. There was no serious or sustained comeback for state intervention and control in the 1990s, and the agenda of mass politics today has become dominated by claims of government efficiency and 'output' rather than democratic control. The alternatives offered by the different parties to voters at election time are now often hard to distinguish from one another, with essentially minor variations on the same broad theme based on top-down elite initiatives rather than bottom-up demands from voters.

The precise meaning of the Third Way in the United Kingdom or the Neue Mitte in Germany, for example, is highly likely to remain shrouded in rhetorical flourishes and studied vagueness. The deliberate opacity of both purposes and ends in terms of such an approach to politics may, however, turn out to be an electorally popular strategy with a 'postmodern' European electorate. It remains virtually impossible to pin down the core content of the Third Way or its indispensable elements. For example, in his speech to the Königswinter conference in Oxford on 25 March 2000, British Prime Minister Tony Blair described the basis of the Third Way or Neue Mitte as 'an active civil society' in which 'people need fixed points of reference; a society without prejudice but not without rules'. People 'want the security of belonging to a community, where bonds of connection exist between citizens'(see the Downing Street website for the full text of the speech, <http://www.number-10.gov.uk/news.asp>).

The whole means of mass representation has also undergone widespread change; new forms of public opinion are much more prominent and extensively used to test the wishes of voters. Opinion polls, focus groups, deliberative democracy, citizens' juries and referenda are all employed to measure the public mood, a far cry indeed from holding public meetings or reading newspaper editorials. These new forms of 'manufactured' public opinion may be statistically accurate and duly sensitive to the swings and roundabouts of public opinion, but they remain uninvolving and uninteresting for many.

With the even more recent development of 'e-democracy' and the continuing exploration of the uses of the Internet for voting on-line, the need to get involved publicly in politics as the only route available has receded even further into the past. It will soon be possible to carry out previously public commitments and engagements without leaving the privacy of one's home, participating in the political process via personal computer rather than personal commitment. A final contextual factor to note here has been developments in the mass media and the way they present politics. Despite the ever-increasing and easy availability of information to the mass audience, 'information deficits' remain for many people. Strong emphasis on the 'horse-race' aspect of elections, a seeming obsession with image and style to the neglect of policy substance, and a critical and probing approach which assumes government failure and shortcomings, are all recent developments in the ways in which the mass audience is presented with political events and personalities.

These contextual developments are all potential influences on rates of political participation. The deliberate blurring of ideological boundaries between the parties seems bound to reduce the incentive to vote. If the choice between parties is unclear, the interest of the ordinary voter is unlikely to be sustained. If there appears to be nothing more at stake at an election than a minor redivision of the economic cake, few will pay much attention. If the media and politicians together cannot find ways of explaining complex technical issues in more comprehensible terms and the latter fail to keep promises or keep well clear of conflicting and self-serving interests, increasing cynicism on the part of voters is only to be expected.

Conclusions

We saw earlier that turnout at national elections in Western Europe in the 1990s had not greatly declined, although the general trend was slightly down compared to earlier decades after 1945. There appeared to be no definitive trend, and instead there were different fluctuations in different countries. However, we also noted that the current attitudes of the European electorate suggested at least scepticism about politicians and their promises, along with the perceived lack of ability of the ordinary citizen to influence the contours of European politics. We also noted the vast changes in the context of political participation, comprising the steady waning of 'ideological input', the substantial redefinition of the ideas and implementation of mass representation and the changing approach of the mass media towards more overt and instinctive criticism of those in power. In this concluding section we want to examine the potential for further change based on these recent developments and to assess whether there is a 'crisis of disengagement' in terms of European political participation. Whether such a development is necessarily a 'bad thing' will also be considered.

Classical liberal democratic theory assumes active citizens, people interested in politics and capable of mobilization by mediating organizations such as political parties and interest groups. The recent evidence suggests that, across Western Europe in terms of partisan attachment for example, most people are simply not engaged in the political process in this way. They no longer feel close to any particular party (if they ever did) and they have more pressing claims on their limited spare time than attending party meetings or conferences.

There also appears to be a general lack of confidence in parties. According to Dalton and Wattenberg (2000a, pp. 264–5) based on the results of the World Values Surveys conducted between 1995–98 in eight OECD nations, parties came last in a list of 15 institutions in terms of the degree of confidence held in them. Some of the other institutions were the police, armed forces, the legal system, the churches, the trade unions, the European Union and the press. The police were the institution in which the greatest average confidence was expressed.

For many, such a result is part of a general weakening of civil society, with the decline in the articulation of collective demands and social group influence, and the rise of specific individually-defined wants. There has been a substantial loss of social cohesion within society. Politics is no longer conducted by warring camps based on primordial tribal divisions as tightly knit sub-cultures have gradually lost their internal coherence. Accompanying this has been the rise of managerialism and technocratic solutions in politics. Basic rights and freedoms have long been secured, leading to questions at elections asking, 'what is really at stake any more?' For some, the 'end of ideology' has finally arrived, having been initially predicted as imminent fully 40 years ago (Bell, 1960).

The context within which these changes have occurred has also been influential. There has been the simultaneous rise of pressures derived from processes of decentralization and internationalization which have so far escaped any effective attempt to democratize them. No longer does the nation-state control the key affairs and interests of its people. Increasingly, strong supra-national forces are exerting enforceable influence on policy areas previously reserved to the competence of national governments such as industrial and social policy.

The rapid development of interactive and virtual technologies will inevitably alter the boundaries of communication between governments and their voters. Given this, political participation is certain to assume a radically different appearance, with a shifting balance between private and public engagement with politics. This will produce both new opportunities for the engaged and the informed, whilst new barriers to effective participation will be erected against those suffering from 'information poverty'. From perspectives rooted in classical democratic theory and the structured certainties of the immediate post-1945 period, these developments and the speed with which they have taken hold have understandably given rise to disquiet, even alarm. Central to these concerns are worries about the 'quality' of political participation and its link to the 'health' of West European democracy as a whole. Specifically, the extent of the 'democratic deficit' at national level, replicating the one already existing at EU level, has provided the focus for these concerns.

However, as we saw earlier, there has not yet been any major decline in voter turnout at national elections in Western Europe. Elections still exert a pull and retain a hold on most European electors as a widely accepted civic duty and as a social norm, regarded as a continuing and still credible means of holding governments to account. It would nevertheless be wrong for the European political elite to blithely assume that this situation will necessarily continue of its own accord. The 'danger' for politicians is that new forms of active political participation will arise outside the 'blocked' channels that they control, rendering the scope and nature of public protest and criticism both erratic and unpredictable. The very predictability of the means of articulation of the public mood was something that European governments could generally rely on in the past. They were able to shape the political landscape without great fear that unconventional channels of protest would suddenly catch the public mood and force them to change. The rules of the political game were agreed and clear.

The apparent process of disengagement from traditional political processes may not be a bad thing if it acts to lessen the control of the political elite to set the political agenda and priorities. A critical citizenry is a vital element in the periodic revitalisation of mass democracy and if ordinary people find no palatable home in 'old' parties or interest groups, then a 'renewal from outside' rather than 'civic disengagement' might provide a more accurate description of recent developments. Through this process, new issues can clamber onto the political agenda rather than being taken up and then emasculated by the self-interested imperatives of old political elites. Grassroots activism encompassing broader, more spontaneous forms of participation should keep the political system fresh and responsive.

There will always be a diverse and pluralistic range of political participation activities within West European democracies, and concentrating on turnout at elections will only ever paint part of the overall picture. In particular, there is no cross-nationally applicable and set level of turnout at elections that establishes beyond doubt the legitimacy of a particular government or the effectiveness of the procedures for holding it to subsequent account. However, a low level of turnout of around 50 per cent does generally produce unequal participation by different social groups and a likely class bias in the political process since the more educated members of the electorate tend to vote more regularly (Lijphart, 1997).

It is important to stress that the growth in the numbers of 'critical citizens' and 'disaffected democrats' does not inevitably signify a crisis of 'civic disengagement'. If parties choose to adapt their internal procedures to these new forces of issue articulation, they themselves can be strengthened in the process. Even strong criticism of the political process is not necessarily a sign of disengagement on the part of voters – indeed it may be the reverse.

Popular satisfaction with a political system is mediated both by accumulated experiences and expectations. Governments will consequently always attempt to 'damp down' the 'unrealistic' expectations of voters when the political context in which the governments are forced to operate is changing so rapidly. In this way, the perception of deteriorating performance on the part of the government can partly be moulded, even if the evaluative criteria of institutional performance necessarily remain subjective and contested.

The delicate balance between criticism and confidence in a liberal democratic political system shifts constantly and sometimes unpredictably. It remains the case that an excess of either will continue to pose fundamental questions affecting the 'performance' of politicians as well as the efficacy and vitality of the links binding ordinary citizens into the workings of the overall political process.

Chapter 6

Party Systems, Electoral Cleavages and Government Stability

PAUL WEBB

The central claim of this chapter is that the mobilization of new and resurgent cleavages since the 1960s has tended to further fragment West European party systems, and in a few cases to polarize them, though not necessarily in terms of left–right ideology. While such developments have often coincided with an increased incidence of minority government and coalitional collapse, it would be quite wrong to infer that party governments have become radically more unstable overall, for Western Europe remains a geo-political region dominated by moderate multi-partyism which is in no sense pathological for democracy.

What do we mean by the terms 'party system' and 'cleavage'? With respect to the former, any 'system' – be it social, political, biological or mechanical – consists of a recurring pattern of interaction between a set of component elements; thus, the term 'party system' refers to a recurrent pattern of interaction between a set of political parties. Moreover, the key dynamics involved in the process of interaction between parties involve both competitive and cooperative behaviour. From this, we may infer that a party system is a particular pattern of competitive and cooperative interactions displayed by a given set of political parties. In addition, it should be noted that parties interact in more than one political arena and at more than one level of political jurisdiction. Specifically, party systems operate in electoral, legislative and executive arenas, and at local, regional, national and European levels of jurisdiction. In view of this, it is apparent that statements to the effect that 'country X has party system type Y' are in reality simplifications which beg questions about which level of political jurisdiction and which arena of party interaction one is talking about. That is, West European countries actually have more than one party system, and quite different patterns of party interaction may be found within these different systems; more succinctly, parties operate within the context of multilevel politics. That

115

said, it remains common practice to speak of 'the party system' within specific countries and to mean by this the pattern of party interaction we find in the various national-level political arenas. This chapter will conform largely to this convention, although it will become apparent that the multilevel nature of politics impacts on national party systems (for instance, where they have fragmented as a result of resurgent centre–periphery tensions or where traditional parties have been forced to respond to the European-issue dimension).

Here we are especially concerned with the impact of socio-political cleavages on West European party systems, an idea that will be forever associated with the names of S.M. Lipset and Stein Rokkan (1967). At its simplest, the term 'cleavage' implies a socio-political faultline between social groups which is powerful enough to structure political – and more specifically, party political – conflict. Bartolini and Mair (1990, p. 215) in reviewing the literature have proposed that the concept of cleavage should be understood as comprising three elements:

> an empirical element, which identifies the empirical referent of the concept, and which we can define in socio-structural terms; a normative element, that is, the set of values and beliefs which provides a sense of identity and role to the empirical element, and which reflects the self-consciousness of the social group(s) involved; and an organisational/behavioural element, that is, the set of individual interactions, institutions, and organisations, such as political parties, which develop as part of the cleavage.

Thus, it is not enough simply for there to be political conflict; there are many political issues which bring quite intense disputes onto the agenda of public affairs without ever generating group consciousness or political organizations that structure debate and behaviour in an enduring fashion. Such issues do not constitute cleavages in Lipset and Rokkan's original sense, then, because they fail to meet what Bartolini and Mair call the normative or organizational/behavioural criteria. To reiterate, a cleavage must incorporate an 'empirical' social-structural division based on an ascriptive or demographic characteristic such as ethnicity, class, religion or gender; the social groups involved must be 'normatively' conscious of the collective identities created by such group memberships; and these collective identities must find expression in political organizations which will pursue the political interests of the groups involved. Typically, though not always, the organizations best-suited to this purpose are political parties, which is why patterns of party competition and/or cooperation can largely be understood as an expression of cleavage structures.

Lipset and Rokkan's classic model of cleavage structuration in Western Europe emphasized the central importance of two great macro-historical processes seemingly rooted far back in Europe's pre-democratic past, but each of which generated cleavages of enduring relevance to the democratic era of party politics. The first of these phenomena was that of national revolution, which refers to the process by which national consciousness developed and nation-states came to be formed. Often the process was complex and slow-moving, but Lipset and Rokkan argued that it fostered two enduring socio-political cleavages which remain with us in contemporary Europe. The first of these is the centre–periphery cleavage. The process of National Revolution typically entailed central nation-building elites seeking to subjugate local cultures and jurisdictions. Their goal was to replace these sub-national identities and loyalties with new national equivalents, but the struggle to build the nation-state sometimes left an enduring legacy of bitterness between centre and periphery. This is particularly true where there are what Rokkan and Lipset referred to as 'ethnically, linguistically or religiously distinct subject populations in the provinces and the peripheries'. In fact, there appeared to be relatively few indications of lasting centre–periphery cleavages in Europe at the time they wrote in the late 1960s, but an obvious recrudescence of such tensions in countries like Spain, the UK and France has been one source of party system change since then, as we shall see.

The second type of cleavage which Rokkan and Lipset claimed to have derived from the process of National Revolution was religious in nature. They saw different types of religious cleavage emerging in various ways from the nation-building process; some countries were left with lines of socio-political tension between Roman Catholic and Protestant communities, whereas other nations have been left with conflict between the Catholic church and a secular state. The potential for Catholic–Protestant tensions developed in the sixteenth and seventeenth centuries as nation-building leaders sought to establish national churches that would be independent of the universal authority claimed by Rome. Where societies were largely Protestantized (as in Scandinavia, for instance), there was little potential for lasting Catholic–Protestant conflict, and little potential for Church–State conflict as Protestant churches quickly accommodated themselves to the demands of nation-states. Neither was there any basis for Catholic–Protestant conflict in countries which remained largely untouched by the Reformation, or where the counter-reformation successfully obliterated it (most obviously true of Latin Southern Europe). However, these countries were affected by tensions between secular nation-building elites and the Catholic church in the eighteenth and nineteenth centuries, a development which generated the potential for what Lipset and Rokkan called 'parties of religious defence'. Countries which were only partially Protestantized were left in a rather different situation. The classic example of this is the Netherlands, which maintained a highly segmented system of internal sub-cultures (or 'pillars') based on different religious denominations until the late twentieth century.

The second kind of macro-historical process identified by Lipset and Rokkan was that of industrial revolution; this, they suggested, generated two further kinds of enduring socio-political cleavage: one between industrial and landed (or urban-rural) interests and another between owners and workers within the industrial sector. While the former has had a fairly limited direct impact on contemporary party politics in Western Europe (and is most obvious in the Agrarian and Centre parties of Scandinavia), the influence of the latter has been pervasive; although industrial class politics has undoubtedly been more important in some countries (notably the Scandinavian polities) than in others, no European society or political system has been untouched by it.

Lipset and Rokkan's account of the development of West European party systems emphasized not only history and structure, but also stability. Famously, they concluded their argument with a statement of what has now become widely known as the 'freezing hypothesis'. That is, across Europe as a whole 'the party systems of the 1960s reflect, with few but significant exceptions, the cleavage structures of the 1920s' (Lipset and Rokkan, 1967, p. 50). The reasons for the apparent freezing of party systems were complex, but essentially reflected the narrowing of electoral markets as party organizations mobilized the bulk of 'available' voters during the era when electoral franchises were democratized; hence, the notion that electoral markets had become relatively 'closed' (Bartolini and Mair, 1990, p. 57). This view may have been warranted at the time Lipset and Rokkan wrote, but within a few years observers started to question its continuing validity as evidence mounted of what appeared to be new levels of voter instability across Europe.

Realignment, dealignment and party system change

Changes to the established pattern of cleavages which Lipset and Rokkan described have affected party systems in two ways: through the emergence of new cleavages which have cut across, and thereby weakened, those already established; and through the sheer erosion (and non-replacement) of old cleavages. While the former process constitutes one of realignment of party programmes and electoral support, the latter amounts to a process of dealignment (Flanagan and Dalton, 1984). According to the realignment perspective, the overall degree to which electoral behaviour is structured by cleavages remains constant in the long run, while the nature of the cleavages changes; according to the dealignment perspective, however, electoral behaviour comes to float more freely of social anchors than hitherto. Although it is not easy to be sure which of these two processes predominates since they share a number of common indicators, it now seems likely that a combination of both has affected West European party systems. What is the evidence?

Realignment

There is evidence that a number of significant cleavages have emerged since Lipset and Rokkan formulated their freezing hypothesis. The impact of these new cleavages varies from case to case: in some instances, the new lines of potential conflict have been largely subsumed by existing party systems as established parties have assimilated the issues concerned through programmatic shifts designed to attract new support; in other cases, (where established parties are less flexible or where institutional barriers to gaining representation are low) new parties have emerged.

A number of cleavages deserve attention. The first is the centre–periphery cleavage, the reemergence of which in some of the regions of West European nation-states took most observers by surprise. As Rokkan and Urwin (1982, p. 1) put it:

> As late as 1960, the likely consensus of opinion upon the violence and irrendentism of the German-speaking population of the Alto-Adige would probably have been that it was an atavistic intrusion into the usually placid waters of Western politics – the exception, as it were, which proved the rule.

Since then it has become clear that this particular 'rule' has been heavily bent, if not broken. The countries where regionally-based ethnic parties have resonated electorally include Belgium (where even the established parties have fragmented into Francophone and Flemish units); the UK (where the Scottish and Welsh nationalists, not to mention the nationalist and republican parties of Northern Ireland, have made a notable impact); Spain (where Basque nationalist parties like Herri Batasuna and Partido Nacionalista Vasco operate); Italy (where the German-speaking minority Sudtiroler Volkspartei has long been sustained by the electorate of the Alto Adige); and Finland (where the Swedish-speaking Svenska Folkepartiet operates). The strength of these cleavages should not only be measured by the electoral presence of such regionalist parties, moreover; it is evident too in the programmatic accommodations of established parties. In the UK, for instance, the two major parties have responded to the emergence of Scottish and Welsh nationalism in different ways, so that they are now differentiated not only by left–right class ideology, but also by attitudes to devolution: while Labour introduced new legislation establishing a Scottish parliament and a Welsh Assembly in 1997, the Conservatives sought to defend the existing territorial constitution of the UK.

The second cleavage to have left its mark on West European party systems since Lipset and Rokkan wrote is that of post-materialism. Most closely associated with the name of Ronald Inglehart (1977), the theory of post-materialism attempts to explain widely noted changes in attitudes towards authority, hierarchy and traditional social morality in Western societies. Essentially, it suggests that the absence of war and the unprecedented spread of material affluence since the 1950s have produced new generations of citizens who place less emphasis on the material achievements which older generations had been unable to take for granted, while aspiring to a new range of non-material 'quality-of-life' goals. This quality-of-life agenda is fairly eclectic and takes in issues of democracy and participation, racial and gender equality, and personal liberty and autonomy. The post-materialist issue par excellence, however, is environmentalism: concern for the quality of the environment exemplifies the view that (to some extent) economic growth and affluence can and should be sacrificed to the dictates of protecting nature and the human ecosphere.

Inglehart and various associates have spent years marshalling an impressive array of empirical evidence relating to the spread of post-materialist values across advanced industrial societies, and the impact of this 'culture shift' on party systems. This evidence suggests that a number of countries (especially Germany, Italy, Denmark and Ireland) have experienced significant growth in the proportions of their citizens who might be described as post-materialist (Dalton, 1996, pp. 96–7). As with the centre–periphery cleavage, the spread of post-materialist values will not necessarily generate new parties able to make their presence felt in national parliaments since this depends on institutional factors such as the type of electoral system and on the strategic choices made by post-materialist actors (Poguntke, 1987). However, virtually all West European countries now have Green parties – the archetypal post-materialist party organizations – and in a number of cases such parties have become very significant to patterns of competition and cooperation between parties: this is best exemplified by the case of Germany, where Green politicians have entered government as a result of coalitions with social democrats (Lees, 2001). Moreover, post-materialism has impacted on established organizations, usually by bringing new generations of left-libertarian actors into centre-left parties (Kitschelt, 1994)

A third new type of cleavage meriting attention derives to a considerable extent from the phenomenon of postwar immigration in West European countries. This can be described as a cleavage between opponents of immigration who wish to defend traditional national identities, and cosmopolitans who support multiculturalism and the rights of ethnic minorities. Though not the sole source of their support, this cleavage has been critical in spawning a clutch of far-right parties in various parts of the continent. To be sure, Europe's far-right parties vary ideologically and in terms of their electoral appeal. Some focus mainly on anti-tax, minimalist state themes, while others make great play of tradition and social authoritarianism; moreover, most offer anti-establishment messages about the alleged shortcomings of the major parties. But the most notable programmatic feature of parties such as the French Front National (FN) and the German Republikaner has been a striking xenophobia towards immigrants and ethnic-minority citizens. Herbert Kitschelt has explained the multifaceted appeal of the far-right in Europe in terms of electoral market opportunities for parties offering a mixture of right-wing economics and social authoritarianism – an attitudinal amalgam located at the ideological antipodes of left- libertarian post-materialism: or as he says, 'postindustrial politics is characterised by a main ideological cleavage dividing left-libertarians from right-authoritarians' (1995, p. 2). Note, too, that the anti-minority/cosmopolitan cleavage does not only distinguish a few fringe parties of the far-right from all other parties in Western Europe; it is manifest or latent to some extent in mainstream party systems as major parties are compelled to respond to the political agendas of immigration and multiculturalism. Indeed, such parties have sometimes been confronted by considerable dilemmas in seeking to locate themselves on this issue dimension, as the case of the Gaullist RPR (Rassemblement pour la République) in France illustrates; as the emblematic party of French nationalism it has sought to respond to the electoral threat posed by the xenophobic FN without forfeiting its status as a party of the legitimate governing mainstream, a balancing act which has not always been easy to perform. By contrast, its main rival on the centre-right of the party system, the UDF (Union pour la Démocratie Français), has generally adopted a less ambivalently cosmopolitan position with regard to immigrants and non-white French citizens.

The final new cleavage which bears examination in the context of contemporary Western Europe actually shares a certain amount of common ground with the fault-line between cosmopolitans and anti-immigrationists: this is the difference between supporters and opponents of European integration. The overlap occurs since some of those keen to defend traditional national identities and prerogatives against minority cultures react in precisely the same way to the perceived threat of supra-nationalism emanating from the EU. Thus, for instance, the FN is decidedly opposed to European integration and the RPR has suffered notably from internal dissent on the question. More generally, Gary Marks (1999, pp. 4–5) has elaborated the reasons why the fit between existing cleavages and the European issue is likely to be imperfect:

> Social democratic parties are pulled in two directions. On the one hand, economic integration threatens social democratic achievements at the national level by intensifying international economic competition and undermining Keynesian responses to it. By making it easier for international capital to locate in the country that provides the most favourable conditions and rules, economic integration increases the substitutability of labour across countries, fosters economic inequality and pressures employers to demand labour flexibility. On the other hand, political integration promises a partial solution to this bleak prospect by recreating a capacity for authoritative regulation – at the European level.

Similar tensions exist for right-of-centre parties, albeit as mirror-images. We have already noted those affecting the RPR, but the British Conservatives offer an equally obvious illustration, the European issue revealing a sometimes acute internal tension between the party's market rationalist and romantic nationalist instincts. While classic Burkean Conservatism embodies the centrality of national traditions, identities and loyalties, market rationalism has long been prominent in the thinking of many Conservatives, and emphasizes the benefits of market allocation and free trade. The difficulty with European integration for Conservatives is that it represents an obvious threat to national sovereignty while simultaneously justifying itself largely in terms of market rationality. Thus, apologists for the goal of European Monetary Union often make their case in terms of its importance for the realization of the single market, the savings to consumers and producers in currency transaction costs, the benefits to industry of stable currencies and interest rates, the consequent boost to long-term growth rates, and so on. Yet the symbolism of abolishing the national currency, and the loss of national autonomy over economic policy, weigh heavily on the Conservative conscience. What should the true Conservative do: defend national sovereignty or pursue the logic of economic reason in an era of global capitalism? During the 1990s, it became obvious that different Conservative politicians had different answers to this question, which precipitated a serious bout of internal conflict with some individuals leaving the party over the issue. More generally, over the course of the decade following the British general election of 1987 the UK's major parties and their supporters in the electorate adjusted their attitudes towards Europe, with Labour becoming a pro- integrationist organization and the Conservatives anti-integrationist (Evans, 1999). At one and the same time, this illustrates the potential for the European cleavage to generate realignments within domestic party systems and the capacity of established parties to assimilate it. Indeed, in general terms it must be emphasized that national party systems across Western Europe have thus far remained relatively impervious to the impact of the European cleavage, a fact which Mair ascribes chiefly to the stunted development of a transnational party system at the European level; this in turn reflects the fact that there is as yet no directly-elected European executive (Mair 2000).

Dealignment

Party-system change is not explicable solely in terms of the cross-cutting effects of new upon old cleavages, and those of the partisan dealignment school often argue that cleavages in general have less structural capacity to influence voter choice than hitherto. Typically, they account for this in terms of the cognitive mobilization of citizens. According to this view the expansion of higher educational provision and mass access to television combine to facilitate the political independence of electors (Barnes and Kaase, 1979). That is, voters become more able to assess information about public affairs without having to rely on party cues, thanks to the role education plays in developing their intellectual skills at precisely the time that they have far greater access to independent sources of non-partisan information from the broadcasting media (Dalton, 2000, p. 32). The cognitive mobilization argument constitutes part of a broad critique of modern political parties which proposes that they are gradually losing their functional relevance for modern democratic politics in a number of ways and are consequently undergoing a process of 'decline'. Amongst other things, it is contended, this shows up in the growing number of sophisticated voters with access to non-partisan sources of political information; such individuals can be independent of parties and can even choose to act through single-interest groups rather than parties should they prefer. Thus, in the context of a sophisticated and rational electorate, the interest groups and mass media come to replace parties in fulfilling key political functions such as political communication and interest articulation. Although cognitive mobilization is by no means the only plausible cause of partisan dealignment, there is telling evidence to confirm its existence.

The most clear-cut evidence consists of the decline in the extent to which voting behaviour is structured by cleavages. Mark Franklin *et al.* (1992) have provided the most comprehensive overview of this subject, although their analysis is somewhat out of date now; nine out of the ten West European countries they examined (Italy being the sole exception) showed a reduction in the overall impact of social structure on voting behaviour between the 1960s (or early 1970s in two cases) and the mid or late 1980s. On average, the percentage of the variation in voting behaviour explained by structural cleavages dropped from 23 per cent to 15 per cent. This clearly suggests that, notwithstanding the cross-cutting effects of new cleavages, electorates are to some extent more dealigned – that is, less anchored to particular parties by virtue of social group identities – than hitherto.

Consistent with this process of dealignment are also various secondary indicators, the best-known of which is the decline of partisan identification: almost all Western societies have reported a significant (in some cases dramatic) decline in the percentage of survey respondents willing to declare a (strong) affinity with any specific party (Dalton, 2000, p. 25). There is even more incontrovertible evidence with respect to the declining number of citizens prepared to join and be active in parties (Katz *et al.*, 1992). By the 1990s, moreover, it became evident that voter turnout at national elections had declined in most West European countries, while measures such as the 'Pedersen index' (Pedersen, 1979) tended to reveal a simultaneous increase in the volatility of electoral behaviour. Although most of these indicators might in principle be explained by purely contingent factors related to the short-term circumstances of particular elections, the number of countries in which they occurred simultaneously is striking; this pattern suggests a broad cross-national phenomenon rather than the product of occasional national peculiarities. It is also interesting to note that these indicators generally coincide with significant levels of voter dissatisfaction with parties in general (Webb *et al.*, forthcoming), all of which suggests that they are tapping a degree of authentic voter disillusionment with party politics.

In summary, then, it seems reasonably clear that the cleavage structures and party systems of Western Europe have been affected by the twin processes of realignment and de-alignment. But does any of this necessarily imply change in the ways that political parties interact in their respective domestic political systems?

Fragmentation, polarization and cabinet stability

Giovanni Sartori (1976) is largely responsible for developing the widely acknowledged notion that two factors have an especially critical bearing on system dynamics: fragmentation and polarization. The fragmentation of a party system refers to the number of significant (or as Sartori says, 'relevant') parties in a system, and it is fascinating to observe that almost (though not quite) every important attempt ever made to categorize party systems relies at least in part on this criterion. Thus, the simplest and most intuitive way of classifying party systems is to differentiate one-party, two-party and multi-party systems. Polarization refers to the ideological distance between the major protagonists in the system. Each of the main types of party system Sartori distinguishes in the context of Western Europe provides insight into the way that fragmentation and polarization can combine to affect the nature of interactions between parties.

The classic Sartorian type is that which he refers to as 'polarized pluralism', a system characterized by the presence of high levels of both fragmentation and polarization. He defines a high level of fragmentation as consisting of at least five or six relevant parties, while he suggests that a polarized system is one defined by the presence of at least one significant anti-system party. The confluence of such levels of fragmentation and polarization brings with it, according to Sartori, a number of important consequences for the way parties interact. First, there are likely to be coalition governments of the centre confronted by 'bilateral oppositions' – that is, government opponents (single parties or blocs) to both the right and the left of the governing parties (assuming a predominantly left–right axis of party competition). Second, the presence of anti-system parties in these bilateral oppositions provides 'centrifugal' ideological pulls on coalitionable parties concerned not to lose support to radicals. Third, the improbability of these bilateral oppositions sharing enough ideological ground to make common cause makes it unlikely that there will be any meaningful alternation in power: the same party or parties remain in government virtually regardless of political circumstances or election results. In the long run this undermines the accountability of party governments.

Sartori's second major systemic variant is less pathological for democracy. This is what he refers to as 'moderate pluralism'. Numerically this is less fragmented than polarized pluralism (Sartori specifies three to five relevant parties), and the degree of ideological polarization is less pronounced (there being no meaningful anti-system parties, for instance). The dynamics of such a system are fundamentally different to those found under polarized pluralism. For one thing, the system is characterized by 'centripetal' rather than 'centrifugal' ideological drives – that is, the major parties are not driven by the presence of anti-system competitors to adopt comparatively radical stances themselves. For another, competition is bipolar with two blocs of parties alternating in office. Sartori's third major type is the two-party system, which in its essential dynamics operates much as moderate pluralism does, although this time the presence of third parties does not prevent major parties from governing alone. It should be added that Sartori further distinguishes 'predominant party systems' in which a single party controls or dominates government over a period of at least three consecutive elections. However, he argues that this is not a true 'class' in its own right, but a variant that occurs within either two-party or multi-party settings when, 'even though no alternation in office actually occurs, alternation is not ruled out and the political system provides ample opportunities for open and effective dissent' (Sartori, 1976, p. 200).

Thus, we gain some notion of the way in which fragmentation and ideological polarization can influence the nature of party interactions. Empirical research has confirmed that they impact on processes of party government in a number of ways. For instance, Arend Lijphart has shown that the extent to which a party system is fragmented correlates strongly (r-squared = 0.87) with the type of government a country has; in essence, the greater the number of parties, the less likely it is that a single-party government or a 'minimum-winning' coalition will be formed (Lijphart, 1999, p. 112). Furthermore, fragmentation appears to affect the average duration of governments in so far as single-party and minimum-winning coalition governments have longer average lifespans (Laver and Schofield, 1990). Polarization can have a similar effect in that, unsurprisingly, the greater the ideological diversity within a government, the shorter its endurance is on average (Warwick, 1994). So, if fragmentation and polarization can affect party system dynamics in a variety of ways, it is surely appropriate to ask what the significance of the cleavage developments we have already traced might be in respect of these systemic features. Has the mobilization of new cleavages and/or erosion of old ones resulted in growing fragmentation or ideological polarization within European party systems? And if so, have such developments impacted on party systems in the expected manner?

The fragmentation of party systems can be measured in a number of ways, the most widely used of which has been developed by Markku Laakso and Rein Taagepera (1979). Their formula for counting the 'effective number of parties' takes account of both the number of parties in the system and their relative strength. This is a very intuitive and useful technique of measurement since it tells us, for instance, that in any system comprised of just two equally strong parties, the effective number will indeed by 2.0, while a system consisting of three equally strong parties will generate an effective number of 3.0, and so on. This measure can be calculated either on the basis of party shares of the popular vote (the effective number of electoral parties, ENEP), or on the basis of shares of seats won in parliament (the effective number of parliamentary parties, ENPP).

According to Taagepera and Grofman (1985) there are good reasons to expect a close relationship between the number of mobilized cleavages and the fragmentation of a party system. They suggest that a two-party system is a logical outcome for a society characterized by a single significant political fault-line, and, thereafter, one further party is needed for each extra cleavage which is mobilized. Although such a formula is inevitably (and intentionally) simplistic, evidence suggests that it comes surprisingly close to capturing the reality of democratic politics; indeed, Lijphart reports a correlation coefficient of 0.84 (1999, p. 88) for the relationship between the effective number of parliamentary parties and the number of mobilized 'issue dimensions' (that is, cleavages) across some 36 democratic societies between 1945 and 1996. Given that this is the case, the emergence of new cleavages since 1970 suggests that we should expect West European party systems to have become increasingly fragmented.

Of course, one would expect the cleavage–fragmentation relationship to be strongly mediated by institutional contexts; in particular, the type of electoral system which a country uses has obvious potential to foster or suppress the translation of cleavages into party representation in national parliaments. While proportional electoral systems tend to foster the translation of cleavages into representation, non-proportional systems have the opposite effect. This is best illustrated by the case of the UK, where the effective number of electoral parties has grown from approximately two to three since the 1960s, but the highly disproportional single-member plurality ('first-past-the-post') electoral system has restricted the effective number of parliamentary parties to two (Webb, 2000, p. 5). In Western Europe the relationship between the number of cleavages and party-system fragmentation has been facilitated by the fact that postwar national parliamentary electoral systems have generally been proportional in nature; France (since 1958) and the UK stand out as the only counter-examples. Thus, electoral systems have rarely constituted much impediment to the likelihood that new cleavages will generate additional parliamentary parties. It is no great surprise, therefore, to discover that most West European countries for which time-series data are available show increases in the effective number of parliamentary parties since the 1960s. Only four of the 13 cases reported in Table 6.1 fail to show increasing fragmentation, and the

Table 6.1 Fragmentation and party governments in Western Europe

Country	Effective number of political parties			Cabinet terminations due to lack of parliamentary support		Change in percentage of minority cabinets**
	1960s	1990s	Change	1950–64	1965–94*	
Austria	2.4	3.4	+1.0	0	0	+4.0
Belgium	3.8	8.5	+4.7	0	0	−0.5
Denmark	4.0	4.5	+0.5	2	4.5	+1.1
Finland	5.5	5.1	−0.4	3	0	−34.3
France	4.6	3.2	−1.4	8	0	−8.3
Germany	2.4	3.3	+0.9	0	1	0.0
Ireland	2.9	3.2	+0.3	3	1.5	−22.5
Italy	3.9	6.9	+3.0	5	5.5	−14.7
Netherlands	5.5	5.1	−0.4	2	0.5	+3.2
Norway	3.6	4.2	+0.6	2	0.5	+69.0
Sweden	3.3	4.0	+0.7	0	0.5	+8.7
Switzerland	5.3	5.8	+0.5	0	0	0.0
United Kingdom	2.5	2.2	−0.3	0	0	+2.2
Average	3.8	4.6	+0.75	23†	13.5†	+0.61

Note: * The actual incidence of cabinet terminations due to lack of parliamentary support during the period 1965–94 is halved in order to account for the fact that the period is approximately twice as long as that reported in the previous column. Taken together, these columns effectively compare the rate at which such terminations occur over any given 15-year period before and after Lipset and Rokkan wrote. ** Change in percentage of minority cabinets uses the same periodization as the previous two columns. † Total, not average.
Sources: Gallagher, Laver and Mair (2001, p. 322); Bartolini and Mair (1990, appendix 2); Lane and Ersson (1999, p. 218–19); Strøm (2000, p. 199).

average effective number grew from 3.8 to 4.6 across Western Europe as a whole between the 1960s and 1990s.

What does this signify for party system dynamics? One might suppose that increasing fragmentation would render the whole business of constructing stable governing majorities more problematic, and this is largely confirmed by Table 6.1. Of the nine cases which have become more fragmented since the 1960s, it is evident that four have experienced an increase in the rate of government terminations due to a lack of parliamentary support (Denmark, Germany, Italy and Sweden), while four have had greater recourse to the formation of minority governments (Austria, Denmark, Norway and Sweden). In all, then, six have experienced increased governmental instability in one or the other of these senses; only Ireland, Belgium and Switzerland have become more fragmented without encountering either consequence (though as we shall see, the former two have experienced a greater propensity for cabinet terminations due to internal discord). Belgium and Switzerland are classic examples of consensus (or 'consociational') democracies which have avoided these developments by dint of forming 'surplus' or 'oversize' cabinets – that is, coalition governments which contain more parties than are strictly necessary in order to control a parliamentary majority. France and Finland, it should be noted, confirm the general nature of the relationship between fragmentation and governing dynamics in the reverse direction: that is, each has become less fragmented since the 1960s and has endured fewer governmental terminations while resorting less frequently to minority government.

So much for fragmentation: what of polarization? Broadly speaking, there are two main ways in which the ideological locations of political parties can be assessed empirically. The first is through the use of 'expert-judgement scales' whereby samples of political scientists are asked to state where they believe parties to be located on various ideological dimensions, and the arithmetic means of these evaluations are then calculated for each party. The difficulty with this approach from our point of view is that it does not yield long time-series since the available scales all start in the 1980s (Knutsen, 1998; Laver, 1998); in other words, the use of such data is pointless for this exercise since it does not allow comparison of levels of polarization before and after the freezing hypothesis was articulated. The second approach, however, is more helpful. This draws on the Comparative Manifestos Project, a laboriously systematic attempt to apply a common interpretive scheme to the official programmes of political parties in democratic societies between 1945 and the late 1980s (Klingemann *et al.*, 1994). Although this means that reliable comparative data are not available for the 1990s, it is at least possible to consider whether party systems became more or less polarized in the two decades after Lipset and Rokkan wrote; this clearly takes in the period in which all of the new and resurgent cleavages outlined above – bar the European one – emerged.

The most systematic recent attempt to use manifesto data in order to assess the overall degree of ideological distance within party systems has been made by Caul and Grey (2000). The measure of ideological 'dispersion' which they devise takes account of the ideological location of every party in a system – not just the major ones, nor even the most extreme ones – and then weights these scores by the shares of the vote won by the respective parties at elections. In this way, larger parties make a greater contribution to the overall ideological diversity of a system than smaller parties. This analysis is only conducted in respect of the left–right dimension, it should be noted, and so does not necessarily take account of the ideological impact of new cleavages. However, it does focus on the one cleavage which is universally salient in West European politics. Their conclusion is unequivocal: '. . . the general trend for most advanced industrial democracies is for the major left and right parties, and for the party system as a whole, to display a pattern of ideological convergence over time' (Caul and Grey, 2000, p. 214). Table 6.2 extracts the West European countries from their analysis and shows that parties converged rather than polarized in seven out of the 11 systems for which we have data.

What are the implications of these findings for party system dynamics? In general, we might reasonably expect higher levels of polarization to coincide with an increase in the incidence of governmental collapse through internal discord between coalition members, or with the formation of 'surplus' cabinets as a way of avoiding such collapses; that is, where the risk of intra-cabinet conflict is high, leading parties may deliberately seek to create 'oversize' coalitions (that is, those with more coalition partners than are strictly necessary in order to control a parliamentary majority) so as to minimize the risk of governmental collapse due to one partner exiting (Luebbert, 1986). Table 6.2 shows that these expectations are partially borne out by developments in Western Europe. Thus, while increased ideological polarization is associated with a higher incidence of cabinet termination through internal dissension in the case of Denmark, it has produced an increase in the number of surplus coalitions in France and Italy; Sweden is the only case of increased polarization to have experienced neither of these hypothesized consequences. The expected relationships hold in the reverse sense for three other cases: that is, reduced polarization has generated fewer cabinet terminations through internal dissension in Austria and Germany, and fewer surplus cabinets in Germany and the Netherlands. In addition, it should be said that Table 6.2 is probably misleading in the case

Table 6.2 *Left–right polarization and party governments in Western Europe*

Country	Average polarization*			Cabinet terminations due to internal dissension		Change in percentage of surplus cabinets***
	1950s	1980s	Change	1950–64	1965–94**	
Austria	38.9	7.6	−31.3	2	0.5	0.0
Belgium	15.9	2.8	−13.1	3	5.5	+33.5
Denmark	22.9	24.6	+1.7	0	1	0.0
France	10.9	31.9	+21.0	6	0.5	+6.9
Germany	20.7	8.2	−12.5	5	1	−47.3
Ireland	36.0	31.7	−4.3	0	1	0.0
Italy	8.8	17.5	+8.7	6	5	+2.3
Netherlands	19.5	2.1	−17.4	0	3	−73.1
Norway	8.5	1.3	−7.2	0	0.5	0.0
Sweden	25.1	27.5	+2.4	1	1	0.0
United Kingdom	9.4	2.6	−5.3	0	0	0.0
Average	19.7	14.3	−4.2	23†	19†	+0.93

Note: * Polarization scores are derived from the comparative manifestos project. ** The actual incidence of cabinet terminations due to internal dissension during the period from 1965–94 is halved in order to account for the fact that the period is approximately twice as long as that reported in the previous column. Taken together, these columns effectively compare the rate at which such terminations occur over any given 15-year period before and after Lipset and Rokkan wrote. *** Change in percentage of surplus cabinets uses the same periodization as the previous two columns. † Total, not average.
Sources: Caul and Grey (2000, p. 215); Lane and Ersson (1999, pp. 213–19); Strøm (2000, p. 199).

of Belgium; it purports to show a case in which substantially less polarization coincides with a considerable increase in the percentage of surplus cabinets and a higher incidence of government collapse through internal dissension. This seeming paradox is almost certainly explained by the fact that our polarization data are limited to the left–right dimension of ideology; while the Belgian parties have undoubtedly converged on left–right issues since the 1960s, the virulence of the resurgent ethnic cleavage between Flanders and Wallonia implies that the parties are actually polarized to a far greater extent on this cross-cutting cleavage. In essence, then, Belgium accords with our expectation that ideological polarization generates cabinet dissension and (as a way of combatting the resultant instability of government) surplus cabinets. Therefore, only Ireland and Norway really seem to run contrary to expectations in having experienced ideological convergence yet suffered slight increases in the rate of cabinet dissension.

Conclusion: the continuing prevalence of moderate pluralism

Overall, Tables 6.1 and 6.2 jointly suggest that cabinets have become more vulnerable to instability (as evidenced by the increasing number of minority governments and terminations) in a number of West European countries thanks to greater party system fragmentation (Scandinavia, Germany, Austria and Italy) and/or ideological polarization (Belgium and Denmark). Were it not for the non-proportional limits to parliamentary representation constituted by electoral institutions, moreover, we would quite probably be able to add France and the UK to this list. In all of these cases, fragmentation and/or polarization appear to derive from the emergence of new cleavages, or the recrudescence of 'pre-industrial' ethnic cleavages. To some extent, however, the potential that new or revived cleavages create for governmental destabilization is offset by the convergence of left–right ideological differences within party systems. Note, too, that ideological convergence has also occurred in respect of the religious cleavage given the advance of secularization across Western societies. This process has not been addressed in detail in this chapter since the appropriate data are not available; however, it is certain that the impact of religious differences on party systems has diminished notably in countries such as the Netherlands, Belgium, Italy, France, Germany and Austria.

So where does this leave the classification of West European party systems at the outset of the twenty-first century? Despite the changes we have traced throughout this chapter, it must be said that little has changed overall in the quarter-century since the publication of Sartori's classic work, *Parties and Party Systems* (1976). At that time, Sartori felt able to classify most West European cases in the category of moderate pluralism (if we include Norway and Sweden, even though both of these countries were characterized by the presence of predominant Social Democratic parties), while identifying two cases of the more pathological category of polarized pluralism (Italy and Finland) and two cases of two-partyism (Austria and the UK). There can be little doubt that moderate pluralism remains overwhelmingly the modal category. All bar Belgium of those that Sartori placed in this category remain unambiguously within it, Norway and Sweden all the more decidedly so since neither now have predominant Social Democratic parties in Sartori's sense. Belgium's continued location there seems harder to justify; however, since it is the most fragmented party system in Western Europe and, as we have seen, the diminution of left–right polarization cannot obscure the severity of rifts between parties on other issue dimensions; this lends party competition a centrifugal quality, all of which points to a condition of polarized pluralism (de Winter and Dumont, 1999).

Turning to Sartori's two cases of polarized pluralism, both have undergone significant changes in the last decade, largely as a result of the end of the Cold War. While no formal manifesto information is available that would permit us to include Finland in Table 6.2, it nevertheless seems quite clear that Finnish party politics has experienced considerable ideological depolarization since 1989; indeed, notwithstanding the continuing fragmentation of the party system there, one commentator has described the 'transformation of closed ideological party behaviour to pragmatic politics' as involving nothing less than a centripetal 'rush towards the political and geographical centre' (Nousiainen, 2000, p. 298). This plainly points to the appropriateness of a designation of moderate pluralism. Italy is less clear-cut. With the end of the Cold War, the historical tension between communism and Christian Democracy in the country collapsed and the old party system with it. What has emerged since still bears all the signs of being transitional; while fragmentation remains high, it is hard to be certain that ideological distance is generally as great given the shift towards the mainstream of the successor parties to the former communists and neo-fascists. While it is true that this convergence is to some extent offset by the emergence of new forms of radicalism along rather different issue dimensions (notably the regionalist Northern League), it should also be said that an inchoate form of bipolar two-bloc politics involving broad but loose coalitions of left and right has emerged. The alternation in power of these blocs since 1994 has far more in common with the essentially centripetal dynamics of moderate pluralism than it does with the now seemingly outmoded centrifugal tendencies of polarized pluralism. On balance, therefore, a tentative designation of moderate pluralism seems most appropriate for contemporary Italy, though things remain delicately poised.

This leaves Sartori's cases of two-partyism. As we have already seen, electoral change since 1970 suggests an underlying shift towards moderate pluralism in the UK, though this is currently suppressed by an electoral system which ensures that the country remains a two-party system at the parliamentary level. Austria is a much less straightforward case. In the 1980s, after a period of Social Democrat predominance, it returned to its former status of moderate pluralism, but in the 1990s it came to exhibit many of the characteristics of polarized pluralism including greater fragmentation and ideological distance thanks to the emergence of the Greens and the right-wing populism of Jörg Haider's FPÖ (Freiheritliche Partei Österreichs) (Luther, 1999). That said, the coalition formed between the centre-right ÖVP (Österreichische Volkspartei) and the FPÖ in 2000 constituted an alternation in power which does not really conform to the precepts of polarized pluralism. Austria, as much as Italy, perhaps, presents the observer with an unclear impression of something which may be half-formed and transitional or may simply be oscillating in an unstable manner. On balance, it is probably best to award it a designation of moderate pluralism, though it currently seems near to the cusp of polarized pluralism.

Overall, then, Western Europe is still dominated by centripetal and moderate forms of multi-partyism. Although the slightly more fragmented nature of most party systems can and often does make the business of constructing enduring and stable coalition governments more problematic than hitherto, it cannot yet be judged to constitute a fundamental challenge to party government. The more significant threat is apparent in the few cases where cleavage change has generated new ideological polarities, though one can only speculate as to whether these changes will prove transitory or enduring.

Chapter 7

Extremist Movements

CAS MUDDE

Proclaimed by Francis Fukuyama as 'the end of history', liberal democracy has become 'the only game in town' throughout Western Europe. But voices of dissent remain, some from the distant past, and some more or less new. This chapter will provide an overview of the main 'extreme' movements in contemporary Western Europe, presenting their history, main ideas and actions, and suggesting current and sometimes new explanations for their success or the lack thereof.

Though much can and has been said about what 'extreme' means, here it will be defined in a fairly broad and general manner, denoting opposition, in terms of ideas or actions, to the fundamental values or institutions of the democratic regime. Though this comes close to the more current definition of extremism as the antithesis of democracy (see for example Backes, 1989), it is not completely the same. First of all, in my definition extreme does not have to present an alternative vision to democracy (as communism or fascism used to do). Second, it does not have to oppose democracy as such, but rather the democratic regime; that is, democracy as it exists within the country or region of the extreme actor. Therefore, some extreme actors actually claim to be the real democrats, opposing a regime which they claim is not or no longer democratic (Canovan, 1999). Third, and last, extreme does not necessarily mean the use of violence.

Despite the absolute triumph of democracy, various extreme movements do exist within contemporary Western Europe. It is not always easy to categorize the different groups, as they are of different shades and colours. Rather than trying to come up with a wholly new, perfect classification scheme, I will group extreme movements on the basis of both their ideological core and practical manifestations into five separate categories, which are partly overlapping in both theory and practice: extreme left, extreme right, territorial extremists, religious fundamentalists, and the 'new fringe'.

Although the old distinction between 'left' and 'right' might provide a useful tool for the media and politicians, for political scientists it can be no more than an imperfect instrument which, though still necessary for a lack of alternatives, is rapidly losing sense in current extreme politics. The category of territorial extremists, that is groups that oppose the existing territorial borders within Western Europe, is fairly diffuse in ideological terms, including members of both the extreme right and the extreme left. However, they should be mentioned separately, as it is particularly the territorial dimension rather than the left or right ideology that defines their importance in contemporary West European politics. The religious fundamentalists are distinguished on the basis of their core religious beliefs, which override all others (including nationalism, socialism or even territorialism).

In the 1990s various extreme groups have come into the spotlight that seem to be relatively new in terms of organizations or issues. Though some share ideological features and issues with most notably the 'old' (that is Marxist) extreme left, and there is a considerable overlap in personnel, the two sub-cultures are intrinsically different and can and should be separated. First of all, the 'new fringe' have their intellectual origins in the student revolts of the late 1960s, rather than in Marxism (Lent, 2001; Pfahl-Traughber, 1998); therefore, ideologically most groups are libertarian, and often despise the authoritarianism of the Marxist-Leninist old extreme left. Second, many activists of the new fringe do not have a past in the extreme left and do not even sympathize with their goals. Third, various movements address issues that simply cannot be captured under the traditional headings of 'left' and 'right'. In the words of one activist-academic: 'We might tip our hats to ideas and organizations past but we know we are our own politics now' (Jordan, 1999, p. 1).

The extreme left

In the late-1940s communist parties profited greatly from their participation in the anti-fascist resistance and gained their biggest electoral victories. In various countries they were, for the first (and often last) time in their existence, included in the first postwar governments. However, with the start of the Cold War, their status and electoral success changed radically: from defender of the nation and strong governmental partner to Soviet Union's fifth column and often weak pariah party. There were some notable exceptions though: in countries like Finland, France and Italy they kept strong parties in terms of electoral support and membership, though generally remaining outside of (national) political power. In the 1970s various communist parties, inspired by the Communist Party of Italy (PCI), developed a Euro-communist ideology. Despite the fact that Euro-communism rejected

Soviet communism and accepted parliamentary democracy, communist parties continued to be treated in a hostile manner by the other parties and remained on the margins of West European politics.

Roughly speaking, three factors may be used to explain the electoral support of communist parties. Of probably the least importance was pure ideological support. Though it was vital, together with the support from the Soviet Union, for the functioning of the party itself, its electorate consisted of a relatively small core of true communist believers. A second explanation for the parties' support was the activities of their often elaborate subcultures, which provided a wide variety of services within local communities. In various strongholds of the PCI in Northern Italy, the party was perceived in a similar clientelistic way as the Christian Democratic party or the Socialist Party in other parts of the country. Support for the PCI was a strategic rather than an ideological choice, as it was simply the best provider in the area.

While ideology explains the core support of the party, and subculture accounts for the rise in support in certain areas, political protest explains the regular fluctuations of electoral support for communist parties. Similarly to the extreme right since the 1980s, communist parties were often voted for by protest voters, who voiced their dissatisfaction with unemployment, social abuses and so forth. Most notably, they would protest against the policies of the social democrats in these domains, claiming that they had 'betrayed the workers'. Protest voting was crucial, for example, in Italy's 'red belt', a poor agricultural area to the North of Rome that became a stronghold of the PCI, or in explaining the strengths of the Communist Party of France (PCF) in departments like Creuze and Correze in France in the early 1950s.

Obviously, the fall of the Berlin Wall has changed the faith of communist parties significantly (Moreau, 1997; Bull, 1994). First of all, many communist parties decided to (finally) renounce the label 'communist' and to fully complete their development towards the democratic left; and in other countries, communist parties were no longer considered as threatening now that the 'evil empire' had ceased to exist. This meant that in some countries, electorally weakened, non-reformed communist parties could finally make it into government; for example, the Party of Italian Communists (PdCI). Overall, however, communist parties in Western Europe have either changed into democratic socialist (for example the East German Party of Democratic Socialism), if not fully-fledged social democratic parties (such as the Democratic Socialists in Italy), or they have become electorally insignificant parties (such as the communist parties in Finland, Greece or Portugal). In some cases, communist parties have ceased to exist independently, reemerging as parts of (non-extreme) 'new politics' parties (such as, GreenLeft in the Netherlands).

The demise of the (real) communist parties has not meant the end of extreme left electoral politics. Though still early days, the last decade has witnessed the resurgence of a new kind of socialist party: the left-wing populists. Parties like the Dutch Socialist Party (SP), the German Party of Democratic Socialism (PDS), or the Scottish Socialist Party (SSP) have started to establish themselves in their respective party systems. Though stemming from different backgrounds, they do share a clear ideological core and a specific political style. Ideologically, they resemble the old party family of the democratic socialists, accepting parliamentary democracy but rejecting capitalism. However, they differ in terms of political style, with the new socialist parties being far less dogmatic (that is, Marxist) and employing a strong populist rhetoric, juxtaposing the 'moral people' against the 'amoral elite'. Being no longer the vanguard of the proletariat, but rather the *vox populi*, these parties put particularism over internationalism, flirting with regionalist (PDS and SSP) and xenophobic (SP) sentiments.

The success of the left-wing populist parties lays both in the demise of the communist parties and in the recent movement to the right of many social democratic parties, such as the Dutch Labour Party under Wim Kok, the German Social Democratic Party under Gerhard Schroeder, and the British Labour Party under Tony Blair. This has opened up the 'left' side of the political spectre, where left-wing populists (and right-wing extremists) are battling for the traditional blue-collar vote. For the moment, the chances of left-wing populist parties gaining power in West European democracies remains remote. However, rather than influencing politics through their policies, the left-wing populist parties do have the potential to influence through their propaganda, undermining the legitimacy of the established party and political system.

The extreme right

Today, the main electoral 'threat' comes from the right of the political spectrum. Since the early 1980s extreme right parties have haunted Western Europe, though at the end of the twentieth century it seems to have become more qualified. What originally looked like a wave that was going to wash the shores of the whole of Western Europe has now turned out to be a series of floods in some countries. At the beginning of the twenty-first century, one could even speak of a general failure of the extreme right, as most countries in Western Europe have only marginal extreme right parties (such as Finland, Germany, Greece, Iceland, Ireland, Luxembourg, Netherlands, Portugal, Spain, Sweden, United Kingdom).

At the same time, extreme right parties are highly successful in a handful of other countries. What had been deemed impossible after the defeat of fascism in the Second World War, became reality in the 1990s: extreme right parties were represented in democratically elected governments in Western Europe. The premiere was for Italy, where Gianfranco Fini's rejuvenated, 'post-fascist' National Alliance (AN) entered the short-lived, right-wing Berlusconi government in 1994. In Austria, Jörg Haider's equally transformed Austrian Freedom Party (FPÖ) joined the Austrian government in 2000. Though parties like the Flemish Block (VB) in Flanders, the Dutch speaking part of Belgium, and the National Front (FN) in France never made it into the national government, their influence on their national politics has hardly been less.

Finally, there are some countries with successful borderline cases, that is parties whose extreme right status is debated among scholars and media alike. Most notably, this includes the Progress Parties in Norway and Denmark, as well as, though to a lesser extent, the Danish People's Party. Sharing a negative position on immigration and an often radical rejection of the elite with the extreme right parties indicated above, these parties miss the combination of nationalism, xenophobia, welfare chauvinism, and a tough law and order stand that defines the extreme right core ideology (Mudde, 2000). The same has been argued for the Northern League (LN) in Italy and the Swiss People's Party, which under the leadership of Christopher Blocher has at times flirted with anti-elitism and xenophobia.

But electoral success tells only part of the story. While extreme right parties might be unsuccessful in countries like Germany and Sweden, extreme right violence presents an increasingly serious threat in these countries. Though far smaller in number of supporters, the wider neo-Nazi movement seems to increase both its numbers and its actions. While it is still far too early to talk about a 'Brown Army Faction', as some media and anti-fascists have done, right-wing terrorism is on the rise in a number of West European countries. Though most racist violence is perpetrated by non-political youths, extreme right groups have started to arm themselves and call for an outright fight against the state. The situation is particularly worrying in Germany and, more surprisingly, Sweden, where neo-Nazi groups like White Aryan Resistance, inspired by examples from the United States, have been involved in various political killings, often against their own, and their campaign of terror has brought fear to its opponents (see Kaplan and Weinberg, 1998; Bjørgo, 1997).

Most explanations of the rise of the extreme right have been aimed at the demand-side, explaining why the 1980s and after have provided a particularly good breeding ground for the extreme right. This type of explanation can be divided into two general sub-groups, cleavage-based and issue-based, though in reality they often overlap. Cleavage-based explanations argue that the post-industrial 'revolution' has changed society fundamentally, giving way to a new cleavage in West European politics dividing the extreme right and the Greens (see for example Kriesi, 1995; Kitschelt and McGann, 1995; Ignazi, 1992). Simply stated, the issue-based explanations can be divided into two groups: xenophobia and resentment (Betz, 1994). The first argues that the influx of large numbers of (non-Western) immigrants and the subsequent development of a multicultural society within West European countries has sparked fears and rejection among the 'indigenous peoples'. The second sees the rise of the extreme right as a reaction to a more general sense of resentment, largely fueled by growing gap between 'the people' and 'the elites'.

The problem with demand-side explanations is that they explain the success of the extreme right in some countries, but do not explain their failure in others. In Germany and the Netherlands, for example, the post-industrial revolution was as pervasive as in other countries and resentment and xenophobia are (virtually) as widespread, yet no extreme right party has been successful. One of the few supply-side explanations is provided by Kitschelt and McGann (1995), who argue that only those extreme right parties are successful that adopt the 'winning formula' of free-market liberalism and authoritarianism. Unfortunately, this theory is flawed, as no extreme right party, not even the successful ones like the VB or FPÖ, adopted such a formula. One of the core ideological features of extreme right parties is actually welfare chauvinism, that is a welfare state for the 'own people', not free-market liberalism. Rather, an answer can be found in party organization (Mudde and Van Holsteyn, 2000) – extreme right parties with well-developed party organizations (such as AN, FPÖ, or VB) have been able to sustain their first electoral successes, while those without a strong organization (such as Dutch Centre Democrats or German Republicans) have become victims of their own success and faltered after good election results led to infighting and defections.

Extreme right violence is more difficult to explain. More so than with electoral behaviour, there is a large gap between ideas and actions. And, though the breeding ground might be highly conducive, extreme right violence is still a phenomenon of a tiny minority. Even in Germany, the Federal Bureau for the Protection of the Constitution estimates the number of (potentially) violent right-wing extremists at some 9000 in a population of over 80 million. At the same time, as already mentioned above, much racist or extreme right violence comes from people with no or weak extreme right links. Among anti-fascists it has been in vogue to argue that extreme right electoral success increases extreme right violence, because it creates a more supportive environment. Because of a lack of reliable comparative data this thesis is hard to test, but the little research that is available argues that it might actually be the other way around. Electoral success of extreme right parties provides a venthole for extreme right sentiments which otherwise would be vented through violence (Koopmans, 1996).

Territorial extremists

Territorial extremists, that is groups that oppose existing territorial borders, exist in only a few countries in Western Europe, but the intensity and violence of the actions of some makes them a principal extremist threat. Though most of these movements are seen as separatist, there are also movements that struggle for (re-)unification or even a combination of the two (see Hewitt and Cheetham, 2000). For example, the VB wants Flanders to split from Belgium (separatism) to then form a Dutch federation with the Netherlands (unification). An even more complex sequence of events is pursued by Basque separatists, who want the respective Basque regions to separate from Spain and France to then unite in one independent Basque state. Not all territorial extremists are involved in a violent struggle, however. In the United Kingdom, for example, both the Party of Wales and the Scottish National Party try to realize their separatist goals purely within the democratic framework, working mainly through electoral politics.

What typifies the most famous cases of terrorist extremist politics is their combination of legal and illegal politics. The largest faction of Irish nationalists, for example, pursue their goal of a united Ireland by means of a terrorist group, the Irish Republican Army (IRA), and a political party, Sinn Fein (We Ourselves, SF). Though there are clear organizational and personal links between the two, for example most SF leaders are former IRA members, they each deal with their own part of the struggle. At times this will lead to frictions between the 'radical' and the 'moderate' factions, stimulated by the British state structures, though overall they will draw one line on the most important issues. While the United Kingdom has accepted the need to treat the SF as a more or less regular political party, not hindering their normal political activities, the Spanish government has taken a fundamentally different approach. Faced by the multiple threat of the terrorist Basque Homeland and Freedom (ETA) and its political arm, People's Unity, it decided to ban the latter. One can question the effect, as its successor, We Basques, won 14 seats in the 1998 regional elections, three seats more than its predecessor had won in 1994.

There is another, less political element to the illegality of many separatist struggles, which is their involvement in organized crime. Though
many (territorialist) terrorist groups originally got involved in organized
crime because of their political struggle – for example, trading drugs for
weapons – some have become virtually indistinguishable from organized crime organizations. In Northern Ireland, for example, groups like
the Ulster Defence Association and the Ulster Volunteer Force have been
mainly involved in turf wars connected to the drugs and protection
trade in parts of Belfast, rather than in fighting their political enemy, the
IRA.

There is a bulk of literature on the why and how of territorial extremism in general, and separatism in particular (see for example Hewitt and
Cheetham, 2000, pp. xiii–xv). Within Western Europe the explanation
of regional economic disparities does explain some cases, for example
Wales and Scotland where the underdeveloped periphery revolts against
the core. Flanders and the Basque Country, on the other hand, rather fit
the rational-choice interpretation, where out of material self-interest
richer regions revolt. Modernization theory might explain why regional
identities became politicized, but it fails to explain when and how territorial extremists will act. This could better be explained by the scope
and quality of representation within the state and by the political
choices of the territorial actor (Ishiyama and Breuning, 1998). In addition, the international context influences the behaviour of territorial
extremists, both through spillover and contagion (Ayres and Saideman,
2000). For example, separatists like the VB feel hugely strengthened in
their quest for independence by the break-up of the Soviet bloc, and has
called for a break-up of Belgium based upon the Czechoslovak 'velvet
split'.

Religious fundamentalism

Though Christianity has lost most of its importance within West
European politics these days, as a result of the continuing process of
secularization, there are still orthodox Christian groups that espouse
extremist views. While not all are politically organized, such as the
Jehovah Witnesses, some do still play a role in politics. For example, the
staunch Catholic and anti-Semitic Opus Dei faction remains influential
within, most notably, South European Christian Democratic parties,
while followers of the late (excommunicated) bishop Lefebvre form the
influential Christian-Solidarity faction with the French FN. Though the
troubles in Northern Ireland are often perceived in terms of a religious
struggle between Protestants and Catholics, it is not really a conflict

between two sets of religious fundamentalists. Though parts of, most notably, the pro-British Protestants come close, such as the reverend Ian Paisley and his Democratic Unionist Party, the struggle is first and foremost territorial (see above), that is between 'loyalists' (pro-British) and 'republicans' (pro-Irish). The few religious fundamentalist parties that make it into parliament can be found in the Netherlands, though of the three only the State Reformed Party can be regarded as truly extreme – as they still adhere to a theocracy.

While Christian fundamentalism seems to be a relic of the past, Islamic fundamentalism, or 'political Islam' (Tibi, 1998), has revealed itself as one of the more sizeable threats of the future. The challenge is not limited to the incursions of foreign terrorists such as those who are believed to have perpetrated the tragic events of 11 September 2001. Islamic fundamentalism has a domestic political variant in Western Europe as well. As a consequence of the mass immigration into Western Europe, most countries have become multicultural societies, whether they want it or not. While much attention has focused on 'ethnic' differences, the process has also transformed Western Europe in religious terms. Most notably, Islam is now the second largest religion in Western Europe, despite representing just 3 per cent of the population. More importantly, contrary to Christianity, it is very much a growing religion. Obviously, Islam harbours many different varieties and only a small minority is extremist. Unfortunately, the image of Islam fundamentalism has become one of the most daunting of our times, easily penetrating the minds of the media and population alike.

Despite the fact that only a minority of Muslims subscribe to a fundamentalist version of Islam, the threat of their organizations has been noted in many European countries. Most notably, there have been worries over organizations linked to fundamentalists abroad (see for example Belaskri, 1999), such as the Algerian Armed Islamic Group, the Palestinian Hamas, or the Turkish Islamic Community, Milli Görüs (IGMG). In 1998 no less than 14 such groups were identified in the United Kingdom, which, according to one author, 'has in recent years become a centre for militant Islamists, either fleeing persecution in their countries of origin or who choose Britain as a safe haven from which to operate' (Whine, 1999, p. 376). While the UK has attracted many Islamists from Asia and the Middle East, France has been the place for Islamic fundamentalists from Northern Africa, particularly from its troubled former colony Algeria (Étienne, 1987).

Not unlike the communist parties of the Cold War period, many religious fundamentalist organizations function as transmission belts for a foreign country; for example, Iran and Saudi Arabia have invested a lot of money into building mosques in Europe through which they spread their official version of 'state Islam' (see for example Lebor, 1997). Similarly, the strength of the local religious fundamentalist groups often reflects their foreign sponsors rather than their local support – although IGMG has some 27 000 members and a far larger number of supporters in Germany alone. While – in contrast now to the United States – terrorist attacks have so far remained a rarity on West European territory, this does not mean that religious fundamentalists have been without impact. Most importantly, many of these organizations actively oppose the integration of immigrants (and their offspring) into their new home country, thereby using threats and terror. This can lead to tensions between the indigenous peoples and the immigrants, as well as within the immigrant communities themselves.

The explanations for the recent rise in religious fundamentalism are both internal and external to West European politics. More generally, authors have pointed to the ongoing process of secularization which fundamentalists perceive as a threat to their way of life (see for example Almond *et al.*, 1995), to the end of the Cold War which has created an increasing antagonism between 'the West' and 'the World of Islam' (see for example Juergensmeyer, 1993), and to the influence of globalization which has led to a defensive reflex of those who feel threatened or confused by the new situation (see for example Tibi, 1998; Misztal and Shupe, 1992). These three major international events, obviously related to each other, have given way to a struggle of 'Jihad vs McWorld' (Barber, 1995).

Within Western Europe there are some specific additional factors that explain the rise of religious fundamentalism, particularly among immigrants and their families. Most notably, the problematic dealings with existing multicultural societies have led to the development of an 'ethnic underclass'. Feeling ignored or even scorned by their (new) country, some immigrants and minorities become susceptible to the message of Islamic fundamentalists who reject Western 'decadence' and 'egocentrism' and instead offer an identity and community which links them to their 'roots'. Moreover, in certain communities Islamic fundamentalists have become involved in community activities, both in a positive (such as providing shelter and food for the poor) and in a negative sense (such as enforcing 'order'). The fact that, on average, Hindu immigrants have fared better than Islamic immigrants in Western Europe, most notably in socio-economic terms, might explain the less prominent rise of Hindu fundamentalism within the region.

A final external reason for the development of Islamic fundamentalist groups in Western Europe is the situation in many Middle Eastern and North African countries where these organizations are involved in a bitter and often violent struggle with the national rulers. For decades countries like France and the United Kingdom have functioned as both safe havens and operation bases for political activists from former colonies, including Islamic fundamentalists.

The 'new fringe'

> Neither the nostalgia of the left, those old bearers of hope, for the times when it knew the correct line, nor the arrogant insecurity of the right that simultaneously declares the grass roots dead while fearing its demands, can alter the fact the new forces for change have coalesced into a new politics. (Jordan, 1999, p. 1)

Among the main new issues that the 'new fringe' addresses are animal rights, environmentalism and opposition to globalization. The new fringe includes a ragbag of groups and individuals, such as the so-called 'eco-warriors' (such as Earth First!), animal-rights activists (for example People for the Ethical Treatment of Animals), gay and lesbian activists (such as OutRage), anti-fascists (such as Anti-Fascist Action), Autonomen ('autonomous' people), and anti-globalists (for example Mayday 2000).

For the moment, these groups are not able to mobilize mass support on a national or international scale, though some of their actions have caused havoc in major cities – such as the annual Chaos Tage (Chaos Days) in the German city of Hannover, or the 'Carnival of Fun' in May 2000 in London. Moreover, while the new fringe has become a significant political factor in some countries, like Germany and Great Britain, it hardly exists in others (most notably in the South of Europe). In general, also where the movement is stronger, organizational structures are weak and the social movement is more important than any of its constituting organizations. In addition, it has developed a 'counter-culture', often referred to as the 'Do-It-Yourself culture' or 'DiY culture' (McKay, 1998), which rather than opposing the dominant culture tries to create an alternative culture outside of it. In some ways the idea is similar to the famous 'parallel polis' of East European dissidents like Vaclav Havel.

However, in recent years one can see the institutionalization of small but well-organized cells, who both within and independent of the broader movement engage in terrorist attacks to further their cause. For some years now the Animal Liberation Front has been damaging property as well as threatening people in their alleged struggle for animal rights, while the Earth Liberation Front has done the same in their fight for the environment. Though often rejected by the leaders of the larger movements, such as Earth First! or the more moderate Friends of the Earth, these small terrorist groups can count on sympathy among parts of the wider subculture (Wall, 1999). Like the extreme left terrorists of the 1970s, such as the Red Brigades or the Baader-Meinhof group, the new fringe terrorists profit from a broader support environment as well as from advocates among the left-wing elites.

Some of the groups of the new fringe have roots in older organizations; for example, the Autonomen and anti-fascists have clear ties to the now largely defunct squatter scene (see for example Pfahl-Traughber, 1998; Buijs, 1995), while members and issues from (former) Third World organizations are prominent among anti-globalization groups. It would go too far to claim that the new fringe is an exclusively left-wing phenomenon. Though its activists might, to a large extent, come from left-wing circles, many are entirely new to politics and do not share traditional left-wing dogmas (this is most notably the case among environmentalists and animal-rights activists; see Wall, 1999). In addition, the main ideas of the movements are also popular at the other side of the political spectrum. Extreme right groups like the International Third Position have long defended the environment and animal rights, and their nationalism puts them at the fore of the anti-globalization struggle. So far, however, the new fringe and the extreme right groups have not been able to come together. One of the main reasons for this is that they increasingly define themselves in negation of the other, as many within the new fringe are deeply involved in antifa (anti-fascist) activities, while the extreme right has become increasingly focused on anti-antifa activities.

Over the past two decades new social movements have split into two groups: those accepted by and often coopted into the political elite, and those fundamentally opposed to the elite. It is in part the 'betrayal' of the old leaders of the social movements that have radicalized the small minority that is increasingly resorting to violent actions to further their cause. However, the new fringe's diversity does not prevent it from mobilizing commonly in certain high-profile cases, such as the violent protests against globalization in Seattle, Melbourne and Prague (CSIS, 2000). Moreover, with the EU as its new target we can expect increasing activities within Western Europe, such as in December 2000 in Nice.

Extreme movements in Western Europe: an assessment

After the end of the Cold War, democracy has also survived its second major competitor within European politics. As a consequence, most extreme movements today no longer draw upon fundamentally different 'grand narratives' which present an alternative to (liberal) democracy, but rather indulge in criticizing parts of the democratic regime or ideology. This can be best seen in the cases of the extreme left and the extreme right, which struggle with finding a new identity that is not communist or fascist, but is at the same time fundamentally different (and therefore recognizable) from liberal democracy.

In the case of the extreme left this has led to the recent emergence of a 'new old left', that is left-wing populism, which combines old socialist values with a populist style of politics. The extreme right has developed differently and more diversely. Not only are there many different strands within the extreme right, the successes of the parties have differed significantly within Western Europe. So far the actual threat of the electoral extreme right has not materialized. In the most successful cases, such as Austria and Italy, the extreme right in government was hardly distinguishable from the mainstream right-wing parties. Their participation might even lead to a transformation into a national conservative party – Gianfranco Fini has often stated that he models his AN on the French Gaullists rather than the FN, while within the FPÖ many see the Bavarian Christian Social Union rather than the Republicans as their main ideological ally. That said, parties like the FN and VB remain both extreme and reasonably successful. Moreover, in many other countries extreme right forces might not be successful in electoral terms, but increasingly pose a threat to the internal order through racist attacks and even terrorism (such as in Germany and Sweden).

A principal terrorist threat still comes from territorial extremists, most notably in France (Corsica), Spain (Basque country) and the United Kingdom (Northern Ireland). An extreme territorialist group whose territory lies outside West European borders, but whose struggle is in part fought within them, is the Kurdish Workers Party. Its struggle is partly financed by the large Kurdish communities in Western Europe, which has led to serious tensions within the immigrant communities and even a ban of the party in Germany (see Grünewald, 1997).

Still, there are two new potential extremist threats to West European politics: Islamic fundamentalism and the 'new fringe'. With regard to the former, the development of an 'ethnic underclass' in many West European countries has created a fertile breeding ground for Islamic fundamentalists to recruit disappointed and frustrated young immigrants and ethnic minorities. Though the numbers are still fairly moderate, their link to extremely violent organizations such as those implicated in the attack on the World Trade Centre on 11 September 2001 and to undemocratic states does raise cause for concern. The threat of the 'new fringe' is more internal, but no less serious. Though they might not pose an electoral threat, elements within the new fringe might become the main terrorist threat of twenty-first century West European politics.

There are two factors that strengthen the extreme movement: the EU and the Internet. As a result of the ongoing political integration, the EU is increasingly becoming a dividing political issue within Europe, both in and outside of the EU. As virtually all mainstream parties are pro-EU, extreme parties of the left and right can pick up the growing anti-EU vote. Rather than taking a purely strategic Eurosceptic position (Taggart, 1998), they oppose the EU in principle, seeing it as an imperialist or capitalist threat. For territorial extremists, the EU has created alternative ways of increasing autonomy. Rather than having to deal exclusively with the national state, which might be negatively inclined towards autonomy claims, they now look to the EU for recognition. Parties like the Scottish SNP or the 'Padanian' LN want to use the new structure of the EU to strengthen their claim for independence, pointing to the redundancy of the national state structure and dismissing the small-scale argument. Thereby, the EU has both strengthened separatist claims, and moderated them (as EU recognition is dependent upon 'good behaviour'). Finally, like the extreme parties of the left and right, the new fringe is increasingly targeting the EU in their anti-globalization struggle, which is able to unite its various strands.

The second factor that influences extreme movements in (and outside of) Western Europe is the Internet. Though the influence on the electoral fortunes of extreme parties might be irrelevant, the Internet can strengthen the conviction and operational scope of smaller and more extreme groups. The Internet provides lone extremists with a 'virtual community', which builds mental strength and could supply ideational or even material assistance. Information can no longer be suppressed, as the 'weakest link' in terms of national legislation decides what is available on the web. Consequently, extremists throughout Western Europe are increasingly using the Internet as their main source of information and mobilization, profiting from the broadly defined freedom of speech in some countries (most notably the United States) to circumvent more limited interpretations at home. They also profit from the newness of the medium, which leaves governments often trailing in terms of surveillance techniques and countermeasures. Finally, the Internet provides a weapon in itself, in terms of propaganda as well as sabotage (such as 'e-mail bombing').

PART III

Governance and Effectiveness: Do State Institutions Deliver on Popular Demands?

Chapter 8

Executive Capacity and Legislative Limits

PAUL HEYWOOD

There has been much discussion in recent years of the impact of global-ization and transnationalism on political organization. Whilst there is as much dispute as agreement over the meaning, extent and even existence of these twin trends, it is undoubtedly the case that all modern states face a series of increasingly similar, yet increasingly complex, policy challenges. In Western Europe we can point to a number of develop-ments over the last decade which have altered the policy environment. First, there has been an internationalization of decision-making in a growing number of spheres, most notably within the EU, where member states find themselves increasingly bound by the need to pool ever-more aspects of sovereignty. Second, the end of the Cold War has seen the collapse of the geo-strategic certainties which characterized the postwar period, and the emergence of new points of tension within the European sphere of influence. Third, the demands placed on governments have become more complex, involving the need to balance apparently contra-dictory demands such as economic growth and environmental protec-tion, or greater social protection and a reduced fiscal burden. Equally, other issues such as immigration have placed additional and often acute pressure on governments as they seek to avoid the charge of construct-ing 'Fortress Europe'.

A fourth development has been the growth of multilevel governance, with the emergence of key decision-making points at various diffuse (and sometimes competing) levels (Sharpe, 1992; Hooghe and Marks, 2001). Such changes have made it more difficult to manage policy chains which often cut across national boundaries and have led to growing institu-tional dependence. Fifth, there has been a reshaping of decision-making networks with financial institutions such as central banks, the mass media and magistrates all playing an increasingly prominent political role, often in competition with more traditional public actors. In conse-quence, there has been a blurring of traditional public/private distinc-tions, exacerbated by a continued balkanization of state apparatuses as new public management reforms have promoted the separation of policy decisions from policy delivery (Heywood and Wright, 1997, p. 91). The net result of such developments has been a growing privatization of the state, or at least of key elements of its public-sector administration. Indeed, Rhodes (1997a, p. 199) has spoken of a 'hollowing-out' of the state, reflecting its loss of coherence and capacity to coordinate or control other actors.

The challenge for analysts is to understand how governance in contemporary Western Europe has been affected by these profound changes in the policy environment. In seeking to provide some answers, this chapter will focus on the executive and legislative branches of government in contemporary Europe, and on the relationships between them. The chapter will be structured in four sections. First, it will be argued that all executives in Western Europe have sought to respond to the more complex policy milieu by placing increased emphasis on the need to improve internal policy coordination, but that this has involved any increase in executive strength being purchased only at the cost of a loss in reach. Second, however, it will be shown that there has also been a divergence of executive policy responses according to which actors, sectors, structures and settings are involved, in turn influenced by specific institutional legacies of decision-making patterns. The third section will analyse the arguments over the declining policy influence of legislatures *vis-à-vis* executives, and seek to identify those factors which may temper such an assessment. Fourth, and finally, it will be concluded that in an ever-more complex policy environment, executives and legislatures are increasingly bound by a shared interest in maintaining the credibility of their claim to be able to govern, expressed through an increased emphasis on efficiency and transparency.

From government to governance: the core executive and the challenge of coordination

In contrast to the traditional (and somewhat sterile) focus on the executive as encompassing prime ministers and their cabinets, the notion of the 'core executive' is intended to capture the sense that a much wider range of actors and organizations is actually involved in the policy process, often through complex networks and communities. Whilst the term 'core executive' is associated primarily with the work of Rhodes and Dunleavy (1995) on the United Kingdom, it has come to be used increasingly in comparative studies of public policy. In the UK, meanwhile, the term has been formally adopted by the Public Record Office as part of a pilot project to develop a searchable on-line catalogue of government department policy records, and includes the Civil Service Department, the Cabinet Office, the Ministry of Defence, the Department of Economic Affairs, the Prime Minister's Office, and HM Treasury (PRO, 1998, 2000). Thus, the notion of core executive moves beyond old-fashioned 'black-box' institutional policy models which posit a clear separation in terms of function and role between the executive, legislature, bureaucracy and judiciary.

In practice, as indicated above, the state has become increasingly fragmented. In Olsen's terms, '[t]he ship of state has become a flotilla, making co-ordination between levels, branches and sectors of government a problem' (Olsen, 1997, p. 162). Nevertheless, one paradoxical feature common to all countries in Western Europe (and beyond) has been that as the political process becomes increasingly complex, so its public presentation becomes more simplistic, evidenced most obviously by a growing personalization of politics. Governments have come to be associated almost exclusively with their lead figures – usually the chief executive and the finance minister. A number of factors have contributed to this development, most obviously the growing media-focus of governments which seek to bypass the traditional role of political parties as channels of popular expression and aggregators of interests. The rise of international summitry within the EU – with key decisions being made at Inter-Governmental Conferences (IGCs) – has reinforced the focus on leaders, who are able to set the political agenda. In turn, the treaty obligations associated with EU membership – in particular economic and monetary union (EMU), but also in areas such as social welfare – have placed increased pressure on governments not only to present a united front in negotiations and so appear to defend national interests, but also to promote budgetary rectitude, thereby reinforcing the prominence of finance ministers. Indeed, when governments appear disunited they face intense media scrutiny over perceived internal battles.

Given the complexity and scale of the demands facing all modern governments, the pressure to appear organized and purposeful can be accommodated only if the core executive is able to coordinate its activities effectively (Davis, 1997). In practice, mechanisms of core executive policy integration are correspondingly complex, and unsurprisingly they sometimes fail to work effectively. A variety of coordination mechanisms can be identified. Several governments have sought to centralize coordination, with prime ministers taking the lead in seeking to impose their authority and thereby reinforcing the personalization of the political process. In the UK, for instance, Tony Blair has often been accused of acting as a 'control freak', appointing so-called cabinet 'enforcers', but even in countries with a strong tradition of ministerial autonomy, such as Germany and the Netherlands, greater emphasis has been placed on the need for government to appear united around the prime minister (Mayntz, 1987; Andeweg, 1991). Traditionally, though, coordination has often been 'negative', reflecting a desire to avoid conflict rather than to promote policy coherence. Indeed, evidence suggests that in spite of a general recognition of the importance and need for greater coordination within European core executives, in practice coordination efforts have been modest and relatively low level. Most attempts to create strategically focused planning units – for instance, the French Commissariat Général du Plan, originally created in 1946 by De Gaulle at the suggestion of Jean Monnet, or the Planning Division in the German Chancellor's Office (Wright and Hayward, 2000, p. 133) – have been less than signal successes. Core executives are less effective than might be imagined in taking a proactive role, and instead can best be understood as arenas in which competing interests compete for ascendancy.

A recent major study into core executive coordination in six West European states (Wright and Hayward, 2000) concluded that there remain substantial obstacles to effective coordination, even though governments in all six countries – Austria, France, Germany, Italy, the Netherlands and Spain – have sought to reduce the coordination burden. Amongst the obstacles to coordination are the perceived costs of undermining existing harmonious, if messy, patterns of interaction by trying to impose centralized control; competing demands for core executive attention, notably the routine business of day-to-day political activity; lack of capacity, either through information overload or through too many competing interests within government; and institutional constraints, particularly in those countries with a tradition of ministerial autonomy, which can be reinforced by the size of the department in question as well as the personality or political strength of the minister in charge. Obviously, where governments enjoy clear majorities, as is currently the case in the UK or Spain for instance, the position of key ministers can be even further enhanced. By the same token, when governments are dependent on coalition partners, as in Germany, or face a situation of so-called cohabitation, as in France, key ministers face greater constraints. Indeed, it has been argued that coalitions lead to greater governmental coherence because they rely on negotiation and mutual respect of interests (Rhodes, 1997a, p. 209).

Partly in response to the growing complexity of the policy challenges they face, governments have also engaged in measures to reduce the scale of activities which need coordination. Such measures have contributed to what has been termed a shift from government to governance (Rhodes, 2000, pp. 5–6), characterized by a tendency to replace responsibility for policy implementation from line bureaucracies to more fragmented service providers. The notion of governance therefore encompasses such developments as the transfer of policy responsibility to third-sector agencies or to specific bodies charged with a particular policy area (for instance, the drugs 'Tsar' in the UK), extensive privatization and contracting-out, or the creation of quasi-markets by splitting purchasers and providers. As Majone (1997, pp. 140–1) points out, even before the wave of privatization under the Thatcher administration, the UK had established a number of specialized regulatory agencies such as the Independent Broadcasting Authority (1972), the Civil Aviation Authority (1972), the Health and Safety Commission (1974), the Equal Opportunities Commission (1976) and the Commission for Racial Equality (1976). Equally, in France – where privatization was also adopted in the mid-1980s primarily on the basis of ideological commitment (Bauer, 1988) – similar developments had included the creation of the Commission des Infractions Fiscales (1977), the Commission Bancaire (1984), the Conseil de la Concurrence (1986) and the Commission de Contrôle des Assurances (1989).

National governments in Europe have also sought to displace policy-making responsibility both upwards, to the European Union level, and downwards to the regional or sub-national level (Wright and Hayward, 2000, p. 34). Taken together, these developments have led to a growth of new networks (as well as leading to an expansion of existing ones) in which the government is not necessarily a central player. Whilst the scope of government control may therefore appear reduced, the need for coordination may have actually increased, since demands for transparency and accountability have led to the emergence of ever-more regulation (Hood *et al.*, 1999): Thus, in the UK, a series of new regulatory agencies was established in the 1980s and 1990s, including the Office of Telecommunications (Oftel), the Office of Gas Supply (Ofgas), the Office of Water Services (Ofwat), the Office of Gas and Electricity Markets (Ofgem), the Office for Standards in Education (Ofsted), and – most recently – the Strategic Rail Authority (SRA). Such development have been parallelled throughout Western Europe as public utilities have been privatized and the Single European Market has generated the need to regulate competition.

Associated with the notion of a shift from government to governance has been an increased emphasis on policy networks and communities, which are seen by some analysts as offering a more realistic account of how the policy process operates than the more traditional emphasis on varieties of pluralism and corporatism (Peterson, 1997; Marsh, 1998; Marsh and Smith, 2000). The rise of multilevel governance, in particular, has rendered significantly more complex the mechanisms and routes of influence that interest groups and peak associations seek to exploit. Rather than the somewhat simplistic relationships between domestic actors posited in pluralist and corporatist models, the idea of policy networks is intended to capture the sense of a complex set of interrelationships and links which traverse national boundaries as required. Although it is possible to distinguish a number of different conceptions of policy networks, the key point which they share is that such networks are based on interdependence and exchange between strategic actors in the policy process. As such actors continue to deal with each other on a repeated basis, so patterns become established and the network starts to assume an autonomous structural identity in which there emerge certain 'rules of the game'. These may vary between different networks, as may the patterns of interaction, but all are based on the notion of a 'power-dependence' relationship in which resources are exchanged between actors and organizations. Power-dependence relationships are asymmetrical in that public actors, such as government departments, exercise a disproportionate influence over access to resources, but all organizations remain dependent on others for their resources (Rhodes, 1997b).

The policy-networks approach is most closely associated with Rhodes, whose focus has been almost exclusively on the UK. He has distinguished between five different types of policy network along a continuum, according to the degree of integration between members. Thus, they range from policy communities characterized by a high degree of integration and cohesion, to issue networks which are loosely integrated and often conflictive. In between, professional, intergovernmental and producer networks are dominated respectively by particular interests (Rhodes, 1997b, pp. 36–9). Other analysts have introduced modifications to the framework, for instance by emphasizing personal relationships, or by drawing a distinction between a 'policy universe' which encompasses all actors with a potential interest in a given policy, and more narrowly defined policy communities (which have a common policy focus) and networks (which link two or more communities) (Wilks and Wright, 1987). The policy-networks approach has been adopted to analyse the policy-making process in a number of West European states as well as the EU itself, often focusing on specific sectors (Grant *et al.*, 1988; Freddi and Bjorkman, 1989; Peterson and Bomberg, 1999). Whilst it is an approach which does recognize the increasing complexity of the policy environment, it has been criticized for an overreliance on imprecise definitions in its attempt to capture that complexity, and for sacrificing analytical purchase to descriptive detail. Dowding (1995) has argued that the policy-networks approach presents a sophisticated map of policy formulation and coordination, rather than an explanatory model with explanatory capacity – a charge forcefully rebutted by Rhodes (1997b, pp. 10–11).

In all six European states covered by the Wright/Hayward project, a mix of internal coordination techniques has been adopted. This mix includes greater emphasis on internal self-government through reforms associated with 'new public management' (NPM); the identification of lead ministries responsible for coordination; attempts to ensure pre-legislation political agreements; the creation of 'super-ministries' to reduce the number of departments involved in legislation; greater emphasis on information flows between officials; the appointment of sympathetic officials in strategic positions within networks; and the construction of binding consensus around core ideas, such as 'modern-ization', 'reconstruction' or 'Europe' (Wright and Hayward, 2000, p. 35). Not all six governments have adopted all the above measures, but most have engaged in a range of activities which have sought to improve internal governmental effectiveness. One feature which does appear to be common to all West European governments is the rise of 'networking' as a means of coordinating governmental activity in the context of growing marketization – that is, the focus on 'competition as the organising principle of service delivery' (Rhodes, 2000, p. 12). Networks are not new of course, they have long been an intrinsic feature of executive coordination – but, ironically enough, new networks have arisen precisely in response to the fragmentation of service delivery which was introduced in part to counteract the existing entrenched networks of producers and suppliers.

In spite of their widespread existence, networks vary significantly throughout West European executives. In France and Spain, for example, there are important networks based on the grands corps or cuerpos, which build on a strong sense of tradition and shared professional background and training. Indeed, so strong are these networks that they can be an obstacle to coordination, particularly when they stand in opposition to rival networks. Other countries, such as Germany, Austria and the Netherlands, have no such grands corps tradition (Wright and Hayward, 2000, p. 36). However, they remain subject to other difficulties, such as networks putting their own interests and survival before the overall aims of the executive, or overlapping membership leading to divided loyalties as well as competing jurisdictions, or – perhaps most damaging – a break-down in trust upon which ultimately all networks depend if coordination is to be effective. Trust develops through routinized patterns of interaction, and is a basic characteristic of effective networks – but it is also a fragile commodity which can be easily damaged by personnel changes or personality clashes. Many European executives have found it difficult to coordinate the activities of departments led by ministers who have poor relationships with their ministerial colleagues. The Blair administration in the UK has been hurt by stories of personal animus between the Chancellor, Gordon Brown, and the Prime Minister's close friend and ally, Peter Mandelson, whilst tensions in Germany between Gerhard Schröder and his high profile Finance Minister, Oskar Lafontaine, also led to the latter leaving the government altogether.

Core executive coordination and national specificity

Networks do not, of course, develop within an institutional vacuum; rather, the institutional context within which they emerge and operate reflects prevailing cultural and political traditions (Weaver and Rockman, 1993). The notion of 'path dependence' (Pierson, 2000) seeks to capture the idea that historical origins and cultural systems exercise significant influence on institutional development, and can help determine whether attempts at innovation will succeed. Institutions tend to have standard operating procedures, reflected in policy frames which routinize the values of the political system. In fact, such frames can operate as constraints on the autonomy of core executive actors, thereby helping to maintain established patterns of coordination. The Wright/Hayward project identified a number of such policy frames, including the ideological weight of a dominant perspective (for instance, the primacy of a single European market), the legitimacy of an accepted political system and constitutional order, the existence of well-worn routines and procedures which penalize non-compliance, the continuation of standing commitments and agreements, and the specific patterns of activity associated with particular policy sectors. Taken together, these policy frames contribute to institutional 'stickiness', which refers to the persistence of set modes of operation (March and Olsen, 1989, p. 106).

Over the last decade, however, conventional policy frames in most West European states have been undermined or unsettled by the emergence of new challenges to the system, including the impact of technological developments, changing patterns of employment, the growing influence of the EU, the internal changes associated with New Public Management initiatives (or some variant thereon), and the greater contestation of public space. Whereas routine, bureaucratically-dominated activities have been able to continue operating within established policy frames, the new challenges have posed coordination problems which have not been so easily accommodated within existing frames. As might be expected, responses to such pressures have varied significantly across countries in line with their particular institutional development, traditions and legacies of decision-making patterns (cf. Elgie, 1995). These in turn shape the political opportunity structures available to core executives.

As the constraints and pressures on the core executive become more complex, so negotiation and cooperation becomes more imperative. However, the manner in which such negotiation and cooperation is handled between core executives, networks and other interested actors depends critically on the particular institutional structure of the country in question, as well as the policy sector involved. Thus, the range of actors involved in the core executive may vary according to the issue at stake. The Wright/Hayward project revealed that in regard to privatization, for instance, coordination was handled by various different ministries: in Austria, the lead ministry with responsibility for the enter-prise in question; in the Netherlands, the Interior Ministry; in France and Spain, the Finance Ministry; and in Italy, the Industry Ministry as well as the Finance Ministry. Other policy areas, such as immigration policy or European Union affairs, demonstrated similar differences over the identity of the key actors involved in core executive coordination (Wright and Hayward, 2000, p. 37). Which ministry takes the lead in a given area can, of course, have a significant impact on the coordination process.

Coordination mechanisms also vary between different countries. In the case of coalition governments, procedures range from highly-struc-tured agreements between potential partners, as in the case of the Netherlands, Austria and Germany, which are regularly reviewed once the coalition government is in place, to relatively loose arrangements between parties, as in France. In Spain, minority governments have avoided formal coalitions, relying instead on informal pacts with regional parties. Usually, the central actors involved in monitoring coali-tion agreements are the core executive and party leaders, although in Italy the prime minister may be the only member of the core executive involved in political summit meetings with party leaders. Approaches to policy coordination also vary. France, despite its less formal approach to using coalition agreements as a policy frame, is alone amongst the major European democracies in operating powerful centralizing mecha-nisms at the heart of government, and also in using cabinet committees to support coordination. In terms of the composition of core executives, the formal role of chief executives, ministers and other key figures can vary significantly, both in terms of formal constitutional position and also practical reality. Thus, in Spain, the prime minister and economy minister operate as a diarchy at the centre of government, whereas in Italy the premier's resources are far more limited (Heywood and Molina, 2000; Cassese, 2000). In the UK, the influence of the prime

minister is crucially conditioned by the size of the parliamentary majority, whilst in all countries issues of personality and character can also
have a major influence on coordination capacity.

Similar variations can be observed in coordination types and styles.
All countries have developed a particular mix of positive and negative
coordination according to historical precedent, institutional design and
the demands of a given policy sector. In broad terms we can distinguish
between a more proactive and directive style, characteristic notably in
France and Spain, and one based more on compromise and negotiation,
the generally prevailing pattern in Austria, Germany and, especially, the
Netherlands. Of course, the extent to which command or consensus
predominates will be influenced not just by institutional legacies or
traditional modes of behaviour in given settings, but also by the personality, drive and determination of key individuals (Hennessy, 2000). For
example, whilst the institutional resources available to Felipe González
as Prime Minister in Spain (1982–96) were extensive, there is little
doubt that his political skills and acumen were a crucial asset in his
control. Similarly, Margaret Thatcher imposed her will on ministers and
civil servants during her premiership (1979–90) through a variety of
means, both subtle and unsubtle, whereas Helmut Kohl and François
Mitterrand were forced to rely on more emollient methods of management. Individual ministers, too, bring very different styles to bear:
witness the contrast between, for instance, Mo Mowlam and Peter
Mandelson as Northern Ireland Ministers in the UK government.

Legislatures and executive limitation

It is logical that, where the executive faces few institutional checks on
its policy-making capacity, the role of the legislature is correspondingly
weakened – and vice versa. Traditionally, a distinction has been drawn
between the Westminster model which emphasizes parliamentary sovereignty exercised through an accountable executive delivered via a first-
past-the-post electoral system, and continental European models which
provide for greater ministerial autonomy but with weak legislatures and
less direct accountability through list-system proportional representation. Another familiar distinction is often drawn between parliamentary
systems (with strong executives and strong political parties) and presidential systems (with weak executives and weak political parties): the
former are held to deliver more uniform patterns of policy-making than,
for example, in the USA, where the President may face rejection of a
significant number of his proposals (John, 1998, p. 42). Such shorthand
idealized models are naturally subject to challenge, not just on the

grounds that they provide an overly simplistic characterization of how political systems function in practice, but also because they are unable to accommodate responses to the changes in the policy environment outlined at the start of this chapter. Moreover, they provide a potentially misleading picture of the relationship between executive and legislature as being inevitably competitive and involving a struggle for power and influence. In reality, the relationship between the two institutions is far more fluid and variable, entailing both cooperation and conflict.

There is a widely held view that the capacity of parliaments to influence the policy process and act as checks on executives has been 'in decline' over recent decades (Judge, 1995). This is particularly the case in regard to economic policy, which has either been claimed as an executive responsibility – for instance, through increasingly centralized control over public expenditure and financial management (Wanna, 1997) – or else delegated in part to non-party political experts in central banks, treasury departments, budget bureaux, national planning commissions and so forth (Majone, 1997; see also Bergman *et al.*, 2000). The argument has gained strength since the 1980s, with the emergence of an international economy and the growing role of bodies such as the Group of Seven (G7), the International Monetary Fund (IMF), the World Bank and the World Trade Organization (WTO), which are seen to have ever-greater control over macroeconomic policy options, and the policy imperatives derived from the Single European Act (1987) and the Treaty on European Union (1993) signed at Maastricht. Moreover, the capacity of the European Commission to issue binding regulations and directives was seen as further undermining the role of national parliaments, which could – at best – seek merely to influence the Commission (in spite of the provisions of the TEU which sought to encourage greater involvement by national parliaments in the activities of the EU). In the United States of America, in particular, there was talk of 'conservative legislatures' which stood in the way of executive action in the increasingly international economic arena: legislative subordination to the executive was seen as both desirable and necessary.

Norton (1996) has distinguished between policy-making legislatures, as in Italy or the Netherlands, which can not only modify or reject the executive's policy initiatives, but also formulate their own alternative or independent proposals, and policy-influencing legislatures, as in France or Ireland, which can amend but not substitute executive policy proposals. He argues that national parliaments have had to adapt to the challenges posed by European integration, and that their capacity to do so has been shaped in each country by its constitutional arrangements, political culture, party system, parliamentary norms and practices, and parliamentary workloads. Olson and Mezey (1991), in assessing the role of parliaments in public policy, similarly emphasize the need to focus on the legislature's relationship with other political institutions (notably, the executive and bureaucracy), its internal structure (political party rules, committee systems, support staff), and sectoral specificity in regard to the policy area in question.

Olson and Mezey (1991) generated and tested a series of hypotheses – focused respectively on external, internal and sectoral factors – about the nature of executive–legislature relationships in presidential and parliamentary systems. Their study was informed by research into France, (West) Germany and the UK, but the analysis can be extended to cover other contemporary West European democracies. In terms of externally-focused factors, the influence of legislatures on the policy-making process should be greater under the following conditions:

- when the political system is open and decentralized rather than exec-utive-dominated, because federal systems tend to disperse authority and create more veto points (Weller, 1997);
- when decisions are 'hived off' to operating agencies, rather than handled directly by the core executive, because there is less direct input and committed investment by the government;
- when electoral systems are candidate-oriented and decentralized, rather than dominated by highly-disciplined political parties, because such parties tend to tie ministers to government (Laver and Shepsle, 1995); and
- when there are significant and functionally specialized active interest groups able to lobby parliamentary representatives, because legisla-tures offer alternative sources of influence to executives and adminis-trative agencies.

In practice, the involvement of parliament in the policy process varies according to the stage in question, being higher in general during the implementation than the deliberation stage. Equally, it appears that parliamentary activity is most apparent when a given piece of legislation has a clear and immediate impact on particular local groups, which then organize to lobby their representatives. Some European parliaments – notably in Germany and the Netherlands – have significant capacity to set their own agendas, and in all countries parliamentary activity (measured in terms of questions and committee work) has increased over the last 10 to 15 years. But in spite of this, European legislatures have shown only a limited ability to influence the policy-making process.

In regard to internally-focused factors, the two critical variables are political parties and the committee structures which operate within parliaments. Thus, parliaments are more likely to be able to influence the policy process to the extent that:

- parties are numerous, weakly organized and fragmented, or relatively autonomous from their leadership, because in such circumstances executives are unable to rely on securing disciplined majority support;
- committee structures within parliament are permanent, with relatively slow turnover in membership, because such committees not only allow members to develop expertise in specific areas, they also tend to assume some autonomy; and
- committee structures parallel those of the administration, so that there is a clear link between policy area, committee oversight and bureaucratic responsibility for implementation.

As Weller (1997, p. 37) points out, the influence of parties on the core executive is not constant: 'For instance, the party's impact on policy may be in decline while its capacity to enforce accountability may be growing more marked.' Clearly, parties are central to the operation of all parliamentary democracies, but the range and type of parties and party system varies significantly across western Europe – not only in terms of 'majoritarian' (for instance, the United Kingdom, France, Greece and possibly Ireland) versus 'consensus' (for instance, Austria, Belgium, Germany, the Netherlands), but also in terms of volatility (high in Italy, France and Norway, but usually low in Germany, Spain and the UK). Majoritarian systems are characterized by what Andeweg and Nijzink (1995) have described as an 'inter-party' mode of interaction between the key actors in the executive and legislature, in which party affiliation is the predominant influence on behaviour, whereas consensus systems exhibit a 'cross-party' mode of interaction characterized by a search for agreement.

Thus, paradoxically, the capacity of parliament to influence the policy process is to some extent contingent on political parties being less rather than more effective and disciplined – even though parties are the lifeblood of any parliamentary system. Both executives and legislatures can be seen as being to some extent in thrall to parties. In general, where parties are weak or poorly organized it is more likely that parliamentary committees will be strong, although Germany and the UK (where parties and committees are powerful) to some extent provide exceptions; equally, where parties are ill-disciplined and committees are weak, as in Greece, parliament is able to play only a limited role in the policy process. Parliamentary committees also tend to be more effective in consensus systems – notably, for example, Austria, Germany and the

Netherlands – since they are the site of much routine legislative work before bills are presented to the legislature, as opposed to majoritarian systems in which the executive usually initiates legislation before it passes to committees for scrutiny. Southern Europe provides the clearest examples of executive dominance: in Spain, Portugal and Greece, parliament has often acted as a docile 'rubber stamp' since the mid-1970s transitions to democracy (Liebert and Cotta, 1990). In the UK, too, parliament is often subservient to the executive – although this is significantly influenced by the size of the government's majority.

Finally, in regard to sector-specific factors, legislatures are less likely to have significant influence over macroeconomic and foreign policy, which tend to be seen as 'reserved domains' for the executive, than other areas such as social policy and welfare distribution. Equally, legislatures are more likely to be able to take policy initiatives in newly emergent and highly salient policy areas (for instance, genetic modification and food safety) when an urgent response is demanded, than in routine areas of low public visibility. Overall, the focus on a range of variables demonstrates that the 'decline of parliament' thesis requires some refinement. Whilst it is true that parliaments are not generally the lead actors in the policy-making process, nonetheless they cannot be dismissed as an irrelevance. Parliaments may have lost formal powers *vis-à-vis* executives in many liberal democracies, but their influence and role should be seen neither as static nor trapped in an inevitable downward spiral. Indeed, whilst the role of legislatures is inevitably bound up with that of executives, what we may be witnessing is a growing normative convergence over the appropriate characteristics and organization of the liberal democratic state in an era of transnationalism and globalization. Rather than an ongoing struggle between two branches of government over their respective competencies, there is evidence of an emerging consensus that the democratic state should emphasize two fundamental priorities: efficiency and transparency.

Conclusion: from control to credibility

This chapter has sought to rehearse the story of how the increasing complexity of the modern policy environment, combined with the demand for governments to appear in control of that environment, has generated pressures which have in turn led to profound changes in the nature of governance in Western Europe. One of the most significant changes relates to the so-called 'hollowing-out' of the democratic state, which has been ceding powers both upwards and downwards to supranational and subnational institutions, as well as sideways to independent agencies and private interests. Whilst the capacity of executives to control the policy environment has in practice been in steady decline over recent decades, the rhetoric of parliamentary democracy seems to point the other way: political leaders routinely make electoral promises which are premised on a supposed control over a macroeconomic policy framework which resists any such central management – especially since the creation of the European Central Bank (ECB), whose regulations are binding (Elgie, 2000). Meanwhile, legislatures have similarly been faced with the reality that their role in the policy-making process has been increasingly marginalized, even though members of parliament must maintain the public facade that they are centrally involved in formulating and shaping policy.

Two questions naturally follow: why has the state ceded these powers, and why do politicians nonetheless claim to be able to make a significant difference over macroeconomic management? The answer to the latter question is more straightforward, given that an electoral platform based on an admission of a limited capacity to effect major policy changes might win credit for honesty but is less likely to attract votes. In any case, a strong (if contestable) argument can be made that executives do indeed make a real difference, that they do have the capacity to manipulate supply-side, or structural macroeconomic policies in line with partisan preferences, despite growing global economic interdependence (Boix, 1998). Certainly, insofar as the ideological divide between social democracy and conservatism retains meaning, it is true that parties of each persuasion have sought to offer competing prescriptions to achieve similar broad policy aims of high employment together with sustained economic growth. Whereas social democratic parties have usually talked up the role of public investment and conservatives have promised to cut taxes, in practice the extent to which executives have actually been able to follow clearly differentiated policies is open to question. In Spain (1996), the United Kingdom (1997) and Germany (1998), the shift from social democratic to conservative government, or vice versa, was not followed by radical changes in macroeconomic management. Yet, in a host of other policy areas ranging from environmental management to social policy, there is evidence that executives can and do make a difference according to partisan persuasion (Schmidt, 1996).

The question of why the state has ceded capacity is less straightforward. As states face ever-more difficult challenges and demands in an ever-more complex setting, they naturally seek mechanisms to help them cope. However, the process of 'hollowing-out' combines proactive and reactive elements, and a number of explanations can be offered for its continued development. Thus, it may be that in an increasingly complex and interdependent policy environment the process of policy-making requires more input and expertise than can be delivered by the executive alone: independent agencies are able to provide such expertise in an adjudicative capacity. Equally, it can be useful to have a separation between government and independent agencies when there is a perceived need to avoid charges of political bias or party political influence – an argument often made to support the establishment of independent central banks. Related to this argument is the view that agencies are able to provide policy continuity, since they are not constrained by the electoral cycle and the need to garner support, thus allowing greater policy flexibility. Another potential advantage provided by agencies is that they may be able to develop closer links to the public, particularly through public hearings and enquiries.

What unites all these explanations is that they reflect a process whereby governments have hived off responsibility in those areas where they have either limited autonomy or limited leverage, whilst being able simultaneously to claim that delegating key powers to independent experts underlines their policy commitment. Indeed, Majone (1997, pp. 144, 148) sees the issue of policy credibility as central to understanding delegation:

> the growing complexity of public policy continues to erode the effectiveness of the traditional command-and-control techniques of government bureaucracy . . . [T]he main reason for delegating . . . [is] to establish a policy credibility which becomes increasingly important as policy objectives can no longer be imposed by legislative or administrative fiat.

What brings executives and legislatures together in contemporary West European democracies is the shared perception that the real threat they face is public cynicism and apathy. Democratic governments need credibility in order to survive – but credibility is threatened if they are consistently unable to deliver on promises. Yet credibility achieved through delegation to independent agencies in turn generates additional problems: there is a tension between the technocratic argument in favour of efficiency, which has been used to support the delegation of economic policy-making in particular to experts and professionals, and the public demand for legislative accountability. Without clear mechanisms for exercising such accountability, democracies become vulnerable to the charge that there is a 'democratic deficit', that public policy is not made on the basis of the public's choice.

Such a tension has been acutely recognized within the EU itself, which has been most obviously open to the charge of democratic deficit. The

EU Commission President, Romano Prodi, has placed much emphasis on the need to do less, but do it better, underlining a commitment to achieving legitimacy by ensuring that action matches rhetoric. This theme was clearly articulated in speech to the European Parliament in Strasbourg in February 2000, in which Prodi underlined the need for the European Union's institutions to be seen to operate in a transparent and accountable way:

> People want a much more participatory, 'hands-on' democracy. They will not support the European project unless they are fully involved in setting goals, making policy and evaluating progress . . . I believe we have to stop thinking in terms of hierarchical layers of competence separated by the subsidiarity principle and start thinking, instead, of a networking arrangement, with all levels of governance shaping, proposing, implementing and monitoring policy together. (Prodi, 2000)

In some senses, the President of the Commission was simply echoing trends which have been emerging at national level in the EU's member states. The reality of modern democratic government is that negotiation at all levels is the key: leaders can no longer seek simply to impose or control (Rhodes, 1997a, p. 219).

The story of the shift from government to governance in West European democracies is thus partly about the growing recognition that in an era of more complex policy challenges, the only viable strategy is to allow for greater specialization through increasing delegation. In order to confront the potential problem of accountability entailed by such a development, both executives and legislatures have a shared interest in promoting efficiency and ensuring higher transparency: the former points to accepting limitations on the reach of government, the latter to the need to ensure that government says what it does, and does what it says.

Chapter 9

Disintegration or Reconfiguration? Organized Interests in Western Europe

RAINER EISING AND MICHELLE CINI

West European systems of interest intermediation are in a state of flux, and making sense of these changes means identifying the factors or pressures that are shaping this reconfiguration of interest organization. This chapter identifies three such factors: first, market or functional pressures which result from an intensification of competition and technological developments; second, ideational pressures, and here we focus on neo-liberalism, alongside the debates and the policies arising from it; and third, institutional effects associated with the proliferation of European-level regulation and the process we call 'Europeanization'. In this chapter we argue that these three factors or pressures are central to any explanation of the reconfiguration of governance systems in Western Europe.

More specifically we argue that they are driving important changes in the organization and practice of interest intermediation. In order to begin to explain these changes we first need to say something more about the pressures themselves before moving on to show how individual interest organizations and national systems of interest intermediation have responded to them. In the main we focus our attention on France, Germany and the United Kingdom, for not only are these the largest countries of Western Europe, but they also represent three quite different types of interest intermediation: statism, corporatism and pluralism.

The nature of change

In some economic sectors such as telecommunications and information technology, and in the fields of financial services and transport, market changes have impacted indirectly on the sectoral organization and representation of interests. For instance, the technological fusion of telecommunications, information technology and the media brings together in a new configuration sectors with very different regulatory traditions and modes of organization. However, this is only the case in highly dynamic technology-led sectors, and cannot explain why we also witness tremendous change in areas where the effect of these functional pressures is not so obvious.

In some of these cases there would seem to be a more indirect cognitive or ideational dynamic at work. Growing awareness and debate about economic globalization, together with the perceived failure of 1970s-style Keynesianism opened the door to new economic policy doctrines in the 1980s, contributing to the rise, for example, of supply-side policies. Underpinned by a belief that 'the competitive market system, left to its own devices, free of government interference, will produce superior results, in terms of efficiency and social justice' (Helm, 1989, p. 12), monetarism and the politics of privatization, liberalization and deregulation formed the core of the neo-liberal reform agenda. This agenda has challenged established systems of production, regulation, welfare and interest intermediation. It has altered relations amongst firms and competitors in the market, as well as amongst employers and employees, and has called into question the role traditionally played by associations as interest intermediaries.

Finally, in several issue areas, the establishment of international regimes and organizations has altered in a much more obvious way the institutional 'target structure' of interest organizations. The emergence of international rules of the game and the sharing of powers amongst international, national and sub-national political institutions can provide powerful incentives for organized interests to be present at all three of these levels. We need to understand not only the role of individuals, social movements and organized interests in international politics, but also how actors situate themselves in networks that cover various spatial levels.

For Western Europe, the most important of these regimes or organizations is regional, and takes the form of a Europeanization of governance structures. We define Europeanization as 'the adaptive response of national institutions and actors to the impact and imperatives of European intervention or particular initiatives' (Colino, 1997, p. 5). It is hardly surprising that analysts of the European Union (EU) have emphasized the importance of institutional factors given that the EU is a highly dynamic, if still evolving, political system. Its authority covers a greater number of policy areas and reaches deeper into the member states than does any other international regime. Moreover, the sharing of national regulatory powers with the institutions of the European Union has transformed the domestic environments of the member states and has embedded domestic actors in a multilevel political system. It has also transformed the arenas in which individual interests are pursued, offering both new opportunities and imposing constraints, whilst also challenging intra-and interorganizational routines and modes of interest intermediation. Europeanization effects can be far-reaching; although we don't pursue this perspective in this chapter, they may even bring about changes in actors' loyalties and identities (see the chapter by Thomas Risse).

Despite the fact that these pressures are felt by all West European states, we do not expect to see an alignment of the way in which interests are organized and articulated in domestic contexts. First of all, neoinstitutional analyses have shown that domestic structures and practices are often quite resilient to change (see Steinmo, Thelen and Longstreth, 1992). Accordingly, the impact of the changes mentioned above on national systems of interest intermediation depends to some extent on preexisting domestic configurations. In this way, the further development of these systems is path-dependent. On this basis we would expect actors operating under different modes of governance, whether these are defined sectorally or nationally, to feel and therefore to react to these pressures in different ways, with different but functionally equivalent solutions emerging in response to the same perceived problem. For these reasons, there is broad agreement in the literature that these factors exert neither a uniform influence across sectors and countries nor that they will necessarily lead to a full-scale convergence of national systems or a regulatory 'race to the bottom' (Berger and Diore, 1996).

In the next section we distinguish between modes of governance, concentrating on the classical distinction often made between pluralism, statism and corporatism. We then turn to look more empirically at the way in which market, ideational and institutional pressures have impacted upon national governance systems and consider some examples of how West European systems of interest intermediation are changing. In these three sections, examples are drawn from various sectors and West European states, allowing us to draw some tentative conclusions that relate the empirical material to our earlier expectations. Thus while we end the chapter by admitting that some of our expectations have clearly not been met, and that the causes and mechanisms of the ongoing reconfiguration of interest organization in Western Europe remain elusive, we also claim to shed light on some of the changes underway.

Modes of governance

Although there is a wide variation in patterns of interest intermediation across both political systems and policy domains, the literature on state–society relations still distinguishes among three major ideal-types of interest intermediation: pluralism, corporatism and statism. These types vary from one another in four ways: in the role of state actors; the patterns of interaction; the dominant actors; and the level and scope of political allocation. In the pluralist mode, the state's role is reduced to that of a referee mediating the pursuit of individual interests. Organized interests representing their memberships engage in lobbying to this end. These actors compete and bargain to build minimum winning coalitions that are generally fluid and dependent on parallel interests. As a liberal state that intervenes relatively little in the affairs of the business community, the United Kingdom is traditionally grouped in the pluralist camp.

At the opposite end of the spectrum, in the statist mode, the state is an authority above society, legitimated by the democratic vote and pursuing a common 'national' interest. State actors are thus the dominant actors in policy formulation, with interest groups playing only a minimal role. Participation in policy formulation is limited to a small number of organized interests. Indeed, many interest organizations tend to be included in policy decisions only after the basic contours of the policy have been outlined, often politicizing the later stages of the policy-making process, so that policy implementation becomes characterized by 'the politics of accommodation' (Schmidt, 1999, p. 167). In Western Europe, France has been identified as having a particularly statist system of interest organization, though Italy and Greece have also been labelled as statist, with interest intermediation in these two countries taking paternalistic and clientelistic forms.

Between the extremes of pluralism and statism lie corporatist and network modes of interest organization. In the corporatist mode, the state performs the role of mediator, integrating the conflicting group interests of peak associations that fully represent their organizational domains. The associational setting is thus highly centralized. In negotiation, the state and the peak associations seek to build consensus over the problems plaguing their particular sectors. Actor constellations are relatively closed and stable, and interest groups are on an equal footing with state actors as they work towards the formulation of binding rules and their effective implementation. As a consequence, at both the formulation and implementation stages of the policy process, interest organizations assume quasi-public functions. In Western Europe, Austria, Sweden, Norway, the Netherlands and to a lesser extent Germany have been identified as possessing corporatist modes of interest intermediation.

A fourth type of governance of relevance to this chapter, labelled 'network governance', is a more recent conceptualization reflecting socio-economic dynamics and institutional changes occurring in Western Europe (see Kohler-Koch and Eising, 1999). This is the mode of interest organization typical of the European level of governance.

Central to this concept of network governance is an assumption that policy-making is largely concerned with problem-solving, and that in solving problems political actors have no choice but to take into account the specific rationalities of highly organized and differentiated social sub-systems (*ibid.*). Thus, in the network mode, the state is said to be vertically and horizontally segmented, with its role more that of 'activator' than 'authoritative allocator'. The process of governing takes place via flexible and loosely-coupled inter-organizational networks which facilitate the building of consensus over controversial issues, and interest groups perform a largely consultative role, even though, for functional reasons, they may also have self-regulatory powers when policy comes to be implemented.

So what effect might our market, ideational and institutional pressures have on interest organization under these different modes of governance? Generally speaking, we might expect to find evidence that market pressures, ideational changes and institutional factors affect statist and corporatist systems of governance to a much greater degree than they do pluralist or network systems. For example, in statist systems we would expect market pressures to diminish the relevance of the state, given that where business activity becomes globalized, the state is likely to have less to offer societal actors by way of knowledge or control over relevant markets. Moreover, in supporting market solutions rather than associational governance, and as international competitive pressures render consensus among business groups more difficult, neo-liberalism and the policies related to it would seem to seriously undermine a corporatist mode of governance. Finally, in the multilevel system of network governance which now characterizes the European Union, we would expect to find less of an impact where there is a congruence (or 'goodness of fit') between the EU mode (usually of network governance) and that found at other 'levels'. As network and pluralist modes of governance are rather similar in certain respects, the most dramatic effects and the most disruptive reconfigurations are therefore likely to be found in cases where corporatism and statism predominate. More generally, though, we would expect to find evidence that patterns of change (or reconfiguration) amongst interests mirror or coincide with those modes of governance identified above.

Market change: technological and competitive pressures

Theories of globalization point to the numerous forces, both technological and competitive, affecting markets within the international political economy. It is supposed that these forces engender a change in the inter-action of societal actors, as they alter opportunity structures, causing actors to adjust their organization, strategies and preferences accord-ingly (Armstrong and Bulmer, 1998). These actors have to adapt to a new global economic, technological and political environment in order to ensure their continued survival. For example, impinging upon labour and product markets, market changes are said to affect the interest defi-nitions of firms, thus reducing the relevance of associations as interest intermediaries for them. With the uncertainty that globalization engen-ders, both firms and individuals, as well as the organizations represent-ing them, seek new ways to minimize the risks involved and profit from the opportunities that the new environment brings.

Large firms have been particularly adept at capitalizing on the oppor-tunities that market changes have offered; but they have done so in diverse ways. While these companies have certainly not become state-less, they have extended their territorial reach considerably. Swedish firms provide a telling case (Pestoff, 2000). Compared to other West European countries, Swedish industry is highly concentrated and inter-nationalized. While in 1965 the 30 largest Swedish firms employed about two-thirds of their staff within Sweden, today they employ more than three-fifths abroad. In the largest West European states, the inter-national activities of the largest firms have increased to a lesser extent. For 84 of the largest 100 German firms, for example, the share of foreign employment as a proportion of total employment increased from an average of 17.8 per cent in 1986 to 27.3 per cent in 1996 (data from the Max Planck Institute for the Study of Societies). Indeed, even if the domestic market is still an important base for production and research facilities, it would appear that the national level is losing some of its relevance for these actors as a consequence of the growth of EU and international regulation and of the internationalization of their economic activities.

As a consequence of these developments, we can hypothesize that large firms are more likely to question the relevance of the role tradi-tionally played by their interest intermediaries in this new environment. They may begin to see them as unnecessary constraints upon their autonomy, and as a result suggest that existing associational structures be reformed. For members of large firms the downsizing and organiza-tional rationalization of associations is often seen as a remedy to the problems caused by market change. In Scandinavia, for example, there is a clear trend 'towards merging the functions of trade associations and employer associations into a single business interest organization' (Pestoff, 2000). In 2000, the activities of the Swedish Federation of Industry were merged with those of the Swedish Employers'

Association to form the Central Organization of Swedish Business and Commerce.

By contrast, we can hypothesize that small firms, or rather those not inextricably linked to large firms in a supplier relationship, are likely to react to more intense competition by making additional demands on political actors via their associations. They will do so in order to enhance their own security. Indeed, in Switzerland, the divergent interests of small and large firms in associational governance are reflected in the failed merger of the Swiss Business Association with the Swiss Employers' Associations. While a small group of industrialists from the highly internationalized Swiss chemical sector planned a merger between these associations to ensure 'closer cooperation' across the divergent issues of social policy, labour relations and economic policy, as well as to 'increase organizational efficiency', their proposal was voted down by many of the small and medium-sized companies in the employers' association (Kriesi, 2000). Not only did the small firms fear that they would be overpowered by the larger firms, but the employers' association itself pointed to the increase in internal complexity that would characterize the merged association, predicting concomitant problems for decision-making. As a result, the streamlining of the Swiss associational landscape has in recent years remained confined to export-orientated sectors such as chemicals and machinery. Both in Sweden and Switzerland, then, the ability of associations to 'discipline' their members has given way to a stronger role for large firms within these associations, undermining an important precondition for corporatist concertation. Where this has not occurred, a divergence of interest amongst association members has led to deadlock or an inability to adapt to the new external pressures.

That it was the highly internationalized chemical industry which pressed for associational change in Switzerland simply highlights the fact that competitive pressures are not felt equally by all sectors of the economy. For example, Lovecy (1999) points to pressures felt in the professional services sectors, such as accountancy and law. For her, the unity which these professional bodies have sought in representing their interests at the European level is a direct consequence of the functional imperatives characterizing these particular sectors. She finds, by contrast, that in a field such as healthcare where the boundaries between national systems are deeply entrenched, professional bodies have generally been insulated from direct global competitive pressures to the extent that national cleavages outweigh sectoral similarities when it comes to representing interests in international forums.

In certain sectors such as telecommunications, information technology, financial services and transport, the effects have been more dramatic. Indeed, in all of these sectors staggering technological and market changes have been witnessed over recent decades. These functional pressures have had important effects on interest organization, and not only at the national level. In telecoms, for example, technological change, the convergence with information technology and sectoral liberalization have paved the way for the reconfiguration of the sector (see the chapter by David Levy). Once the monolithic postal and telecommunications administrations began to be broken up, the telecoms market became increasingly differentiated. New entrants and users became more vocal both at the level of the European Union and at the global level (Bartle, 1999). The investments made by the major telecommunications companies have become far more internationalized and integrated; and global commercial alliances such GlobalOne, bringing together France Telecom, Deutsche Telekom and Sprint, have been institutionalized.

One of the consequences of these changes has been an increase both at the EU level and at the global level in issue-specific interest alliances and in interest organizations constructed on the basis of direct firm membership. Yet even in these similar sectors the relationships between global and EU-level interest organizations and activities have not followed a single overarching logic. For instance, while the International Alliance for the Distribution by Cable was transformed into an EU-level organization – the European Cable Communications Association – the International Telecommunications Users Group gradually took over the functions of the EC Telecommunications Users Association. While this indicates that European and global issues have become more closely entwined in telecommunications, the case of the cable organizations and telecoms users demonstrates the considerable discretion that actors have with regard to the market effects and the different responses that have resulted.

Ideational effects: the neo-liberal surge

The demise in the 1970s of Keynesianism as the dominant economic paradigm, and the rise of neo-liberalism in the 1980s, both underpinned and justified the introduction of deregulatory, monetarist and privatization policies by governments of both right and left. When examining the effects of neo-liberalism on organized interests, this is certainly one area to be considered. However, the ascendance of neo-liberalism did not lead to any wholesale importation of policies of this sort into Western Europe. While it led to the introduction of neo-liberal policies in some countries and in certain sectors, it also opened the door to what became a far-reaching debate about the extent to which market solutions to economic (and political) problems were appropriate in all cases, given the diversity of sectoral contexts and political systems within the region.

By way of an example, this debate, which focused attention on the limits of regulation and the role of governance mechanisms beyond the state, contributed to a 'renaissance of concertation through social pacts' in the 1990s (Ebbinghaus and Hassel, 1999, p. 6; see also Schmitter and Grote, 1997). Relatively stable tripartite agreements were concluded amongst the state, trade unions and employers' associations in Ireland, Finland, Italy, the Netherlands and Denmark. However, in those countries where stable agreements were negotiated, the nature of those agreements differed substantially from the neo-corporatist concertation and the Keynesian wage policies of the 1950s to 1970s; that is, from a system of 'wage containment in exchange for near-full employment and side-payments in increased, state-provided, welfare' (Schmitter and Grote, 1997, p. 14). The new social pacts of the 1990s have both a wider and a narrower scope: wider in the sense that they imply, whether simultaneously or sequentially, a reform of the welfare state, labour relations and employment policies; but narrower in the sense that they are closely tied to the strengthening of national competitiveness and the reform of public finance as embodied in the convergence criteria for Economic and Monetary Union. Thus, social pacts combine liberalization and flexibility on the one hand, but on the other they also provide some compensation for labour (Ebbinghaus and Hassel, 1999).

However, in Greece, Spain, Portugal, Belgium, Germany and Sweden such pacts either excluded one of the social partners or they failed altogether; and in some countries such concertation has not been a major element in the reform of the welfare state and of labour relations. In statist France, for example, there is no evidence of increased cooperation between the French state and the 'social partners'. Quite the contrary in fact: in France, the abandonment of national wage bargaining and the decentralization of labour relations in the 1980s led to the introduction of plant-level wage bargaining, and even, according to Ebbinghaus and Hassel (1999), to employer-imposed wage settlements. Despite a high concentration of state power, the French state has not been able to compensate for the distrust that still exists between business associations and unions, and between firms and wage earners.

In the United Kingdom the retrenchment of the welfare state and the reform of labour relations was the result of unilateral state action. Despite the election of a Labour government in 1997 there were subsequently no significant moves towards strengthening trade unions and reintroducing tripartite negotiations. However, these two cases should not lead us to conclude that the effects of neo-liberalism imply any convergence upon a single model. While competitive and financial pressures induced statist France and the neo-liberal British Conservative government to adopt a more market-oriented and pluralistic organization of labour relations, the same cannot be said of all West European states. Moreover, as France and Britain do not have the same mode of governance, we might have expected them to react very differently to the neo-liberal surge. In fact, without exaggerating the similarities, there has been a move in the same general direction, albeit from a very different point of departure.

On the face of it, we might have presupposed that the introduction of a neo-liberal agenda would induce a weakening of organized interests across the board in Western Europe. After all, from a neo-liberal standpoint associations are often deemed little more than cartels of actors intent on protecting the interests of their members in a conspiracy against the public interest and free trade. However, from the above example we might surmise that the surge of neo-liberal ideas that has swept Western Europe has been received very differently in different states. While the position of and relationship between the social partners has certainly altered across Western Europe, the way in which they have changed has varied – and in ways which do not coincide neatly with our earlier expectations.

Institutional pressures: interest organization in a multilevel system

The European Union is now responsible for a vast array of policies. With the dramatic increase in its powers and competencies in a series of treaty revisions from the Single European Act in 1986 to Nice in 2001, the economic and political fates of the West (and soon the East) European states are bound together in new policy interdependencies. These changes have altered the context within which interest intermediation occurs. While European integration extends the problem-solving reach of those states involved, it also constrains their autonomous policy-making capacity. The EU and member state institutions have now become embedded in a system of multilevel decision-making, a system which binds together state institutions at multiple levels at all stages in the policy process. The increasing number of policies dealt with now in one form or another at the European level has prompted interest organizations to promote their cases more readily before the EU institutions. The European Commission, fulfilling as it does many of the EU's executive and administrative functions, and the European Parliament which has gained in legislative power over the course of the last two decades, are both important addressees of interest-group concerns. In addition, given their key position in the policy-making process, members of the Council of Ministers and of its administrative sub-structure are often targeted by national interest groups, even if obtaining direct access to the Council is more difficult. Indeed, most interest groups have little choice but to approach the Council through their national ministries. However, if the extension of qualified majority decision-making has robbed individual members of the Council of some of their veto options, it has also meant that interest groups are now forced to form cross-country alliances. Note also that adjudication by the European Court of Justice (and the Court of First Instance), based in Luxembourg, also offers an important avenue for the pursuit of interests.

There is a huge amount of interest-group activity in Brussels, Strasbourg and Luxembourg, and the number of groups operating around the European institutions gives some indication of the extent of that activity. In Spring 2000, for example, the European Commission's Secretariat-General listed approximately 900 EU associations. Moreover, in the late 1990s approximately 350 large firms were said to have set up offices in Brussels in order to gain better access to the EU institutions, enabling them to coordinate their work with other interest groups. As market integration has been the foundation stone of the European integration process since its inception, economic interest groups (that is, producer groups and employer groups) are particularly well-represented at the European level. By comparison, the representation of general interests (environmental, social and welfare groups, trade unions, religious organizations, human rights groups and so forth) is much more limited. So while about 80 per cent of EU groups represent agricultural, industrial or service interests, only about 20 per cent fall into the general interests category. The institutionalization of civil dialogue and the establishment of consultation committees composed of social or environmental NGOs only partly makes up for this representation deficit. Indeed, owing to the complexity of the EU system, the lack of a European 'public' and the difficulties encouraging a transnational form of mobilization, social movements have barely Europeanized their activities.

Nevertheless, the institutional properties of the EU system and the fragility of its democratic legitimacy have contributed to the emergence of a network mode of governance at the EU level. For the EU's institutions, and particularly for the European Commission, the construction of European networks has become a matter of organizational survival (Metcalfe, 2000). The diffusion of authority in the EU and the limited capacity of the EU institutions to fulfil the functions they must perform force them to be open to societal and economic actors who not only provide them with expertise but also with a measure of legitimacy. The EU institutions have also supported the development of 'umbrella' interest groups (or Euro-groups) at the EU level as these groups are able to aggregate the positions of their national members, thus reducing decision costs. Therefore, even if we can identify certain corporatist traits in the making of EU social policy (the peak associations of business, UNICE and CEEP, and labour, ETUC, are able to formulate rules in certain areas), and even if there is some evidence of a statist pattern of policy formation in the treaty revisions such as those establishing Economic and Monetary Union, the network mode of governance can still be identified as the dominant mode of interest organization (Kohler-Koch and Eising, 1999). This mode of interest intermediation has gained broad acceptance amongst political, societal and economic actors as it allows actors affected by EU policy to be integrated into the EU system.

Thus EU associations are frequently in touch with the European institutions. However, this does not tell us whether these contacts mainly serve informational purposes or whether they qualify as processes of interest intermediation. Regardless, we may tentatively conclude that EU associations have evolved into genuine interlocutors between their national members and the EU institutions. Their intermediary role is underlined by the fact that they have quite frequent contacts with national governments, either through their members or directly through their own staff.

The multilevel character of the European Union ensures that interest representation is not restricted to EU-level organizations. National interest organizations understand the need to coordinate activities at both the EU and the national level. Data from a recent survey conducted at the Mannheim Centre for European Social Research illustrates this point in identifying the number of contacts made between national trade associations and state institutions in three EU states (Eising, 2000b). The survey was addressed to 1998 trade associations from the United Kingdom, France and Germany, and at the level of the European Union to 68 large firms as well (40.9 per cent responded). In 1998–99, roughly two-thirds of British German and French trade associations represented their interests to both the EU institutions and the national political institutions. Around two-thirds of the EU associations also maintained contacts with national political institutions through their national members, as well as having some direct contact. Overall, the findings of this survey suggest that we are witnessing the emergence of a truly multilevel system of interest intermediation.

It is the institutional features of this multilevel system that to a large extent determine the access that firms and national trade associations have to political institutions. The number of contacts actors have with the European Commission, the European Parliament and the Council of Ministers varies according to both the division of labour amongst these organizations, and to the main operating level of the associations but less so with regard to the national modes of interest intermediation. Thus 65 per cent of the EU associations said they had monthly or weekly contact with the European Commission, while this holds for only approximately 30 percent of the German trade associations and an even smaller proportion of the British and the French associations (roughly 15 per cent and 20 per cent respectively). Large firms have better access to the European Commission than trade associations, however, with almost 82 per cent of them having at least monthly contact with the European Commission. Firms, EU associations and national associations had far fewer contacts with the European Parliament and the Council of Ministers than with the Commission. Not surprisingly, perhaps, the European Commission is by far the most important addressee of interest group concerns at the EU level.

At the domestic level the number of contacts that interest organizations have with political institutions 'at home' is also of relevance when EU affairs are being discussed. Here groups also have more contact with national executives than they do with legislatures. Despite the existence of a multilevel system of governance, national governments are still highly relevant for national interest organizations. Over half of the German associations maintain at least monthly contacts with their government in EU affairs. This holds for around 40 per cent of UK associations and French associations. Perhaps surprisingly almost a quarter of EU associations also have at least monthly contact with national governments, either through their members or directly. This suggests that national associations have included the EU level in their lobbying strategies but pay more attention to domestic institutions when it comes to lobbying in the EU. Compared to associations that tend to be embedded in one level of governance, large firms have evolved into professional two-level players. Almost 80 per cent of the large firms maintain at least monthly contact with national governments, with the same figure thus maintaining frequent contact with both the national and the EU executives.

Therefore, while German associations have relatively good access to the European Commission this is less the case for associations from the other two countries surveyed. What might account for this difference? One tentative conclusion we might draw from these data is that it is in fact German corporatist practices that are able to flourish best within the EU's network mode of governance. The long-standing relationships between trade associations and the state actors and the institutionalized channels of interest representation at the domestic level resonate well with the EU's network mode of governance. Indeed, a survey of business interest groups in corporatist Denmark also found that the shifting of policy-making competencies to the European level did not lead to any drop in contact between the national state and private actors. Quite the contrary, in fact, as several national interest groups intensified their contacts with the national political institutions (Sidenius, 1999). Thus, there can be no presumption that ties among national actors loosen as a result of the integration process; only that these ties will become integrated into a multilevel system of interest organization.

Differences in national modes of interest intermediation must be particularly pronounced for them to show in access patterns within the EU institutions. Against our expectations, for example, the more informal British policy style does not permit the UK associations to access the Commission more easily than, say, the French associations. Indeed, it would seem that of all modes of interest organization, it is corporatism which best prepares trade associations for participation in the EU policy process. It should be added, however, that the broader findings of the research project summarized here show that while different modes of interest intermediation do affect the strategies of individual associations, they are less relevant than the division of labour that exists between the EU and national associations and the EU's institutions.

The Europeanization of policy alters the opportunity structure for individual actors. For these actors systemic adaptation costs are but one element in their overall cost–benefit ratio, and a change in the domestic status quo might even be advantageous for them. For example, in the case of professional services, increasing access to the ECJ allowed 'policy outsiders' at the national level in the UK and France to move centre-stage at the EU level, enabling individual members of the professions and service recipients 'to challenge and, when successful, overturn the kinds of entrenched national and sub-national restrictive practices which have been the product of alliance-building between those who are "policy-insiders" within the member states' sectoral governance structures' (Lovecy, 1999, p. 148). In other words, the new practice of litigation caused a process of governance transformation 'by the back door'. Similarly, the British Union for the Abolition of Vivisection was 'struck by the accessibility of the European Parliament and Commission and the openness of its officials compared to the UK' (Fisher, 1994, p. 232). By extending its activities to Brussels and mobilizing an almost EU-wide opposition to the testing of cosmetics on animals, this national public-interest group influenced the Commission and the Council decision to end (subject to certain qualifications) this form of animal experimentation.

Such instances make it difficult to assess whether on balance private or public actors have gained in the process of European integration. According to Edgar Grande (1996), the embeddedness of public actors in the horizontal and vertical negotiations characteristic of EU decision-making may allow them to gain autonomy *vis-à-vis* private actors. A strategy of self-binding may provide a convenient means of turning down the demands of societal and economic interest organizations.

Thus, we seem to be witnessing contradictory results from the empirical studies reviewed. On the one hand, easy access to EU institutions, resource dependencies and the need for functional representation would appear to tip the balance in favour of big private players. For instance, the first of the EU's major information technology research programmes, ESPRIT, was launched by a coalition of large firms and the Commission against the preferences of member-state administrations. Yet on the other hand, the complexity of the EU system and the centrality of the public actors in decision-making process make it difficult for interest groups to have a decisive impact. In recent years, evidence from the sectoral liberalization of public service sectors such as electricity, gas, transport and telecommunications have been used to substantiate this point. In these cases fundamental reforms were often decided in the face of resistance from large and powerful economic actors with entrenched political ties to national state actors.

Conclusions

We began this chapter by claiming that although interest intermediation in Western Europe is currently in a state of flux, we should not assume that this implies a process of convergence or the creation of a West European model of interest organization. In other words, organized interests will feel and react to the pressures and challenges they face differently in different sectors and countries. Taking this premise further, we suggested that the 'mode of governance' (pluralism, corporatism, statism and network governance), might be the key to understanding this variation. So while we can say that there is a reconfiguration of interest organization throughout Europe, the effects that will be felt as a consequence will be subject to substantial variation.

To explore this hypothesis, three pressures facing interest organization in Western Europe were identified. Market pressures were said to arise out of intensified competition and technological change; ideational pressures highlighted the rise of neo-liberalism as the dominant economic ideology, focusing on the debates and policies that arose as a consequence; and institutional pressures in the form of a process of

Europeanization emphasized the effect of the expansion of the scope and intensity of EU regulatory activity since the mid-1980s.

On the basis of the examples presented in this chapter, what then are the conclusions to be drawn? Clearly, we must concede that our expectations have not been met in the sense that modes of governance alone do not provide an adequate explanation of variation when seeking to explain the reconfiguration of interest organization in Western Europe. It would seem, then, that corporatist and statist systems of governance on the one hand, and the pluralist and network systems on the other are likely to see as much variation within as between them. In looking at market pressures upon interest organization, for example, we found evidence that there was no single logic of reconfiguration even in rather similar high-tech sectors. If anything, the examples used suggested that differences between large and small firms and large and small states were as, if not more, important than the dominant mode of governance. Considering the effects of neo-liberalism, we again found evidence that patterns of adaptation did not mirror modes of governance. In France and the UK, for example, fairly similar patterns were identified, a factor that could not have been predicted on the basis of our initial working hypothesis. Finally, our review of the Europeanization of interest intermediation also produced some unexpected results. Most notably, it was found that associations operating within a German corporatist context were better able than French and UK actors to access the EU institutions, a finding which would seem to undermine those intuitive arguments made about the importance of 'goodness of fit' between the EU and national levels of governance.

While we stick by our contention that the reconfiguration of interest intermediation does not imply a convergence of systems of interest organization, a clear pattern which would explain the variation in responses from interests remains elusive, even if certain potential variables have suggested themselves in the empirical examples above (sector type, county size, or size of corporate actor, for example). Yet even if modes of governance alone do not provide the answer, this does not mean that we need dismiss them as unimportant. Rather, it suggests, perhaps unsurprisingly, that a plausible explanation of variation is likely to be somewhat more complex that was envisaged in the early sections of this chapter.

Chapter 10

Political Corruption, Democracy, and Governance in Western Europe

PAUL HEYWOOD, VÉRONIQUE PUJAS AND
MARTIN RHODES

Political corruption was seen until recently as a serious problem only in non-democratic regimes and developing nations, and significant just at local or municipal levels in established western democracies. However, the revelation of major corruption scandals during the 1980s and 1990s in several European democracies has prompted a critical reassessment of the forms, nature and extent of political corruption. Much of the literature which has appeared during the last decade on corruption in western Europe has assumed, first, that high-level political corruption has mainly occurred 'below the olive line' – that is, in the Catholic countries of southern Europe (most notably, Italy, Spain and France); and second, that major corruption scandals have in particular implicated members of the socialist 'party family' (Little and Posada-Carbó, 1996; Levi and Nelken, 1996). If such assumptions ever held any descriptive validity, their explanatory purchase was always limited. In fact, the recent revelations of high-level corruption scandals in countries such as Belgium, the Netherlands and Germany, as well as within the European Union, have undermined even their accuracy as description. Even in the United Kingdom, usually seen as basically free of political corruption, concern has grown in recent years over standards in public life.

This chapter focuses on three separate, yet related, issues: the particular nature of high-level political corruption in West European democracies; competing approaches to explain the incidence of such corruption; and the impact of political corruption on the nature of democratic governance. Of course, given that definitions of political corruption are highly contested (Peters and Welch, 1978; Johnston, 1996), any analysis needs to specify what is understood by the term. Illegality is central to many definitions of political corruption, because it provides a basis for comparative analysis. Such an approach, however,

184

confronts a two-fold problem: first, laws are not necessarily consistent in interpretation or application across different countries. What is illegal in one country may not be in another, leading to situations in which similar acts can be defined as corrupt or not according only to where they take place. The financing of political parties, which is a key feature of much contemporary concern over corruption, provides a good example: the rules on party financing in some countries are much stricter than in others, and there is little doubt that some well-established practices in Britain – such as voluntary private contributions, even from overseas, to party funds – would prompt investigation in several other democracies.

Second, the recourse to legal norms in definitions of political corruption forgoes any possibility of capturing a more nebulous aspect of the phenomenon. All democracies rest on some basic principles, one of which is the public accountability of decision-making. But accountability can be enforced only if government activity is transparent: citizens cannot hold their elected leaders to account for activities of which they are unaware. This truism highlights one of the central conundrums in constructing a definition of political corruption. It could be argued that one of the most sinister forms of political corruption in a democracy is when the 'democratic transcript' is betrayed: that is, when members of the political class act in such a way as to prevent or circumvent the exercise of accountability, by actively seeking to ensure that the electorate is not properly informed about a given issue. Such activities deliberately subvert transparency without 'causing any immediate, specific, personal and justiciable injury to anyone' (Fuke, 1989). Thompson (1993) refers to 'mediated corruption' in trying to capture the essence of such activities, which concern the process of democratic politics and connect to more classical understandings of the concept based on the moral health of societies (Johnston, 1996). Such a form of political corruption is peculiar to democracies precisely because of their claim to legitimize decision-making through public accountability – a fact which fundamentally sets them apart from non-democracies. Political corruption is therefore understood in this context as activity which, for financial gain or some other in-kind benefit, abuses the duties and responsibilities of public office.

Corruption scandals in contemporary Western Europe

The wave of corruption scandals across West European states over the last decade demonstrates a number of common features, in regard not just to the nature of the scandals themselves, but also their revelation.

Indeed, one striking feature of high-level corruption scandals in Western Europe over the last decade is that so many have involved the illegal funding of political parties – particularly in Belgium, France, Germany, Italy and Spain. Even in the United Kingdom, largely seen as free of high-level political corruption in the modern era, concern has grown in recent years over standards in public life generally, and party funding specifically. In its Fifth Report, on the problem of party political funding in the UK, the Committee on Standards in Public Life commented:

> There is no overt corruption in the constituencies and no overt trade in honours. Yet in broad outline what today concerns the public is the inscrutability of the sources from which the parties derive their money. People ask: Who is paying? And how much? In return for what? Is it British or foreign money? No satisfactory answers are vouchsafed. (Standards in Public Life, 1998: paragraph 2.6)

Concern in the UK was prompted by the issue of donations to the major political parties, notably the 'Ecclestone affair', in which it emerged that the Formula One boss had given the Labour Party £1 million (€1.6 million) at a time when the new government was seeking to exempt the sport from European Union legislation to banish tobacco advertising at sports events (Thompson, 2000, p. 174). Prior to this, however, the Conservative Party had been under intense scrutiny over the willingness of some MPs to act on behalf of private interests in return for payment ('cash-for-questions') as well as the party's readiness to accept major undeclared overseas donations.

Other notable scandals related to party funding in Europe have included the Augusta-Dassault military contracts affair in Belgium surrounding the sale of fighter planes, which led to the prosecution of the former Socialist economy minister, Willy Claes, and his resignation in 1995 as NATO Secretary-General. As with the Conservatives in Britain, accusations of graft and sleaze helped bring down the Belgian government. In Spain, the Socialist government of Felipe González became similarly mired in corruption scandals during the early 1990s, notably the Filesa and Time-Export cases which involved fictitious consultancy work in return for party political donations, and the so-called GAL scandal in which it was revealed that Interior Ministry reserve funds had been used to set up anti-terrorist assassination squads during the early 1980s. González lost the 1996 elections after 14 years in power. Another scandal involving a Socialist party was the Urba affair, which came to light in France early in the Mitterrand presidency and again involved fictitious contracts to generate party funds. Italy stood as a case apart, given the scale of systemic corruption revealed during the tangentopoli scandals of the early 1990s, which had no real parallel in any other established European democracy. In general, though, it was easy to see how the conclusion could be drawn during the mid-1990s that socialist parties were particularly susceptible to corruption.

Such assumptions have had to be revised in the light of further party funding scandals which emerged at the end of the 1990s. In particular, the revelation that Helmut Kohl, German Chancellor between 1983 and 1997, had kept secret party accounts for the Christian Democratic Union (CDU) undermined the notion that Germany stood apart from its southern neighbours in terms of high-level party political corruption. Referred to in the German press as 'Don Kohleone', the former chancellor's refusal to name the donors compounded his apparent readiness to break German laws which forbid the keeping of secret accounts. Scandals involving the Social Democrats (SPD) were described in *The Economist* (3 February 2000) as 'small beer compared with the Christian Democrats' elaborate system of anonymous cash donations, party slush funds worth many millions of D-marks, and secret foreign accounts built up over decades.' Kohl was subsequently alleged to be implicated in the major French 'Elf affair', in which the oil company apparently operated a huge slush fund during the presidency of François Mitterrand. Authorities in Germany have investigated the purchase by the former state-owned company of a German oil refinery in 1992, with money allegedly funnelled to Kohl's reelection campaign. The Elf scandal also involved allegations against a number of other senior politicians and business people, including former Prime Minister Edith Cresson, the former Finance Minister Dominique Strauss-Kahn and – most notably – former Foreign Office Minister and President of the Constitutional Council Roland Dumas who, in May 2001, was handed a 30 months prison sentence for corruption.

The Elf affair generated huge media interest, not least because it also involved the ex-mistress of Dumas, Christine Deviers-Joncour, who gave the title 'Whore of the Republic' to her own account of her role (Deviers-Joncour, 1999) and claimed she was paid £6.6 million (€10.7 million) by the oil company to put pressure on Dumas to reverse the French government's refusal to sell frigates to Taiwan. Deviers-Joncour was imprisoned as a result of the scandal, along with three others. In another book, Pierre Lethier (2001), a former secret service agent who allegedly was the conduit for 'commissions' paid in Germany by Elf, claimed that the oil company paid off several Africans in favour of the French state. Although the Elf affair mainly touched on leading figures from the Mitterrand era, including the late President and his son, Jean-Christophe, the presidency of Jacques Chirac also found itself involved in a series of high-profile scandals by the end of the 1990s. Again, one of the central accusations amidst allegations of personal enrichment and misuse of public office was that Chirac had been involved in illegal funding of his party, the Rassemblement pour la République (RPR). Immune from investigation whilst in office, Chirac was caught up in the mysterious case of a video-taped testimony by an RPR official, Jean-Claude Méry, which was made public in September 2000 (after Méry's death) by the Socialist politician, Dominique Strauss-Kahn, himself under investigation for false account-ing. Meanwhile, the Secretary-General of the French Communist Party, Robert Hue, was also charged with illegal fund-raising, and the former RPR Premier, Alain Juppé, was under investigation for his activities when in charge of the Paris city budget during Chirac's long period as mayor of the French capital (1977–95).

Explaining political corruption: social capital versus incentive structures

There are two broad approaches to explaining the prevalence of high-level political corruption in contemporary democracies. On the one hand, some analysts have stressed the importance of cultural factors in providing a climate which is conducive to corruption. In particular, the notion of social capital (Putnam, 1993) – that is, the networks of civic engagement which allow people to develop social trust and norms of reciprocity – has been widely cited as a positive good which can help inhibit the spread of corruption. Where norms of reciprocity and social trust are well-developed, it is held, corruption will not prosper; where they are lacking, the opportunities to engage in corrupt practice will be greatly increased. Thus, Tanzi (1994, 1998) points to a division between an efficient, rule-bound north and a back-scratching, favour-driven south: 'the very features that make a country a less cold and indifferent place are the same that increase the difficulty of enforcing arm's length rules so essential for modern efficient markets and governments.' On the other hand, it has been argued that high-level political corruption, like all other forms of corruption, is more a function of specific incentives (Rose-Ackerman, 1999). Individuals – wherever they are – voluntarily engage in corrupt activity when the perceived returns outweigh the potential costs, and therefore the key to reducing corruption lies in altering the incentive structure.

That political parties have been at the centre of so many high-level corruption scandals points to the need to focus on common patterns, which suggest there may well be particular incentives, as well as opportunity structures, characteristic of established western democracies which have increased the propensity to high-level political corruption. They also suggest that institutional factors, rather than social capital, are more likely to offer insights into the apparent rise in high-level political corruption throughout Europe (Pujas and Rhodes, 1999a). As della Porta (2001, p. 1) has commented, 'Clearly, incentives to corruption increase (as they do for any other illegal activity) as the probability of being discovered and punished decreases – that is, the less efficient the control mechanisms are.' However, incentives are not related solely to the likelihood or otherwise of discovery. There are other factors which also need to be considered, including the lack of political will to strengthen anti-corruption legislation, a culture of secrecy within West European governments, and a failure to provide adequate protection for 'whistleblowers'. A further factor of signal importance in the emergence of high-level political corruption concerns the financing of political parties and the regulations by which it is monitored and controlled. Peter Eigen, chairman of Transparency International, commented in October 2000:

> The current wave of corruption scandals we are witnessing across Europe is not about personal enrichment – it's about the purchase of access to policy-makers, and political parties are the prime target in this game. (Transparency International, 2000a)

Many countries have in the past allowed tax deductions on bribes distributed to foreign officials in order to win lucrative contracts, including Austria, Belgium, Denmark, France, Germany, Luxembourg, the Netherlands, Norway, Portugal, Sweden and Switzerland (Milliet-Einbinder, 2000). The 1997 OECD Convention on Combatting Bribery of Foreign Public Officials in International Business Transactions, Phase One of which entered into force in April 1999, was adopted by all 29 OECD members – but by June 2000 only 21 states had ratified the Convention, amongst which just nine were in Europe (Austria, Belgium, Finland, Germany, Greece, Spain, Switzerland, Sweden and the United Kingdom). Whilst the OECD initiative suggests that some progress is being made, it remains the case that changes in the law may not produce changes in practice. Moreover, there is evidence that European states have been ready to fall back on arguments about national security to cover their actions. During the Elf case, referred to above, when judge Renaud van Ruymbeke asked French customs officials to provide a list of bribes declared by Elf-Aquitaine, the request was refused on the grounds that the information constituted a 'state secret' and to release it would compromise national security. In the United Kingdom in 1992, lawyers acting for the defence in the Matrix Churchill affair – which involved the sale of machine tools to Iraq in contravention of a ban on exports of defence equipment – found their requests for the release of documents held by the Department of Trade and Industry blocked by the issuing of Public Interest Immunity (PII) certificates signed by four ministers. The PII certificates were signed on the grounds that national security was at stake. Similarly, during the GAL trial in Spain in the mid-1990s, Prime Minister González referred to 'reasons of state' for the non-disclosure of information.

González also provides a representative example of what might be termed the 'untouchable' status of serving leaders in many West European states. His own position was never seen as seriously threatened by the GAL affair whilst in office, even though his personal reputation and that of his government was seriously damaged by the string of corruption scandals which emerged during the early 1990s. In some countries, such as France, the head of state is immune from investigation. In others, although there may be no formal prohibition there is often little that can be done in practical terms to force compliance with judicial investigations. The recourse to 'reasons of state' is consistent with the idea that there are certain activities within the domain of political leaders which must remain secret and hidden, and that intelligence services may be used to serve the political ends of the government. In France, the arrest in April 2000 under strange circumstances of Brigitte Henri, head of the intelligence agency (RG) regional office in Grenoble, aroused suspicion that her investigations of corruption and financial fraud by senior politicians in the RPR threatened to embarrass the President, Chirac. In spite of detailed reports compiled by Henri on illicit funding of Gaullist party activities, no formal investigations were launched by the justice or interior ministries. 'Reasons of state' have also been used to justify 'reserve' or secret funds available to governments: in Spain, the GAL were financed using interior ministry reserve funds, whilst in France it is widely believed that incoming governments have access to a 'special fund', comprising up to 0.1 per cent of the state budget. The use of such funds is naturally not accessible to audit committees, thereby undermining the commitment to transparency and accountability which underpins democratic governance.

A culture of confidentiality within government and public administration in most West European states also militates against the revelation of malpractice and corruption (Vincent, 2000). Although often portrayed in the media as heroes for confronting the excesses of their employers, whistleblowers in large organizations are very often systematically targeted and discredited. The Government Accountability Project (GAP), based in Seattle, describes standard tactics used against whistleblowers, which include questioning their motives, manufacturing a poor record, threatening, isolating or humiliating them, setting them up for failure, prosecuting them, and blighting their career. The costs of whistleblowing can thus be high, in spite of the fact that many government departments and public organizations have codes or conventions to 'protect' whistleblowers. The case of Paul van Buitenen, the EU Commission official who was a member of an audit team and wrote a report on fraud in the Commission, is instructive: suspended and subjected to disciplinary procedures, van Buitenen found his attempts to return to his job blocked even though the Commission Executive resigned *en masse* in March 1999 after a scathing independent report into its activities. Indeed, in contrast to the USA, the term 'whistleblowing' has no legal definition in EU or UK law, although in the latter case the Public Interest Disclosure Act of 1998 was designed to promote greater openness in the workplace and involved an amendment of the 1996 Employment Protection Act. The new act would not, however, have protected either Clive Ponting or Sarah Tisdall, who were prosecuted under the Official Secrets Act for leaking documents about the sinking of the Argentinian ship *The General Belgrano* and the siting of US missiles.

Political corruption and party finances

If the above factors help elucidate the institutional context within which high-level political corruption is able to develop, resist detection and even flourish, they do not in themselves explain the incentives to engage in corrupt activity. For any given individual, there may be a number of incentives ranging from personal venality to misplaced loyalty or commitment to a cause. Much of the work which has focused on incentives stresses an economic imperative, usually in terms of self-interested individuals engaging in rent-seeking behaviour (Rose-Ackerman, 1999). However, the common elements of many high-level corruption scandals across Western Europe – particularly those in which political parties are the intended beneficiaries – suggest the need to look beyond individual motivation towards more generic incentives. Two factors are significant in this regard: need and opportunity. In respect of need, an issue of central importance is the growing financial demands placed on political parties and their difficulties in meeting them: in most West European states, membership dues barely cover the most basic costs and are nowhere near enough to meet the demands of virtually permanent media campaigns (*The Economist*, 27 January 2000). In the words of the Neill Committee's report on parties in the UK, which are equally applicable to all West European democracies:

> Without doubt, the parties' belief that elections can only be won by the expenditure (mainly on advertising) of vast sums of money has given rise to something of an arms race. This in turn has put enormous pressure on party fundraisers to devise imaginative ways of attracting donations. (paragraph 5.3)

In terms of opportunity, emphasis should be placed on the nature of party finance regulation, the system of checks and balances, and the existence of new possibilities for corrupt activity related to the blurring of the public/private boundary.

The financing of political parties has historically been a source of controversy and debate (Ware, 1998). In the 1950s and 1960s, public funding of parties was widely – though by no means universally – adopted as a means of securing the operation of democracy. The arguments in favour of public financing were essentially two-fold: on the one hand it was held to secure greater equality of access to resources, according to transparent formulae, which would underpin freedom of political expression; on the other it offered a means of regulating and controlling spending, for instance by specifying maximum limits on expenditure and requiring that sources of finance through donations be revealed. In broad terms, three approaches to party funding can be identified (see Table 10.1): states which have a high degree of state control over party financing (Austria, Belgium, France, Greece, Ireland, the Netherlands and Switzerland), states which follow a more market-led approach, with no state funding (the United Kingdom), and states which have a public–private mix of funding (Germany, Italy, Spain and Sweden). France allowed a public–private mix until 1995 when private financing was abolished (with some exceptions) following a string of scandals involving major French firms. The adoption of state funding has contributed to what Katz and Mair (1995) termed 'cartel parties', characterized by management through a professional core of salaried officials, and typically rely heavily on state subsidies. Resting on the twin pillars of the state and civil society, their ambiguous position can lead to the blurring of the distinction between these two spheres, as party bureaucracies effectively become para-state organizations.

Lyrintzis (1984, pp. 103–4) has spoken of 'bureaucratic clientelism', when parties use the resources of the state to build up clienteles by granting favours and resources:

> Bureaucratic clientelism . . . consists of systematic infiltration of the state machine by party devotees and the allocation of favours through it. It is characterised by an organised expansion of existing

Table 10.1 Party funding in selected European states

Country	State funding of political parties	Donations from firms or trade unions	Foreign donations	Accounts published	Level above which donations are declared	Limits on donations and party spending
Belgium	Yes	No	Yes	Yes	BEF 5000 (€124)	National and candidate spending limits; some donor limits
France	Yes	No (since 1995) but some exceptions	No	Yes	FFR 1000 (€153)	Limits on spending; FFR 50 000 (€7622) limit on individual donations
Germany	Yes	Yes (no tax exemptions)	No	Yes	DEM 20 000 (€10 225)	None
Italy	Yes	Yes	Yes	Yes	ITL 5 000 000 (€2583)	National and candidate spending limits; some donor limits
Spain	Yes	Yes	No	Yes	5 per cent of state aid	National and candidate spending limits; some donor limits
Sweden	Yes	Yes	Yes	Yes	None	None
United Kingdom	No	Yes	No*	No**	£5000 (€8090)	Candidate spending limits; recommended limit for national spending; no donation limit

Notes: * Since February 2001; ** no legal requirements, but parties publish basic accounts.
Source: The Economist, 27 January 2000; the *Guardian*, 18 January 2001.

posts and departments in the public sector and the addition of new ones in an attempt to secure power and maintain a party's electoral base.

A variation on 'bureaucratic clientelism' is what might be termed 'institutional clientelism', characteristic of several developed democracies in which the state has been 'hollowed out'. As many of the activities and responsibilities of the state have been reassigned, with competences transferred to sub-national governments, semi-autonomous regulatory bodies, quangos and 'third-sector' organizations (voluntary, non-profit or charitable organizations which have become the 'private agents of public policy'), so opportunities for patronage have increased. Whilst patronage may not in itself be politically corrupt, it can easily shade into the kind of 'mediated corruption' (referred to above) which undermines the democratic process. Moreover, it could be argued that the privatization of state-owned assets and the 'hiving off' of state activities have created new opportunity structures for political corruption. These structures have been exploited by political parties seeking to confront the financial demands imposed by the changing nature of electoral competition in advanced democracies, and have led to the emergence of a form of institutional clientelism in which political parties and private financial interests have sought to extract mutually beneficial advantage from privatization initiatives and deregulation.

Examples of such activity can be found in countries as ostensibly different as Spain (southern, recently democratized, with a weak civil society and a reputation for high levels of corruption) and the United Kingdom (northern, one of the world's oldest democracies, with an active civil society and a reputation for very low levels of corruption), suggesting that opportunity structures represent a critical variable. In Spain, the Socialist administrations of Felipe González (1982–96) systematically used their control of the state machinery to reward party members and sympathisers by giving them jobs in the public administration. Between 1982 and 1994, more than half a million new state jobs were created (Beltrán 1996, p. 269). The PSOE (Partido Socialista Obrero Español) also made direct appointments to some 25 000 administrative posts between 1984 and 1987 (Gillespie, 1989, pp. 83–4), largely related to the new autonomous regions. Given the small number of party members such patronage was highly significant, with some 70 per cent of party members being either functionaries or public office holders by the 1990s (Gillespie, 1994, p. 55). The PSOE did not engage in distributing jobs (or promises of jobs) on a scale similar to the Christian Democratic and Socialist leaders in southern Italy; instead, rather than develop Italian-style relationships of exchange between party representatives and voters, the PSOE was more concerned to establish links with business firms and entrepreneurs in order to secure party funding (Cazorla, 1994).

In the UK, whilst there is no real evidence of party loyalty being rewarded with jobs in the public administration (widely seen as being virtually free of corruption), state resources can be used to promote party interests, as some believe has been happening on an increasing scale since the 1980s. A perennial issue of concern has been the use of the honours system which is widely seen as being open to abuse. It has been estimated that under Margaret Thatcher, 'of 174 private-sector industrialists given peerages or knighthoods, 85 were connected with companies that had given a total of £13.6 million (€22 million) to the Conservative Party or to front organizations laundering money for the party' (Adonis, 1997, p. 114). Industrialists were apparently 10 times more likely to be awarded honours if their firms had donated money to the Conservative Party. Other means by which loyalty can be rewarded include former ministers being offered highly paid directorships in the private sector, in some cases even in firms they had been involved in privatizing. Equally, the continued creation of quangos – responsible by the mid-1990s for some 20 per cent of public spending – provided opportunity structures for corruption. Reports by the Audit Commission have regularly highlighted concerns about the suitability of some of the appointments made to and by quangos, with growing evidence of misuse of funds and poor management of budgets.

In both the UK and Spain, the 'hollowing-out' of the state, parallel with deregulation and privatization initiatives, have provided powerful possibilities for institutional corruption. As Rose-Ackerman (1999, p. 35) has observed, 'the process of transferring assets to private owner-ship is fraught with corrupt opportunities'. For instance, uncertainties over the valuation of state enterprises can favour corrupt insiders in the bidding process. In Spain, in particular, privatization processes have been shrouded in secrecy in respect to their precise structure and status (Chari, 1999). Meanwhile, in the UK, contracting-out, or 'outsourcing' of state supplies, has further contributed to the sense that accountability and transparency are wanting. As Doig and Wilson (1997) concluded, the risks of corruption are greater under contracting-out. Political parties – especially those in power – have shifted their interests increasingly towards cultivating relationships with the business and financial worlds on whom they often depend for financial support, and away from their own members.

Nearly all major political parties in Europe have faced the 'double whammy' of increased costs and declining membership (Katz *et al.*,

1992). For some parties, notably those in the Iberian democracies, this problem has been compounded by the fact that they have operated under democratic conditions only since the mid-1970s, and therefore never enjoyed the financial benefits of mass membership. However, even mass parties in the 1950s and 1960s were never able to cover the costs of election campaigns from membership dues and relied on outside donations. As the costs of politics have spiralled, together with the number of elections in an era of multilevel governance, so the need to attract funding has exponentially increased. Political parties are effectively impelled to seek new means of raising their income, and the development of illicit mechanisms to do so should come as no surprise. As Ware (1998, p. 236) observes, 'The demand for money makes even highly questionable sources attractive to parties, and it is important to find ways of keeping such funds hidden from public view.' The incentive to seek such funds is particularly high when mechanisms of regulation and accountability are found wanting – widely held to be the case in many democracies.

Political corruption and the contestation of governance

If it is true that the need to find additional resources in the context of declining memberships has provided a powerful incentive for political parties to become involved in corrupt activity, and that the blurring of the distinction between public and private sectors has provided an ideal opportunity structure, this supports the idea that institutional factors are more important than cultural ones in accounting for much contemporary high-level political corruption in Western Europe (Pujas and Rhodes, 1999a). However, whilst opportunities for parties to engage in corrupt fund-raising may have increased in the last two decades, the existence of party-related corruption is hardly new. For instance, in the so-called Flick scandal which emerged in the early 1980s, politicians were accused of taking cash in return for granting tax breaks. It was alleged that Flick funds had been used to support the Spanish Socialist Party during the mid-1970s. In early 2000, it emerged that the German state had earmarked up to £10 million (€16 million) via the federal intelligence services to support democratic parties in Iberia during the 1970s and 1980s (*Guardian*, 2 February 2000). Similarly, in Italy, the appropriation of public resources by state functionaries, entrepreneurs and members of the criminal world was a systemic feature of the postwar political arrangements superintended by the Christian Democrats and Socialists (della Porta and Vannucci, 1999).

What may be new, however, is the likelihood that a scandal will be produced once the evidence of corruption has been exposed. This directly raises the issue of the relationship between the objective circumstances of corrupt activity and the proliferation of corruption scandals across all European countries. As argued by Pujas and Rhodes (1999b), one of the explanations for the sudden wave of scandals that broke across southern Europe in the 1990s was a redefinition of relations between parties and between political and other social actors – notably the media and the magistracy. On the one hand corruption has been politicized to the extent that political parties that once competed on ideology but colluded in corruption, completely revised their tactics as the salience of older *choix de société* issues declined. As the party platforms of the left and right have gradually converged, and as the pressure to make policies on technical, legal-rational grounds has increased, so the grounds of political competition have correspondingly shifted. In some countries, the 1980s and 1990s did witness an increase in political competition – either with the appearance of new parties (such as the Italian Lega Nord) or as a function of exacerbated factional strife within large party structures (the Spanish PSOE, split between *renovadores* and *guerristas*, and the French RPR). But a more general trend has been for parties to engage in corruption-linked mudslinging as a proxy for past ideological conflict. As the salience of 'clean government' has risen in public opinion, so has the opportunity for parties to engage in 'holier-than-thou' political tactics in their effort to attract and cement in place political support from growing numbers of floating and ideologically disoriented voters.

Of course, political parties do not compete in a vacuum. One of the key characteristics of the new wave of scandals of the 1990s was the emergence of a new breed of anti-corruption magistrates and a press and wider media much less supine and in thrall to political parties or rich proprietors than in the past (della Porta, 2001). In the southern European countries, this process could be seen in part as one of democratic 'maturation', as judges and newspapers emerged from highly 'corporatist', post-authoritarian constraints. But the revelations of recent large-scale scandals in some of the supposedly 'less corrupt' northern countries suggests that all countries may find themselves in 'cycles of contestation', as elites rotate in power and as the attention of the public is alerted to (or tires of) media exposures. Certainly the renovation and modernization of political movements in a number of countries has had a generational effect, as younger politicians have sought to displace or distance themselves from their older political forebears. In many countries, changes in the career patterns and personalities of crusading judges and journalists – and, perhaps more critically, their political backing and public support – will also feed into the cycle. A cycle of this kind may help explain the current acquiescence and apathy of the press and public opinion in Italy which stands in marked contrast to the explosion of protest, media attention and political denunciation of scandal in Italy in the early 1990s. For it is not as if the problem has 'gone away'. In the run up to the 2001 election of Silvio Berlusconi – a man who regularly denounced the 'hero judges' of the anti-corruption crusades as politically motivated 'reds' and who has himself been the subject of various corruption indictments – there was little sign of the public indignation that led to the collapse of the Christian Democrat and Socialist Parties in 1992 and 1993. Few of those indicted ever stood trial in Italy, while some of the key figures in the anti-corruption magistracy have resigned or abandoned the pursuit of still open legal cases. It may even be that in the Italian case the political catharsis of the scandals in the early 1990s has exhausted the public's appetite (and that of many politicians) for further political upheaval.

The Italian example may also point to a broader phenomenon in which certain democracies remain resistant to fundamental changes in established behaviour, either because their elites are incapable of developing and implementing effective new rules, or because the fragility of their regulatory frameworks means that probity and accountability in public life are never fully embedded in norms and institutions. As Philp (2000) has argued, well-regulated and institutionalized political systems require two types of accountability – the formal (based on rules) and the political (based on mutually-recognized standards of behaviour). Anti-corruption measures may be able to strengthen the former, but the latter (based on parliamentary or public endorsement) are much harder to develop and embed. If the hypothesis concerning the existence of a cycle of contestation is correct, then in some countries the layers of political accountability may gradually be put in place, but continued vigilance and repetitive waves of protest and scandal may be required to make them effective. Yet in the advanced democracies, new forms of public management and the devolution of public services to private agencies have not just created new incentives and opportunities for corruption, as already discussed; they have also blurred the lines between public servants and political masters and thus between formal and political accountability.

In an ideal democratic world, 'formal accountability procedures enhance authority where they signal reasons for trust in the political system and confidence in those who rule' (Philp, 2000, p. 10). 'Trust' and 'confidence', of course, bring us back to the notion of social capital; however, the concept of social capital is notoriously difficult to use as a measuring stick or analytical tool when thinking about the corruption proclivities of diverse polities. Social capital – if conceived in terms of a dense network of trust-based relationships, linking the individual through the family to the community at large – may even be strengthened as the general level of confidence in politicians declines. Thus, the contestation of governance associated with corruption scandals may be well-suited to the delegitimization of one set of elites but much less-suited to the legitimization of a new one. If, in the meantime, people fall back on more traditional, depoliticized forms of association as party membership and ideological identification decline, then social capital could conceivably increase as public support for elites erodes. Like formal accountability, alternation in power is a central feature of a healthy well-functioning democracy, but the extent to which alternation can in itself contribute to the creation of relations of confidence and trust where they do not already exist is open to question. Indeed, to take the Italian case again, the experience of scandal on a wide scale seems to have contributed to voter cynicism and apathy given the decline in voter turnout, especially among the young. If the scrutiny exercised by the electorate is impaired, then one of the key elements of democratic legitimacy also fails – and the incentives to engage in corrupt behaviour may thereby be increased.

Conclusions

Creating 'integrity' in public behaviour will, in the end, depend on the creation of a virtuous circle between formal rules of accountability, informal accountability, the constant and assiduous scrutiny of a genuinely free and diversified media (a key element of informal accountability), trust in political procedures and access to power. It is not the mere existence of these factors that will reduce the incentives for corrupt behaviour, but their interaction. To that extent, although it may seem trite to say so, governance must be permanently contested in the day-to-day operation of the polity, rather than depend on the periodic clean-up and catharsis imparted by system-shaking scandal. But contestation is not the same as competition, and competition for power is not the same as the active challenging of power. Nor does competition in the market (a fanciful notion which is blind to the reality that markets have a natural tendency to concentrate power) necessarily rule out corruption among politicians and public servants. Thus the emphasis by the growing multilateral crusade against corruption led by international organizations and NGOs on a generic notion of 'good governance', based on the extension of western conceptions of free markets and competition between elites and accompanied by a proliferation of formal rules, may well be misplaced (IMF, 1997; Transparency International, 2000b).

Neither market competition nor political competition necessarily safeguards a system against corrupt behaviour. And the expansion of formal rules may simply complicate the system, providing new incentives for illicit activity unless public scrutiny and the informal side of the accountability equation is not also strengthened.

Chapter 11

Territorial Politics and the New Regionalism

MICHAEL KEATING

One of the striking features of modern European politics is the reemergence of territory; a new regionalism is changing the political geography both of individual states and of Europe as a whole. Yet it is an elusive phenomenon, taking different forms in different places, linked to a variety of social and political movements and operating at several geographical scales. We can speak of economic regions, cultural regions, political regions and administrative regions, which may or may not coincide in space. The scale of regions goes from the European Union, considered by international-relations specialists as an example of 'regional' integration, to the 'city region' consisting of an urban area and its hinterland. What the various meanings have in common is that they refer to emerging social and political arenas beyond the nation-state.

It is a commonplace that the European state is currently undergoing major transformations. It is challenged from above, by the complex of processes captured by the shorthand term 'globalization' and by European integration; from below, by the emergence of regionalist, localist and minority nationalist movements; and laterally by the advance of the market and of civil society. As a result the state is being restructured both functionally and territorially, and its claims to a capacity for broad social regulation are questioned. This challenges integrationist theories of state-building and development which tended to see integration as a one-way process (Deutsch, 1966), usually equated with modernization and progress. These accounts have gradually given way to more subtle and less determinist analyses of the links between territory, function and political authority over time. In the 1960s and 1970s, Stein Rokkan (1980) traced the evolution of the European state system on a grand scale and pointed to continuing fault-lines and instances of imperfect integration. In the 1980s and 1990s social scientists posed further questions about the evolution of states, why we ended up with the ones we have, and what might have happened had circumstances been different (Tilly, 1990; Spruyt, 1994). From the

1990s, major historiographical disputes erupted in several countries on the sources of state legitimacy, the rights of minorities and the existence of pluralistic and more open traditions of statehood. It is no coincidence that these historiographical controversies should have exploded just at the time when the authority of the state in social and economic regulation is being called into question. We are now being forced to realize how strongly the social sciences were influenced by the nation-state framework in which they developed. Political scientists are increasingly inclined to see national integration as a continued exercise in statecraft and management rather than as a one-off process (Keating, 1988). Jurists are demystifying the state as the source of all law, and looking at legal pluralism and the emergence of normative orders beyond the state (McCormick, 1999). Social geographers and economic sociologists are examining systems of social regulation and economic production rooted in territories below and beyond the state.

The reconfiguration of the state has taken many forms but our interest here is the territorial dimension and the emergence of regions as new systems of social regulation and collective action, below the state and, to some degree, beyond it. The 'new regionalism' (Keating, 1998) is a complex set of processes and influences, since the interplay of function, identity, political mobilization, systems of representation and government varies across the states of Europe and increasingly within them. Three dimensions are of critical importance: economic restructuring; new social and political movements; and institutional change. The interplay among these in the context of global and European integration goes a long way to explain the complexity and diversity of the phenomenon.

Economic restructuring

There has in recent years been a radical change in thinking about economic development and its relationship with territory. Generally, in neo-classical and Keynesian economic theory territory is not considered an important factor in itself. Location matters only as it affects the distance of a firm from its raw materials and its markets and this is fundamentally a matter of cost or the availability of transport infrastructure. It is thus possible for a government, taxes and subsidies to persuade investors to locate their plants in its preferred places. In a closed national economy (such as most European states after the 1930s depression), these have no alternative but to comply. Following the Second World War, governments, faced with problems of underdevelopment in some regions and obsolescence in others (notably in the older industrial areas of the United Kingdom), put in place ever-more elaborate mechanisms to manage their spatial economies by diverting investment to areas of need. At a time of overall full employment, this was presented as a zero-sum policy in which the needy areas would benefit from added investment, the booming areas from the relief of pressure, and the national economy from mobilizing resources in peripheral areas that would otherwise remain idle. The broad aim was to reintegrate declining areas into national economies, while preparing to face European competition and the opening of global markets. Policies, initially based on fiscal incentives and grants and on planning controls, gradually became more sophisticated as governments engaged in spatial planning (especially in France, Scandinavia and the Netherlands) and sought to build 'growth poles' around key sectors. Policy was overwhelmingly top-down, aimed at integrating the regions into the national economy, but as strategies became more elaborate governments sought partners on the ground among local political and economic elites. In France, Italy, Belgium and the United Kingdom, regional development councils were established to engage in concerted action and integrate central and local efforts. These were not generally a great success, caught as they were between central demands and local needs, but they did succeed in politicizing what was until then a rather technical exercise. In France, Italy and Belgium, regional planning councils gave way over time to elected regional government, while in the United Kingdom they atrophied until their abolition in 1979, but were revived in a new form in England in 1999. In Germany, there was a less corporatist approach to regional development which was handled intergovernmentally though the Joint Tasks Framework between the federal government and the Länder.

Centralized regional policies increasingly came into question after the oil crisis of the 1970s. With the end of full employment, the consensus on diversionary policy collapsed and regions had to compete for development. Some of the large developments sponsored by governments failed to take root or to spark self-sustaining growth around them, giving rise to the jibe that they were 'cathedrals in the desert'. It Italy, the system of regional development had been captured by the *partitocrazia* and subordinated to a clientelistic logic of divisible benefits, with projects being broken up into small pieces and losing their critical mass. With the opening of markets and increased capital mobility, governments were unable to prevent firms locating in boom areas since they would otherwise flee the country altogether. Regional policy thus lost its economic rationale and was sustained only for social and political reasons. This led to a change of focus from large regions and into smaller-scale local and urban initiatives.

At the same time, there has been a change in academic thinking about regional and local development, which has supported the move away from top-down planning and towards more locally-based approaches. The new scholarly thinking is rich and complex and it is difficult in a short summary to do it justice, but some themes stand out. One is a new emphasis on place, considered as more than mere location (Agnew, 1987) but as a complex of social relationships, norms, institutions and understandings. This idea draws on the literature on economic sociology (Swedberg, 1993) and on the social construction of the market (Bagnasco and Trigilia, 1993) to show that economic development is more than about merely assembling factors of production in a physical space. The social structure of places is important, so that parachuting an investment into an inappropriate locale is unlikely to lead to success. Successful regions are said to possess social capital (Coleman, 1988; Putnam *et al.*, 1993), by which is meant patterns of social relationships and trust that permit a balance of cooperation and competition, allowing the production of public goods and long-term collective investment (Sabel, 1993). Economists have long recognized traded dependencies based on the linkages among producers and suppliers or complementary firms in traditional industrial districts – and that these formed the basis for the growth-pole strategies of the past. The new approaches adds untraded interdependencies (Courchene, 1995; Morgan, 1995; Scott, 1998) arising from the 'milieu' or informal patterns of cooperation and support, and the proximity of innovators, research facilities and associations within a region. These sustain networks and foster the associational economy (Cooke and Morgan, 1998) which combines market competition with social cooperation. Another key idea is that of the learning region (Morgan, 1995) in which innovation is self-sustaining. The focus here is not on the large firms of the past, but on small businesses engaged in flexible production in response to changing markets. Economies of scale are achieved not within the firm, as in conventional theory, but at the level of the local system of production. Such economies are particularly important for small and medium-sized firms based on flexible specialization.

So the locality, from being a mere space in which market forces operate, becomes a key element in production itself. The basis unit of production is no longer the individual firm, but the whole productive space of the region. The old idea of comparative advantage under which every region had a place in the national and international division of labour, underlying traditional regional policy, has given way to absolute or competitive advantage (Scott, 1998) in which regions, not just firms, compete for investment, markets and technology. This has radical implications for politics since it postulates a common regional interest in competition overriding other solidarities of class, sector, gender, age or ethnicity. It encourages a neo-mercantilist form of politics in which politicians can portray the region as pitched into ceaseless competition for market advantage. How much such political appeals are based on hard economic reality, and how much on the political interpretation of it, is another question.

Regional development policy has been refocused. It is more decentralized to the regional or local level where the capacity for horizontal integration and knowledge of problems is greatest (Cappellin, 1995). It places less emphasis now on physical infrastructure and more on human resources development. Training policies have widely been decentralized to complement other instruments of intervention and education has often been tied into economic policy in a more direct way than before. There is also a strong emphasis on research, development and technology transfer through networks and linkages among firms and between them, universities, research centres and governments. There is less emphasis on synoptic planning or large-scale intervention and more on 'steering' and selective intervention to remedy market failures. There is a focus on the need to determine the region's niche in the global economy and to foster clusters of industries that can exploit this best and sustain each other. Endogenous and self-sustaining growth is the new formula for success. Neither big government nor big business can save the regions but, by proper organization, dense networks of small and medium-sized firms can forge a productive system to take on global competition.

These policy ideas have been developed and diffused, through academic networks, conferences, consultants, interregional associations and European Union (EU) regional policies across Europe, so as almost to amount to a new consensus. The Commission, as a requirement for funding, has insisted on a shift in priorities away from hard infrastructure, and on partnership arrangements with all levels of government and the private sector. New member states have had to adopt regional structures in accordance with best modern practice, and prospective member states are encouraged, through the PHARE programme, to regionalize themselves. Regional leaders throughout Europe have adopted a similar discourse, stressing markets, public–private partnership and the need for stronger regional institutions. Indeed the model of the networked or learning region has become something of a received wisdom. A cynic might even detect a circular process in which academics sell the idea to policy-makers; they adopt the corresponding rhetoric and then other academics come and study it as part of the social reality.

There has indeed emerged a new generation of prophets of the new regionalism as an encompassing system of social regulation – there are clear parallels with the way in which other partial ideas like Keynesianism or post-Fordism have been applied to the entire social world. Kenichi Ohmae (1995), writing from a neo-liberal perspective, jumps directly from the emergence of economic regions to the end of the nation-state. He portrays a world of thrusting, dynamic regions jostling for advantage in world competition, although anyone with the least familiarity with some of his examples will harbour their doubts. Putnam (1993) has extrapolated from a much-contested study of Italian regions into a whole theory of society, including democratic performance and economic growth. Cooke and Morgan (1998) see the new regionalist paradigm as both more economically efficient and socially just than its neo-classical or neo-liberal alternatives. It lends itself to a 'third-way' type of politics between neo-liberalism and social democracy. The left like it because of its criticisms of unbridled capitalism, and the right because it is against big government and social engineering. These claims have in turn sparked a series of repostes, based on (a) the inadequacies of the model, and (b) the dangers of extrapolating from functional economic change to political and institutional restructuring without taking into account politics, culture and the influence of institutions themselves (Pintarits, 1996).

Critics of the model often claim that it generalizes excessively from a few cases, firstly in central Italy, then in southern Germany (Hadjmichaelis and Papamics, 1991; Ritaine, 1989; Lovering, 1999). They criticize the portrayal of small firms as the salvation of the region. Small firms might be important generators of jobs and innovation but they are very often dependent on the presence of large firms or government. The growth of business services, for example, is often the result of large firms outsourcing these services rather than a form of endogenous development. By no means are all regions characterized by flexible specialization. Indeed, insofar as the model is based on the need to tailor policies to the needs of specific locations and the recognition that there is no 'one best way' to success, one might ask whether there is a model at all (Storper, 1997). Imitation of success stories in other regions is likely to be counter-productive, because the circumstances are different and because the other region has got their first occupying that niche in the international division of production.

It does seem that something is happening here, that the relationship between territory and economic change is changing, but the functionalist explanation that political form follows economic function is no more persuasive here than it is as a theory of European integration. Regions are emerging as a key level of economic change in Europe, but the way they are doing so depends on the balance of social and political forces in each case. The neo-mercantilist strategy seeks to subordinate all considerations to that of competitive growth, but this is as much a matter of political choice as economic imperative. There are many ways in which regions might react to the demands of economic change and the opening of global markets. Since the region is not a fixed concrete reality but a socially constructed system of action, we need to ask just how it is constructed and what is the balance of social and political forces within it. Even restricting the analysis to the field of economic development, we can see that there is more than one way of adapting to global competition and the response will depend on the balance of forces within the region, or the 'regional development coalition'.

In an earlier work (Keating, 1998) I identified four ideal types of regional development coalition. In the low cost or 'sweatshop' model, the region is a policy-taker, seeking to attract investment through keeping social overheads down, low taxation, lax regulation, low wages and an absence of trade unions. This model, common in the southern states of the USA, is generally disdained in Europe as a form of 'social dumping' and restrained by national and European rules, but it can be discerned nonetheless. A second model, 'bourgeois regionalism' is a high-cost strategy for development, emphasizing heavy investment in infrastructure, technology, training and education in order to stimulate and attract high value-added activities. It is associated with regions which have their own network of indigenous business elites and a favourable position in world markets. The 'social democratic' model is also a high-cost one, but includes labour and social interests in the dominant coalition and emphasizes social spending as well as investment. Finally, the 'nation building' model is primarily political in intent, seeking to enhance territorial autonomy and to incorporate a strong cultural and political dimension. Economic development may be an important goal of nation-builders but, given its ambitious aims, the coalition needs a wide social and political base and cannot pursue growth at the expense of social cohesion. These four types are not exclusive and any given case is likely to show a combination of the elements depending on the local political balance and institutional opportunities. We must, therefore, study politics and institutions in their own right.

The politics of regions

Social and political interests have also changed their focus in response to the new regionalism, but in varying ways. Capital has been consolidating at the European and global levels through mergers and alliances but, given the new importance of territory, business has also become more conscious of the local and regional level. Business interests have become more or less active members of regional development coalitions across Europe and have favoured institutional reforms to give more focus to regional development and business support. They have not, however, favoured elected regional governments, fearing that these could be used to impose extra regulation or be dominated by labour and social interests. Trade unions have traditionally been rather centralist, looking to the state to provide equality of labour regulation and welfare services and fearing the division of the working-class movement. Since the 1970s, however, there has been a certain trend to decentralization, as unions have become involved in local struggles over plant closures and have rediscovered territory as a basis for social solidarity. Like the social democratic parties, they have refurbished older traditions of localism and, while previously inclined to corporatist arrangements for regional government in which they would be directly represented, now tend to support elected regional governments and the strengthening of local governments. New social movements, especially environmentalists, have been committed to regional and local action in principle and as a level at which they can more easily organize. The result has been a certain shift of regionalism, previously associated over much of Europe with conservatism, towards the progressive or left-wing pole. Social democratic parties have rediscovered localist or regionalist traditions from their past, although these still sit uneasily with their legacy of statism, Jacobinism and centralization.

In stark contrast is a right-wing regionalism found in wealthy regions, complaining about that the need to support their needy compatriots through welfare provision and transfers is hindering their ability to compete in European markets. In the old closed national economy, these transfers would mostly come back to the wealthy regions in the form of orders for their goods, while solidarity was recognized as the price for national unity. In the single European market, these conditions no longer hold and some regionalists prefer to stress the need to compete in broader context. Italy's Lega Nord combines this complaint with a strident xenophobia and populism. In Flanders and Bavaria, regionalists complain about the burden of transfers, although both have been net beneficiaries in the past. The wealthier Spanish autonomous communities complain about the need to support the rest. Elsewhere regionalism has been associated with traditional Christian democracy, which has often played the regionalist card against the centralized secular state, and which can link regionalism to doctrines of subsidiarity.

Some regions have a historic sense of identity, a distinct culture or their own language. The United Kingdom and Spain recognize the existence of distinct nations (UK) or nationalities (Spain) within the state. Such language is impermissible in France, despite the existence of cultural minorities and movements in Corsica, the Basque Country, Brittany, Occitania and Alsace. In Belgium the language issue has led to the federal division of the state, with two homogeneous language communities in Flanders and Wallonia, a small Germany community and a bilingual capital region of Brussels. Some cultural groups straddle state boundaries, as in Catalonia and the Basque Country, while in Denmark, Sweden, the United Kingdom, Belgium, the Netherlands and Italy there are minorities that are culturally or politically identified with the population of a neighbouring state. Historic and cultural regions have gained in prominence in recent years and minority nationalist movements have sought to use the new regionalism and European integration as instruments to gain more·autonomy without having to set up a separate state.

Data on public opinion are uneven and inconsistent and the different meanings of regionalism across Europe make it difficult to make rigorous comparisons, but some trends are apparent (Keating, 1998). There has been a general convergence of values across territories, largely due to secularization, but at the same time an increasing but highly uneven sense of regional identity. It appears that old regionalism, rooted tradition, conservative values, defensiveness and ruralism – entrenched in clientelistic networks – is giving way to a new regionalism based on modernization and change and appealing to younger and more upwardly mobile people. Where there are deep or historic sources of identity, as in stateless nations like Scotland or Catalonia, there are strong dual or multiple identities as people learn to operate at different political levels for different purposes. Here, too, territorial identities take on a cultural significance and underpin broader demands for autonomy. Regionalism has also tapped into a more general movement for decentralization, pluralism and participative government, reinforcing its modernizing credentials.

Regional politics thus takes a variety of forms and is linked to a variety of other political movements and demands. There has been a general move away from the integrative regionalisms of the 1960s, which sought to eliminate disparities and disadvantages and equalize social and economic conditions across states, to an autonomist regionalism resting on theories of endogenous development and demands for the decentralization of power. In the past regions stood in a dyadic relationship with the state, exchanging political support for protection against the market and policy concessions. With the state's ability to manage its spatial economy now reduced, regions are faced more directly with the global and European market. In the past they were integrated into states in a national division of labour; now they are in competition in wider markets. This in turn has affected the politics of regions, and interregional disparities may grow as regions are able to compete more or less effectively. Support for anti-disparity and equalization policies has fallen, as wealthier regions see less for themselves in these. So in the past, territorial redistribution could be supported by wealthy regions as the price for maintaining national markets and in the knowledge that many of the transfers would come back in the form of orders for their goods. Now that access not just to national but to global markets is secure, unity is less vital, and there is no guarantee that transfers will come back rather than being spent elsewhere. It is not surprising, then, that in Germany, Italy, Spain, Belgium and the United Kingdom, increasing complaints are heard from wealthy regions about the cost of supporting their poorer compatriots. Within regions, the emphasis is increasingly on competitiveness as a zero-sum game, biassing the policy agenda to development policies and away from social integration. This neo-mercantilist logic may partly be the result of inescapable facts, but one has to see it also as a political strategy on the part of certain elites within the region to play the competitiveness card in internal political arguments.

Regional institutions

Over recent decades, all the large Western European states and some of the smaller ones have established a meso- or intermediate level of government between the state and the municipal level, but it takes very different forms depending on the motives behind its establishment. One motive is functional efficiency, the desire to establish mechanisms for decision-making and coordination corresponding to the emerging functional systems, notably in relation to economic development. In the 1960s and 1970 the leitmotiv was regional planning and integration. Nowadays the emphasis is on the promotion of endogenous development and entrepreneurship. Training and active labour market policy has increasingly been devolved to regional levels and linked both to education and to economic development. Another function that has been widely regionalized is health planning and administration. Governments have also been accused of offloading the more burdensome or politically unprofitable tasks, especially in the allocation of scarce resources, to lower levels. The other motive for establishing regional government is more political, the need to respond to pressures from the ground level, notably in the case of multinational states or those with strong cultural minorities. Regionalization may also be a response to pressures for state reform and democratization more generally, as in the establishment of the German federal state after the war, or the persistent but inconclusive debates about federalization or devolution in Italy.

The weakest form of regionalization is functional decentralization, in which regional institutions, sometimes indirectly elected or corporatist, perform specific tasks. This is essentially the case in France, where the principal task of the regions is in planning and programming of investments in cooperation with central and local governments. Since they were directly elected in 1986 the have been more politicized, but without becoming a main focus of political debate and interest. Much the same can be said of Italian regions whose administration and budgets are dominated by the health service, although they have been directly elected since 1970. Functional regionalism has been reintroduced to England with the Regional Development Agencies and nominated chambers to shadow them, although in some regions there are pressures to move beyond this to elected regional government. The functional model has also generally been adopted in those countries that have introduced regions at the behest of the European Commission (see below).

A stronger form is devolution where the state entrusts regions with broad political and administrative responsibilities but stopping short of federation, which would make them full partners under the constitution. Devolution best describes the Spanish system of autonomous communities, although these do have a degree of constitutional protection, and the Belgian regions and communities before the reforms of 1993. Since 1998–99, devolved governments have existed in Scotland, Wales and Northern Ireland, with widely differing powers and roles. Although the UK government insists that parliamentary sovereignty is unaffected and that devolution could be suspended at any time, the fact that the three assemblies were endorsed by referendum would make it politically very difficult for Westminster to recover its powers. Since the late 1990s there has been a lot of debate in Italy about devolution as a way of reconciling the unitary state with the pressures for radical reform or federalization. One feature of devolution is that, with the centre maintaining at least a theoretical hold over the whole state, it is easier for it to contemplate asymmetrical arrangements. The United Kingdom, Spain and Italy all allow special status for individual regions, as to a lesser degree does France in the case of Corsica and Alsace. Proposals for further asymmetrical devolution in Spain, however, are controversial and in France are extremely so, as reaction to the proposals for further devolution to Corsica have shown.

The strongest form of regional government is federalism, in which the division of powers is constitutionally entrenched, so limiting the scope of the central government and parliament. Germany and Austria have had federal systems of government since their return to democracy after the war, while Belgium has been a federal state since 1993. Germany and Austria are divided in a symmetrical way into Länder while Belgium, because of the complexity of its problems, has a complicated system of dual federalism. To manage the linguistic-ethnic question there are three language communities, the Flemish, the French and the German which handle education and personal services. To deal with regional matters there are three territorial regions, Flanders, Wallonia and Brussels, handling economic and physical development. In practice, the Flemish region and community have merged but, because of the issue of Brussels, this has not been possible for the French and Walloon governments. A feature of Europe's three federal systems is that not only do the regions have a measure of autonomous government, but they are also represented in central decision-making through second chambers of parliament. The absence of such representation has been a source of some controversy in Spain and the United Kingdom.

Another form of regional government merges with the municipal category; this is the urban metropolitan region or city region. In several countries, it is not the large provincial-level region but the city that has emerged as the motor of change and most functionally relevant unit. In others there is a competition between city and regional elites to occupy the policy space in economic development and establish themselves as the nodes of decision-making networks. In France, the cities have generally gained more from decentralization than the regions, and this may also prove true in Italy where the direct election of the mayors in the 1990s allowed them to enhance their political standing while discussions on reforming the regions meandered without end. Metropolitan city regions were in vogue in the 1960s and 1970s as a way of improving planning and service provision and bringing together city centres and their hinterlands, but the movement petered out in the 1980s as a result of political opposition and disenchantment with big government. From the late 1990s the issue came back on the agenda but, given the political difficulty of reforming local government stuctures, this has taken the form of encouragement to voluntary cooperation among municipalities, as in France, Italy or Spain, or of weak metropolitan government as in the arrangements for London after 2000.

Regions and European integration

European integration has transformed the regional question in Europe in both its economic and its political aspects (Jones and Keating, 1995).

Economically it has favoured the 'new regionalism', with regions competing for advantage in the single market, and with a new pattern of winners and losers. At one time these disparities were portrayed as a centre–periphery question, with the 'golden triangle' drawing in resources at the expense of the outer areas. In the 1980s, some French economists replaced this with the image of the 'blue banana', a belt of developed regions from northern Italy through Flanders to southern England, which curiously reflected not only the trading routes of the early modern era, but also the 'shatter belt' of culturally distinct regions which scholars have discerned between the German and Latin cultural areas. Other analysts have pointed to more complex patterns of disparity, within as well as between regions, preferring the image of the mosaic. At one time, peripheral regions adversely affected by market integration tended to be disproportionately opposed to the European project, fearing increased economic and political marginalization. This is still true in Scandinavia, but elsewhere peripheral regions have changed tack and now seek to engage in the European political venture, encouraged by the Structural Funds, and are often among the most enthusiastic Europeans. Indeed the need to organize themselves for European economic competition and to influence European policy has been a factor in stimulating regional consciousness and mobilization itself.

A more directly political effect concerns the distribution of powers within states. Since it is states that are represented in the Council of Ministers, the increased scope of European policies has allowed national governments, acting on the principle that European affairs are foreign policy and therefore their exclusive responsibility, to negotiate on matters such as agriculture, training or the environment, which are constitutionally devolved to the regions. As early as the 1960s, the German Länder, sought to match European integration with a greater role for themselves in Germany's European strategy. In the Treaty on European Union (Maastricht) they obtained a clause allowing regions, where these have autonomous governments with a ministerial structure, to represent their states in the Council of Ministers. Thus far this clause has been used in Germany, Austria and Belgium, while Scottish and Welsh ministers have participated in UK delegations. There is no constitutional or legal obstacle to its being extended to Spain, but political difficulties have so far prevented it. It has also featured in proposals for constitutional reform in Italy. The Maastricht Treaty also established a Committee of the Regions with rights of consultation with the Council, the Commission and later the European Parliament on matters of regional concern. It has become a regular part of the EU machinery but the differences of interests among regions and its purely consultative status has limited its real power. Maastricht was the high point of the 'Europe of the Regions' movement in which regions sought recognition as a 'third level' of European government. In the negotiations for the Amsterdam Treaty they sought a further extension of their role, including the right to go to the European Court to uphold the principle of subsidiarity, but achieved little. Regions have also been active lobbyists in Brussels and over 200 have established a presence there in the form of delegations of permanent offices.

Regions have also been implicated in the EU's own spatial anti-disparity policy. This started in 1975 after the accession of the United Kingdom with a double logic (Hooghe and Keating, 1994). It was intended to counteract the adverse effects on regions of market integration; and to compensate the UK for the fact that it was a net contributor to the budget. This policy logic and intergovernmental logic have long been in tension and until 1988 the latter prevailed. Funds dispensed under the European Regional Development Fund (ERDF) were received by national governments, which regarded them as compensation for their own national regional policies rather than passing the money on to the regions. In 1988, however, a major reform doubled the size of the funds, grouped the ERDF with the European Social Fund and the Guidance section of the Agriculture Fund into the Structural Funds instrument, and sought to make this into an instrument of genuine European policy rather than a mere intergovernmental compensation mechanism. European-wide criteria and a single European map of eligible areas were established, regions were to be involved in the management of the funds in partnership with the Commission and national governments, and the principle of additionality was to ensure that the money was passed on to the regions. Although regions and the Commission shared the objective of partnership and of reducing the role of national governments, they were not entirely successful and the funds remained an object of contention. Further reforms in 1993 and 1999 simplified procedures and strengthened the hand of national governments. Nonetheless, the Structural Funds have had an impact on regional mobilization, and brought discussions of Europe to the centre of debate within regions (Hooghe, 1996). They have also forced governments in states without a regional tier to establish some form of regional administration and planning. Even the candidate countries of central and eastern Europe are being pressed to set up regional government in order to qualify for and to manage the Structural Funds. EU initiatives have also been important in stimulating cross-border cooperation and the emergence of regions covering more than one state, although so far such regions have not taken on a political life of their own (Balme, 1996).

Understanding change

One distinct feature of the new regionalism is that it is no longer contained by the nation state on any of its dimensions. Rather than serving complementary functions in a national division of labour, regions compete in global and European markets. Cultural and historic regions cross state frontiers, and regional leaders seek political support, economic resources and cultural sustenance outside state boundaries through an emerging para-diplomacy and strategic alliances with other territorial actors. European policies penetrate national space, bringing regions into contact with each other and the Commission so that state territories are simultaneously Europeanized and regionalized. This is a complex political order, comparable, although not identical to, the pre-state European order of overlapping and underlapping sovereignties, different types of authority in the state, the economy and civil society, and competing forms of legitimacy. Despite loose talk of a neo-medievalism, or analogies with the Holy Roman Empire, however, it is distinctly modern in that it coexists with universal norms of liberal democracy. Political scientists, seeking to make sense of it, have come up with a plethora of new concepts and neologisms, none of which quite fits the bill.

Perhaps the most widespread notion in contemporary analysis is that of 'governance'. This is a broad term for which at least six different meanings have been identified, but the basic idea is that government, identified with the traditional hierarchical state form, has given way to a world of diffused authority in which the boundaries between public and private are blurred. Hierarchy gives way to networks of horizontal and vertical cooperation across the whole gamut of organizations in the public sphere, including governments at all levels, private firms, and associations. Applied to local and regional restructuring, this takes the form of 'multilevel governance' (Marks, 1993) in which the state shares power with emerging bodies above and below it as well as with the institutions of market and civil society. There are a number of problems with this concept. In the first place, it relies heavily on a mythical view of a past in which authority was monopolized by a centralized state which, in turn, was the only actor in the international system. At best this describes an aspiration of European states from the mid-nineteenth century until the late twentieth century, not the historical experience of European space. Even in the archetypal centralized hierarchical state, France, researchers for over 30 years have emphasized the complex dispersal of power and the need for continuous negotiation. Students of federalism, especially in Germany, have long recognized the interdependence of tiers of government and the complex patterns of cooperation and competition that this produces. In the minority nations of Europe the legitimacy of the state has always been seen as somewhat conditional and resting on a range of explicit and implicit concessions. In other words, there is nothing new about territorial politics.

Another problem with multilevel governance is its high level of generality and abstraction. A concept, to be useful in making sense of a changing world, must be operationalizable, and theories must be testable and should help to explain things we would otherwise not understand. Multilevel governance has been criticized as non-operationalizable or testable. It is never clear, in fact, whether it is meant to be an operational theory, a descriptive metaphor, or a general comment on the state of the world. It does not seem to be possible to contrast instances of multilevel governance with instances where it is absent, or to calibrate degrees of multilevel governance. If multilevel governance is everything, then perhaps it is nothing – or maybe no more than a descriptive metaphor. The concept is loosely pluralistic in its emphasis on the dispersal of authority, and like so much pluralist theory suffers from a severe level-of-analysis problem. At some level of analysis every social phenomenon is plural, since we can go on disaggregating until we come down to the level of the individual. This is very easy since the state, the region, Europe, social class or gender are no more than abstract concepts.

It is more difficult, but nonetheless essential, to choose appropriate levels of reaggregation. This is the work of theory. Theories of governance, which have their origins in organization theory, tend to take the organization as the unit of analysis. This in turn has a number of effects. It fillets out of the analysis other social aggregates like class, gender or residential location, which undergird much of the struggle over power and resources in society. This in turn confirms the pluralist analysis since organizations are easily disaggregated and pluralistic theory becomes self-confirming. Eventually, disaggregation takes us down to the individual actor, yet theories of social action built purely from an individual basis are notoriously unreliable. So pluralism, and multilevel governance with it, becomes no more than an artefact of methodology; if you look for it anywhere at all, you will find it. It is also a fundamentally conservative concept since in its effort at mirroring the emerging order it fails to question its normative bias or to provide normative concepts able to sustain a critique.

The alternative approach is that of 'territorial politics'. This starts from the importance of territory as the essential element in regionalism and to see how regions are built as systems of social regulation and then, in some cases, constitute themselves as actors within the state and transnational order (Keating, 1997). This allows us to avoid the twin perils of defining regions out of existence on the grounds that they are so different, and of reifying them. Regions are territorial spaces with more or less defined and known boundaries. They may be economic spaces of which there are two recognized types; regions dominated by a single sector, and regions in which different sectors complement each other to make up a production system. Some may have their own culture, language and sense of identity. They may be political spaces, with their own media, sustaining a public debate in which issues are appraised for their territorial impact. There may be regionally-based interest groups and a territorial policy community. Finally, regions may be more or less institutionalized and autonomous. It is the coincidence of these diverse meanings of the region that determines the strength of regionalism and its nature. There are cases, such as the French or Italian regions, of administrative bodies with a degree of autonomy and powers, but which do not correspond to political spaces or to the new patterns of economic dynamism (Bagnasco and Uberti, 1997). Until 1999, Scotland was a political space, but without its own autonomous institutions. There are also cultural and linguistic regions, like Catalonia or the Basque Country, that span state boundaries. In France this disjuncture may not be accidental – critics allege that the boundaries of the regions were drawn up precisely to break up historic regions like Brittany, Normandy or Languedoc and weaken regionalist potential. The territorial politics framework allows us to appreciate the diversity of regionalism without losing sight of the common elements. It allows us to examine the construction of regions and the way in which territory intersects with other social cleavages, and to explore issues of power and influence. It also allows us to post normative questions avoided by the multilevel governance approach, questions about democratic control and accountability, and the classic political question of who gets what.

The key to understanding territorial politics in Europe is its very diversity (Keating and Loughlin, 1997). There are stateless nations, cultural regions, economic regions, city regions and provinces. Regions are not about to replace states as the primary instrument of social regulation in Europe, but alongside states they are finding their own place in the emerging continental order. As Europe integrates more closely and states surrender more powers of regulation to the European Union (or choose to exercise these powers jointly as some would put it), they will further lose their ability to regulate their own spatial economies. Regional actors will in consequence have an incentive to organize themselves for economic and political competition in Europe as well as within the state. Some will prove better at this than others, having a better market position and a greater capacity for organization. This is likely to increase interregional inequalities, especially after the enlargement to include poorer regions to the east. This can only accentuate interregional competition and diversity among regions.

PART IV

Resilience: Can States Respond to New Challenges and Demands?

Chapter 12

Environmental Challenges

NEIL CARTER

Western European states are confronting a wide range of environmental challenges. Once environmental policy was primarily concerned with nature conservation and local pollution; today it encompasses complex problems such as climate change, loss of bio-diversity and genetic modification, and encroaches upon many other policy fields including energy, transport and agriculture. All countries therefore need to develop their environmental capacity, which is 'a society's ability to identify and solve environmental problems'. To this end all Western European governments have declared their commitment to the principles of sustainable development.

The first part of this chapter identifies the key political and policy challenges posed by environmental problems. Progress towards better environmental governance is then assessed by examining the integration of environmental considerations into policy-making processes and the use of new policy instruments, followed by an assessment of how governments have responded to the key contemporary environmental challenges of climate change and GM foods.

The environment as a political issue

The environmental capacity of the state partly reflects the extent to which environmentalism is institutionalized, measured by the degree of public concern about environmental issues, the receptiveness of the media and the influence of environmental groups and green parties. The stronger and deeper the degree of institutionalization, the greater the pressure on governments to respond to environmental issues.

The growing political importance of the environment is partly a reflection of public concern about the issue. A 1999 poll reported that 69 per cent of European Union (EU) citizens regarded environmental protection and the fight against pollution as 'an immediate and urgent problem' (with only 4 per cent regarding it as 'not really a problem'), and 56 per cent of EU citizens agreed that we must 'fundamentally change our way of life and development if we want to halt the deterioration of the environment' (Eurobarometer, 1999, p. 10). The focus of concern varies over time: acid rain and ozone depletion were big issues in the 1980s, whereas today climate change and genetically modified organisms (GMOs) generate more anxiety. The level of public concern also fluctuates, having peaked across Western Europe in the late 1980s, then declining during the recession of the early 1990s. Subsequently, it has been rekindled by specific disasters and controversies such as the Belgian dioxin scare and the furore over GM products during 1998–99.

This public concern is reflected in the growth of environmental activism. Many individuals now regularly engage in numerous acts of ecological citizenship, ranging from recycling bottles and composting waste, to green consumerism and ethical investment. Environmental groups, judged by the size and scale of their activities, have become a significant force, particularly across northern Europe; for example, membership of environmental groups is approximately 3.5 million in Germany and 3.7 million in the Netherlands. In each country, membership is typically concentrated in a few large organizations, usually the major international groups – Greenpeace, Friends of the Earth and the World Wide Fund for Nature – and long-standing national groups such as the Dutch *Natuurmonumenten* and *Danmarks Naturfredningsforening*. Thus the environmental lobby can mobilize significant resources, including a mass membership, large budgets and professional staff, to further their interests in national, EU and international arenas. Governments have increasingly brought these groups into the policy process through regular consultation and involvement in implementation. Alongside the major established groups is a vibrant grassroots sector consisting mainly of local groups opposing specific developments, such as a proposed incinerator or toxic waste dump, but also direct action eco-protesters such as Earth First!, anti-nuclear activists and the UK anti-roads movement who are prepared to use confrontational methods to achieve their aims. Direct action has achieved some spectacular successes, notably the Greenpeace campaign that prevented the Brent Spar oil rig being dumped at sea, and governments often struggle to find the right response to these unconventional methods.

Green parties are now an established part of the political landscape, regularly securing a respectable 5 to 8 per cent vote share in Austria, Finland, France, Germany, Luxembourg and Switzerland. The two Belgian green parties have the most consistent and strongest electoral record, winning a combined 14.4 per cent in the 1999 national election. The Greens have also gradually strengthened their position in the European Parliament, where the election of 38 Members of European Parliament (MEPs) in 1999 made them the fourth largest party grouping.

Subsequently, Germany appointed the first Green Party EU Commissioner, Michaele Schreyer. A significant recent development has been the entry of green parties into government coalitions in Belgium, Finland, France, Germany and Italy. As new, junior coalition partners the Greens in government have not yet produced a dramatic transformation in environmental policy. However, the environmental achievements of the German red-green coalition since 1998 include the introduction of several eco-taxes and a programme for the gradual phase-out of nuclear reactors, which suggests that a sustained Green presence in government would result in a more progressive approach towards environmental protection. Green parties have contributed to a broader party politicization of the environment, encouraging established parties such as the German Social Democrats (SPD) to adopt greener programmes. However, a green party is not a prerequisite for party politicization; in Denmark, Norway and Sweden established parties became relatively 'green' in response to public concern before a green party emerged.

Although environmental issues are now firmly on the political agenda, their significance must be set in perspective. The environment still has low electoral salience everywhere, exercising little influence over voting behaviour. Consequently, while established parties have strengthened their environmental programmes and adopted a greener rhetoric, few have embraced environmental issues wholeheartedly. Environmental groups may have acquired more formal power, but in most core policy areas industrial interests still wield far greater influence. Nor should the environmental sentiments of the wider public be exaggerated, for whilst people frequently express concern about the state of the environment, they also want governments to maximize economic growth, protect jobs and cut taxes. Put differently, are people prepared to bear the costs and make the lifestyle sacrifices necessary to protect the environment?

The policy challenge

Environmental issues have several characteristics that pose unusually challenging problems for policy-makers. Many problems of the global community, such as climate change and ozone depletion, are transboundary in that they do not respect national borders and can only be solved by international cooperation. Yet there is great scope for freeriding: if one nation reduces its greenhouse gas emissions it cannot prevent other nations benefiting from its actions. Environmental policies must recognize the interdependence of natural and human systems; problems need to be treated holistically, rather than by addressing individual parts in isolation. In addition, scientific uncertainty suffuses environmental issues. Is climate change caused by natural fluctuations in temperature patterns or by human activities? Are GMOs dangerous to natural habitats? Policy-makers want certainty, but science struggles to provide it. The scientific knowledge informing our understanding of environmental problems is often based on a contestable theory and evidence that can be interpreted in several different ways. Scientific judgements are always provisional and open to revision, particularly regarding unfolding problems such as climate change and GMOs. The problem of uncertainty is exacerbated by the irreversibility of many environmental problems. If GMOs can damage natural ecosystems and cause irreparable harm to bio-diversity, then policy-makers may have only one chance of making the correct decision.

There are also significant political and institutional obstacles constraining the capacity of governments to respond to environmental pressures. The central problem is the classic trade-off between environmental protection and economic growth. Many environmental policies impose costly regulations or taxes on industry which may reduce competitiveness and result in job losses, encouraging the affected interests – industry, farmers, trade unions, consumers – to offer strong resistance to government proposals. The administrative fragmentation of government into policy sectors – finance, industry, energy, agriculture, transport – is a further barrier to coordinated environmental policy. These core economic ministries have traditionally acted as sponsors for the key industrial groups within each policy sphere, so they give priority to their own narrow sectoral objectives over environmental considerations.

Although there have been some significant improvements in the quality of the environment since the 1970s, notably in reducing sulphur dioxide, lead and phosphorous emissions into air and water, there has been an overall deterioration in the state of the European environment. It became clear that the traditional approach to environmental policy – reactive, tactical, piecemeal and end-of-pipe – was inadequate. Instead, West European governments have turned to the alternative policy paradigm of sustainable development, set out in the 1987 Brundtland Report (WCED, 1987) and the Agenda 21 document endorsed at the 1992 UN Earth Summit in Rio. The appeal of sustainable development lies in its claim that the economic growth versus environment trade-off can be resolved. No longer need these two objectives be in conflict (a zero-sum game); instead, sustainable development offers a positive-sum game in which economic and social development that provides for basic human needs removes inequalities and improves the material quality of life, and is compatible with environmental protection.

Whilst sustainable development is a complex and contested concept with many different meanings, it is possible to identify several core principles. First, the need for equity between current and future generations (intergenerational) and within society today (intragenerational). Secondly, policy-makers should apply the precautionary principle so that 'where there are threats of serious or irreversible damage, lack of full scientific certainty shall not be used as a reason for postponing cost-effective measures to prevent environmental degradation' (UNCED, 1992: principle 15). Thirdly, governments must adopt an integrated and planned approach to the environment that builds environmental considerations into all aspects of policy-making. Finally, there is a need for greater democracy to widen participation in decision-making.

One criticism of sustainable development is that it is does not offer a clear blueprint for action, particularly in providing a practical agenda for industrialized nations. Several European nations have witnessed the emergence of a variation of sustainable development, known as ecological modernization, that seems more appropriate to their needs. The states where this is most advanced are the 'pioneers' of progressive European environmental policy, in Scandinavia, Austria, Germany and the Netherlands (Andersen and Liefferink, 1997). Ecological modernization is built on the positive-sum claim that *pollution prevention pays*; in short, business can profit by protecting the environment (Hajer, 1995). Ecological modernization emphasizes the role of the market and technology in finding solutions to environmental degradation. Governments should employ market-based instruments (MBIs), such as eco-taxes and tradeable permits, which internalize the costs of environmental damage into the price of a good, so that businesses and consumers have a financial incentive to change their behaviour. Green technologies can save firms money by cutting energy costs and waste, and they provide solutions to (some) problems, such as the development of substitutes for the ozone-depleting chemicals used in refrigerators and fire extinguishers. Whilst the need for integration and the precautionary principle remain central to ecological modernization, elements of the broader social agenda of sustainable development, such as the need for equity and democracy, tend to be downplayed.

A government that fully embraces sustainable development or ecological modernization should have the anticipatory, comprehensive and strategic capacity to deal with complex environmental challenges. The rest of this chapter examines the commitment of European governments to these ideas, by examining progress towards environmental governance and then assessing how they have faced the challenges of climate change and GM foods.

Environmental governance

Environmental governance requires governments to transform themselves by changing both the way they make policy decisions and the instruments they use to implement those policies.

Policy-making: integration and planning

Environmental governance involves improving the coordination of environmental concerns across government and ensuring that environmental considerations are incorporated into routine decision-making in each sector.

The EU is now the primary focus of environmental decision-making for member states and, on balance, has played a progressive role in environmental policy. Since the First Environmental Action Plan (EAP) in 1973, major regulatory achievements in specific policy areas include improvements in bathing and drinking water quality, air pollution and waste policy. The Fifth EAP (1992–2000), Towards Sustainability, was explicitly committed to the principles of sustainable development and outlined a bold strategy to improve integration. It focused on five key sectors – tourism, industry, energy, transport and agriculture – and proposed a wide range of policy initiatives and instruments including sustainable tourism, industrial eco-audits, eco-labels and set-aside schemes protecting environmentally sensitive areas. However, although some initiatives have been implemented, most Commission directorate-generals continue to give priority to their own narrow sectoral interests and show little interest in sustainable development. And member states have done little to improve matters. Thus the failure to reform the Common Agricultural Policy (CAP) which provides the huge financial incentives such as guaranteed farm prices and export subsidies that underpin the intensification of European agricultural production, completely outweighs any marginal benefits from set-aside schemes. There is little to suggest that the Sixth EAP, Environment 2010: Our Future, Our Choice (2001–10), will overcome the obstacles that contributed to the failure of the Fifth programme.

At a national level, progress varies considerably. Every Western European government has consolidated an increasing range of environmental responsibilities under the control of a specialized environment ministry. These ministries have given greater prominence to environmental matters within government and improved the coordination of programmes in traditional 'environmental' areas such as pollution control and nature conservation. Stronger ministries, particularly in northern Europe, have also provided a focus for coalitions of environmental and consumer interests to mobilize against powerful producer interests such as farmers and energy utilities. However, environmental ministries have lacked the power to impose integration on other policy sectors. Consequently, some governments, notably Northern European, have introduced reforms aimed at integrating environmental considerations into all sectors in a more routine way. Norway and Denmark require each sectoral ministry to ensure that planning and development follow the principles of sustainable development. Some governments have also sought to establish a firmer structural underpinning to this functional integration by amalgamating environmental and economic responsibilities; for example, the Danes merged the energy and environment ministries, although the danger here is that the outcome may be a large, unwieldy and internally divided ministry, such as the UK Department of Environment, Transport and the Regions formed in 1997. Other initiatives include new cabinet committees, interdepartmental working groups, specialist advisory groups and sustainable development roundtables to work alongside the formal administrative structure. Thus Finland set up a National Commission on Sustainable Development in 1993 whose members included the prime minister, senior ministers and representatives from local government, churches, business, trade unions and the media. The British government merged several such bodies into a new Sustainable Development Commission in 2000, chaired by the environmentalist, Jonathan Porritt, with the role of advocating and monitoring the implementation of sustainable development across government. Whilst these bodies provide useful talking shops and feed ideas into the policy process, overall their impact, to date, has generally been limited (Lafferty and Meadowcroft, 2000).

In an effort to improve strategic environmental planning, most Western European governments have produced a national sustainable development or environment plan. Typically, these plans set out long-term goals, policies and targets for sustainable development. However, most plans are stronger in rhetoric than substance: the goals are generally inadequate; there are few new policy initiatives; the commitments are vague; and only a handful of targets are identified. Their timidity reflects the compromises that governments have had to make with powerful economic interests. Although some national plans, such as the Portuguese, have already been virtually shelved, elsewhere, as in the UK, new strategy documents have produced successively stronger plans.

The series of Dutch National Environmental Policy Plans (NEPP) published since 1989 represent the most comprehensive, ambitious and successful model of planning. Rather than reorganize the structure of government, the NEPP framework has tried to develop policy-planning processes that establish coordination and integration. The first NEPP set

50 strategic objectives, with over 200 staged quantitative targets aimed at achieving sustainability by 2010. The objective of reducing acidification, for example, was accompanied by costed targets setting out percentage reductions in the level of emissions of critical chemicals such as sulphur dioxide and nitrogen oxide, which in turn were broken down into individual targets for different activities such as traffic, energy supply, industry and households. This target-setting approach was repeated for other environmental problems, including climate change, eutrophication and waste disposal. Subsequent NEPPs have concentrated on ensuring the implementation of the original objectives and identifying options for future development. Despite some implementation difficulties for key pollutants such as sulphur dioxide, nitrogen oxide and phosphates, 'evaluation studies indicate that environmental policy in the Netherlands has, in recent years, achieved a marked reduction of pressures on and threats to the environment' (Hanf and van de Gronden, 1998, p. 178).

The Dutch do not have a monopoly on innovative planning mechanisms; several countries have made significant improvements in the quality of monitoring and measurement mechanisms. Germany has outlined an 'Environment Barometer' setting out indicators and targets for air quality, soil, nature protection, water, energy and raw materials. The British government published a set of 15 'headline' sustainable development indicators in 1999, backed up by a further set of over 150 indicators. But it remains to be seen how seriously governments treat these targets and monitoring systems. The Local Agenda 21 process has also seen important community initiatives, notably in Sweden, the Netherlands and the UK, involving local authorities taking a leading role in planning sustainable development and encouraging the participation of a wide range of local actors in this process.

Although the overall impact of these administrative reforms is limited, they represent a small step towards a more strategic and integrated approach to environmental policy. However, a major obstacle is the unwillingness of core polluting sectors to accept their environmental responsibilities. One lesson of the successful NEPP is that effective planning requires strong, sustained political leadership that can be institutionalized through legislation, institutional reform, target-setting and monitoring so that momentum is maintained when governments change.

Policy instruments

Environmental policy has traditionally depended on regulatory, or 'command and control', instruments. Most international agreements adopt this approach, whether banning whaling or the manufacture of ozone-depleting chemicals. EU directives rely heavily on standard-setting, for example, by regulating the level of pollutants allowed in drinking water. If Western European governments are moving towards ecological modernization we should expect greater flexibility in the use of policy instruments, such as voluntary agreements or MBIs, that try to change the behaviour of industry and consumers.

Environmental voluntary agreements have become increasingly common: there were over 300 such agreements within the EU by 1997, with Germany and the Netherlands accounting for around two-thirds of the total (EEA, 1997). A central feature of the Dutch NEPP is the 'target group' policy involving structured consultation and negotiation of the targets in the form of voluntary agreements, or covenants, between government representatives and key industrial interest groups. The intention is to persuade these target groups to accept a greater share of the responsibility for environmental protection by encouraging them to develop a sense of ownership of the targets, whilst allowing these groups the flexibility to achieve them in their own way. Whereas the Dutch have concluded agreements in almost all policy areas, other countries have just a handful of agreements concentrated in a few core polluting areas, notably the chemical industry. The voluntary agreements are often quite unambitious, involving commitments at a lowest-common-denominator level acceptable to the least enthusiastic signatories to the agreement. An industry will only accept a voluntary agreement to forestall the threat of a tougher regulation or eco-tax, so it is likely to set easier targets and more relaxed deadlines than the government might impose by other means. The absence of sanctions makes freeriding a real possibility.

Governments have also shown greater willingness to use market-based instruments, notably eco-taxes, over the last decade. For example, nine EU member states now tax waste disposal compared to just two in the early 1990s. Yet they are still used sparingly: the total EU tax revenues raised from environmental taxes (on energy, transport and pollution) was only 6.7 per cent in 1997 (EEA, 2000a, p. 2). Successful eco-taxes include Dutch water pollution charges which have reduced organic emissions into waterways at low cost and encouraged firms to introduce cleaner technologies, and Swedish taxes on sulphur dioxide and nitrogen oxide which have led to significant emission reductions. Many countries introduced tax differentiation between leaded and unleaded petrol to encourage consumers to use unleaded petrol, prior to the eventual ban on leaded petrol throughout the EU in 2000.

Eco-taxes are becoming increasingly attractive as part of a general shift in the burden of taxation from environmental 'goods', such as enterprise, employment and savings, on to environmental 'bads', such as pollution and inefficient use of energy and resources. Proponents argue that a 'double dividend' is possible: eco-taxes can protect the environment and by removing inefficient subsidies and tax distortions they can also stimulate employment. Several governments have introduced tax packages that apply these principles. For example, the Finnish coalition government in 1997 made cuts to income and labour taxes that were partly compensated by a landfill tax and increased energy taxes. Similarly, the German SPD-Green government introduced staged increases in energy taxes in April 1999 with the revenues funding reductions in the social security contributions of employers and employees to stimulate employment.

The growing interest in voluntary agreements and MBIs indicates the increasing influence of ecological modernization in government. However, MBIs encounter significant political obstacles in wider society. In short, every tax creates winners and losers. Eco- taxes impose costs on industry or citizens, so they are often fiercely resisted. Industry argues that eco-taxes increase costs and reduce international competitiveness, while consumers dislike higher prices on key items such as petrol. A government cannot achieve ecological modernization alone; but there is little evidence that either industry or the consumer has yet been converted.

Climate change

Climate change illustrates many of the problems confronting the implementation of sustainable development as it is transnational, probably irreversible and clouded in scientific uncertainty. Its solutions confront the economic growth versus environment trade-off because the precautionary principle requires policies that will require substantive short-term material sacrifices in exchange for the satisfaction of protecting the planet for future generations. In short, there are many short-term losers and few immediate winners. Not surprisingly, few people perceive climate change in the positive-sum terms of sustainable development or ecological modernization.

The EU has made an important contribution to international climate change diplomacy. Since the UN Framework Convention on Climate Change was agreed at the Rio Earth Summit in 1992, EU member states have taken a leading role in trying to turn its worthy rhetoric into substance. By agreeing a common platform, EU member states have been able to wield considerable weight at the bargaining table, particularly in negotiating the 1997 Kyoto Protocol which committed developed countries to reducing their overall emissions of greenhouse gases by at least 5 per cent below 1990 levels throughout the 2008–12 period (EEA, 2000b, p. 16). The EU adopted a burden-sharing approach which promised an overall EU cut in carbon emissions by 8 per cent, with individual member states agreeing different emission targets according to economic circumstances. The common platform allowed the EU to secure commitments from key actors, notably the USA which is responsible for 25 per cent of global greenhouse gas emissions and therefore critical to the success of the Protocol.

Although the modest Kyoto commitments would have only a limited impact on climate change, they represent an important first step. The Kyoto Protocol also proposed an international emissions-trading regime to enable industrialized countries to buy and sell emission credits amongst themselves. Unfortunately, at the critical follow-up meeting at the Hague in November 2000 which was intended to firm-up the Kyoto commitments, negotiations broke down due to the intransigence of the so-called 'umbrella group' of countries headed by the USA, Japan and Australia. This group would only concede emission cuts if they were allowed to use carbon sinks, such as forests, to offset their high emissions.

The US government renounced the Kyoto protocol during the first months of President George W. Bush's administration in 2001. Subsequently, at meetings in Bonn and Marrakesh, the rest of the world nevertheless reached a binding agreement on the implementation of the protocol. That agreement made allowance for carbon sinks and specified rules for ensuing compliance with Kyoto commitments.

If it is difficult agreeing emission targets, it is even harder to implement them. The limited commitment of European governments to climate-change prevention is illustrated by current progress towards the Kyoto targets. Although overall EU carbon emissions almost stabilized between 1990–98, emissions fell in just three EU states – Germany, Luxembourg and the United Kingdom – which are also those most likely to meet their Kyoto commitments (EEA, 2000b). Yet Germany and Britain benefited from fortuitous one-off events that may mean these cuts are unsustainable in the longer term: namely the huge energy efficiency improvements arising from German reunification and related economic restructuring, and the rapid switch from coal to gas in British electricity generation. Current upward trends in carbon emissions suggest that with continued economic growth over the next decade the EU is unlikely to meet even the modest Kyoto targets.

Over 90 per cent of EU carbon emissions come from fossil fuels, which accounted for 79 per cent of gross energy consumption in 1997 (42 per cent oil, 21 per cent gas, 16 per cent solid fuels, mostly coal and lignite). The key contributors are the energy-generation and transport sectors which account for 32 per cent and 24 per cent of total CO_2 emissions respectively (EEA, 2000b, pp. 6–7). Any significant reductions in carbon emissions will require fundamental policy changes in these two sectors.

Energy generation

A sustainable energy-generation policy would see a major reduction in the current dependency on fossil fuels. The two main sustainable alternatives are nuclear and renewable energy.

Nuclear power is a highly controversial 'environmental' option. Whilst it produces zero carbon emissions, the wider threat of radioactive contamination from accidents and long-term storage of spent fuel and waste is potentially even more catastrophic than climate change. Furthermore, the nuclear industry is in deep crisis. European public opinion has turned sharply against nuclear power, especially since the 1986 Chernobyl accident which resulted in radioactive fall-out right across the continent. The nuclear industry has also failed to deliver its original promise to be safe, reliable and cheap. Many countries had invested heavily in the nuclear sector, particularly after the 1973 oil crisis, so that nuclear power currently contributes around one-third of EU electricity. Yet expansion has come to a virtual standstill, with no new nuclear plants under construction in Western Europe during 2000, and a moratorium on expansion in five of the eight EU states with nuclear power. Even in pro-nuclear France the traditional bipartisan enthusiasm for nuclear power has weakened, especially since Les Verts entered government in 1997. Elsewhere, the entry of green parties into government in Belgium and Germany has resulted in the launch of long-term nuclear phase-out programmes, and Swedish Social Democrat government, which is dependent on Green and Left Party support, closed the Barseback-1 reactor in 1999.

Ironically, as the nuclear sector declines it will be partly replaced by coal-generated energy, thereby increasing carbon emissions. Indeed, the climate change imperative may yet offer the nuclear industry a lifeline. Significantly, the European Commission adopted a green paper on energy supply in November 2000 which suggests that carbon emission-reduction targets may only be met by building new nuclear reactors to replace the declining stock.

The uncertain future of nuclear energy reinforces the importance of expanding renewable energy sources, such as hydroelectric power (HEP), biomass, wind, geothermal and solar power, which emit low or zero carbon. The growth potential for HEP, which supplies 13 per cent of EU electricity (and most Norwegian electricity) is now limited everywhere by strong conservationist opposition to the damage to habitats and communities arising from the construction of large dams. Most governments have only recently treated other forms of renewable energy seriously: they contributed just 1.6 per cent of EU electricity generation in 1997. The wind and biomass power industries offer most potential. The Danes have pioneered wind energy: Denmark's turbine industry is a world market leader and generous price tariffs have helped boost the domestic sector. Germany has the largest wind industry in Europe and with the nuclear industry in terminal decline the government has set ambitious targets for renewable energy, backed by annual subsidies of 2 billion euros. Biomass generation is expanding quickly from a similarly small base, especially in Finland and the Netherlands.

Nonetheless, the EU target of doubling the share of energy supply provided by renewables to 12 per cent by 2010 looks unrealistic. The nascent renewables sector faces many obstacles, and the new technologies have experienced many teething problems. In Britain, where there is huge potential for wind energy, public resistance to the construction of wind farms in areas of natural beauty has stymied the development of wind energy since the mid-1990s, forcing the government to redirect attention to less-intrusive (but more expensive) offshore wind farms. The major problem is that renewable energy struggles to compete effectively with fossil fuels on price, primarily because the liberalization of European energy markets has driven down the price of energy. Moreover, large subsidies are still paid to some fossil fuel industries, notably the coal industry, which is hardly evidence of an integrated climate change strategy. A possible counter-balance may come from European Commission guidelines announced in December 2000 – based on the polluter pays principle – allowing member states to fund up to 50 per cent of the investment costs of renewable energy projects.

Furthermore, a carbon tax on fossil fuels would make renewable energy more price-competitive, especially if the revenues were invested in the renewables sector for research and design, subsidies and preferential agreements. A carbon tax would also provide a financial incentive for industry to improve energy conservation. However, carbon taxes pose a classic freerider problem: unless states coordinate their actions by imposing a uniform carbon tax, then industry in countries where a tax is levied will be competitively disadvantaged. A stiff carbon tax imposed on Swedish industry in 1991 was reduced a year later with the government declaring that the resulting competitive advantage to domestic industry would create over 10 000 jobs, although it has subsequently been increased for energy-intensive industries. Similarly, fierce industry lobbying ensured that the climate-change levy introduced in the UK in 2001 was a watered-down version of the original proposal. Although eight EU member states had introduced carbon taxes by 2001, in order to be politically acceptable, most are set too low to change behaviour. The continuing absence of a stringent EU carbon tax (a proposal in the mid-1990s encountered strong opposition from industry and key member states, notably the UK and France) suggests a lack of commitment to climate change.

Transport

Transport presents even more intractable problems than energy generation. Carbon emissions from the EU transport sector increased by 15.3 per cent between 1990 and 1998, primarily due to the inexorable growth in road traffic, although air transport is a rapidly growing source. Emissions from transport grew in every EU member state: Spain, Germany and France showed the largest absolute increase, but the largest relative increase was in countries with lower car ownership, such as Portugal (42 per cent) and Ireland (77 per cent).

Transport policy-makers have traditionally pinned hope on the technological fix of developing 'greener' motor vehicles, through engine modifications, anti-pollution devices and alternative fuels. However, the rapid growth in the volume of road traffic has outstripped improvements in energy efficiency. Clearly, a sustainable transport policy must produce a significant reduction in road traffic, yet no country has made serious progress in this direction. The powerful road lobby – a broad coalition of oil companies, vehicle manufacturers, road builders and driving organizations – has ensured that transport ministries usually give priority to the road sector. The result in most countries is a long-standing policy of predict and provide: predict the amount of traffic growth and provide the roads needed to carry it. Taxes on motoring, such as sales, vehicle and fuel taxes, cover only a small proportion of the external costs of motoring, whilst road users benefit from many subsidies such as tax allowances for company cars.

Transport policy-makers are gradually using MBIs to alter travelling habits. Fuel taxes and road-pricing systems provide a financial incentive not to use a car whilst generating revenue to invest in the public transport network, improving bus and train services. Without the carrot of reliable, efficient, convenient and affordable public transport, it is unlikely that people will be persuaded to leave their cars at home. But where vehicle and fuel taxes have been increased for explicitly environmental reasons, as in Britain, Norway, Sweden and the Netherlands, it has had little impact on car ownership or aggregate car use. The inelasticity of demand for petrol means that only a stringent increase – perhaps over 40 per cent – would alter consumption significantly, but this would be very regressive with a disproportionately harmful impact on those with low incomes and rural dwellers. Politicians are understandably apprehensive about such a radical step, especially since the wave of popular protests against high fuel prices orchestrated by road hauliers and farmers that swept across Western Europe during August and September 2000. Whilst high fuel prices were partly due to increased crude oil prices, popular resentment focused on the burden of government taxes. The speed with which these protests produced a serious fuel crisis, particularly in France and Britain where petrol ran out and aeroplanes were grounded, prompted concessions from several governments in the form of reduced duties. The fuel protests underline the importance of public opinion in addressing climate change. Whilst industry is frequently condemned for its resistance to progressive environmental protection measures, the unwillingness of consumers to accept lifestyle sacrifices is also a major obstacle to climate-change prevention.

Overall, although most governments have started to develop more sustainable energy and transport policies, there are few signs of the radical paradigm shift for a serious impact on greenhouse gas emissions.

Food scares and GM crops

Genetically modified foods display many of the classic characteristics of environmental problems: scientific uncertainty, the potential for irreversible harm and the need for international cooperation. There is fierce conflict between proponents and opponents of GM foods. The main potential benefits are that the resistance of GM crops to pesticides, as well as to disease, pests, weeds and extreme weather conditions, should cut costs and increase yields. More controversially, proponents claim GM crops are good for the environment because they require fewer pesticides. The biotechnology industry also offers huge commercial opportunities and European companies, notably in Britain, France, Germany and Switzerland, have been market leaders. However, critics argue that GM crops pose a major potential threat to bio-diversity. If cross-pollination from GM plants results in the spread of pesticide resistant genes in the wild population, then weeds and pests could spread uncontrollably and the species composition of wildlife communities could be altered with devastating consequences. There is also concern about the unknown health risks that consuming GM foods may have on human health.

The rapid escalation of GM crops onto the political agenda in the late 1990s has to be understood in the context of recent food scares in Europe, notably the BSE crisis which originated in Britain and the dioxins that infected the food chain in Belgium and neighbouring states.

First, these food scares have contributed to growing concern about the threat to human health and the environment from intensive agriculture. Food production in Western Europe is dominated by big agro-business whose relentless pursuit of profit has resulted in the widespread use of agrochemicals, antibiotics and related factory-farming methods. It is likely that the BSE crisis arose from a 'cost-cutting' measure typical of modern agro-business, when poorly rendered meat was mixed in cattle feed.

Second, the BSE crisis demonstrated the potential costs of failing to apply the precautionary principle. After BSE was classified as a notifiable disease in 1988 the Conservative government, backed by most leading scientists, repeatedly reassured the public that there was no possibility of BSE jumping the species barrier into the human food chain. The British policy tradition of acting only on firm scientific evidence of a demonstrable risk, rather than the precautionary principle that justifies action where there is a potential risk, meant that any scientist raising doubts (without hard evidence) about the safety of beef was ignored. The government was understandably reluctant to introduce precautionary measures that would impose a heavy financial burden on farmers and damage public confidence in beef, but the folly of this strategy was exposed in 1996 when the government announced the discovery of a link between BSE and new variant Creutzfeld-Jakob disease which turned BSE into a European human health crisis, resulting in the imposition of a EU ban on the export of British beef. Unfortunately, rather than apply the precautionary principle themselves, neighbouring countries preferred to define BSE as a 'British problem' and so failed to adopt the same stringent regulations governing cattle feed and the rendering of cattle as applied in Britain. This shortsightedness led to a new crisis provoked by the discovery of BSE in cattle in France, Germany and elsewhere during 2000–01, prompting a collapse in beef sales and new EU-wide regulations.

Finally, the BSE crisis resulted in a significant decline in public trust of scientists and government. BSE raised serious doubts about the reliability of so-called 'scientific' evidence and the kind of risk analysis that was used to reassure the public for years. The public regarded the British government's handling of the BSE saga as a mendacious attempt to cover up errors and protect producer interests at the cost of public health. Consequently, public opinion seems instinctively to favour the precautionary principle.

These lessons from the BSE crisis help explain the dramatic transformation of GM foods from a backroom technical debate amongst experts into a hot political issue. Until the mid-1990s, the development of a GM regulatory regime in Europe had remained in the hands of political, scientific and industry elites. In adopting a 1990 directive governing the release of GM products, the European Commission was trying to balance the need for adequate regulation whilst not impeding the commercial development of the biotechnology industry. Although this regulatory framework required states to take 'preventive action' to avoid 'irreversible' environmental damage, the dominance of pro-biotechnology governments, such as France and the UK, meant that, in practice, the key criteria driving regulatory approval were the internal market and international competitiveness. The risks posed by GM products were regarded as no worse than those arising from existing intensive farming methods and the notion that the actual process of genetic modification might have some unknown impact on the environment, a view held by smaller states, such as Austria and Denmark, was dismissed. Consequently, 18 GM products had been approved by 1998.

Then the GM issue was catapulted into the public eye. A key factor in this turnaround was the European Commission's approval of imported US maize and soya which coincided with Monsanto deciding to stop separating GM and non-GM soya supplies. These decisions provided an opportunity for consumer and environmental groups to force the issue onto the political agenda by arguing that the lack of segregation and labelling of GM foods would deny consumers the right to choose not to eat them. Public concern was further exacerbated when, in July 1998, British scientist Arpad Pusztai discovered adverse effects in rats fed with GM potato. Although his findings were widely criticized by official scientific bodies which argued that GM products posed no danger to human health, the recent memory of the BSE crisis meant that the British public had little trust in such scientific reassurances. Subsequently, 20 leading scientists issued a statement of support for Pusztai. American scientists later found that the pollen produced by GM corn was lethal to the caterpillar of the Monarch butterfly. The media launched high-profile campaigns against these 'Frankenstein foods'. European consumers took direct action by refusing to purchase GM products and major supermarkets, having previously protested that it was impossible to separate GM products or to label them, withdrew food containing GM products from their shelves.

Governments responded by introducing new legislation requiring the labelling of GM products; some countries implemented bans on GM crops even when they had received EU approval, an action which the European Court of Justice later upheld. Although the Council of Ministers rejected a formal moratorium on all new varieties of GM applications, France, Austria, Italy, Denmark and Luxembourg announced they would block the issue of any new licences until new EU regulations were in place. With no new GM crops approved since 1998, an effective moratorium existed. In Britain, the biotechnology industry agreed a voluntary moratorium on commercial planting of GM crops until 2003 pending the outcome of crop trials, but Greenpeace and other anti-GM groups attracted enormous publicity by taking direct action that destroyed these crops in the fields, persuading many farmers to withdraw from the experiments. In a major U-turn, Prime Minister Tony Blair, an ardent supporter of biotechnology who a year earlier had called on the public to 'resist the tyranny of pressure groups', acknowledged 'legitimate public concern' about GMOs (*Financial Times*, 28 February 2000).

The decision to invoke the precautionary principle by banning GM crops was a manifestation of governments losing control of events rather than displaying a planned commitment to sustainable development. This major policy change was forced on governments by bottom-up public pressure, as a powerful alliance of environmentalists, greens, consumer groups and farmers – with other political parties jumping on the bandwagon – cleverly exploited media interest to whip up a frenzy of public concern during 1998–99. The consumer boycott of GM foods divided business interests by turning supermarkets and many food suppliers against the biotechnology industry. Conversely, the transparent vulnerability of European governments to the GM campaigners indicates that grassroots mobilization, drawing on a new repertoire of action which includes innovative use of the internet, is becoming an increasingly powerful and unpredictable force in environmental politics.

Can this grassroots victory be sustained? The future politics of GM foods will be contested on a wider international stage. Consumer resistance in Europe has had major repercussions in the USA where, having originally accepted GM foods with little opposition, there is now a strong backlash from consumers and farmers. The US and Japanese governments and biotechnology multinationals such as Monsanto want to use World Trade Organization rules that require 'sufficient scientific evidence' of danger to overturn the EU moratorium on GM crops (although the Cartegena Protocol on Biosafety [2000] allows individual nations to invoke the precautionary principle to prevent the import of GM crops on environmental grounds or to require them to be labelled). Under pressure from member-state governments, the European Parliament finally agreed tough new regulations for the approval of GM crops in February 2001. However, the *de facto* moratorium persisted because Austria, Denmark, France, Greece, Italy and Luxembourg immediately declared that they would not support any further authorizations of GM crops until tougher regulations governing the tracing and labelling of GMOs through the food chain were put in place.

Coping with environmental challenges

Environmental policy is in a period of flux throughout Europe as governments respond to new challenges. The principles of sustainable development and ecological modernization are slowly being implemented, albeit in a piecemeal way. The 'pioneer' countries of northern Europe have made most progress, using existing corporatist structures to nurture closer state–industry cooperation in pursuit of ecological modernization, and the framework provided by EU environmental policy has strengthened the capacity of all member states to deal with new problems.

Yet there is little evidence of genuine environmental governance even in the pioneer states of northern Europe, and there has been no major transformation in the way policy-makers think about these challenges. Environmental considerations have not been integrated into routine decision-making, particularly in key sectors dominated by powerful producer interests such as transport, energy and agriculture. The unwillingness of most countries to introduce targets and monitoring systems along the lines of the Dutch NEPP makes it difficult to hold government to account. Although eco-taxes are used more widely, they are always fiercely resisted and rarely set high enough to change the behaviour of either industry or consumers. In practice, it seems that the principles of ecological modernization, notably that pollution prevention pays, have only limited appeal in industry boardrooms. The absence of a comprehensive and radical approach to climate change shows that, despite widespread acceptance of the rhetoric of sustainable development, the economy versus environment trade-off still dominates the way environmental problems are perceived.

Here the contrast between climate change and the GM cases is instructive. Crucially, the public perceives a direct and tangible risk to their own health from GM foods and has nothing to lose by rejecting them. While GM foods benefit the biotechnology industry and, possibly, farmers, there is little in it for consumers. Food will not taste better and it may even be dangerous, so why should European consumers accept it? No longer willing to trust the reassurances of government or scientists, the public now instinctively supports the application of the precautionary principle. However, the threats from climate change are more intangible and mainly affect future generations, whilst the solutions impose significant personal costs.

One lesson is that governments cannot hope to solve a complex environmental problem like climate change, where the solutions involve far-reaching changes that reach all parts of the economy and society, without the support of wider civil society. Industry is an obvious villain, and the ecological modernization strategy of using the market, technology and closer cooperation between government and industry needs to be pursued with much greater enthusiasm. But wider public support is also needed, notably for policies to conserve energy and reduce car use. Somehow the climate-change threat must be made more tangible and visible in order to elicit the kind of public response seen towards GM crops. This will require a much greater institutionalization of environmental concerns by using education, the media, cooperation with environmental groups and encouraging active participation throughout civil society in order to nurture a wider grassroots 'ecological citizenship'. Such a programme demands strong leadership. Unfortunately, determined national leadership commitment to sustainable development remains noticeable only by its absence amongst the political elites of Western Europe.

Chapter 13

The Information Society

DAVID A. L. LEVY

The term 'Information Society' (IS) refers to policies directed towards the converging sectors of telecommunications (telecoms), IT, the Internet and broadcasting. It also includes attempts to use these technologies to modernize and expand access to government services, and to reduce inequalities in technology usage. For Western European governments and EU policy makers the 'Information Society' has at least two meanings. First, there is the practical problem of understanding and responding to the social, industrial, economic and regulatory challenges posed by these converging sectors. A plethora of expert reports, Green Papers and discussion documents at the EU level and in most West European countries have posed very similar questions: How should regulation be adapted in the face of the convergence of previously separate sectors? How can Internet penetration be increased? What will create greater confidence in e-commerce? Most difficult of all, is there any role for national policy given an increasingly globalized communications industry sharing a strong preference for *laissez-faire* solutions?

In marked contrast to this practical agenda is a second, more voluntaristic, political agenda. Here the 'Information Society' takes on the character of mobilizing myth, a leitmotif for modernization and competitiveness, a symbol of the commitment to create 'the most competitive and dynamic knowledge-driven economy in the world'. According to this interpretation, Europe's major nations can be masters of their own destiny. They can formulate win–win policies which not only ensure both competitiveness and a more humane, distinctively European approach to the 'Information Society', but also favour growth and cultural diversity as well as inaugurate the e-society and promote the growth of e-commerce. It was this approach which informed Commission President Romano Prodi's launch of his e-Europe initiative in the Autumn of 1999. e-Europe has since become a unifying theme for many of the Commission's actions on competitiveness, growth, employment and regulatory reform as well as those strictly related to the IS itself (EC, 2000c, 2000d).

This chapter examines these two dimensions of the IS – the practical policy suggestions and the attempts to create a mobilizing idea – at both the national level (in France, Germany and the UK), and also at the EU level. Three questions are addressed. First, what are the key policy challenges presented by the IS and how have different countries responded? Second, where does policy leadership occur in IS affairs – primarily at the national, the EU or the international level? Third, is there an emerging EU policy consensus over IS policies and who are the main players pushing for one?

National responses to the challenges of the Information Society

In policy terms, a marked convergence between Europe's major nations in response to the IS has been evident since the mid-1990s. Most engaged in facilitating and regulating digital television, reviewing regulation in the communications sector, liberalizing telecoms and, most recently, promoting Internet penetration and addressing the risks of an information poor/information rich social divide. However, even though the policy agenda was shared, the ways in which these issues were tackled has varied greatly. National cultural and political preoccupations counted a great deal, even if changes were often presented as driven purely by exogenous factors and as critical to modernization and competitiveness (Levy, 1997).

Liberalizing telecoms and infrastructure

The UK was the first major European country to liberalize its telecoms industry, dismantling its telecoms monopoly in the 1980s more than a decade before France and Germany. Part of a wider agenda of privatization, it was felt by the Conservative government that if competition were introduced, and British Telecom (BT) was prevented from offering television, then the innovative energy of the newly created UK cable industry would be unleashed. This in turn would leave private enterprise free to create wired cities – offering telephony and TV – with accompanying benefits for the economy. The result was a system of asymmetric regulation in which the incumbent, BT, was subjected to rigorous control whilst cable companies were consistently favoured. The UK experiment succeeded in creating a powerful independent regulator (OFTEL) and also a new class of popular shareholder with shares in the privatized BT. But the wired cities never happened in the decade following privatization. In part this was because the UK cable sector was extremely slow to build networks. Cable was highly fragmented and, unlike the satellite operator BSkyB, had no compelling content of its own to persuade terrestrial TV viewers to become subscribers. Cable operators were reduced to offering cheap telephony and operating as retailers of BSkyB's programming. BT's dominance of the residential market continued throughout the late 1980s and 1990s, and serious competition only took off with the development of a mass mobile telephone market in the late 1990s and growing interest in the Internet.

France and Germany liberalized their telecoms industries much later. France created an independent telecoms regulator in 1997 but the government retained control of France Telecom. Similarly in Germany, an independent regulator was created in 1998 and only in 2000 was Deutsche Telekom privatized. Although both countries shared the UK's excitement about the potential that cable offered, they saw it as part of a political as much as an economic agenda, and insisted on a leading role for government. The motivation for the development of cable in Germany came partly from the desire of the Christian Democratic government to challenge the dominance of what were perceived as SPD-dominated public-service broadcasters. In France, cable was designed to create a nationally controlled network that could combat the influx of largely US TV programmes on satellite. German networks were built using old-fashioned coaxial cable, and hence of limited use for eventual IS applications. French cable was higher quality, but plans for a national fibre-optic network foundered for lack of money.

The French and German approaches to cable closely matched those elsewhere in the EU. In countries where telecoms liberalization was slow to develop, cable networks built with state subsidies ended up being controlled by the national telephone company rather than competing with it. The consequences were long-lived. By 1997, even after the liberalization of telecoms, major cable networks were still owned by the major telecommunications companies in half of the EU's member states.

By the late 1990s the first stage of telecoms liberalization was complete. Admittedly there were problems about entry rights for new companies in some areas and some countries had moved further than others in creating genuinely independent regulators. Equally, while the market for mobile telephony had developed rapidly, in some countries this was used to consolidate the power of the incumbent telecommunications company, whereas in others, such as the UK, there was vigorous competition in the mobile market.

The main regulatory problems concerned the second wave of liberalization, in particular the speed with which the incumbent undertook local-loop unbundling (LLU) in its fixed-line and residential networks. Where LLU had been implemented, new entrants could offer broadband access to consumers using so-called DSL technology. DSL technology's great strength was its ability to offer always-on Internet access at up to 10 times the speed of conventional dial-up modems through existing copper-wire lines, whilst simultaneously allowing conventional phone use. However, DSL only works relatively close to the local telephone exchange and new entrants required access to the local loop or the 'last mile' of copper wire from the exchange to the consumer. They also needed to install their equipment in the incumbent operators' exchange, and access to technical information. Disputes centred around all these issues in each of the countries under discussion here, but on LLU in particular the UK lost its earlier lead. By early 2001, LLU was not widely available in BT exchanges and few third parties were able to offer DSL access through BT's lines by June 2001, the official date for LLU to be complete in the UK. In January 2001, the Commission's regular report on the telecoms market found that while local-loop unbundling was 'operational' in Denmark, Germany, the Netherlands, Austria, Finland and Sweden, discussions and technical tests were continuing in the UK and France (EC, 2000b).

Digital broadcasting and regulatory convergence

Digital TV (DTV) raised a dilemma for national policy-makers, and provides a good illustration of how digital technology was bringing about convergence in the previously discrete industries of telecommunications, IT and broadcasting. After all, it meant not just an increased choice of channels, but also the possibility of receiving them through a broader range of devices and delivery systems, as well as using the TV for everything from watching programmes, to ordering videos, sending e-mail and engaging in e-commerce. For some this led to the assumption that the separate regulation of the three sectors was no longer viable. However, others could point to continuing differences between TV and other sectors. Unlike IT or telecommunications, TV was not just a device or transmission system, but also a source of influence over the social, political and cultural lives of western societies. This alone meant that politicians and policy-makers viewed it quite differently to other IS sectors.

Also, DTV technology and business models raise different and potentially more complex regulatory problems than telecoms and IT. Whereas Internet users can access whatever content they want, in DTV the programmes and services viewers can access depend on what the network operator makes available and on the technical capability of the digital set-top box or decoder. Telecoms and the Internet have benefited from the network effects made possible by their connectedness and interoperability, but DTV remains a series of closed networks where operators supply non-interoperable equipment as a way of locking consumers into their services.

Finally, the shift to DTV opened up three difficult issues. The first was the moment at which digital transmission might be so widespread that the existing analogue terrestrial signals could be switched off without endangering the existence of TV as a universal medium. The second was how the analogue spectrum might then be reused or sold on by government. And the third was the extent to which governments could control what their citizens watched once analogue transmission was phased out. Clearly there would be greater opportunities for control with a digital terrestrial transmission system or cable, since both are managed by national (or regional, in the case of Germany) licensing authorities. Thus, while there were strong calls particularly at the European level for the convergence of regulatory approaches to the IS to include TV, there were equally strong political, cultural, technical and competition reasons for national policy-makers to treat DTV differently.

There was no reluctance among national governments to reform the regulatory system for TV. Since the mid-1990s an unprecedented wave of broadcasting and media policy reform has occurred in the EU's major member states – France, Britain, Germany, Italy and Spain all made substantial changes in broadcasting legislation. Politicians regularly cited technological change and digitalization as a strong exogenous pressure for reform, and shared a common concern to maintain or reassert their regulatory authority. But the ways in which this was attempted reflected the particular traditions and circumstances of each country.

France: defending culture
French approaches to digital regulation were coloured by a long-standing view of communications policy as a modern-day Maginot line against industrial and cultural incursion. In the mid-1990s France perceived herself as technologically backward. Cable and satellite TV penetration was only 10 per cent of Germany's, there were only half as many Internet users as in the UK or Germany, and France was near the bottom of the European league table for mobile telephones. France also felt ideologically isolated in international organizations such as the World Trade Organization (and, increasingly on audio-visual matters, within the EU as well), and culturally threatened by the popularity of American programming. For some time French policy had been directed at building strong national media companies and promoting modernization of the country's infrastructure, while keeping Hollywood away from French TV and cinema screens. With the advent of digital broadcasting these traditional preoccupations remained, but increased

emphasis was placed on the industrial and economic, rather than cultural, aspects of broadcasting policy (Levy, 2001).

The Broadcasting Bill first discussed in 1997 was only finally passed, in much-revised form, in June 2000. The law had four key features. First, France's public service broadcaster, France Television, was granted more reliable multi-year funding in return for a reduction in advertising. Second, the future of digital terrestrial television in France was confirmed, with France Television expected to play a leading role. Third, media ownership rules were relaxed. Finally, France implemented the provisions of the EU 1995 Advanced TV Standards Directive, governing third-party access to digital set-top boxes.

Regulating access to set-top boxes was important in the UK in opening up the satellite television network to third-party broadcasters. But in France, competition was ensured through other measures. The government had already created a competitor to the leading pay broadcaster, Canal Plus, by sponsoring the creation of Télévision par Satellite (TPS), a joint venture between private and public broadcasters. For its first three years of operation TPS alone was allowed to transmit France TV channels, allowing it to gain subscribers in those areas where terrestrial reception was poor. Another feature of the French approach was the emphasis on digital terrestrial broadcasting (DTT). Whereas DTT in the UK was used to free-up the terrestrial spectrum, in France it was clearly intended to ensure a public sphere, with strong emphasis on using DTT for public-service broadcasters and community rather than commercial operators. It remains unclear whether this will help DTT succeed in France or, rather, reduce any commercial incentive to subsidize consumer equipment, thereby placing it at a disadvantage to satellite and cable.

French approaches to DTV thus reflected a mix of cultural and more commercial views of TV. As home to Europe's largest pay broadcaster – Canal Plus – France could never ignore the commercial side of TV. But the policy rhetoric surrounding DTV was still heavily influenced by cultural concerns, reflected in a resistance to creating converged regulation. The spheres of the telecoms regulator (the ART) and the Conseil Supérieure de l'audiovisuel (CSA) were kept separate. And while other countries suggested a diminishing role for content regulation in an age of convergence, in France the legitimacy of such regulation and public intervention over content remained paramount.

Germany: federalism first

In contrast to Britain and France, German approaches to the regulation of DTV often seemed somewhat perverse. Discussion of the IS quickly led to constitutional debate because the new multimedia services appeared to challenge the existing separation between Federal jurisdiction over telecoms and Länder responsibility for broadcasting. This debate meant there was never any serious question of achieving a converged regulatory structure. Instead there were often messy compromises in the treatment of IS services leading in 1997 to an Interstate Treaty on New Media Services, and a Federal Information and Communication Services Act which also dealt with new media services, both operating alongside a revised Interstate Treaty on Broadcasting.

With new media services, a distinction was drawn between those regulated at the Federal level, those providing access to the Internet or other networks, and services offered for information or communication. The Interstate Treaty, meanwhile, applied to 'All information and communication services (media services) in form of text, audio or video that are directed at the general public'. Where services straddle the two levels, jurisdiction is determined according to whether or not they have any editorial input or impact. The system's complexity stems from the fact that the Länder drew up the Media Services Treaty to prevent Federal legislation encroaching on their regulatory domain. German approaches have been more conventional in the broadcasting sphere, where the Länder are in clear control. In some areas – such as media ownership – the aim has been to liberalize controls and create a more competitive German media sector, but the growth rate of digital pay TV has been slower in Germany than in either Britain or France. This may be because the European competition authorities prevented the merger of the two major German media companies – Bertelsmann and Kirch – leaving the latter to develop digital pay TV on its own. However, the plentiful supply of free TV (the average household has access to 30 free channels) has certainly contributed to the lag.

UK: ensuring control and protecting universal access

The UK's reactions to DTV were different again. With the exception of media ownership, reregulation rather than deregulation was the hallmark of measures introduced in 1996. Tough regulations were imposed to ensure third-party access through digital set-top boxes, a 'must-carry' regime was created to ensure the carriage of public service channels on digital cable networks, and the 'listed events' provisions (aimed at preventing key sporting events being shown only on pay channels) were reinforced. Two features that distinguished UK digital broadcasting policy were the emphasis given to Digital Terrestrial TV (DTT) and to the regulation of conditional access. Both reflected a similar preoccupation to ensure that digital TV developed on a different model from that of analogue pay TV.

UK policies to promote DTT in the mid-1990s not only placed it at odds with its more cautious neighbours, but appeared to be a surprising attempt at industrial policy by a normally *laissez-faire* Conservative government. From the government's perspective, DTT had several advantages: it could provide guaranteed coverage for the existing public-service terrestrial channels; offer a nationwide distribution system under government control; open the possibility of an eventual switch-off of analogue terrestrial transmission and consequent auction of the spectrum; and create a rival digital system to BSkyB's digital satellite services. Since the early 1990s, BSkyB had established a seemingly unbreakable hold over analogue pay television, mainly through its control of premium sports rights. BSkyB was 40 per cent owned and effectively controlled by Rupert Murdoch's News International, whose newspapers in turn accounted for 30 per cent of newspaper circulation, and the government was not keen to see Murdoch's hold on the media increased (Levy, 1997).

Interest in switching off analogue terrestrial transmissions increased after the hugely successful sell-off of third-generation mobile licences, which brought in around £20 billion (€32 billion) for the Treasury. Political difficulties raised by talk of analogue switch off led the government to develop a new term, 'digital switchover', to offer reassurance about the continued universal availability of TV transmissions. In September 1999 the government offered a window of 2006 to 2010 for switchover, subject to digital services being as widely available as analogue TV (99.4 per cent of the population) and 95 per cent of consumers having access to affordable digital equipment. Exactly how these targets were to be met, though, remained unclear.

Towards the end of 2000 a White Paper on the future of Communications marked a new development in UK policy (DTI/DCMS, 2000). The White Paper had three aims: to make the UK home to the most dynamic and competitive communications and media market in the world; to ensure universal access to a choice of diverse services of the highest quality; and to ensure that citizens and consumers are safeguarded. Key proposals included the creation of a converged regulator – OFCOM – dealing with infrastructure and content issues across the sector, limited liberalization of the rules on media ownership allowing some further consolidation in the ownership of the main free-to-air commercial terrestrial broadcaster, ITV, and obligations to ensure the universal availability of free-to-air public-service television channels across all the digital TV platforms. In spite of being dubbed a 'Communications' White Paper, the document is more preoccupied with the broadcasting sector than with IT or telephony. Nevertheless, the commitment to a converged regulator marks a new departure. The challenge for such a body will be to balance not just the conflicting demands of different sectors, but also economic and infrastructure versus content-focused regulation. Equally demanding will be the need to fit national regulation of broadcasting into a framework established at the EU level.

Encouraging e-commerce and creating the e-society

Perhaps it is understandable that broadcasting is an area where divergences between approaches most reflect the different national traditions and preoccupations and where, as a result, exogenous pressures for reform are highly subject to cultural, social and political mediation. But there have also been marked differences in promoting e-commerce and improving universal access and IT literacy, which are much less politically charged.

Britain, France and Germany all saw the Internet, and the promise of much extended e-commerce, as a great opportunity for boosting growth and competitiveness. But there were also serious risks: to social inclusion if some groups could not gain access to the new technology; of competitive disadvantage if, for example, Internet penetration in one country did not keep pace with that elsewhere; and of a loss of government control in terms of the rules that could be imposed on e-commerce companies. These concerns all demanded different forms of public intervention. In contrast was the view shared by US business and some EU member states that innovation in the IS was best promoted by government withdrawal, not more intervention. In practice, the policies pursued by most member states towards the IS sought some balance between these different pressures.

France, Germany and the UK instigated a series of plans for the IS in the late 1990s (EC, 2000a). The French IS strategy was launched in January 1998 through an Action Plan to 'prepare the entry of France into the Information Society'. Six priority areas focused on education, culture, using IT as a tool for modernizing public services, promoting the use of IT in companies, encouraging innovation and research in IT and the Internet, and updating the regulatory framework to promote secure payment systems on the Internet. The French focus on culture was quite distinctive among EU countries, and involved supporting the creation of multimedia materials and services, digitizing France's cultural heritage and distributing cultural data on the Internet, and reinforcing the international presence of France and the French language. It also reflected the extent to which the French saw the IS as a cultural as well as a commercial challenge.

A French government review of progress in 2000, following expenditure of 760 million French francs (€116 million) over three years, was

positive; 100 per cent of primary schools had been connected to the
Internet, the civil service had caught up with the private sector in terms of
Internet use, support mechanisms had been established to help in the transition to the IS, and a new programme was developed to combat the 'digital divide'. French concerns about culture were revealed early in 2001
when the Culture Minister, Catherine Tasca, suggested that levies on digital recording media (designed to compensate artists for private copying)
should be extended to include PCs. The proposal was rejected, but it highlighted an area where the desire for rapid rollout of IS technologies
conflicted with traditional French concerns. Indeed, the proposal was in
direct conflict with the campaigns by French Internet and IT companies
for more government encouragement of their sector, through lighter regulation and new local flat-rate telephone charging schemes to allow unlim-
ited Internet use. One campaign for flat-rate charging launched in
February 2001 pointed out that only 19 per cent of French households
were Internet connected, compared to 29 per cent in Germany, 35 per cent
in the UK, and over 50 per cent in Scandinavia and the USA.

The German authorities were similarly concerned to facilitate e-
commerce. The government's 1999 Plan for the Information Age
included some familiar themes: ensuring broad access to new media and
building competence; increasing supplier and consumer confidence in
electronic trading; and modernizing the state through 'e-government'.
Thus, the plan sought to increase Internet subscriptions from 9 per cent
of the population in 1999 to 40 per cent in 2005 and to boost the use
of the Internet by small firms, to equip all schools with PCs and Internet
connections by 2001 and to integrate new media into lifelong learning
programmes, and to encourage the use of electronic tendering and tax
returns (EC, 2000a).

Some of these aims came up against other more traditional national
concerns. Measures to liberalize e-commerce and to base regulation, as
proposed by the EU, on the country-of-origin principle, ran counter to
long-established German rules outlawing comparative advertising, or
even automatic searching for the lowest possible price, one of the main
consumer benefits of the Internet. In late 2000 two German courts ruled
that so-called power shopping, where consumers band together to
create sufficient market power to get a larger discount, contravened a
1933 German law prohibiting discounts other than up to 3 per cent for
individual cash-paying customers. Equally, attempts to promote the IS
through confidence-building measures designed to protect minors came
up against the divided competence between the Federal government and
the Länder. Progress towards e-government faced a less tangible obstacle, namely the traditionalist hierarchy of many German civil servants,
until relatively recently reflected in an inverse relationship between

seniority and the likelihood of an individual having a computer on their desk or indeed any computer skills.

The UK liked to see itself as in the European vanguard of approaches towards creating a business and consumer-friendly IS. Cultural and constitutional considerations proved less of an obstacle than in France or Germany and the UK made rapid progress towards creating greater Internet penetration, advancing e-government and placing the issue of how to create an inclusive IS at the top of the agenda.

Under the Blair administration, the key features of its IS strategy became clear in May 1998. Strong emphasis was placed on facilitating private-sector initiatives in e-commerce, with a government role in harnessing new technology in education, preventing a gulf between information haves and have-nots, promoting competition and competitiveness, ensuring the quality of new services matched the best in traditional delivery systems, using new technology in the delivery of government services and making them more readily available to consumers and citizens.

UK e-commerce and IS initiatives were characterized by a proliferation of action programmes, specialist units, targets and progress reviews. The aim was to put Britain at the cutting-edge of the IS in Europe, and progress reviews were frequently linked with initiatives on private-sector competitiveness and improving the electronic delivery of government services. In September 1999 the Cabinet Office Performance and Innovation Unit published a report, *e-commerce@its.best.uk*, listing 60 targets. The report recommended the appointment of a minister responsible for e-commerce and the creation of the post of e-Envoy, tasked with spreading e-commerce in industry and government. Together, the minister and the e Envoy produce monthly reports assessing progress in meeting the commitments set out in the 1999 report.

One priority for the government was to extend Internet access and increase the efficiency of government service delivery. The 2001 launch of the government portal *ukonline.gov.uk* was one of the most important elements of this programme. Tony Blair set the target of universal Internet access by 2005. By the end of 2000 the figure for home access was around 30 per cent, but there remained a distinct lack of clarity over how the government might judge when its target had been met. Did universal access include at work as well as at home? Did access close to home (such as in a public library) count? And did access to a walled garden of preselected sites through a digital TV count as Internet access at all, since as far as e-commerce was concerned consumers might find themselves limited to simply one on-line trader for each service (Tambini, 2000).

Vague answers to such questions led some to wonder whether the primary goal was more about demonstrating a modernizing government at work, than about delivering concrete services. While e-government initiatives flourished, very few people had started using them by early 2001. And while the creation of the e-Envoy demonstrated commitment, a parliamentary committee also criticized the e-Envoy's office for being too much like a propaganda arm of government.

It seems clear that the UK gave great attention to promoting e-commerce, but capturing the rhetorical lead was perhaps easier than changing reality and, as remarked above, the UK's early lead in telecoms liberalization was lost through delays in achieving local-loop unbundling. In 2000 a World Information Society Index placed the UK twelfth out of 55 countries and fifth amongst EU member states (EC, 2000a).

Policy leadership: national or supranational

As is clear from the preceding discussion, there were very many national policy responses to the IS. It is worth asking, however, how far these responses were just a reaction to technological developments or whether they were structured, at least in part, by policy discussions and developments taking place at the international level.

Since one of the principal drivers of IS policy was a desire for competitiveness, it is natural that there were constant pressures to look beyond national borders to compare performance in the IS sector and find lessons. This kind of policy transfer between national and supranational responses to the IS occurred in three ways. The first was in the emergence of new IS policy communities involving governments and key industry players in fora such as the OECD and the EU. The second was the EU's role in setting the policy agenda after 1997 through its emphasis on regulatory responses to convergence and telecoms liberalization and the Prodi initiative for e-Europe. Finally, there was the legislative momentum created by EU initiatives in areas such as e-commerce, copyright and telecoms. This section seeks to assess the extent to which, taken together, these three developments provide evidence of policy leadership developing beyond the nation-state in the IS arena, and, if so, how much of it rested with the EU or other international groupings.

The development of IS services was accompanied by the emergence of new policy communities. Among contributory factors was a sense of frustration in several companies involved in IS services at existing regulatory frameworks, as well as a natural tendency for government experts and firms involved in IS services to want to gather together in international fora and discuss ideas. The result of these trends was that the new policy communities started to see themselves as pioneers and evangelists for largely technocratic solutions to regulatory problems that had for too long been dominated by political and cultural concerns.

The OECD provided an arena for the transfer of ideas from a US-dominated IS community to the EU and beyond. One 1997 OECD paper called for the elimination of 'the traditional regulatory paradigm based on strict communication service boundaries' (cited in Levy, 2001). Later that year a pioneering OECD work on the impact of 'webcasting' (the use of the Internet to deliver broadcast-type audio and video services) concluded that: '[t]he more webcasting comes to resemble traditional services the greater the challenge will become to the existing regulatory frameworks' (OECD, 1997). In more recent years the OECD has provided an important forum for the development of ideas on facilitating e-commerce and building trust in new electronic networks, discussing privacy, and examining the impact of differing local-access pricing schemes on Internet take-up and possibilities for e-commerce.

The OECD's reflections coincided with those of others concerned with telecoms policy-making, both at the national level and within the EU. Telecoms operators and regulators were quick to see the development of IS services as an opportunity for the approaches adopted in telecoms to be applied on a wider scale. Broadcasting regulation, one of the most traditionally resistant areas to such treatment, was amongst the first to be called into question by the trend towards convergence. In the UK, OFTEL had argued from as early as 1995 that as:

> the traditional scarcity of broadcasting channels becomes an issue of the past, and as traditional telecommunications systems begin to offer video-based services, broadcast services will become increasingly difficult to distinguish from other services [and] . . . the traditional regulatory distinctions between broadcasting and telecommunications will be difficult to sustain. (OFTEL, 1995)

But at the time this idea was seen as being at the margins of available political options. It was only with the development of EU interest in ideas of regulatory convergence that more radical ideas of how to approach the IS found, if not exactly an advocate, at least an arena in which they might be articulated.

The EU's 1997 Green Paper on Convergence grew out of earlier discussions within the OECD, together with developing thinking by European advocates of radical regulatory reform of the communications sector (EC, 1997). The Green Paper offered an analysis of the obstacles to convergence, including differing approaches to the classification of new services, differing licensing regimes in different countries, and the contrasting approaches adopted to spectrum allocation in telecommunications and broadcasting. Several proposals were advanced to deal with these 'potential obstacles', including greater reliance on self-regulation, as on the Internet, and a common set of principles for national licensing authorities. The key section of the Green Paper discussed three policy responses to regulating for convergence: building on current regulatory structures, primarily at the national level; developing a separate regulatory model for new activities that could not be satisfactorily classified under telecommunications or broadcasting; and moving towards a new regulatory model to cover the whole range of existing and new services. The Commission's Information Society Directorate had a clear preference for the third option. Indeed, in a speech made shortly before publication of the Green Paper, Commissioner Bangemann (who was then responsible for IS policy) had expressed his desire that the future 'regulatory framework for communications and media in Europe . . . must be 'technology neutral', simplified, uniform, and not fragmented, so that it genuinely reflects the converged environment' (cited in Levy, 2001).

These radical ideas never came to pass, largely because member states, broadcasters and the European Parliament opposed them – in part because of the transfer of competence they required in broadcasting policy from member states to the Commission. This defeat of the more radical Commission ideas on the treatment of the regulatory framework for the IS and the converging communications sector was significant but relatively short-lived. The compromise solution that emerged was for a reform of the regulation of all communications infrastructure, giving the Commission a greatly increased role in setting agreed policy objectives and establishing regulatory principles, while policy implementation and all questions of content regulation were left to member states. Thus, even though the Commission's early attempt at leadership had failed, in the long term it was to emerge with greater oversight, and supervision of all national communications regulation.

The Commission's pattern of intervention in telecoms, promoting deregulation at the national level followed by reregulation at the EU level, was to reemerge in the ideas proposed as part of its 1999 Communications Review and subsequent directives on the entire communications sector. Other than a regulation designed to speed up progress towards local-loop unbundling (LLU), there were also directives on the regulatory framework, on access and interconnection and on universal service and users' rights. The directives excluded almost all references to content-related issues, but were otherwise far-reaching and marked a transfer of responsibility from the member states to the EU.

The Framework Directive established policy objectives that all national regulators were obliged to follow, a further optional set of regulatory measures, and a prohibition on intervention against any operator who did not have 'significant market power', that is 40–50 per cent of the market. All these measures were generally welcomed by those incumbent operators who hoped to expand outside their national territory and by mobile operators. Both groups saw restrictions on the freedom of national regulatory authorities as helping them in territories where otherwise the national regulator might favour its own incumbent. Mobile operators particularly liked the idea that their status as new, and largely unregulated, entrants would be difficult to call into question since national regulators could not act against firms who were not dominant.

The Commission's role as policy leader and agenda-setter in IS policy-making was more clear-cut with the transition from the early Information Society Action Plan, hatched under Bangemann, to Prodi's e-Europe initiative. e-Europe was launched in December 1999 with the key objectives of bringing all Europeans into the digital age and online, creating a digitally literate Europe supported by an entrepreneurial culture, and ensuring that the process was socially inclusive and developed consumer trust. The initiative was endorsed by member states at the so-called 'dot com' Lisbon Summit in March 2000, the first occasion when heads of government really engaged at EU level with the implications of new technologies for employment and growth. The summit also produced political agreement for a fast-track approach to LLU with a commitment to implementation by the end of the year (EC, 2000d). The subsequent June summit at Feira in Portugal was used to create an e-Europe Action Plan, and the Nice Summit in December 2000 provided an opportunity for progress reports on developments since Lisbon. While Europe's relatively low levels of Internet penetration were a constant theme of these summits, the contrast was also made with the opportunities presented by Europe's lead over the USA in mobile telephony, thanks to a European-wide standard, GSM. The hope was that as the Internet moved from the fixed PC to the mobile phone and digital TV, Europe might catch up lost ground.

The impact of e-Europe was felt in two main respects. Similar initiatives were rapidly adopted in all the major member states, with clear programmes and targets against which regular progress reports were produced. The UK's reports from the office of the e-Envoy predated e-Europe, but they reflected an approach which was rapidly extended across the EU.

Reporting on the progress of e-Europe to the Nice European Council in December 2000, the European Commission (2000c, p. 2) lauded its early results:

Since its launch, e-Europe has had a broad policy impact, strengthening existing initiatives and fostering the development of new ones. It has become a policy concept, not only at European level, but in member states at national and regional level. 'e-Initiatives' of one kind or another are now generalised within the Union, with the launch by individual member states and regions of new initiatives and support programmes.

Concrete EU-level legislative progress included the Regulation on local-loop unbundling, rapid steps taken on the rest of the Communications Review package and the adoption early in 2000 of the e-commerce Directive providing a legal framework for the provision of services in Europe. Further steps involved the e-money Directive and the progress made on the Copyright Directive, which was finally adopted by the European Parliament in February 2001 (EC, 2000c). Many members of the European Parliament saw the Copyright Directive as the most heavily lobbied directive ever. The discussions in the Council of Ministers over the course of 1999–2000 were equally fraught. Ultimately, the Parliament and Commission's desire for the new Directive to be passed into law led them to accept a much weaker harmonizing measure than either institution might have liked. A raft of – admittedly rather minor – national exceptions to copyright rules were incorporated into the final Directive by member states.

IS issues were highly susceptible to policy leadership coming from the EU and the international arenas. The development of new IS-focused policy communities, whether at the OECD or EU level, had a clear impact. Sometimes, as with the EU debate on regulatory convergence, these communities could overreach themselves and were reined in by national governments. But this was more likely to occur in areas where there was a clear cultural interest than in most other IS debates. Perhaps the greatest impact of EU policy leadership was in setting the framework within which IS issues were debated, in identifying key targets, and of course through the concrete legislative decisions taken at EU level.

For this policy leadership to be accepted, however, member states and industry needed to be persuaded of the need for action as well as that this could best be achieved at the EU level. Interestingly, in the case of e-Europe there was a close alliance between the UK government and the measures proposed by Romano Prodi and implemented by the Information Society Commissioner, Erkki Liikanen. The language of e-Europe fitted well with the Blair government's preoccupation with modernization, and at least in the early part of Prodi's term of office there were particularly close links between 10 Downing Street and his office. While industry groups would often complain that e-Europe was more about rhetoric than substance, and worried about EU meddling in what they saw as a regulation-free zone, most IT and telecoms companies had higher hopes of satisfactory results being achieved at the EU than at national levels. The EU legislative process was more susceptible to pressure from the newer industrial sectors and many of the players' businesses specifically required an EU-wide policy rather than a series of national approaches. Ideally, many would have liked a global approach via the WTO or OECD, but there was always scope to engage at all three levels in the hope that policies rebuffed in one might succeed at another. In addition there was frequent policy spillover between debates and initiatives at each of these different levels.

An emerging European policy consensus on the Information Society?

Clearly, the IS places traditional patterns of national decision-making under pressure. However the emerging consensus between EU member states over the need to address Europe's perceived competitive disadvantage in the new IS masks differences over the level at which action should take place, and the balance between facilitating e-commerce or creating and sustaining a more inclusive e-society. Amongst those who emphasize the social and cultural impacts of the IS there is a further fragmentation over whether the threat, and therefore appropriate level of response, is primarily to national or to an EU culture.

There is no doubt that converging and globalizing technologies create new policy pressures and change established patterns of agenda-setting. Nationally-based interest groups within the IS industries are more likely to adopt policy demands which have been formulated in an international setting. The strength of a new *laissez-faire* Internet business culture has also helped contribute to an increasingly vocal and homogenous industry view within Western Europe that is often indistinguishable from that adopted across the Atlantic. Convergence meanwhile breaks down established policy communities at the national and European level, exposing broadcasting regulation to demands that it be aligned with the treatment of telecoms, while past settlements in telecoms come under challenge from the demands of the IT industry (such as for unmetered Internet access).

These trends are too contradictory and insufficiently well-established for them to lead on their own to the creation of a new policy consensus. But they do place established national policy approaches and structures under pressure, creating new opportunities for EU and other international policy-makers. Since these have less of a vested interest than national administrations in existing regulatory traditions, they have generally been enthusiastic about extending the EU telecoms approach of national deregulation followed by EU-level reregulation across the converging industries. In this, EU policy-makers can often rely on the support of the new policy communities active in debates within the OECD and the WTO as well as within the EU's elaborate networks. In recent years such communities have included large elements of both EU- and US-owned IT companies, the mobile phone operators and manufacturers such as Nokia and Ericsson, as well as national telecommunications companies which hope a shift in the level of regulation will allow them to penetrate new European markets. These groups can often point to functional arguments for extra-territorial policy-making. It is easy to make the case for the nation-state being too small an entity to create policy frameworks for the Internet, e-commerce or copyright, all of which clearly cross national boundaries. However, arguments such as these were not always persuasive, partly because states would sometimes defend their competence, and also because several industries themselves chose to segment national markets. Thus, on occasion, the film and video industry would insist that technology made national cultural policies unnecessary, but would then introduce country-specific region codes on DVDs in order to protect their release windows for different markets. Similarly, IT firms at the forefront of claims that national regulation was redundant in regard to the Internet would then resort to that same regulation to defend themselves against infringements of their copyright.

What is the case, however, is that more than in many other sectors, policies towards the Information Society are being framed at the European rather than the nation-state level. Broadcasting – because of its cultural and social significance – remains an exception to this developing trend, but the trend is nevertheless becoming increasingly well-established. National policies towards the IS still have different flavours but they are all developed with considerable regard to policy debates, initiatives and legislation framed at the EU level. Thus, the Information Society not only presents a serious policy challenge to Europe's member states, it also contains within it a challenge to the continuation of key areas of national policy-making.

Chapter 14

European Immigration Policies at the Crossroads

CHRISTIAN JOPPKE

A recent study by the United Nations Population Division (2000) revealed the shocking proportions of population decline in developed Western societies. If one assumes an average net migration of 300 000 people until 2050 ('Scenario I'), the European Union (EU) would comprise 40 million less people in 2050 than in 1995 – a loss equivalent to the combined present population of the seven smallest member states (p. 85). In order to keep the size of the working population at its 1995 level ('Scenario III'), the EU would have to recruit almost 80 million new migrants in the next 50 years, which amounts to an average of 1.4 million migrants per year – more than twice above the current level. And in order to keep the 'potential support ratio' of active to retired people at its 1995 value ('Scenario V'), the EU would have to accept a staggering 701 million immigrants over the same period, which is an average of 12.7 million per year.

This is no news to demographers – individual country studies had long revealed similar trends. Moreover, the absurdly high numbers of Scenario V, which estimates the required support structure for pension schemes as currently devised, suggest that immigration can hardly be The Solution to the problem of shrinking and ageing populations. Accordingly, as a German demographer comments on the UN study, 'there is no demographer who would recommend an active immigration policy as a remedy to shrinking birth rates' (*Frankfurter Allgemeine Zeitung*, 12 April 2000). However, the at least partial need for such a policy in contemporary Europe is increasingly difficult to refute (*The Economist*, 6 May 2000). French Interior Minister Chevènement, not known for expansive views on immigration, recently confronted his EU colleagues with the disturbing UN data, which in his view show the need for an active immigration policy in the European Union (*Frankfurter Allgemeine Zeitung*, 31 July 2000). However, against the objective need for a 'soliciting' immigration policy stands a long-lasting legacy of European immigration policies, both at national and supranational levels, geared towards the opposite logic of 'stemming'.

The first part of this chapter elaborates on the different logics of soliciting and stemming immigration policies, pointing in particular to some dilemmas inherent in the stemming policies that have come to predominate in Europe after the first oil crisis of 1973. In a second step, I show that the pending Europeanization of the immigration function has been in the spirit of stemming too, which is doubly determined by the stemming policies of member states and the new regime's compensatory function for the dissolution of internal borders within the EU. The third part discusses the strategies and problems connected with stemming unwanted migration at Europe's new external borders to the east and the south. I close with a brief discussion of the cautious turn towards soliciting immigration policies in Europe, which was brought into the open by Germany's 'green card' scheme in spring 2000, but which is hampered by some structural hurdles such as a hostile mass public and the logic of party competition.

'Soliciting' and 'stemming'

Soliciting and stemming are everywhere the two faces of immigration policy. They differ in their relationship to the underlying migrant flows: soliciting is about the creation of flows; stemming presupposes existing flows, and seeks to contain them. While analytically to be kept distinct, soliciting and stemming often overlap empirically. The relationship may be causal; an example is the soliciting guestworker policies in continental Europe, which created the ethnic networks and pathways that subsequently became the object of stemming policies. Or a soliciting policy may take on elements of stemming; an example being the recently reactivated 'deeming' schemes in US quota immigration which make it more difficult for resident immigrants to sponsor their family members, and which are obviously designed to reduce immigration flows. Finally, a soliciting policy is sometimes seen as the best way of stemming a flow – this is one rationale for the second-generation guestworker programme established by Germany with its East European neighbours in the 1990s, and it is the main pragmatic argument by those who would like to see legal quota immigration established in Europe.

In contrast to the United States, which – like all new settler nations – has both soliciting and stemming immigration policies, in contemporary Europe immigration policies are exclusively about stemming (see the overview in Guiraudon and Joppke, 2001). This has deep historical roots, not least the aversion of ethnic nation-states to welcome newcomers. The two distinct immigration experiences of postwar European states, guest-worker and post- colonial immigration, reinforced this aversion (see Joppke, 1999). Both types of immigration, as different as they are, have at least one thing in common: they happened by default. They were unintended consequence of the pursuit of other interests – the political interest in empire, or the economic interest in manpower. As 'immigration', that is the permanent settlement of aliens, both guestworker and post-colonial immigration was unwanted. This makes the European immigration experience fundamentally different from the American one, where legal quota immigration is wanted immigration. Next to being unwanted as 'immigration', guestworker and post-colonial immigration was perceived in Europe as a one-time experience. This again differs from US-type legal quota immigration, which has been a recurrent experience – even at the height of nativist restrictions in the 1920s it could only be drastically reduced, not entirely abolished. The unwanted immigration of guestworkers and post-colonials has even powerfully reaffirmed the rejection of US-type recurrent legal immigration. European states, so to speak, made an exception in the case of guestworkers and post-colonials. And courting these exceptional immigrants with generous integration offers, such as reformed citizenship laws for (the descendants of) guestworkers and anti-discrimination and race relations laws for post- colonials, is promised on closing the doors for all others. There is no American (or Canadian or Australian) equivalent to the peculiarly European tying of 'good' immigrant integration to immigration policies whose sole purpose is to prevent more to come.

Whatever their historical origins and rationales, European immigration policies geared towards stemming are notoriously suspected of being deficient. This suspicion is expressed in the recent scholarly debate on the authority and capacity (or 'sovereignty') of states to control the movement of people across borders (Guiraudon and Lahav, 2000). With regard to soliciting policies, sovereignty is a non-issue – the requisite flows are only if states have decided to have them. By contrast, inherent in the logic of stemming policies is the charge that they are deficient: they are activated by already existing flows which are, as such, a violation of the no-immigration norm that drives the stemming exercise. In crafting stemming policies, states are like detectives – only a crime activates them. Being by definition *ex post*, stemming policies are chronically exposed to the deficiency charge. This chronic deficiency is aggravated by the fact that states are dealing with resourceful migrants who are constantly circumventing existing controls – the historical evolution in Europe from the guestworker recruitment stop in the mid-1970s, to restricting asylum in the 1980s and early 1990s, and to combatting illegal immigration and organized human smuggling since the mid-1990s could be retold in terms of a cat-and-mouse game in which the clever-chased forever finds another escape (or 'loophole').

If one takes the *ex post* nature of stemming policies into account, the widespread notion of 'control crisis' (Cornelius *et al.*, 1994) is misguided. In fact, it is raised whenever resourceful migrants create the need for a new stemming policy. A good example is the wave of mass asylum-seeking after the opening of the Berlin Wall, which was effectively responded to by state-level restrictions of constitutional asylum rights and a European-level coordination of asylum responsibilities. If one applies a long-term view, the effectiveness, rather than deficiency of stemming policies moves to the fore. A recent comparison of immigration control in eight European countries concludes: 'There is no significant control crisis present in Europe today . . . On the contrary, [there is] steadily higher sophistication in terms of flow control and internal surveillance' (Brochmann and Hammar, 1999, p. 298).

Next to being chronically deficient due to their *ex post* nature, stemming policies have a second structural problem – once in place it is difficult to get rid of them, or, as in the case of Europe, to complement them with soliciting policies should the need arise. This is not just a result of entrenchment and path-dependency. It seems to be an Iron Law of the mass public in immigrant-receiving states to be negatively disposed to new immigration, even in the transoceanic new settler nations (Simon and Lynch, 1999). Stemming policies cannot but reinforce this negative view, because they are premised on a picture of migrants as resourceful cheaters. The legitimacy of soliciting policies rests on a fundamentally different picture of migrants, as in the interest of the receiving society. The current European movement towards legal quota immigration not only has to overcome a mass public who are everywhere hostile towards immigration, in Europe as much as overseas, but a mass public whose negative instincts have been further fuelled by three decades of immigration policies in the negative spirit of stemming only. Among previous immigration foes, the new migrant image sometimes takes on rather crude contours which is visibly coloured by the old: 'We need more foreigners of use to us and less who utilise us', say the new immigration enthusiasts in the German CDU (*Die Zeit*, 6 July 2000).

In between immigration that is to be stemmed and immigration that is solicited is as-of-right immigration. Examples are the family unification of settled labour migrants, or asylum. Like immigration that is subject to stemming, as-of-right immigration is essentially unwanted – receiving states would rather prefer not to have it. But like solicited immigration, as-of-right immigration is legitimate and lawful, and cannot be prevented by liberal states unless they violate liberal principles. A proper interpretation of as-of-right immigration has been the true subject of the scholarly debate over the resilience or decline of state sovereignty in immigration control. Some have argued that international or 'global' norms force states to accept unwanted as-of-right immigrants, and they see state sovereignty in decline (most explicitly Jacobson, 1996). Others have identified domestic norms and processes as responsible for this outcome, thus arguing in favour of resilient but 'self-limited' sovereignty (Joppke, 1998, 2001).

The sovereignty debate has somewhat suffered from an exaggerated division between domestic-level and global-level norms and processes, instead of looking at their interconnections. And to the degree that global norms are externalizations of domestic principles and traditions of long-entrenched liberal states, the distinction between global and domestic norms becomes spurious. Moreover, perhaps more relevant than quibbling about the origins and location of rights constraints is to look at how states have actually responded to them. In a stimulating overview, Guiraudon and Lahav (2000) have shown that European states have responded to global and domestic rights constraints by shifting the locus of immigration control 'upward' to intergovernmental bodies not subject to judicial review and the critical gaze of civil society (most notably the European Union), 'downward' to local governments which, more than national governments, feel the nervous breath of an immigrant-hostile publics in their necks (cf. Money, 1999; Karapin, 1999), and 'outward' to non-state actors such as airlines and ordinary citizens which release the state as such of the control burden.

Perhaps not quite captured by this tripartite distinction is a more fundamental distinction, between 'internal' and 'external' immigration controls (for this, see Brochmann and Hammar, 1999). Examples of internal controls are employer sanctions or mandatory ID cards; examples of external controls are visa schemes, physical border reinforcements, the safe-third-country rule in asylum policy, or the creation of extraterritorial 'anomalous zones' (Neuman, 1997) in which the rule of law does not apply. While immigrant-receiving states have perfected both control strategies, the advantage of an external strategy is to circumvent rights without openly violating them. By contrast, internal controls require rights restrictions, which often also affect non-immigrants. For this there are clear legal and moral limits in liberal states. An example is the notorious *Certificat d'hebergement*, by means of which the French government sought to turn its entire citizenry into police spies, and which had to be revoked under an avalanche of public protest (see Hollifield, 1999).

'Europe' as a tool of stemming

In the context of zero-immigration policies at the member-state level, the Europeanization of the immigration function had to occur in the spirit of stemming. However, the polemical notion of Fortress Europe obscures that there is not one, but two European migration regimes, whose guiding principles and legal infrastructures are radically different (see Koslowski, 1998). First, there is a supranational regime governing intra-European migration; and, secondly, an intergovernmental regime governing external migration (and thus: 'immigration' proper) into the EU. The intra-European regime is grounded in the founding treaty of the European Community, which guarantees free movement rights for workers, self-employed persons and service providers. However, it did not spring from a free agreement between states, but had to be imposed on recalcitrant but increasingly disempowered 'member states' by the supranational institutions created to implement the EC Treaty, most notably the European Court of Justice (see Joppke, 2001). This coercive logic makes the development of free movement in the EC different from previous free-movement regimes within Europe, such as the Nordic labour market and passport union of the 1950s, which remained purely intergovernmental and did not take on a supranational dimension with own courts and jurisdictions. Since the internal free-movement regime is best interpreted in terms of *de facto* state-building, it should not be called an 'immigration' regime at all. Witness that the 'migrant workers' in the earlier literature (see for example Garth, 1986) have all but disappeared, and that since 1992 internal border-crossers are officially codified as EU 'citizens'.

The astonishing erosion of the capacity of European Union states to control movements across their internal borders, especially since the Single European Act of 1985, has moved the control of external borders to the top of the political agenda. The notion of Fortress Europe is thus doubly determined – by the zero-immigration policies of member states, and by the compensating function of the emergent external migration regime. In contrast to the well-established intra-European regime, Europe's external migration regime is protean, and it has for long resisted the pull of supranationalization. Its philosophy differs fundamentally from that of the intra-European regime: not rights, but security; not free movement, but the prevention of migration from outside the EU. It thus incorporates the guestworker and post-colonial experiences of European states, whose quintessence is: Never Again! The intergovernmental nature of the external migration regime means that most of its provisions are soft law only, good (or bad, according to taste) intentions that are not legally binding and enforceable by a supranational watchdog, such as the ECJ. However, because the purpose of this regime is to help European states to better stem unwanted immigration, (some of) these states have taken a keen interest in further developing it.

This development has occurred within two separate but overlapping fora. One is the Schengen forum, in which five of the six founding states of the EC (excluding Italy) decided to move ahead quicker than the rest in realizing the single-market objective and, consequently, in coordinating the control of external borders in the form of a common visa scheme, cooperation on asylum and technological information exchange (the so-called Schengen Information System). A second forum has been a variety of schemes for 'ad hoc cooperation' among the interior ministries and police officials of all member states on those domestic security concerns that have an external dimension, such as, initially, terrorism and drug trafficking, and over time also immigration and asylum issues. Its perhaps most important result has been the Dublin Convention of 1990, whose purpose is to combat 'asylum shopping' through holding the state of first contact responsible for handling an asylum application, and ruling out the possibility of a rejected applicant trying again in a second convention state.

While for long a tool of member states to more effectively stem unwanted immigration, the external migration regime was pushed by the imperative of harmonization into a supranational direction. A first step in this was the Maastricht Treaty, which formalized the variety of *ad hoc* cooperation in the (still intergovernmental) Third Pillar. The outcome, though, has been slim: a joint (though non-binding) definition of refugee, and five (legally binding) 'joint actions' on rather marginal items, such as school travel for children of third-country nationals (Guiraudon, 2000, p. 254). This will change with the second and decisive step towards supranationalism in the Amsterdam Treaty, in which the entire immigration and asylum complex of the Third Pillar, plus the non-EU Schengen *acquis*, were moved into the supranational First Pillar, although mellowed by a lot of transition and opt-out clauses that guarantee a strong intergovernmental component in the immediate future. The respective Title IV of the Amsterdam Treaty calls for the creation of an 'area of freedom, security and justice', an order of words which deserves scrutiny. Putting freedom first articulates the original impulse of the European project, the removal of barriers for free market exchanges. Placing 'security' ahead of 'justice' (the code word for immigrant rights) reflects the spirit of stemming unwanted immigration, out of which the external migration regime is made.

This is not to say, however, that the last-mentioned justice concern will remain without teeth. In giving more authority to the European

Commission and the European Court of Justice, the Amsterdam Treaty also lets loose their liberal rights – creating rather than – restricting instincts in the immigration field. The European Commission, which has the official mandate to propose a common EU asylum and immigration policy within five years, has already indicated that 'humanist' criteria will fare prominently in it (*Frankfurter Allgemeine Zeitung*, 6 July 2000). A proposed directive on family unification for third-state nationals (including temporary refugees), for instance, goes well beyond the family rights for migrants provided by most member states, and in the opinion of a German critic it would entail 100 000 new as-of-right immigrants per year (Bosbach, 2000, p. 11). The European Commission, along with the plethora of non-governmental migrant organizations aligned with and financed by it, has long been a champion of the rights of settled immigrants who have so far been blatantly left out of the ambit of European Community law. They are bound to be the first beneficiary of the pending supranationalization of the external migration regime.

Before Amsterdam, there has been much criticism, especially by non-governmental organizations and academics (see for example Geddes, 1995) of the secrecy and conspiratorial nature of the emergent external migration regime. The respective member-state officials tended to meet informally, leaving no written trace of their decisions, and supranational watchdogs such as the European Commission were generally excluded. As Sandra Lavenex (1999b, p. 113) astutely observed, intergovernmental cooperation on immigration (due to its roots in terrorism and drug control) was from the start dominated by security-focused interior ministry officials, thus crowding out the rights concerns that at national level have always been articulated by the foreign, social or labour ministries, but who were never part of the originally internal-security focused intergovernmental cooperation on asylum and immigration. The critique of this arrangement is summed up in the label 'democratic deficit'. This label is premised on a strong and highly questionable counterfactual: that a 'democratic' European immigration policy would look fundamentally different (read: be more generous and expansive) (see the excellent critique of the 'democratic deficit' argument by Caine, 2000). Considering that the overwhelming majorities in all European states are negatively disposed toward new immigration, notional zero-immigration policies at national and European levels are exactly in line with the preferences of the mass public; in this sense, they are democratic. It is therefore more appropriate to speak about a liberal deficit of the external migration regime: insufficient incorporation by actors other than interior ministry officials and security specialists and insufficient judicial oversight, so that the liberal-constitutional principle of divided powers and the rule of law is violated. However, this liberal deficit in the external migration regime has in principle been remedied by the Amsterdam Treaty.

'Europe' as a tool of stemming is nowhere more visible than in the regional asylum regime that has emerged since the late 1980s under the auspices of the European Union. Against current attempts to fuse both under the imperative of stemming, it has to be stated upfront that immigration and asylum policy are based on fundamentally different principles. The principle of immigration policy is state interest; the principle of asylum is the right of individuals for elementary protection. The sharp contrast between both is certainly blunted by an international asylum law according to which the right of asylum is technically not a right of the individual to enjoy asylum, but the right of the state to grant it. Secondly, one must not deny that asylum also serves state interests. The institution of asylum emerged in response to the rise of modern nation-states in Europe, which streamlined their populations along first religious, then ideological, and finally ethnic lines (see Zolberg *et al.*, 1989, chapter 1). Asylum was the safety valve that made these homogenizing efforts by states easier to accomplish. Accordingly, states have an interest in asylum too; otherwise an international asylum and refugee regime would never have seen the light of day.

Having said this, the original impetus of asylum as instituted under the auspices of the United Nations Organization after the Second World War – to acknowledge a universal human right for elementary protection – is almost invisible in the EU asylum regime. Its most distinct feature, established by the Dublin Convention of 1990, is perhaps the farming-out of asylum responsibilities through the 'safe-third-country' clause. This meant initially that the EU state of first contact was responsible for considering an asylum claim; the London Resolution of 1992 unilaterally extended the clause to non-EU countries (in effect, the EU applicant states to the east), thus erecting a buffer zone surrounding the EU. The EU asylum regime is thus built in the spirit of external immigration control: its main purpose is to deny territorial access to unwanted asylum-seekers. The second key feature of the EU asylum regime is a refugee definition narrower than the UN definition: only persecution by state actors is acknowledged, thus precluding civil war victims from consideration for refugee status. The UN definition of refugee via 'well-founded fear of persecution' presumes but does not explicitly say that persecution has to originate from (or be authorized by) a state, thus allowing a less narrow interpretation. Thirdly, the distribution of asylum responsibilities in terms of the safe-third-country clause has not been accompanied by a sufficient substantive harmonization of asylum rules, which raises serious equity concerns (see Peers,

1998). To the degree that an emergent 'Europe' will have to revolve around a human-rights identity, the latter is certainly not visible in its asylum regime as currently devised.

Stemming in East and South

Due to the geographical positioning of First and Third Worlds, global migrations move 'compass-like' from South to North and from East to West. European vulnerabilities to unwanted immigration are accordingly biggest at the southern and eastern peripheries. The dismantling of communism and the uniting of Europe have suddenly thrown both peripheries into sharp relief, as the old system of either impenetrable borders (to the East) or tiered borders (to the South) has been replaced by one external border with considerably less-developed parts of the world, none of which imposes any exit restrictions on their people. As a result Europe acquired equivalents to the Rio Grande, the US-Mexican desert river that divides First and Third Worlds on the North American continent. Examples are the Oder-Neisse line that divides Germany and Poland or the Strait of Gibraltar, the perilous waters that separate Spain from North Africa.

Considering that all three borders, including the American one, have become emblems of human tragedy, organized crime and defensive fortification by receiving states, the hope that more generous immigration policies in Europe could soften its new external borders may be premature – at least the US case disproves this nexus, which is currently driving the perhaps elusive chase for a 'comprehensive' immigration policy at the EU level.

While similar in dividing highly unevenly developed parts of the world, the two European external borders differ in one important respect from one another. The southern border through the Mediterranean Sea is a permanent border, forever dividing Europe from the African continent. By contrast, the eastern border is a moving border – after Poland's accession to the EU, the Oder-Neisse line will cease to be Europe's external border, and this has important implications for immigration control.

East

Cynically speaking, the European stemming exercise in the east is greatly facilitated by the existence of EU applicant states, such as Poland, Hungary or the Czech Republic, whose willingness to join the EU is traded against current member states' delegation of (some of) their immigration control problems. Examples are the farming-out of asylum responsibilities according to the 1992 London Resolution on 'safe third countries', or – more recently – the tying of EU membership to full compliance with the Schengen *acquis*. In one author's view, the accession lever amounts 'to a serious interference in these [east-central European] states' internal and home affairs and to their unilateral adaptation to Western perceptions of threat and Western operative methods' (Lavenex, 1999a, p. 85). She even concludes that immigration and asylum 'would not constitute a major concern in [these states] without pressure from the EU' (*ibid.*). Such reasoning ignores the benefits accruing to East European migrants from the underlying bargain with EU states; and it downplays the external migration pressures in the region which are quite independent of EU accession. Let me comment on both in turn.

The price for turning Eastern Europe into a buffer zone for extra-European migrants has been the selective opening of EU states for East European migrants, in terms of waived visa requirements for short-term visitors and new guestworker schemes. These measures correspond perfectly to the dominant type of 'pendular' migrant in the east, who seeks only short-term, income-adding employment in the west, rather than permanent settlement. As a result of pendular migration accommodated by suitable policies, the much-feared 'flood from the East' did not materialize after the fall of the Iron Curtain.

In a brilliant analysis, Ewa Morawska (1999) has characterized the new pendular migrants as *Arbeits-* and *Handelstouristen* (working- and trading-tourists). While distinct through a certain *debrouillard* outlook acquired under communism, these pendular migrants share with their much-studied peers at the US–Mexican border their reliance on ethnic networks – between 40 and 70 per cent of tourist-workers are estimated to have been helped by kin or friends abroad (Morawska, 1999, p. 8). Sociological studies show that such network migration is very difficult to control by receiving states (Massey *et al.*, 1998). Unlike the US government, which embarked on a 'march of folly' (Massey, 1998) against network- based illegal immigration from Mexico, thus inadvertently turning pendular into permanent migration, European states, above all Germany, got it right by allowing these networks to thrive – not because of having the right theory of the nature of the flows, but for extrinsic foreign policy and economic reasons. If framed by adequate policies, there are inbuilt stop factors to east–west pendular migration (Morawska, 1999, p. 18f). Trading-tourists, who live from circumventing customs regulations, are bound to decline with the emergence of border-spanning, EU-supported 'micro-regions' with well-developed legal commercial infrastructures. The pool of tourist-workers, estimated

at 600 000 to 700 000 (p. 5) is unlikely to increase, due to the satura-
tion of ethnic networks, rising domestic wages in the course of EU-
spurred development and social disincentives such as the 'lack of
respect' that East Europeans fear to encounter across the border.

Accordingly, the immigration problematic at Europe's eastern periph-
ery is not one of indigenous migrants, but of external migrants using
East European countries as transit zones for further westbound travels.
To contain them is the whole purpose of the EU accession lever. The
Czech Republic and Poland have become transit zones for some of
Eurasia's major human smuggling pathways, originating in Turkey and
with Germany as a destination point (*The Economist*, 20 February
1999). Run by mafia rings based in Istanbul, Tirana and other cities in
Eastern Europe, the smuggling of people into the EU has turned into a
$3–4 billion (€3.4–4.6 billion) business a year. Detected illegal transit
travellers, who tend to be without documents to avoid deportation,
usually request asylum and then disappear to await another opportunity
for heading west. In Poland, 50 per cent of asylum cases in 1996 were
discontinued because the applicants had disappeared; and 30 000 illegal
transit travellers are believed to have succeeded in moving from Poland
to Germany in the same year (Morawska, 1999, p. 28). To combat organized illegal transit migration is the purpose of the so-called Budapest
Process, regular meetings between EU and Eastern European interior
ministers which coordinate the exchange of western training and technology for eastern help in preventing westbound illegal immigration
(Lavenex, 1999a, pp. 102–4). A major innovation in this context is
cross-border police cooperation, 'with permanent exchange of notes,
common training, and daily communication' (Bohrt, 1999, p. 12), as is
now the practice at the German–Polish and German–Czech borders.
This heralds a 'return to spatial approaches to security and control'
(*ibid.*, p. 3), which had once been replaced by the linear borders and
clearly demarcated sovereignties of nation-states.

There is still no denying that the incentive of EU accession is endow-
ing East European states with 'sheriff's deputy' immigration policies that
are problematic in several respects. For one, they feed resentment as they
force these states to cut off vital relations with some of their eastern
neighbours, such as Russia, Belarus or the Ukraine. Secondly, they are
often deficient from a human-rights point of view. This is especially visible in asylum policy. When West European states moved to restrict
asylum rights from the early 1980s on, this occurred against the backdrop of long-standing liberal traditions and legal cultures that put brakes
on the restrictionist impulse. By contrast, East European states, cut off
from liberal traditions by communism, are building asylum regimes that
are from the start tainted by the post-1980s fusion of illegal immigration

and asylum seeking. For example, East European states have immediately applied the 'safe-third-country' principle to their own eastern neighbours. At the same time, western material aids in the immigration field only marginally cover asylum: only 13 per cent of the DM120 million (€61.3 million) offered by Germany to Poland in the context of their bilateral readmission agreement was earmarked for the building of an asylum infrastructure; the vast 'rest' was dedicated to better equip border authorities and the police (Lavenex, 1999a, p. 88).

The high-level Reflection Group on 'The Nature of the New Border', chaired by Giuliano Amato, concluded:

> The EU's external border cannot be treated simply as a physical line on the ground to be defended solely by the apparatus of repression. The attempt to make it impermeable is doomed to ineffectiveness and can increase instability by disrupting economic and cultural ties between neighbours. (Amato and Batt, 1999, p. 61)

An immigration policy 'fixated on techniques of control at the border' (*ibid.*, p. 8) indeed conflicts with other, foreign policy objectives of the EU, and it may even be ineffective in their own terms as it only drive up the prices and thus the profits of criminal trade in humans (for a similar critique of the US border enforcement towards Mexico see Andreas 2000).

South

Often referred to as Europe's 'soft underbelly', the South is no less than the East exposed to illegal immigration, particularly of the organized kind. No day passes in which Italian newspapers do not report about new boatloads of trafficked migrants from Albania and other parts of the world washed up on the shores of Puglia – if they reach those shores and are not thrown into the sea by increasingly brutal *scafisti* (*la Repubblica*, 9 August 2000). There are also similar solutions in the South and East to stem this inflow, most notably readmission agreements and police cooperation with sending states. Only, these have much less bite due to the absence of the EU accession lever – for Albania or Morocco illegal (transit) migration is a trump to squeeze out concessions from Italy or Spain, not a liability that stands in the way of EU membership. After two Italian officers of the *Guardia di Finanza* were killed in a collision with ruthless *scafisti* in the Golf of Otranto in late July 1999, a fuming Prime Minister Amato went to Tirana to demand a more effective clampdown on smugglers, including Italian–Albanian police cooperation on Albanian soil (*la Repubblica*, 29 July 2000).

Having thought to have reached an agreement, Prime Minister Amato, upon his return to Italy, had to hear from Albania that there was 'no anti-scafisti plan with Italy', and that Albania was anyway not prepared to 'play with the concept of national sovereignty', as its chief of government, Meidani, put it (*la Repubblica*, 30 July 2000). This is notwithstanding the considerable development aids of Lit 266 billion (€116.7 million) that Albania has received between 1998 and 2000 as price for its cooperation in combatting human trafficking across the Adriatic (*ibid.*).

Spain has faced similar difficulties with Morocco. A readmission agreement sweetened by Spanish financial aids exists since 1992, but Morocco has been reluctant to fulfill its part of the bargain, even regarding readmitting its own nationals. Most annoyingly for Spain, Morocco refuses to readmit the considerable number of transit migrants, mainly sub-Saharan Africans, who try to reach Spain's two North African enclave cities, Ceuta and Melilla, from where they have unhindered passage to the Spanish mainland (*Migration News Sheet*, June 2000). While, short of parachuting out of the sky, these African migrants must have transited through Morocco to reach these colonial cities, Moroccan authorities demand concrete proofs, which of course cannot be had due to the logic of illicit travelling. Such intransigent behaviour, which in the Moroccan case is fed by resentment against Spanish colonial presence, contrasts markedly with the anticipatory fulfilment of EU norms by East European states, even by those without immediate prospects of joining the club (see Lavenex, 1999a, chapter 4).

However, the main target of the 'soft underbelly' charge is not so much lax border enforcement, which is anyway an image increasingly out of step with reality. Rather, this charge addresses the *de facto* toleration of vast illegal immigrant populations on southern European soil, which are lured into the light by periodical amnesty campaigns. This constellation is a compromise between two contradictory imperatives: EU-imposed restrictionism (after all, for the English word 'soft underbelly' there is no equivalent in any Roman language) and liberal domestic elites who are aware of the crucial dependence of their vast informal economies on immigrants, and, remembering their own emigrant pasts, seek to set a generous 'left-catholic' counterpoint to the petty restrictionism prevailing in the Protestant North. In this spirit, an Italian interior minister once presented an immigration law, which came to be named after him (Lex Martelli), as in the 'duty to help the development of the South of the world and to welcome its populations' (Christensen, 1997, p. 482). No British, French or German interior minister has ever been heard striking an even vaguely similar chord. The two contradictory imperatives of EU-imposed restrictions and homegrown liberal instincts have at times produced rather bizarre flowers. For instance,

Spain's first immigration law, passed on the eve of accession to the European Community in 1985 and labelled by a critic as a 'police' law that completely disregards the area of integration and immigrant rights (Arango, 2000), is entitled 'Organic Law on the Rights and Liberties of Foreigners in Spain'.

Southern European states' wavering between not stemming but also not openly welcoming immigration is expressed in at least two forms: the lack, until very recently, of something akin to legal-permanent resident status, which makes the distinction between 'legal' and 'illegal' immigrant populations a dubious one, because temporarily legal immigrants are inevitably pushed back to illegal status; and, especially in the case of Italy, a chronic laxity to enforce deportation orders which has raised the ire of the north-western part of Schengenland, true destination point of many a migrant setting foot on Italy first.

Regarding legal status, it has to be seen that the belated introduction of the first immigration laws in the mid-1980s artificially illegalized the *de facto* immigrants already residing on southern European soil, by requiring from them work and residence permits that they initially could not possess. But the legal production of illegality has been more subtle still. Until 1996, there was only a variety of temporary legal resident statuses in Spain, but no permanent legal status for aliens. Spain's periodic legalization programmes 'built in' a loss of legal status overtime, by tying residence renewals to the persistence of the original conditions (most difficult to fulfill, a formal work contract – see Calavita, 1998, p. 550). Accordingly, of the original 128 000 applicants for legalization in 1991, only 64 per cent were still legal after two years. In fact, the 1985 immigration law produced a catch-22 of mutually dependent labour contract, work permit and residence permit, with the lengthy procedures and delays in acquiring one of them cancelling out the possibility of getting the other(s). As Calavita concludes her critical look at Spain, 'legal status is always a fragile state and almost inevitably gives way to periods of illegality' (p. 556).

Regarding deportations, until most recently Italian law made a distinction between criminal and administrative deportations, with the possibility of detention only regarding the former. Because illegal entry was long considered an 'administrative violation' only, detention was ruled out in this case. This led to the notorious practice that caught illegal border-crossers would be formally asked to turn themselves in for deportation on the appointed day – and never be seen again. No wonder that only 15 per cent of deportation orders could be executed, most of them criminal deportees rather than illegal entrants or overstayers. The whole point of the Dini Decree of 1995, forced upon an unwilling centre-left government by the restrictionist Lega Nord, was to provide for swifter deportations. However, in one of the more farcical episodes of Italian immigration policy, the actual measures introduced targeted only crime-based deportations, and thus 'ironically impacted only the most easily deportable class of aliens' (Christensen, 1997, p. 496). Italy's chronic deportation laxity reached crisis proportions with the mass arrival of Kurdish refugees in winter 1997, the majority of them using the loophole to join their ethnic kin in Germany and the Netherlands. Upon the massive threat by northern EU states to exclude Italy from the Schengen Agreement, a provision in the new immigration law of 1998, passed only after strenuous debate and over the opposition of the Catholic Church, finally allowed the detention of entry-and-stay violators, but only up to 30 days, too short in many cases to process the legal appeals. The new law, as a result of which euphemistically called 'reception centres' have come to litter Italy's southern coastline, has still led to a significant increase of deportations: in 1998, there were 54 000 of them, about 10 times above the annual figure in the previous years (*Migration News Sheet*, April 1999). However, after a strange delay of two years, local judges in Milan have recently found the new detention practice in violation of the liberty rights guaranteed by the constitution, releasing a good number of caught clandistini. This is likely to open up another round in Italy's unending detention saga (*La Repubblica*, 5 November 2000).

A third peculiarity of southern European immigration policies is the, however tentative and incomplete, introduction of legal quota immigration. This indicates the desire of these states for a 'soliciting' rather than exclusively 'stemming'-oriented approach. Italy introduced legal quota in the Lex Martelli of 1990. However, the responsible Foreign Ministry set the figure at 'zero' in the first year. In subsequent years the respective decrees simply authorized entries that had already occurred; the decree for 1996, for example, was issued in late December 1996 (Sciortino, 1999, p. 243). In Spain, also, the introduction of annual quotas for labour migrants in 1994 remained limited to a few sectors (such as agriculture and domestic services), and they functioned mainly as legalization devices – nine out of ten workers benefiting from them were already irregularly employed in Spain (Arango, 2000, p. 270). But in introducing the very concept of legal quota immigration, southern European states have pioneered an entirely different, 'soliciting' approach to immigration policy.

Toward soliciting

It is perhaps no accident that a southern European at the helm of the European Commission's Justice and Home Affairs unit, the Portuguese

Antonio Vitorino, is pushing for a EU immigration policy that includes legal quota for labour migrants. Interestingly, he presents his case as in the interest of a more effective stemming exercise: 'I believe that such a [legal quota] policy will also have a major impact on reducing smuggling and the illegal entry of immigration' (Vitorino, 2000). However, without the bottom-up pressure from member states this top-down effort would come to nil, as the long list of unsuccessful attempts by the European Commission to find new ways in immigration policy shows (see Papademetriou, 1996). This pressure now exists. In the single most important change on the European immigration scene since the closing of guestworker recruitment in the early 1970s, Germany's recent introduction of a 'green-card' scheme for foreign computer specialists could pave the way from an exclusively stemming – oriented to a soliciting immigration policy. The timid 'green-card' scheme which consists of only 20 000 sector-specific visas – the allusion to the American 'green card' is false – is limited to five years of work and stay, and is just the tip of the iceberg. Similar bottlenecks for skilled labour exist in the German biotech, construction and health sectors; the employers' union estimated an overall need of some 1.5 million migrants to keep the economy competitive. Similar calls for skilled migrants have been raised in France and Britain (*The Economist*, 9 September 2000). In an interesting north–south divide, southern Europe is more interested in unskilled foreign labour. Italy's farmers' federation called for 65 000 seasonal fruit pickers to be admitted in 2000 (*The Economist*, 5 August 2000), and Spanish farmers have difficulties in filling some 350 000 jobs per year, spurring the government so sign seasonal labour agreements with Morocco and other states (*Migration News Sheet*, November 1999). North and South, skilled or unskilled, the change towards soliciting immigration policies is ringing in Europe.

The German 'green-card' policy, originally branded by Chancellor Schröder as a singular measure without broader implications, has immediately kicked off a cross-party discussion over an active 'immigration policy' to replace the defensive 'foreigner policy' of now. The German debate shows some of the issues and obstacles that have to cleared on the way towards a soliciting immigration policy. First, the public does not want it. The support for legal quota immigration, in the context of a new immigration law, has declined from 55 per cent in 1993 to 37 per cent in 2000. Various polls show that 55 to 65 per cent of Germans oppose even the smallish green-card programme (*Migration News*, June 2000). Accordingly, politicians of all parties ceremonially confirm that a broad consensus is necessary to implement the change. But this goes against the logic of a political system divided into government and opposition, where the whole point of an 'opposition' is to propose B when the government suggests A. Accordingly, there are now two separate expert commissions to explore the possibility of a new immigration policy, one set up by the CDU/CSU in June, and a second by the SPD/Green government in July. To make things worse, the government coup to win the liberal CDU politician Rita Suessmuth as chair of its commission – a 'consensus', after all, is needed – has been received with shouts of 'betrayal' and the shunning of the popular politician within her own party. A 'consensus' is not the likely outcome of all this.

The main source of disagreement is the relationship between as-of-right immigration and the new wanted immigration: additive or substitutive. The Minister President of the Saar, Peter Mueller, one of the new immigration enthusiasts in the CDU, calls for 300 000 net immigrants per year – which is exactly the number of ethnic Germans, asylum-seekers and family migrants that Germany is forced to accept 'as-of-right' every year. Accordingly, the strategy of the CDU is 'to create a free space for wanted immigration through limiting unwanted immigration', as an influential position paper put it (Bosbach, 2000, p. 15). This implies a slimming of family immigration through quota-based queuing and a drastic reduction of the maximum age of foreign children allowed to join their parents; most crucially, it implies a transformation from the constitutional asylum right into an 'institutional guarantee' with lesser judicial protections. Still, in 1997, Germany's major conservative immigration lawyer had rejected legal quota immigration because, in recognition of existing 'legal entitlements', the quota would have to be set at zero (Hailbronner, 1997, p. 42). These previously untouched 'legal entitlements' are exactly the stake of Germany's new immigration debate.

Whatever its outcome, Germany's immigration debate may force the revision of a dearly held view. The image is still that all want to come, if they are graciously let in. Contrary to expectations, however, the wanted Indians from Bangalore have so far not rushed on the half-hearted German 'green card' – their preference is for the real one, the American.

Chapter 15

Crime, Trafficking, Prostitution and Drugs

GIOVANNA CAMPANI

The Maastricht Treaty on European Union, which became effective on 1 November 1993, added a new dimension to European integration: cooperation in the fields of Justice and Home Affairs (the so-called 'Third Pillar'). With the Treaty of Amsterdam, in 1997, immigration, asylum and visa policy were transferred from the Third to the First Pillar. This cooperation means that the following are recognized fields of interest for the member states and for the European Union (EU): asylum, immigration, external border control (that is the borders of the Union, given the dismantling of the internal borders among the participating states on the basis of the Schengen Accord), drug addiction, fraud, customs, terrorism, unlawful drug trafficking and other forms of international crime.

The reinforced judicial and police cooperation sought first by the Maastricht Treaty and confirmed by the Amsterdam Treaty, follows the experience of the 1970s when the European Council established the TREVI group (Terrorism, Radicalism, Extremism, Violence International) which had the task of coordinating anti-terrorist measures. During the 1970s, the focus of judicial and police cooperation inside the European Community was almost exclusively on political terrorism. Under the current expanded system of cooperation, the focus has broadened to the control of immigration, the prevention of illegal immigration, drug-related crimes and organized crime.

This shift in the goals and content of European cooperation corresponds to a new international context and a new conception of the relationship between international and internal security. The non-violent collapse of the Soviet Union has reduced inter-bloc ideological rivalry, while the terrorism that was also related to that conflict has also all but disappeared. But still, the world has not become a safe place. On the contrary – as the events of 11 September 2001 make clear – new security threats and conflicts have appeared. And international terrorism is only one manifestation of the change. In more general terms, the link between international and internal security has taken new forms. Internal security in Europe is no longer conceived simply in terms of external aggression. Hence rather than focus attention on the 'war against terrorism', this chapter builds upon the realization that new factors of insecurity have to be considered, including areas of internal instability. Illegal migration and transnational crime are linked most evidently in the growing phenomenon of trafficking in human beings.

New forms of transnational police and judicial cooperation have been generated by an acknowledgement that national security systems are far from adequate in dealing with the mounting threat to public security created by transnational crime organizations (Attina, 1997, p. 11). The EU's response has been to follow two parallel strategies. The first is to participate – as a Union as well as each member state – in the international cooperation promoted by international institutions, and foremost among them the United Nations (UN). Second, it has developed its own specific institutions, such as Europol, to carry out the new fight against crime. But at the same time there remain important distinctions among the EU member states in migratory policy, prostitution and especially drug consumption. The fight against criminal organizations may also be perceived differently from one country to the next, as in the contrast between Italy where there is a tradition of local organized crime, and Germany which has to deal with penetration by East European mafias.

The lords of crime

In 1998, the Swiss journalist Jean Ziegler published *The Lords of Crime: The New Mafias against Democracy*, in which he assessed the risk presented by the growth of international organized crime for European democracy. International 'organized crime' is crime committed by groups of people with stable, hierarchical forms of organization which perpetrate often violent illegal action across borders (Attina, 1997, p. 2).

The criminal organizations that are responsible for organized crime are also often, in common discourse and in the media, called 'mafia'. Sometimes organized crime and mafia are used as synonymous terms, but mafia also has a more specific meaning. There are many different definitions of organized crime and/or mafia, but what is generally accepted is that a division of labour, a hierarchical structure and a systematic distribution of the spoils of crime are not in themselves enough to define a mafia. A gang that robs a bank is not necessarily a mafia: 'Neither organisation nor violence associated with criminal activity is sufficient to define a mafia' (Anderson, 1995).

First of all, to be a mafia it is necessary to have a quasi-permanent, large-scale structure with internal organization. Another characteristic of mafia is the conscious effort to control the market for crime (Schelling, 1971); mafias enforce agreements among the members of the group and outsiders and punish or demand redress for violation of their codes. Mafias also devote resources not only to ensuring that members do not cooperate with the police, but also to corrupting the legal and regulatory authorities (Anderson, 1995). But if these are the general characteristics, each criminal organization or mafia has its own story in each specific national context, for even if the dubious honour of originating the name belongs to Italy, and more precisely Sicily, there are numerous 'mafias' present internationally.

As is well-known, the term 'mafia' – an Arab word meaning boldness and courage, but also pride and arrogance – was originally the name of the criminal organization which emerged in Sicily in the second half of the nineteenth century, and more precisely after the unification of Italy in 1870 (Catanzaro, 1992). According to scholars, the Sicilian mafia had its origin in a vacuum of power bred from the inability or the unwillingness of the state to ensure public order. Over hundreds of years, Sicilian society turned away from state power to private means of protecting property and ensuring order (Catanzaro, 1992). The mafia system – or 'state in the state' – was brought to the United States in the years of the great Italian migration at the end of the nineteenth and beginning of the twentieth centuries. Originally a system of protection of the Sicilian ethnic group against other ethnic groups, the mafia – then called Cosa Nostra – found an opportunity to increase its power during Prohibition (when the sale and consumption of alcoholic beverages was outlawed). The Prohibition created a major illegal market, and illegal market enterprises generated cash that could then be used for bribery as well as investment in other industries (Anderson, 1995, p. 6). But the Sicilian mafia is not just an historic phenomenon; it is a contemporary reality. The fight against the mafia remains a task of every Italian government and in spite of some successes obtained in recent years, the organization is far from being defeated (Arlacchi, 1986). Moreover, in Italy, organized crime has several faces. Apart from the Sicilian mafia there are three other regional crime organizations: the Camorra (which is as old as the mafia) in the area of Naples and more widely in the region of Campania, the 'n'drangheta' in Calabria and the Sacra Corona Unita in Puglia. This last organization has established solid links with criminal organizations which are active on the other side of the Adriatic, in Albania and Montenegro.

Inside the European Union, Italy is the country where organized crime is apparently the strongest, with control of large areas of the country. I say, apparently, since Ziegler (1998) – whose fieldwork has been mainly done in Germany – gives data about its expanding role all over the European Union. Nowadays various crime organizations – including the Albanian, Russian, Chechen, Ukrainian and Turkish mafias – are spreading transnationally, establishing local bases across the EU. The Colombian drug cartels of Medellin and Cali, and the Chinese triads are operating in Paris, Amsterdam, Berlin and Vienna. Organized crime from Eastern Europe – Poland, Rumania and, more particularly, Russia – has grown rapidly in the last 10 to 15 years and is particularly active in France and Germany. Albanian and other Balkan criminal organizations are very active in Italy where they have begun to dominate street trade in drugs and prostitutes, entering in competition with the local mafias.

The cross-border activities of such groups will be facilitated by the enlargement of the EU towards the East. For in the last 10 years the economic and political transition, social instability, ethnic conflicts and wars in the former USSR, in Eastern Europe and in the Balkans have provided fertile ground for the growth of organized crime. The Russian 'Red Mafia' is considered by some (for example, Anderson, 1995) to be a 'legacy of communism', because of the existence in the Soviet Union of an excessive degree of bureaucratic power characterized by bribery and extortion and an underground economy parallel to the legal or planned economy. With the collapse of the Soviet State, this parallel economy and society has come to the fore. Since the end of the 1980s, the Balkans has become an area where organized crime has grown quickly, thanks to the trafficking of drugs, weapons and human beings. Paradoxically, even the billions of dollars in international aid that have gone to the region following the destruction of war in Bosnia Herzegovina, Kosovo and Albania have helped fuel the accumulation of monetary and material resources by criminal organizations linked to corrupt politicians. If Serbia – while under the control of Slobodan Milosovic – is the most evident case, in both Montenegro and Albania there are multiple connections between organized crime and political power (LIMES, 2000).

The transnational success of these mafias is the result of three forms of organization coming together which until now have functioned separately: an economic and financial organization, designed to make profits; a military organization, using violence in order to control a particular territory; and a kinship group and ethnic structure linked to the previous two (Ziegler, 1998). But their growth across borders has also been facilitated by other forms of internationalization.

Globalization and criminal business

The connection between the international expansion of modern capitalism and financial crime can be interpreted according to two different points of view. The first considers that the flood of illicit transactions and offences under national law or international agreements are the incidental malfunctions of free-market economies and democracy. The answer is to bolster the legal fight against these malfunctions through new and stricter laws and stronger action at the transnational level. A second point of view considers these illicit transactions to be inevitable in a system based on the interpenetration of governments, transnational corporations and mafias (for example, De Brie, 2000). For in the global economy, financial crime is becoming a common practice with banks and business sometimes consciously, sometimes unwittingly, becoming involved. In a context of insider-dealing and speculation, fraudulent balance sheets, the rigging of accounts and transfer prices, the use of offshore subsidiaries and shell companies to avoid and evade tax and the corruption of government officials, organized crime can launder and recycle the fabulous proceeds of its activities (De Brie, 2000).

Whichever view one takes, according to the estimates of different international sources (the United Nations, Interpol), these proceeds are indeed huge. If in 1996, the proceeds of all crime business were estimated at around $500 billion (€569 billion) (Giacomelli, 1996, quoted in Attina, 1997), today this sum covers just the annual profits from drug trafficking (cannabis, cocaine, heroin) and is equal to 8 to 10 per cent of total world trade. This is larger than the oil and gas trade, larger than the chemical and pharmaceutical business and twice as large as the motor vehicle industry. According to De Brie (2000, p. 3), in all, and counting only activities with a transnational dimension, the world's gross criminal product totals above $1000 billion (€1139 billion) a year, or nearly 20 per cent of world trade. These activities include a combination of the 'traditional' and 'new', including gambling, smuggling and counterfeiting (estimated alone at $100 billion: €114 billion), computer piracy (estimated at $200 billion: €228 billion) and trafficking in works of art and antiquities, in stolen cars and parts, in protected species and human organs, and so forth.

Trafficking in people has become the fastest-growing 'new' form of transnational crime. Pino Arlacchi, Executive Director of the UN Office for Drug Control and Crime Prevention, declared recently that it is estimated that at present up to ten million international migrants are subjected to illegal practices of this type (*Reuters*, 30 March 2000). 'Hardly a global issue in the 1980s' (Kyle, 1998), trafficking in people is now estimated to be worth between $7 billion (€8 billion) per year (Caldwell *et al.*, 1997, quoting the UN) and $12.5 billion (€14.2 billion) per year (estimations of the

International Organization for Migration). Considering that trafficking is constantly growing, these estimations are probably lower than the actual figures. Among the smuggled migrants many women are forced into prostitution, contributing further to the profits of crime. The sex business or sex industry is at the border of legal and illegal practices and is partly controlled by criminal organizations. So is pornography, where the attempt to satisfy the 'specific needs' of particular groups of customers (such as paedophiles) has produced a worrying increase in the exploitation of children, including smuggling and kidnapping.

Thanks to the degree of financial power created by these activities, organized crime has been able to exert more and more influence on economic, social and political life, but also over systems of justice and public administrations, with political corruption an ever-growing problem (see the chapter by Heywood, Rhodes and Pujas). In order to continue to recycle and launder the proceeds of crime, criminal organizations are ready to corrupt governments and regulatory authorities. In the United Nations Laundering Conference of March 2000, Pino Arlacchi stated that the fight against money laundering had taken on a new urgency because of the enormous flow of criminal cash inundating the world banking system; but this fight is made very difficult by the unclear distinction between legal and illegal financial flows.

Drugs and drug addiction in the European Union

The narcotics trade is still the biggest profit-earner for organized crime. It is not a recent phenomenon, but it is growing, despite the programmes put in place to fight it by states and international organizations. According to the United Nations which in 1991 created the UN Drug Control Programme (UNDCP) based in Vienna, the illegal trade in narcotics has a market of about 190 million addicts and users worldwide, and, as already noted, is estimated to be worth between $400 and $500 billion (€456–569 billion) per year. The Paris-based International Police Organization (Interpol) says that drug business is second only to the world's arms trade which is estimated at more than $800 billion (€910 billion) annually.

In Europe, the illicit drugs trade and consumption is expanding rapidly in the East. Since the fall of the Berlin Wall in 1989, drug-related problems have been growing: drug consumption among young people has risen and cross-border drug trafficking and money laundering have expanded. The Russian mafia is particularly active in this trade, especially in heroin which is produced in the Central Asia republics of the former USSR, northern Pakistan and Afghanistan (Ziegler, 1998). Drugs are smuggled into Western Europe via the Balkans. Nevertheless, it is difficult to establish whether the Western European drugs market has become more important, because the data coming from seizures indicate an increase in drug supply and availability but also reflect law enforcement priorities and strategies.

Nevertheless, the use of serious drugs in the EU and deaths from drugs seem to have stabilized across the EU. According to the European Monitoring Centre for Drugs and Drug Addiction based in Lisbon, which publishes the annual report of the state of the drugs problem in the EU every year, there are an estimated 1.5 million mainly heroin users aged 15 to 64 in the member states. An estimated one million are likely to meet the criteria for dependence, but, nevertheless, heroin dependence is not increasing. 'Known users are largely an ageing population with serious health, social and psychic problems, although indications of heroin use among younger groups are noted' (EMCDDA, 2000, p. 7). Even the number of deaths because of drugs has stabilized across the European Union. According to the Report, stable or decreasing rates may be linked to the stable or decreasing prevalence of heroin, safer use or increased access to treatment, especially substitution programmes (Farell, 1996).

The use of cannabis is quite widespread in the EU, and at least 45 million Europeans have tried cannabis at least once: 'curiosity is a primary motive for trying cannabis and the use is more experimental or intermittent than persistent' (EMCDDA, 2000, p. 4). Amphetamines and ecstasy are the second-most commonly used drugs in Europe. The use of ecstasy is common in discos, bars and clubs, but, after a sudden spurt of growth in the mid-1990s its use now seems to be decreasing.

The stability in the use of some drugs, alongside a decrease or slow growth in others, can be attributed in part to the effect of European policies, which are becoming more balanced in approach with greater emphasis being placed on demand reduction via prevention, treatment and social rehabilitation rather than the reduction of supply by repression. These aims are promoted by the European Union Drugs strategy (2000–4) which was adopted at the Helsinki Meeting of the European Council in December 1999. This strategy insists, of course, on reducing the availability of illicit drugs and the repression of drug-related crimes (particularly selling) and money laundering, but the de-penalization of drug-use offences is becoming more common. A consensus is emerging that drug users should not be imprisoned because of their addiction, and alternatives provided in law are increasingly used. Given the fact that selling drugs to acquire money to finance a drug habit is a common behaviour among users, a difference is increasingly being made in all the member states of the Union between selling small quantities and large-scale trafficking.

Given the relative stability of the Western European drugs market, organized crime has found a large new market in Eastern Europe, where living conditions have worsened for many people in the last 10 years and where a crisis of social values among some parts of the population is creating problems of social alienation. The enlargement of the European Union towards the East also creates potential new dangers and problems. For this reason, cooperation between the Union and the new candidate members has already begun in this area.

Trafficking in human beings: migration as big business

Following the deaths of 58 Chinese migrants trying to reach Britain in September 2000, Pino Arlacchi announced that:

> This is the fastest-growing criminal market in the world, because of the number of people who are involved, the scale of profits being generated for criminal organisations and because of its multiform nature. We don't just have sexual exploitation. We don't just have economic slavery, which includes two things: forced labour and debt enslavement. We have also a lot of exploitation of migrants. And we have classic slavery. (*New York Times*, 29 September 2000)

As one of the main destinations of illegal migration, Europe is highly concerned with the trafficking of human beings. People are smuggled mainly from Eastern Europe, the Balkans and the Middle East, and there is also some trafficking between Morocco and Spain (Eichenhofer, 1999). Once again, the Russian mafias as well as Eastern European criminal organizations seem to be very active in this area. The economy of Albania has in fact become highly dependent on the trafficking of migrants (Strazzari and Dognini, 2000); small boats filled with illegal migrants, who pay large amounts of money depending on their country of origin and the security of the trip, cross the Otranto channel between Albania and Italy every night. These boats also smuggle heroin, cannabis, cigarettes and weapons. Another border which sees a great deal of illegal migration is that between Slovenia and the region of Frioul in northern Italy. Increasing controls on the Otranto channel have led more migrants and those who traffic in them to use this border, and the anti-mafia police in Trieste estimate that some 35 000 illegal migrants cross it every year. It is also the main route taken by prostitutes illegally entering Italy from Eastern Europe.

It is likely that new criminal networks have grown thanks to trafficking. But not all the actors involved in trafficking are part of criminal networks: while large criminal organizations (Russian mafia, Ukrainian mafia) handle trafficking at the transnational level, at the local level small-time criminals and private citizens are involved in sending and receiving migrants. Taking again the example of Albania, trafficking has become a collective activity in the towns of Vlore and Durres and a way of life for thousands of people. This makes it quite difficult to comprehend and characterize the full extent of the organization of the trafficking – from the point of origin, through the stages of journeys, to the support networks in the receiving country. To cite Kyle (1998):

> Traditionally, many potential migrants have sought help from networks of family or friends who have emigrated before them. The networks and members of the ethnic community facilitated migration. They provided initial information, helped obtain the legal documents required, and found work. More recently, these traditional networks have been substituted or incorporated in trafficking operations. Traffickers of humans now operate internationally or in multiple markets and cultures.

Though Kyle's statement may exaggerate the extent to which traditional networks have been replaced by trafficking, with the blocking of labour flows into many developed countries in the 1990s, old networks were no longer able to fulfil their role successfully without often turning to illegal practices. The combination of legal and illegal practices in the phase of entry into the new country has been present throughout the history of migration, but it was of limited importance when obtaining official permits was a simple practice for migrants as it was in northern Europe (Germany, France) in the 1960s. In the contemporary period, tighter restrictions have gone hand in hand with greater migratory pressures from different countries and continents towards developed countries. The integrated global economy has at least one principal contradiction: 'while free trade allows for the growing mobility of capital and goods, this liberalisation is not extended to human beings' (Seabrook, 1996).

The 'push factors' include the deterioration of living conditions in many Third World countries, as well as in Eastern Europe where the economic transition after the fall of communism has created harder times for some parts of the population in many of the post-communist democracies. And more often than not, those who want to emigrate find individual solutions and revert to trafficking networks. Emigration at all costs, even through traffickers, represents, in the words of Ruggiero (1997) 'individual resistance by way of physical relocation'.

But this individual resistance may also have a cost in terms of development potential in the countries of origin. Within the developed countries' economies, there is an ever-present 'grey-area' of black-market jobs, for which subservient and flexible labourers, like the clandestine labourers, are needed. In these grey areas there are varied spheres of activity, ranging from productive semi-legal activity to the openly criminal:

> These quasi-legal productive sectors border on openly criminal economies, which draw profits from illegal labour and trafficking of human beings. In some cases, organised crime straddles the semi-legal economy and offers a variety of work opportunities to the individuals being trafficked in Europe. (Ruggiero, 1997, p. 241)

Often the illegal, trafficked immigrant can find work within the same enterprises with 'subsidiaries' in Western Europe run by organized crime (such as restaurants, casinos, trafficking, housing complexes, brothels). Within this 'grey area' between the legal and illegal, there are numerous activities linked with services, including private personal services. The increase in female migration in the past 20 years can be explained in this way: in southern Europe, for example, immigrant women initially came to work as domestic servants. Other than the growth of domestic labour, after a period of decline during the 1960s, and in the care-giving professions (nurses, carers for the elderly), the increase in services also relates to less salubrious consumer habits in the developed world (Campani, 1997). In recent years, activities linked to sex tourism and the entertainment industry have also become more prevalent, and it is to this subject that we now turn.

The trafficking of women for sexual exploitation

The trafficking of women for sexual exploitation is just one component of global trafficking in human beings, but one that is constantly on the rise. Organized crime (often in collaboration with petty crime) has a strong presence in this activity. As with trafficking in general, the trafficking of women is certainly not a new phenomenon but it has taken on new dimensions and characteristics in recent years (Cazals, 1995).

In fact, the first International Accord on the suppression of 'white slavery' (as trafficking was called at the time) was signed in 18 May 1904, and was followed by the International Convention (again for the suppression of white slavery) of 4 May 1910 and by the International Convention of 30 September 1921 on the trading of women and children. In 1922, the Society of Nations Conference established an advisory committee on trading in women and children, and in 1933 the first International Convention on the Trading of Women and Children was adopted. After the Second World War, the United Nations took up the theme again and in the seventeenth session in 1948, the Economic and Social Council invited the General Secretary of the United Nations to draw up plans for a new Convention of a general scope covering trading in women and children and the prevention of prostitution. A new development in the Convention of 1949 was the connection established between trade and prostitution; until then the two problems had been kept separate. In the debate on prostitution today, there is a tendency to question this connection between the exploitation of prostitution and trafficking.

Compared to the era in which the first conventions were signed, the directions of trade or trafficking flows have changed. The white-slavery policy assumed north–south or north–north flows, as confirmed by studies conducted in the 1930s. Today, the trafficking of women flows from south to north, or south–south or east–west, and the numbers involved have massively increased. The women who are trafficked come from the poor countries – which are also emigration countries – and are brought to the rich, immigration countries (Campani, 1989). Especially in Asia, women are trafficked to countries in which there is also sex tourism, a much more recent phenomenon, particularly in Thailand (Boonchalanski and Guest, 1994). Japan legally hires Philippine and Thai women for its entertainment industry, but many women are also trafficked illegally.

In Europe, trafficking in women has grown particularly since 1989, following the changes that have taken place in Eastern Europe. The European Commission's report on the trafficking of women for sexual exploitation reports that:

> There is no doubt that the trafficking of women by organised crime is on the rise. Although there are no exact figures ... the IOM (International Organisation for Migration 1996) estimates that in 1995, about 500,000 women have been trafficked, the majority of them illegal, towards countries of the European Union, and studies of the NGO International Campaign against Child Prostitution in Tourism in Asia has recently noted the trend of trafficking of a high number of women and girls in Russia, the Ukraine and Byelorussia towards the West. The figures presented by national NGOs also suggest an increase in the number of women coming from Central and Eastern Europe. (Commission of the European Communities, 1996)

The 'push-factors' in the former Soviet Union and Eastern Europe are easy to understand. During the economic transition unemployment has grown enormously, affecting men less than women, who represent between 60 and 90 per cent of the newly unemployed in countries like Ukraine, Moldavia and Byelorussia. Given diminishing employment opportunities at home, the opportunity of going abroad for work, often with financial and travel 'assistance' from the recruiter (who may also be a trafficker), may be too good to pass up. In Kiev, St Petersburg, Alma-Ata, Tashkent and elsewhere, criminal organizations have opened modelling agencies or employment agencies for young dancers, running advertisements in local papers. Outright abductions also take place. Once they are recruited into the network, girls and women are then sold into international commercial sex markets.

In the Balkans, trafficking of women increased after the war in the former Yugoslavia. A particular case is that of Albanian women who, since 1993–94, have been trafficked into Italy and pushed into prostitution. This can take place via friendship and acquaintance networks, and sometimes even through amorous relationships. In some cases, though less commonly, the girls are the victims of abductions. To reach Italy the girls follow the same routes as other illegal immigrants, travelling in small boats crossing the Otranto channel. The relation between the trafficked girls, subsequently forced to practice prostitution on the streets, and the pimps is often a direct one. The pimps are generally small-time criminals, often young, who in search of easy money do not hesitate to throw onto the streets their female schoolmates, childhood female friends and even their fiancées (Campani, Carchedi and Picciolini, 1997).

If Eastern Europe and the Balkans have become one of the main places of origin for women trafficked into the European Union, the following flows are also important:

- some African countries, for example Nigeria and Ghana, from where women are trafficked into Italy and Germany respectively (Ruggiero, 1997);
- various countries of Latin America, for example Dominicans trafficked into Spain and Dominicans and Brazilians into Switzerland;
- and various Asian countries (for example Thailand and the Philippines) who export women to Europe, frequently in the form of mail-brides and in quite large numbers to Germany, where as early as 1990 there were some 20 000 Philippine women (Council of Europe, 1991).

Trafficked and enslaved women have been found in all Western European countries: Germany is one of the main destination countries, with around 10 000 trafficked women (OIM figures), while Italy has an estimated 18–25 000 (Campani, 1997). Holland, Belgium and France also have large numbers.

Those crime organizations most involved in trafficking for sexual exploitation are the mafias of the former Soviet Union and of the new Republics (Ukraine, Byelorussia, and so on) and the criminal gangs of the Balkans. These same groups are taking control of the prostitution market in Western Europe at different levels. Organized crime controls brothels, eros centres and apartment prostitution, while smaller criminal organizations seem to control street prostitution. For example, in Italy organized crime does not have complete control over Albanian prostitution. Criminal organizations from Eastern Europe, primarily the Russian mafia, also control much of the pornography industry, which has been displaced from Scandinavia to Eastern Europe. They have also been known to be involved in the trafficking and sexual exploitation of children and the production of videocassettes for paedophiles.

European crime prevention policy

Judicial and police cooperation among the countries of the then European Community started in the 1970s, at the time aimed mostly at fighting political terrorism. Italy and Germany had to contend with internal terrorist groups (the Italian Red Brigades, neo-fascist groups, the German Red Army faction) while Great Britain had to deal with IRA terrorism. Meanwhile all three, as well as France, also had to deal with other forms of international terrorism. In 1975, the TREVI group (Terrorism, Radicalism, Extremism and Violence International) – the intergovernmental forum of the Ministries of Justice and Home Affairs – was established by the European Council of Rome in order to increase practical cooperation in security, policing and border control. The Interior Ministers of the participating member states met twice a year in the context of this organization. Although primarily aimed at fighting terrorism, TREVI actually became the prototype organization for the Third Pillar of the Treaty on European Union in 1993 (Boettcher, 2000, p. 3).

During the 1980s, European integration was relaunched under the Commission Presidency of Jacques Delors, with one aim being the eventual elimination of internal border controls within the Community. In 1985, the Schengen Accord (named after the town in Luxembourg where it was signed) brought Belgium, France, Luxembourg and the Netherlands together as a first stage towards this goal. But the full Schengen Agreement was only signed (also in Schengen) in 1990. The complete treaty deals with the question of policing and security, the abolition of controls at internal borders, the creation of a Schengen information system to track the movement of persons, the transport and traffic of goods and the protection of personal data. With the abolition of internal borders, a stronger degree of judicial and police cooperation became necessary to ensure both internal security and that of the external borders. The member states were also concerned to control immigration and prevent illegal immigration (Ahnfelt and From, 1993). Those countries that could not provide guarantees in this respect were excluded from the agreement. In the meantime, in the 1980s and 1990s, a new threat emerged from organized crime.

The European Union (or Maastricht) Treaty, represented a further step forward in judicial and police cooperation. Article K, Title VI 'Cooperation in the Fields of Justice and Home Affairs' is the basis for such coordination. Justice and Home Affairs forms the Third Pillar of the Treaty, the Second Pillar being foreign and defence affairs. The Maastricht Treaty also provided for the establishment of Europol – the European police – but this organization was not fully in place until 1 July 1999. According to Article 2 of the Europol Convention, the mandate of Europol is

> to improve the effectiveness and co-operation of the competent authorities in the Member States in preventing and combatting terrorism, unlawful drug trafficking and other serious forms of international crime where there are factual indications that an organised criminal structure is involved and two or more Member States are affected.

The Amsterdam Treaty in 1997 set forth the Union's policies towards the free movement of persons, but it also introduced a new notion: 'an area of freedom, security and justice' inside the EU's borders. It is the first Article under Title IIIa, Article 73(i), which establishes the goal of 'an area of freedom, security and justice'. In order to reach this goal, the Treaty transferred immigration, asylum and visa policy from the Third to the First Pillar, making them Communitarian policies. The transfer of immigration to the First Pillar has diminished the Third Pillar which now consists of police and judicial cooperation and drugs policy. It is nevertheless evident that the Third Pillar is extremely important for the creation of a European space of freedom of movement, security and justice. Cooperation in justice and internal affairs, on which, in the end, the fight against crime depends, is therefore not implemented as a 'Communitarian policy', as is the case for the common agricultural policy or regional policies, and, since Amsterdam, asylum, immigration and external borders. Member states retain greater intergovernmental influence in this field, and so too do all other instances of the European Union in which the states take part directly.

What then are the instruments foreseen by the Treaties of Maastricht and Amsterdam for implementing a common policy in the fight against organized crime and its activities? Maastricht established that anti-crime measures had to take the form of conventions and joint actions. But the conventions are effectively treaties and require ratification in every member state before they come into force. Consequently, this requirement has meant that none of the six conventions signed since the creation of the Third Pillar have yet been ratified. To reinforce cooperation in the fight against crime, the Treaty of Amsterdam established that in order to facilitate a faster implementation of new anti-crime laws a convention can come into force in those member states which have ratified the convention, even if others decline.

Beyond the Treaties, the fight against organized crime was a major topic for discussion in the European Council of Dublin in 1996, the European Council of Amsterdam in 1997, the European Council of Vienna in 1998, the Council of Tampere in 1999 and finally the European Council of Helsinki in 1999. In the European Council of Dublin, a working group was established to set out a project of action against organized crime. The group produced a Plan of Action which, among other suggestions and initiatives, created the Multidisciplinary Group on Crime and networks of cooperation in the field of justice. The Council of Tampere was an 'extraordinary' Council, exclusively reserved for cooperation in matters of justice and internal affairs, and in the last few years cooperation has been reinforced. Europol has been empowered with collecting highly sensitive data on individuals by the member states, notwithstanding the intense debate on the need to preserve privacy. A Unit for Police and Customs Cooperation has been created and a global strategy to fight against drugs has been proposed and implemented.

Different programmes managed by the General Directorate for Justice and Home Affairs of the European Union have been implemented: these include STOP (trafficking in human beings), DAPHNE (violence against women and children), OISIN (police cooperation) and FALCONE (fight against criminality) – from the name of an Italian judge, Giovanni Falcone, killed by the mafia in May 1992. A European Union Drugs Strategy has been elaborated; new attention is being given to the Internet, cybercrime and the safe use of Internet by children; and at the same time the European Union continues to take part in all transnational initiatives proposed by the United Nations and to establish transnational bilateral agreements for countries engaged in the fight against crime.

Conclusions

Organized crime is a major threat in the global world because of its forms of organization, financial power and capacity for crossing borders – not just between nations but between the spheres of economic and political power, both nationally and transnationally. In this sense it has successfully been adapting to and expanding along with the process of globalization. Single countries are unable to respond to this global threat, against which transnational instruments are needed. International organizations, led by the United Nations, have created specific programmes to promote the fight against crime, but their results are far from being satisfactory.

Europe is particularly exposed to the activities of criminal organizations because of its proximity to areas of political, social and economic instability like the former USSR and the Balkans. In the transition from the communist system to the liberal economy – creating in some countries a veritable no-man's land without rules – criminal organizations have found ready opportunities for expansion. Eastern Europe and the Balkans are at the centre of trafficking of all forms – trafficking in illegal migrants, in women for sexual exploitation, in children for black work and sexual exploitation or even the illegal marketing of body organs. Russia has recently appeared to be one of the places where paedophiles can easily find children to be abused for the production of pornography, which can in turn be sold on the international market via the Internet. For these reasons, the fight against criminal organizations has appeared to be a priority in the implementation of common European policies.

The European experience of fighting against organized criminality in the context of greater political integration may also be of interest for the rest of the world. By strengthening the linkages among member states, the European Union can move beyond *ad hoc* working groups, committees and programmes towards a global political approach and management of the issue. In its search for a model where citizens enjoy a maximum of human rights, the European Union is establishing the right to security as a basic element. The Treaty of Amsterdam spoke of an area of freedom, security and justice, and the instruments to guarantee it are not only of a repressive nature. On the contrary, a civil society which is aware of the dangers represented by criminal organizations, which has a minimum of common values, and which supports solidarity amongst its members can thereby create powerful obstacles to the spread of organized crime. The strategies against drugs, the new organizations (Europol) and the new programmes (STOP, DAPHNE, FALCONE) proposed by the European Union to fight against criminal organizations are all key steps in ensuring that the footholds for organized criminal activity are not further increased in line with political and economic integration.

Nevertheless, in the interest of its citizens, and in order to create a real space of freedom, security and justice, the European Union along with other international organizations must also pay greater attention to the structural causes of the growth of organized crime. These include the impoverishment of peoples in adjacent and Third World Countries, the erosion or collapse of the rule of law in some former communist countries, corruption (including that in its own member states), and the poorly regulated international system of financial transactions that helps fuel (and is fuelled by) international crime.

Guide to Further Reading

Chapter 1 Europe at the Crossroads

Given the range of issue areas touched on by European integration, the challenge of keeping up with events across the Union is a daunting one for any individual. There are a number of excellent textbooks on the European Union, but nevertheless the first place to look for current developments is edited volumes rather than single-author monographs: Cram, Dinan and Nugent (1999) provide an institution-by-institution and policy-by-policy account; Cowles and Smith (2000) offer a more broadly thematic overview; Wallace and Wallace (2000) and Monar and Wessels (2001) are somewhere in between. In addition, two journals (both published by Blackwell) provide annual reviews of developments in the European Union: *Industrial Relations Journal* and *Journal of Common Market Studies*. Finally, the weekly newspaper *European Voice* has emerged as a key source of reporting and analysis. The newspaper is printed on paper, but can also be accessed via the internet at: http://www.european-voice.com.

Chapter 2 Globalization, EMU and Welfare State Futures

The literature on welfare states and Europe has grown considerably over the past few years both as a reflection of concern about the impact of globalization and in anticipation of the launch of Europe's economic and monetary union (EMU). The globalization focus in the literature touches on topics ranging from macroeconomic strategies (Notermans, 2000; Franzese, 2002) and wage bargaining regimes (Iversen, 1999; Iversen, Pontusson and Soskice, 2000) to partisan politics (Garrett, 1998), societal change (Esping-Andersen, 1999) and institutional reform (Esping-Andersen and Regini, 2000). That branch of the literature that anticipates EMU builds on this wide-ranging set of concerns in order to map the evolution of European welfare states within a broader regional context. The argument is not so much that EMU challenges the welfare state, but rather that EMU should be considered in the context of wider challenges. Ferrera and Rhodes (2000), Pierson (2001), and Scharpf and Schmidt (2000a, 2000b) bring together both thematic and country case studies of such adaptation in process. In doing so, these volumes further develop and extend the analysis found – *inter alia* – in such collections as Kitschelt *et al.* (1999) and Hollingsworth and Boyer (1997).

Chapter 3   Reorganizing Security in Europe

Given the fast pace of change in the area, the literature on European security tends to develop as much through the principal journals as through single-authored or edited books. The more policy-oriented journals, such as *International Affairs* and *Survival*, provide regular coverage of developments. More specialized analysis can be found in the pages of the *European Journal of International Relations, The European Foreign Affairs Review, The Journal of Common Market Studies* and *International Security*. Students are also advised to consult the websites of both NATO (http://www.nato.int) and the Western European Union (http://www.weu.int), where it is possible not only to access the latest communiques but also to find archives containing the texts of past agreements or decisions. Broad overviews focusing mostly on the conceptual debates about security are provided in Hodge (1999b) and Croft and Terriff (2000). Finally, there are a number of edited volumes, such as Peterson and Sjursen (1998) and Howorth and Menon (1997), that can be used to provide a starting point for analysis of developments regarding the European Union's common foreign and security policy.

Chapter 4   Nationalism and Collective Identities: Europe versus the Nation-State?

The literature on European identity has exploded in recent years. An interdisciplinary and annotated on-line bibliography on the topic which essentially covers the literature of the 1990s has more than 800 entries (available at http://www.iue.it/RSC/IDNET). Anderson (1991), Eisenstadt and Giesen (1995) and Oakes, Haslam and Turner (1994) tackle theoretical issues pertaining to the concept of collective identity from the perspectives of political science, sociology and social psychology. Survey data on European and national identities are discussed in Duchesne and Frognier (1995) and Marks (1998). Strath (2000) and Jenkins and Sofos (1996) approach the topic from a historical perspective. Elite identities between Europe and the nation-state are covered by Banchoff (1999) and Marcussen *et al.* (1999); Eder and Giesen (1999) cover the important topic of European citizenship and European identity; and, finally, a forthcoming book by Herrmann, Brewer and Risse represents the state of the art on the subject from a variety of disciplinary perspectives.

Chapter 5   Participation and Voting

For a long-term postwar perspective on electoral participation, see Topf (1995a and 1995b), Hayward (1996) and Charlot (1996); for newer data and analysis see the various chapters in Pharr and Putnam (2000), Klingemann (1999), Dalton (1999) and Norris (1999). The Eurobarometer website is also useful for exploring some of the wider issues (http://europa.eu.int/comm/dg10/epo/).

Chapter 6   Party Systems, Electoral Cleavages and Government Stability

The literature on parties and electorates has the virtue of being at the same time enduring and dynamic. Some of the more classical work found in Lipset (1960), Dahl (1966), LaPalombara and Weiner (1966), Inglehart (1977), Bartolini and Mair (1990) and Mair (1990) remains relevant both for course use and for framing research questions. Readers looking to survey the broad range of developments are advised to consult a more synthetic volume like Ware (1996). More recent (or recently updated) analysis can be found in Inglehart (1997), Müller and Strøm (1999) and – particularly – Dalton and Wattenberg (2000b).

Chapter 7   Extremist Movements

The most useful descriptive survey of extremist groups in Europe is Camus (1999). For studies of the post-Cold War extreme left, see Bell (1993), Bull and Heywood (1994) and Moreau *et al.* (1998); on the extreme right in Western Europe see Betz (1994), Hainsworth (2000)and the special issue 'Far Right in Europe: In or Out of the Cold' of *Parliamentary Affairs*, vol 53(3) (July 2000); on territorial extremists see Hewitt and Cheetham (2000) and Ishiyama and Breuning (1998); on Islamic fundamentalism in Western Europe see Kepel (1997) and Sfeir (1997); and on the 'new fringe' see McKay (1998), Wall (1999) and Lent (2001).

Chapter 8   Executive Capacity and Legislative Limits

Useful recent studies of the core executive and its operation in comparative perspective include Weller, Bakvis and Rhodes (1997), Steunenberg and van Vught (1997) and Peters, Rhodes and Wright (2000). An excellent account of the challenges surrounding coordination is Wright and Hayward (2000). For the European Union dimension see Peterson and Bomberg (1999). On the broader issues of governance and institutional structures, Weaver and Rockman (1993) remains a key starting point, but see also the important study by Laver and Shepsle (1995) and the UK-focused studies by Rhodes (1997b and 2000). On the changing role of legislatures, Olson and Mezey (1991) is a good introduction to some key themes, but see also Döring (1995), Norton (1996) and Bergman, Müller and Strøm (2000).

Chapter 9   Disintegration or Reconfiguration? Organized Interests in Western Europe

There is a vast literature on organized interests in Western Europe, with much of it focusing on the organization and activities of European interest groups and the lobbying of the European institutions. Greenwood (1997) provides a solid introduction to this literature, while the essays in Greenwood and Aspinwall (1998) offer more in the way of case studies. There are fewer books dealing with the impact of globalization and Europeanization on domestic interest organization. Beyond Kohler-Koch and Eising (1999), which is a recent addition to this literature, reference has to be made to working papers and articles such as those published in the *Journal of European Public Policy* (see Grande, 1996, for example).

Chapter 10   Political Corruption, Democracy and Governance in Western Europe

Much has been published on corruption in recent years, but little has been explicitly comparative. The most wide-ranging account on its causes and consequences is Rose-Ackerman (1999). Case study-based accounts of corruption in Western Europe can be found in Little and Posada-Carbó (1996) and della Porta and Mény (1997). See also Williams, Moran and Flanary (2000) for corruption in the developed world. For more detailed accounts of corruption in particular countries see, on Italy, the outstanding work by della Porta and Vannucci (1999); on France, Mény (1992); on Spain, Nieto (1997).

Chapter 11   Territorial Politics and the New Regionalism

The literature on territory is broad. Keating (1998) provides a good starting point on the role of territory in Western Europe, with his wide-ranging discussion of the role of regions. For an overview of regional mobilization in the European Union, see Marks *et al.* (1996), Keating and Jones (1995) and Hooghe (1995). Still within the context of the European Union, Jachtenfuchs (1995), Scharpf (1994) and Hooghe and Marks (2001) provide a theoretical framework for the role of sub-state actors, and Leonardi (1995) assesses EU cohesion policy. For a discussion of territorial patterns of party support in European states, see Caramani (1996). Finally, the journal *Regional and Federal Studies* publishes a diverse range of articles relating to territorial politics.

Chapter 12   Environmental Challenges

Comparative European country studies of environmental policy include Andersen and Liefferink (1997) and Hanf and Jansen (1998). An introductory coverage of EU environmental policy can be found in most EU textbooks, but the chapters on environmental policy (Sbragia) and biotechnology policy (Patterson) in Wallace and Wallace (2000) are a good starting point. For more detailed coverage see Zito (2000). For further discussion of sustainable development and ecological modernization see Weale (1992), Hajer (1995), Dryzek (1997) and Mol and Sonnenfeld (2000). Lafferty and Meadowcroft (2000) offer a comparative analysis of progress in implementing sustainable development, while Golub (1998) examines the use of different policy instruments. The journal *Environmental Politics* is a good source of articles on European environmental policy, movements and green parties.

Chapter 13   The Information Society

The breadth of the term Information Society and the speed of developments in this field mean that the literature is quite diffuse and rapidly overtaken by events. On broadcasting, Levy (2001) provides a useful overview of national and European Union developments up to the end of 1999, while Humphreys' (1998) focus is more on national trends. The best overview of information society initiatives is in the EU commissioned survey (EC, 2000a) on 'Public Strategies for the Information Society'. The annual reports from the EU on the implementation of telecoms liberalization (EC, 2000b) provide a rich source of information, both on EU initiatives and national implementation.

Chapter 14   European Immigration Policies at the Crossroads

The literature on European immigration policies is vast and difficult to survey. Descriptive country- and (sub)policy-specific case studies predominate, while theoretically guided explanatory and comparative work is rare. The key text for theorizing immigration policy in cross-sectional and cross-national perspectives is Freeman (1995). Further elaborations on this can be found in Money (1999) and Joppke (1998). A good descriptive (if slightly outdated) overview of immigration policies in several European (and non-European) states is still Cornelius *et al.* (1994). More theoretically guided and up-to-date discussions of problems of immigration control in Western states are Andreas (2001), Andreas and Snyder (2000) and Guiraudon and Joppke (2001). Indispensable for the tracing of current events in this area is the *Migration News Sheet*, published monthly by the Migration Policy Group in Brussels.

Chapter 15   Crime, Trafficking, Prostitution and Drugs

Work in this area tends to specialize both on particular actors and on particular problems. For analysis of the mafia see Catanzaro (1992), Anderson (1995) and Ziegler (1998). For more specific analysis of the trafficking of women see Campagni (1989 and 1997), Williams (1999) and de Stoop (1992) – which unfortunately is only available in Dutch. For a comprehensive analysis of the international drugs trade, see Labrousse and Laniel (2001).

Bibliography

Adonis, A. (1997) 'The UK: Civic Virtue Put to the Test', in D. della Porta and Y. Mény (eds), *Democracy and Corruption in Europe*. London: Pinter, pp. 103–17.

Aggestam, L. (2000) 'Europe Puissance: French Influence and European Independence', in H. Sjursen (ed), 'Redefining European Security? The Role of the European Union in European Security Structures.' ARENA Report no. 7/2000. Oslo: ARENA, pp. 67–82.

Agnew, J. (1987) *Place and Politics: The Geographical Mediation of State and Society*. London: Allen & Unwin.

Ahnfelt E. and J. From (1993) 'European Policing', in S.S. Andersen and K.A. Eliassen (eds), *Making Policy in Europe*. London: Sage, pp. 187–212.

Alber, J. and G. Standing (2000) 'Social Dumping, Catch-up or Convergence? Europe in a Comparative Global Context', *Journal of European Social Policy*, vol. 10(2), pp. 99–119.

Allan, J.P. and L.A. Scruggs (2000) 'Three Worlds Divided or Convergent? Comparing European Welfare States in the late 1990s'. Paper presented at the 12th International Conference of Europeanists, Chicago, 30 March–1 April.

Almond, G.A., E. Sivan and R.S. Appleby (1995) 'Explaining Fundamentalisms', in M.E. Marty and R.S. Appleby (eds), *Fundamentalisms Comprehended*. Chicago: University of Chicago Press, pp. 425–44.

Amato, G. and J. Batt (1999) *The Long-Term Implications of EU Enlargement: The Nature of the New Border*. Florence: European University Institute.

Andersen, M. S. and D. Liefferink (eds) (1997) *European Environmental Policy: The Pioneers*. Manchester: Manchester University Press.

Anderson, A. (1995) 'The Red Mafia: A Legacy of Communism', in E.P. Lazear (ed.), *Economic Transition in Eastern Europe and Russia: Realities of Reform*. Stanford: The Hoover Institution Press.

Anderson, B. (1991) *Imagined Communities. Reflections on the Origin and Spread of Nationalism*. London: Verso.

Andeweg, R. (1991) 'The Dutch Prime Minister: Not Just Chairman, Not Yet Chief?', in G.W. Jones (ed.), *West European Prime Ministers*. London: Frank Cass, pp. 116–32.

Andeweg, R. (1996) 'Elite–Mass Linkages in Europe: Legitimacy Crisis or Party Crisis?', in J. Hayward (ed.), *Elitism, Populism, and European Politics*. Oxford: Clarendon Press, pp. 143–63.

Andeweg, R. and L. Nijzink (1995) 'Beyond the Two-Body Image: Relations Between Ministers and MPs', in H. Döring (ed.), *Parliaments and Majority Rule in Western Europe*. New York: St Martin's Press, pp. 152–78.

Andreas, P. (2000) 'The Transformation of Migrant Smuggling Across the U.S.–Mexico Border', in D. Kyle and R. Koslowski (eds), *Global Human*

Smuggling: Comparative Perspectives. Baltimore: Johns Hopkins University Press.

Andreas, P. (2001) *Border Games*. Ithaca: Cornell University Press.

Andreas, P., and T. Snyder (eds) (2000) *The Wall Around the West*. Lanham, Md.: Rowman & Littlefield.

Andreatta, F., and C. Hill (1997) 'Italy', in J. Howorth and A. Menon (eds), *The European Union and National Defence Policy*. London: Routledge, pp. 66-86.

Arango, J. (2000) 'Becoming a Country of Immigration at the End of the Twentieth Century: The Case of Spain', in R. King *et al.* (eds), *Eldorado or Fortress*. Basingstoke: Macmillan.

Arlacchi, P. (1986) *Mafia Business: The Mafia Ethic and the Spirit of Capitalism*. London: Verso.

Armstrong, K., and S. Bulmer (1999) *The Governance of the Single European Market*. Manchester: Manchester University Press.

Artis, M., and W. Zhang (1999) 'Further Evidence on the International Business Cycle and the ERM: Is there a European Business Cycle?', *Oxford Economic Papers*, no. 51, pp. 120–32.

Attina, F. (1997) 'Globalization and Crime. The emerging role of International Institutions', *Jean Monnet Working Papers in Comparative and International Politics*. Catania: University of Catania.

Ayres, R.W., and S. Saideman (2000) 'Is Separatism as Contagious as the Common Cold or as Cancer? Testing International and Domestic Explanations', *Nationalism and Ethnic Politics*, vol. 6(3), pp. 91–113.

Backes, U. (1989) *Politischer Extremismus in demokratischen Verfassungsstaaten: Elemente einer normativen Rahmentheorie*. Opladen: Westdeutscher.

Bagnasco, A., and M. Oberti (1997) 'Le trompe-oeil des régions en Italie', in P. Le Galès and C. Lequesne (eds), *Les paradoxes des régions en Europe*. Paris: La Découverte.

Bagnasco, A. and C. Trigilia (1993) *La construction social du marché*. Cachan: Editions ENS Cachan.

Bailey, R. (1983) *The European Connection: Implications of EEC Membership*. Oxford: Pergamon Press.

Baldwin, D.A. (1997) 'The Concept of Security'. *Review of International Studies*, vol. 23(1), pp. 5–26.

Balme, R. (ed.) (1996) *Les politiques du néo-régionalisme*. Paris: Economica.

Banchoff, T. (1999a) 'German Identity and European Integration'. *European Journal of International Relations*, vol. 5(3), pp. 259–89.

Banchoff, T. (1999b) *The German Problem Transformed: Institutions, Politics, and Foreign Policy, 1945–1995*. Ann Arbor: University of Michigan Press.

Barber, B.R. (1995) *Jihad vs. McWorld*. New York: Times Books.

Barnard, C. (2000) 'Social Dumping and the Race to the Bottom: Some Lessons for the European Union from Delaware?' *European Law Review*, 25, pp. 57–78.

Bartle, I. (1999) 'Transnational Interests in the European Union: Globalization and Changing Organization in Telecommunications and Electricity'. *Journal of Common Market Studies*, vol. 37(3), pp. 363–83.

Bartolini, S. and P. Mair (1990) *Identity, Competition and Electoral Availability: The Stabilisation of European Electorates, 1885–1985*. Cambridge: Cambridge University Press.

Bauer, M. (1988) 'The Politics of State-Directed Privatisation: The Case of France 1986-89', *West European Politics*, vol. 11(4), pp. 49–61.

Belaskri, Y. (1999) 'Islamic Fundamentalism and "Social Europe" ', in J.-Y. Camus (ed.), *Extremism in Europe: 1998 Survey*. Paris: Éditions de l'aube/CERA, pp. 411–20.

Bell, D. (1960) *The End of Ideology: The Exhaustion of Political Ideas in the Fifties*. New York: Free Press.

Bell, D.S. (ed.) (1993) *Western European Communists and the Collapse of Communism*. Oxford: Berg.

Beltrán, M. (1996) 'Las Administraciones públicas', in J. Tusell, et al. *Entre dos siglos. Reflexiones sobre la democracia española*. Madrid: Alianza, pp. 265–93.

Bentivogli, C., and P. Pagano (1999) 'Regional Disparities and Labour Mobility: the Euro-11 versus the USA', *Labour*, vol. 13(3), pp. 737–60.

Berger, S. and R. Dore (eds) (1996) *National Diversity and Global Capitalism*. Ithaca: Cornell University Press.

Bergman, T., W.C. Müller, and K. Strøm (2000) 'Introduction: Parliamentary Democracy and the Chain of Delegation', *European Journal of Political Research*, vol. 37(3), pp. 255–60.

Betz, H.-G. (1994) *Radical Right-Wing Populism in Western Europe*. Basingstoke: Macmillan.

Bjørgo, T. (1997). *Racist and Right-Wing Violence in Scandinavia: Patterns, Perpetrators, and Responses*. Oslo: Tano Aschehoug.

Boeri, T. (2000). 'Social Europe: Dramatic Visions and Real Complexity', *Discussion Paper No. 2371*. London: Centre for Economic Policy Research.

Bohnen, J. (1997) 'Germany', in J. Howorth and A. Menon (eds), *The European Union and National Defence Policy*. London: Routledge, pp. 49–65.

Bohrt, E. (1999) 'Illegal Migrations and Cross-Border Crime'. Paper prepared for the Reflection Group on 'The Nature of the New Border'. Florence: European University Institute.

Boix, C. (1998) *Political Parties, Growth and Equality*. Cambridge: Cambridge University Press.

Boonchalanski, W. and P. Guest (1994) *Prostitution in Thailand*. Salaya: Institute of Population and Social Research, Mahidol University.

Bosbach, W. (2000) 'Zuwanderungsbegrenzung und Zuwanderungssteuerung im Interesse unseres Landes'. Discussion paper of the Executive Board of the CDU/CSU Parliamentary Group, Luckenwalde (21 June).

Brochmann, G. and T. Hammar (eds) (1999) *Mechanisms of Immigration Control*. Berg: Oxford.

Buijs, F.J. (1995) *Overtuiging en geweld: Vreedzame en gewelddadige acties tegen de apartheid*. Amsterdam: Babylon-De Geus.

Bull, M.J. (1994) 'The West European Communist Movement: Past, Present, and Future', in M.J. Bull and P. Heywood (eds), *West European Communist Parties after the Revolutions of 1989*. Basingstoke: Macmillan, pp. 203–22.

Bull, M.J. and P. Heywood (eds) (1994) *West European Communist Parties after the Revolutions of 1989*. Basingstoke: Macmillan.

Buzan, B. (1991) *People, States and Fear: An Agenda for International Security Studies in the Post-cold War Era*. Boulder: Lynne Rienner, second edition.

Caine, B. (2000) 'Is the Democracy Deficit a Deficiency'. Paper presented at the Conference on 'Beyond Centre-Periphery'. Florence: European University Institute (19–20 May).

Calavita, K. (1998) 'Immigration, Law, and Marginalisation in a Global Economy: Notes from Spain'. *Law and Society Review*, vol. 32(4), pp. 529–66.

Caldwell, G., S. Galster and N. Steinzor (1997) 'Crime and Servitude'. Presentation at conference on 'The Trafficking of NIS Women Abroad'. Moscow: Global Survival Network (November 3–5).

Campani, G. (1989) 'Du Tiers Monde à l'Italie: une nouvelle migration féminine'. *Revue Européenne des Migrations Internationales*, vol. 5(2), pp. 29–47.

Campani, G. (1997) 'Present Trends in Women's Migration: the Emergence of Social Actors', in D. Joly (ed), *Scapegoats and Social Actors*. Warwick: CRER, pp. 192–217.

Campani, G., Carchedi, F., Picciolini, A. (1997) 'Le traffic des femmes immigrées à des fins d'exploitation sexuelle en Italie'. *Migrations et Societé*, 9(52), pp. 105–14.

Camus, J.-Y. (ed.) (1999) *Extremism in Europe: 1998 Survey*. Paris: Éditions de l'aube/CERA.

Canadian Security Intelligence Service (CSIS) (2000) 'Anti-globalisation: A Spreading Phenomenon', Report 2000/08. Toronto: CSIS.

Canovan, M. (1999) 'Trust the People! Populism and the Two Faces of Democracy', *Political Studies*, vol. 47(1), pp. 2–16.

Cappellin, R. (1995) 'Una politica regionale nazionale 'orientata al mercato' tra i nuovi modelli organizzativi e federalismo', in G. Gorla and O.V. Colonna (eds), *Regioni e Sviluppo: Modelli, politiche e riforme*. Milan: Franco Angeli, pp. 331–53.

Caramani, D. (1996) 'The Nationalization of Electoral Politics: A Conceptual Approach', *West European Politics*, vol. 19(2), pp. 205–24.

Cassese, S. (2000) 'The Prime Minister's "Staff": The Case of Italy', in B.G. Peters, R.A.W. Rhodes and V. Wright (eds), *Administering the Summit*. London: Macmillan, pp. 101–09.

Catanzaro, R. (1992) *Men of Respect: A Social History of the Sicilian Mafia*. New York: Free Press.

Caul, M., and M. Grey (2000) 'From Platform Declarations to Policy Outcomes: Changing Party Profiles and Partisan Influence over Policy', in R. Dalton and M. Wattenberg (eds), *Parties Without Partisans: Political Change in Advanced Industrial Democracies*. Oxford: Oxford University Press, pp. 208–37.

Cazals, A. (1995) *Prostitution et proxenetisme en Europe*. Paris: La Documentation française.

Cazorla, J. (1994) 'El clientelismo de partido en España ante la opinion pública.

El medio rural, la administración y las empresas', Working Paper No. 86. Barcelona: Institut de Ciències Polítiques i Socials.

Cecchini, P., E. Jones and J. Lorentzen (2001) 'Europe and the Concept of Enlargement', *Survival*, vol. 43(1), pp. 155–65.

Chari, R. S. (1999) 'Spanish Socialists, Privatising the Right Way?', in P. Heywood (ed.), *Politics and Policy in Democratic Spain*. London: Frank Cass, pp. 163–79.

Charlot, J. (1996) 'From Representative to Responsive Government?', in J. Hayward (ed.), *Elitism, Populism, and European Politics*. Oxford: Clarendon Press, pp. 88–100.

Christensen, D. (1997) 'Leaving the Back Door Open', *Georgetown Immigration Law Journal*, vol. 11(3), pp. 461–505.

Churchill, W. (1953) 'Speech on 11 May'. House of Commons 513 895.

Chuter, D. (1997) 'The United Kingdom', in J. Howorth and A. Menon (eds), *The European Union and National Defence Policy*. London: Routledge, pp. 105–20.

Coleman, J. (1988) 'Social Capital in the Creation of Human Capital', *American Journal of Sociology*, 94: supplement, pp. S95–S120.

Colino, C. (1997) 'The Manifold "Europeanization" of the Audiovisual Sector: Expanding European Initiatives and German Domestic Responses'. Paper presented at the final workshop on 'The European Policy Process' organised by the Human Capital and Mobility Network. Dublin: University College Dublin (8–10 May).

Committee on Standards in Public Life (1998) 'Standards in Public Life: The Funding of Political Parties in the United Kingdom'. London: The Stationery Office, Cm 4057–I and Cm 4057–II.

Cooke, P., and K. Morgan (1998) *The Associational Economy: Firms, Regions, and Innovation*. Oxford: Oxford University Press.

Cornelius, W. *et al.* (eds) (1994) *Controlling Immigration*. Stanford: Stanford University Press.

Courchene, T. (1995) 'Celebrating Flexibility: An Interpretative Essay on the Evolution of Canadian Federalism'. Montreal: C.D. Howe Institute, Benefactors Lecture.

Cowles, M.G., and M. Smith (eds) (2000) *The State of the European Union, Volume 5: Risks, Reforms, Resistance, and Revival*. Oxford: Oxford University Press.

Cram, L., D. Dinan and N. Nugent (eds) (1999) *Developments in the European Union*. London: Palgrave.

Croft, S. and T. Terriff (eds) (2000) *Critical Reflections on Security and Change*. London: Frank Cass.

Dahl, R.A. (ed.) (1966) *Political Oppositions in Western Democracies*. New Haven: Yale University Press.

Dalton, R.J. (1996) *Citizen Politics: Public Opinion and Political Parties*. Chatham: Chatham House, second edition.

Dalton, R. (1999) 'Political Support in Advanced Industrial Democracies', in P. Norris (ed.), *Critical Citizens. Global Support for Democratic Governance*. Oxford: Oxford University Press, pp. 57–77.

Dalton, R.J. (2000) 'The Decline of Party Identification', in R.J. Dalton and M.P. Wattenberg (eds), *Parties without Partisans: Political Change in Advanced Industrial Democracies*. Oxford: Oxford University Press, pp. 20–36.

Dalton, R. J. and M.P. Wattenberg (2000a) 'Partisan Change and the Democratic Process', in R.J. Dalton and M.P. Wattenberg (eds), *Parties Without Partisans. Political Change in Advanced Industrial Democracies*. Oxford: Oxford University Press, pp. 261–85.

Dalton, R.J. and M.P. Wattenberg (eds) (2000b) *Parties Without Partisans. Political Change in Advanced Industrial Democracies*. Oxford: Oxford University Press.

Davis, G. (1997) 'Executive Coordination Mechanisms', in P. Weller, H. Bakvis and R.A.W. Rhodes (eds), *The Hollow Crown*. London: Macmillan, pp. 126–47.

De Brie, C. (2000) 'Thick as Thieves. Crime: the World's Biggest Free Enterprise', *Le Monde diplomatique* (February).

De Grauwe, P. and F. Skudelny (1999) 'Social Conflict and Growth in Euroland'. Discussion Paper No. 2186. London: Centre for Economic Policy Research.

De Stoop, C. (1992) *Zij zijn zo lief, meneer: Over vrouwenhandelaars, meisjes-balletten, en de bende van de miljardair*. Leuven: Kritak.

De Winter, L. and P. Dumont (1999) 'Belgium: Party Systems on the Eve of Destruction', in D. Broughton and M. Donovan (eds), *Changing Party Systems in Western Europe*. London: Routledge, pp. 183–206.

Dehejia, V.H. and P. Genschel (1999) 'Tax Competition in the European Union', *Politics and Society*, vol. 27(3), pp. 403–30.

della Porta, D. (2001) 'A Judges' Revolution? Political Corruption and the Judiciary in Italy', *European Journal of Political Research*, vol. 39(1), pp. 1–21.

della Porta, D. and Y. Mény (eds) (1997) *Democracy and Corruption in Europe*. London: Pinter.

della Porta, D. and A. Vannucci (1999) *Corrupt Exchanges*. Hathorne: Aldine de Gruyter.

Deutsch, K. (1966) *Nationalism and Social Communication: An Inquiry into the Foundations of Nationality*. Cambridge: MIT Press.

Deviers-Joncour, C. (1999) *La putain de la république*. Paris: J'ai lu.

Doig, A. and J. Wilson (1997) 'Contracts and UK Local Government: Old Problems, New Permutations'. Mimeo. Liverpool: Liverpool Business School.

Dolvik, J.E. (2000) 'Economic and Monetary Union: Implications for Industrial Bargaining in Europe', *European Trade Union Institute Paper*, DWP 2000.01.04. Brussels: European Trade Union Institute.

Döring, H. (ed.) (1995) *Parliaments and Majority Rule in Western Europe*. New York: St Martin's Press.

Dowding, K. (1995) 'Model or Metaphor? A Critical Review of the Policy Network Approach', *Political Studies*, vol. 43(1), pp. 136–58.

Dryzek, J. (1997) *The Politics of the Earth*. Oxford: Oxford University Press.

DTI/DCMS (2000) *White Paper: A New Future for Communications*. London: DTI.

Duchesne, S. and Frognier, A.-P. (1995) 'Is There a European Identity?', in O. Niedermayer and R. Sinnott (eds), *Public Opinion and Internationalised Governance*. Oxford: Oxford University Press.

Easton, D. (1979) *A Systems Analysis of Political Life*. New York: John Wiley, 2nd edn.

Ebbinghaus, B. and A. Hassel (1999) 'Striking Deals: Concertation in the Reform of Continental Welfare States', Discussion Paper no. 99/3. Cologne: Max Planck Institute for the Study of Societies.

Ebbinghaus, B. and P. Manow (2001) *Comparing Welfare Capitalism: Social Policy and Political Economy in Europe, Japan and the USA*. London: Routledge.

Eder, K. and B. Giesen (eds) (1999) *European Citizenship and National Legacies*. Oxford: Oxford University Press.

EEA (European Environment Agency) (1997) *Environmental Agreements: Environmental Effectiveness*. Copenhagen: EEA.

EEA (European Environment Agency) (2000a) *Recent Developments in the Use of Environmental Taxes in the European Union*. Copenhagen: EEA.

EEA (European Environment Agency) (2000b) *European Community and Member States Greenhouse Gas Emission Trends 1990–1998*. Copenhagen: EEA.

Eichenhofer, E. (1999) 'Migration und Illegalitaet', *IMIS Schriften no. 7*. Osnabrük: Universitaetsverlag Rash.

Eisenstadt, S.N. and B. Giesen (1995) 'The Construction of Collective Identity', *European Journal of Sociology*, vol. 36(1), pp. 72–102.

Eising, R. (2000a) *Liberalisierung und Europäisierung. Die regulative Reform der Elektrizitätsversorgung in Großbritannien, der Europäischen Gemeinschaft und der Bundesrepublik Deutschland*. Opladen: Leske & Budrich.

Eising, R. (2000b) 'Business Interests in the European Union', European Forum Seminar Paper EUR/20. Florence: European University Institute (January).

Elgie, R. (1995) *Political Leadership in Liberal Democracies*. London: Macmillan.

Elgie, R. (2000) 'The Politics of the European Central Bank: Principal–Agent Theory and the Democratic Deficit', Working Documents in the Study of European Governance no. 3. Nottingham: Centre for the Study of European Governance, University of Nottingham (October).

Eriksen, E.O., J. Weigård (1999) *Kommunikativ handling og deliberativt deokrati: Jürgen Habermas teori om politikk og samfunn*. Oslo: Fagbokforlaget.

Eriksen, E.O., and J.E. Fossum (2000) 'Post–National Integration', in E.O. Eriksen and J.E. Fossum (eds), *Democracy in the European Union: Integration through Deliberation?* London: Routledge, pp. 1–28.

Esping-Andersen, G. (1990) *The Three Worlds of Welfare Capitalism*. Cambridge: Polity.

Esping-Andersen, G. (1999) *Social Foundations of Post-industrial Economies*. Oxford, Oxford University Press.

Esping-Andersen, G. and M. Regini (eds) (2000) *Why Deregulate Labour Markets?* Oxford: Oxford University Press.

Étienne, B. (1987) *L'islamisme radical.* Paris: Hachette.

Eurobarometer (1999) *Public Opinion in the European Union: Report Number 51.* Brussels: European Commission.

Eurobarometer (2000) *Public Opinion in the European Union: Report Number 52.* Brussels: European Commission.

European Commission (EC 1997) 'Green Paper on the Convergence of the Telecommunications, Media and Information Technology Sectors and the Implications for Regulation: Towards an Information Society Approach'. Brussels: European Commission.

European Commission (EC 2000a) 'Public Strategies for the Information Society in the Member States of the European Union'. Brussels: European Commission, Directorate General for the Information Society (September).

European Commission (EC 2000b) 'Sixth Report on the Implementation of the Telecommunications Regulatory Package'. Brussels: European Commission COM (2000) 814 (7 December).

European Commission (EC 2000c) 'The eEurope 2002 update: Prepared by the European Commission for the European Council in Nice'. Brussels: European Commission.

European Commission (EC 2000d) 'Commission Adopts Progress Report on the eEurope Initiative: A Top Priority for the Lisbon European Council'. Brussels: European Commission Press Release IP/00/239.

European Commission (2000e) *Public Finances in EMU-2000.* Brussels: European Commission, Directorate General for Economic and Financial Affairs.

European Council (1997) 'Amsterdam European Council, 16 and 17 June 1997: Presidency Conclusions.' Brussels: Commission of the European Communities, SI (97) 500, 17 June.

European Council (2000a) 'Draft Presidency Report on the European Security and Defence Policy'. Brussels: Council of Ministers, 14056/3/00, 13 December.

European Council (2000b) 'Treaty of Nice: Provisional Text Approved by the Intergovernmental Conference on Institutional Reform'. Brussels: Council of Ministers, SN 533/00, 12 December.

European Monitoring Centre for Drugs and Drug Addiction (EMCDDA 2000) *Annual Report on the State of the Drugs Problem in the European Union.* Luxemburg: EMCDDA.

Evans, G. (1999) 'Europe: A New Electoral Cleavage?', in G. Evans and P. Norris (eds), *Critical Elections: British Parties and Voters in Long-Term Perspective.* London: Sage Publications, pp. 207–22.

Faist, T. (2001) 'Social Citizenship in the European Union: Nested Citizenship'. *Journal of Common Market Studies*, vol. 39(1), pp. 37–58.

Farell, G. (1996) 'Cocaine and Heroin in Europe, 1983–1993: A Cross-National Comparison of Trafficking and Prices', *British Journal of Criminology*, vol. 36(2), pp. 225–81

Ferrera, M., A. Hemerijck and M. Rhodes (2000) *The Future of Social Europe:*

Recasting Work and Welfare in the New Economy. Lisbon: CELTA/Ministério do Trabalho e da Solidariedade.

Ferrara, M. and M. Rhodes (eds) (2000) *Recasting European Welfare States*. London: Frank Cass.

Fisher, C. (1994) 'The Lobby to Stop Testing Cosmetics on Animals', in R.H. Pedler and M.C.P.M. Van Schendelen (eds), *Lobbying the European Union*. Aldershot: Dartmouth, pp. 227–40.

Fiske, S. and S. Taylor (1984) *Social Cognition*. New York: Random House.

Flanagan, S.C. and R. Dalton (1984) 'Parties under Stress: Realignment and Dealignment in Advanced Industrial Societies', *West European Politics*, vol. 7(1), pp. 7–23.

Flynn, G. (ed) (1995) *The Remaking of the Hexagon: The New France in the New Europe*. Boulder: Westview.

Franklin, M.N., T.T. Mackie and H. Valen (eds) (1992) *Electoral Change: Responses to Evolving Social and Attitudinal Structures in Western Countries*. Cambridge: Cambridge University Press.

Franzese, R.J. (2002) *Macroeconomic Policies of Developed Democracies*. Cambridge: Cambridge University Press.

Freddi, G. and J.W. Björkman (eds) (1989) *Controlling Medical Professionals: The Comparative Politics of Health Governance*. London: Sage.

Freeman, Gary (1995) 'Modes of Immigration Politics in Liberal Democratic States', *International Migration Review*, vol. 29(4), pp. 881–902.

Fuke, T. (1989) 'Remedies in Japanese Administrative Law', *Civil Justice Quarterly*, 8, pp. 226–35.

Furet, F., J. Juilllard and P. Rosanvallon (1988) *La République du centre. La fin de l'exception francaise*. Paris: Calmann-Lévy.

Gallagher, M., M. Laver and P. Mair (2001) *Representative Government in Modern Europe: Institutions, Parties, and Governments*. London: McGraw-Hill, 3rd edn.

Garrett, G. (1998) *Partisan Politics in the Global Economy*. Cambridge: Cambridge University Press.

Garth, B. (1986) 'Migrant Workers and Rights of Mobility in the EC and the US', in M. Cappelletti, M. Seccombe and J. Weiler (eds), *Integration Through Law*. Berlin: de Gruyter, pp. 85–163.

Geddes, A. (1995) 'Immigrant and Ethnic Minorities and the EU Democratic Deficit', *Journal of Common Market Studies*, vol. 33(2), pp. 197–218.

George, S. (1994) *An Awkward Partner. Britain in the European Community*. Oxford: Oxford University Press.

Giacomelli, G. (1996) 'Take the Profit out of Crime by Policing the Money Laundries', *International Herald Tribune* (December 4).

Giesen, B. (1999) 'Collective Identity and Citizenship in Germany and France', in K. Eder and B. Giesen (eds), *European Citizenship and the National Legacies*. Oxford: Oxford University Press.

Gill, S. (1998) 'European Governance and New Constitutionalism: Economic and Monetary Union and Alternatives to Disciplinary Neoliberalism in Europe', *New Political Economy*, vol. 3(1), pp. 5–26.

Gillespie, R. (1989) 'Spanish Socialism in the 1980s', in T. Gallagher and

A. Williams (eds), *Southern European Socialism*. Manchester: Manchester University Press, pp. 59–85.

Gillespie, R. (1994) 'The Resurgence of Factionalism in the Spanish Socialist Workers' Party', in D. Bell and E. Shaw (eds), *Conflict and Cohesion in Western European Social Democratic Parties*. London: Pinter, pp. 50–69.

Goetschy, J. (2000) 'European Union and National Social Pacts: Employment and Social Protection put to the Test of Joint Regulation', in G. Fajertag and P. Pochet (eds), *Social Pacts in Europe: New Dynamics*. Brussels: European Trade Union Institute/Observatoire Social Européen, pp. 41–60.

Golub, J. (ed.) (1998) *New Instruments for Environmental Policy in the EU*. London: Routledge.

Grande, E. (1996) 'The State and Interest Groups in a Framework of Multi-level Decision-Making: The Case of the European Union', *Journal of European Public Policy*, vol. 3(3), pp. 318–38.

Grant, W., W. Paterson and C. Whiston (1988) *Government and the Chemical Industry*. Oxford: Clarendon Press.

Greenwood, J. (1997) *Representing Interests in the European Union*. Basingstoke: Macmillan.

Greenwood, J. and M. Aspinwall (eds) (1998) *Collective Action in the European Union*. London: Routledge.

Grünewald, K. (1997) 'Lagebild Ausländerextremismus unter besonderer Berücksichtigung der Arbeiterpartei Kurdistans (PKK)', *Texte zur Inneren Sicherheit*, 1, pp. 127–50.

Guiraudon, V. (2000) 'European Integration and Migration Policy', *Journal of Common Market Studies*, vol. 38(2), pp. 249–69.

Guiraudon, V. and C. Joppke (eds) (2001) *Controlling a New Migration World*. London: Routledge.

Guiraudon, V. and G. Lahav (2000) 'A Reappraisal of the State Sovereignty Debate', *Comparative Political Studies*, vol. 33(2), pp. 163–95.

Haas, E.B. (1958) *The Uniting of Europe: Political, Social, and Economic Forces 1950–57*. Stanford: Stanford University Press.

Habermas, J. (1999) 'Bestiality and Humanity: A War on the Border Between Legality and Morality', *Constellations*, vol. 6(3), pp. 263–73.

Hadjimichaelis, C. and N. Papamicos (1991) ' "Local" Development in Southern Europe: Myths and Realities', in E. Bergman, G. Maier and F. Tödtling (eds), *Regions Reconsidered: Economic Networks, Innovation and Local Development in Industrialised Countries*. London: Mansell.

Hainsworth, P. (ed.) (2000) *The Politics of the Extreme Right: From the Margins to the Mainstream*. London: Pinter.

Hajer, M. (1995) *The Politics of Environmental Discourse: Ecological Modernisation and the Policy Process*. Oxford: Oxford University Press.

Hanf, K. and E. van de Gronden (1998) 'The Netherlands: Joint Regulation and Sustainable Development', in K. Hanf and A.-I. Jansen (eds), *Governance and Environment in Western Europe*. Harlow: Addison Wesley Longman, pp. 152–80.

Hanf, K. and A.-I. Jansen (eds) (1998) *Governance and Environment in Western Europe*. Harlow: Addison Wesley Longman.

Hayward, J. (ed.) (1996) *Elitism, Populism, and European Politics*. Oxford: Clarendon Press.

Held, D. (1987) *Models of Democracy*. Cambridge: Polity Press.

Held, D. (1993) 'Democracy: From City-States to a Cosmopolitan Order?', in D. Held (ed.), *Prospects for Democracy: North, South, East, West*. Cambridge: Polity, pp. 13–52.

Helm, D. (1989) 'The Economic Borders of the State', in D. Helm (ed.), *The Economic Borders of the State*. Oxford: Oxford University Press, pp. 9–45.

Hennessy, P. (2000) *The Prime Minister: The Office and Its Holders since 1945*. London: Allen Lane.

Herrmann, R.K, M. Brewer and T. Risse (eds) (forthcoming) *Identities in Europe and the Institutions of the European Union*.

Hewitt, C. and T. Cheetham (2000) *Encyclopedia of Modern Separatist Movements*. Santa Barbara: ABC-CLIO.

Heywood, P. and I. Molina (2000) 'A Quasi-Presidential Premiership: Administering the Executive Summit in Spain', in B.G. Peters, R.A.W. Rhodes and V. Wright (eds), *Administering the Summit*. London: Macmillan, pp. 110–33.

Heywood, P. and V. Wright (1997) 'Executives, Bureaucracies and Decision-Making', in M. Rhodes, P. Heywood and V. Wright (eds), *Developments in West European Politics*. London: Macmillan, pp. 75–94.

Hodge, C.C. (1999a) 'Germany: Is Sound Diplomacy the Better Part of Security?', in C.C. Hodge (ed.), *Redefining European Security*. London and New York: Garland Publishing Company, pp. 181–201.

Hodge, C.C. (ed.) (1999b) *Redefining European Security*. London and New York: Garland Publishing Company.

Hollifield, J. (1999) 'On the Limits of Immigration Control in France', in G. Brochmann and T. Hammar (eds), *Mechanisms of Immigration Control*. Berg: Oxford, pp. 59–95.

Hollingsworth, J.R. and R. Boyer (eds) (1997) *Contemporary Capitalism: The Embeddedness of Institutions*. Cambridge: Cambridge University Press.

Holmberg, S. (1999) 'Down and Down We Go: Political Trust in Sweden', in P. Norris (ed.), *Critical Citizens: Global Support for Democratic Governance*. Oxford: Oxford University Press, pp. 103–22.

Hood, C., C. Scott, O. James, G. Jones and T.Travers (1999) *Regulation Inside Government: Waste-Watchers, Quality Police and Sleaze Busters*. Oxford: Oxford University Press.

Hooghe, L. (1995) 'Subnational mobilization in the European Union', *West European Politics*, vol. 18(3), pp. 175–98.

Hooghe, L. (ed.) (1996) *Cohesion Policy and European Integration: Building Multi-Level Governance*. Oxford: Clarendon.

Hooghe, L. and M. Keating (1994) 'The Politics of EU Regional Policy', *Journal of European Public Policy*, vol. 1(3) (September) pp. 368–93.

Hooghe, L. and G. Marks (2001) *Multi-Level Governance and European Integration*. Boulder: Rowman and Littlefield.

Howorth, J. (1997) 'France', in J. Howorth and A. Menon (eds), *The European Union and National Defence Policy*. London: Routledge, pp. 23–48.

Howorth, J. (2000) 'Britain, NATO and CEDSP: Fixed Strategy, Changing Tactics', in H. Sjursen (ed.), 'Redefining European Security? The Role of the European Union in European Security Structures', *ARENA Report No. 7/2000.* Oslo: ARENA, pp. 47–65.

Humphreys, P.J. (1998) *Mass Media and Media Policy in Western Europe.* Manchester: Manchester University Press.

Howorth, J. and A. Menon (eds) (1997) *The European Union and National Defence Policy.* London: Routledge.

IDEA (1999) *Voter Turnout from 1945 to 1998: A Global Report on Political Participation.* http://www.idea.int/Voter_turnout/.

Ignazi, P. (1992) 'The Silent Counter-Revolution: Hypotheses on the Emergence of Extreme Right-Wing Parties in Europe', *European Journal of Political Research*, vol. 22(1–2), pp. 3–34.

IMF (1997) *Good Governance: The IMF's Role.* Washington, DC: International Monetary Fund.

Inglehart, R. (1977) *The Silent Revolution: Changing Values and Political Styles Among Western Publics.* Princeton: Princeton University Press.

Inglehart, R. (1997) *Modernization and Postmodernization: Cultural, Economic, and Political Change in 43 Societies.* Princeton: Princeton University Press.

International Organization for Migration (IOM) (1996) *Trafficking in Women for Sexual Exploitation, National Reports: Italy, Austria.* Geneva: IOM.

Ishiyama, J.T. and M. Breuning (1998) *Ethnopolitics in the New Europe.* Boulder: Lynne Rienner.

Iversen, T. (1999) *Contested Economic Institutions: The Politics of Macroeconomics and Wage Bargaining in Advanced Democracies.* Cambridge: Cambridge University Press.

Iversen, T., J. Pontusson and D. Soskice (eds) (2000) *Unions, Employers, and Central Banks: Macroeconomic Coordination and Institutional Change in Social Market Economies.* Cambridge: Cambridge University Press.

Jachtenfuchs, M. (1995) 'Theoretical Perspectives on European Governance', *European Law Journal*, vol. 1(2), pp. 115–33.

Jacobson, D. (1996) *Rights Across Borders.* Baltimore: Johns Hopkins University Press.

Jenkins, B. and S.A. Sofos (eds) (1996) *Nation and Identity in Contemporary Europe.* London: Routledge.

John, P. (1998) *Analysing Public Policy.* London: Pinter.

Johnston, M. (1996) 'The Search for Definitions: The Vitality of Politics and the Issue of Corruption', *International Social Science Journal*, 149, pp. 321–35.

Jones, B. and M. Keating (eds) (1995) *The European Union and the Regions.* Oxford: Clarendon.

Jones, E. (2000) 'The Politics of Europe 1999: Spring Cleaning', *Industrial Relations Journal*, vol. 4(31), pp. 247–60.

Jones, E. (2001) 'The Politics of Europe 2000: Unity through Diversity', *Industrial Relations Journal*, vol. 4(32), pp. 362–79.

Joppke, C. (1998) 'Why Liberal States Accept Unwanted Immigration', *World Politics*, vol. 50(2), pp. 266–93.

Joppke, C. (1999) *Immigration and the Nation-State*. Oxford: Oxford University Press.

Joppke, C. (2001) 'The Legal-Domestic Sources of Immigrant Rights', *Comparative Political Studies*, 34(4), pp. 339–66.

Jordan, T. (1999) 'The Hardest Question: An Introduction to the New Politics of Change', in T. Jordan and A. Lent (eds), *Storming the Millennium: The New Politics of Change*. London: Lawrence & Wishart, pp. 1–14.

Judge, D. (1995) 'The Failure of National Parliaments?', *West European Politics*, vol. 18(3), pp. 79–100.

Juergensmeyer, M. (1993) *The New Cold War? Religious Nationalism Confronts the Secular State*. Berkeley: University of California Press.

Kaplan, J. and L. Weinberg (1998) *The Emergence of a Euro-American Radical Right*. New Brunswick: Rutgers University Press.

Karapin, R. (1999) 'The Politics of Immigration Control in Britain and Germany', *Comparative Politics*, vol. 31(4), pp. 423–44.

Katz, R.S., P. Mair *et al.* (1992) 'The Membership of Parties in European Democracies, 1960-90', *European Journal of Political Research*, vol. 22(3), pp. 329–45.

Katz, R.S. and P. Mair (1995) 'Changing Models of Party Organisation and Party Democracy: The Emergence of the Cartel Party', *Party Politics*, vol. 1(1), pp. 5–28.

Katzenstein, P.J. (ed.) (1997) *Tamed Power: Germany in Europe*. Ithaca: Cornell University Press.

Keating, M. (1988) *State and Regional Nationalism: Territorial Politics and the European State*. London: Harvester Wheatsheaf.

Keating, M. (1997) 'The Invention of Regions: Political Restructuring and Territorial Government in Western Europe', *Environment and Planning C: Government and Policy*, vol. 15(4), pp. 383–98.

Keating, M. (1998) *The New Regionalism in Western Europe: Territorial Restructuring and Political Change*. Aldershot: Edward Elgar.

Keating, M. and B. Jones (eds) (1995) *Regions in the European Community*. Oxford: Oxford University Press.

Keating, M. and J. Loughlin (eds) (1997) *The Political Economy of Regionalism*. London: Frank Cass.

Kepel, G. (1997) *Allah in the West: Islamic Movements in America and Europe*. Cambridge: Polity.

Kielmansegg, P.G. (1996) 'Integration und Demokratie', in M. Jachtenfuchs and B. Kohler-Koch (eds), *Europäische Integration*. Opladen: Leske & Budrich, pp. 47–71.

Kitschelt, H. (1994) *The Transformation of European Social Democracy*. Cambridge: Cambridge University Press.

Kitschelt, H. and A.J. McGann (1995) *The Radical Right in Western Europe: A Comparative Analysis*. Ann Arbor: University of Michigan Press.

Kitschelt, H., P. Lange, G. Marks and J.D. Stephens (eds) (1999) *Continuity and Change in Contemporary Capitalism*. Cambridge: Cambridge University Press.

Klingemann, H.-D. (1999) 'Mapping Political Support in the 1990s: A Global Analysis', in P. Norris (ed.), *Critical Citizens: Global Support for Democratic Governance*. Oxford: Oxford University Press, pp. 31–56.

Klingemann, H.-D., R. Hofferbert and I. Budge (1994) *Parties, Policies and Democracy*. Boulder: Westview Press.

Knutsen, O. (1998) 'Expert Judgements of the Left-Right Location of Political Parties: A Comparative Longitudinal Study', *West European Politics*, vol. 21(2), pp. 63–94.

Kohler-Koch, B. and R. Eising (eds) (1999) *The Transformation of Governance in the European Union*. London: Routledge.

Koopmans, Ruud (1996) 'Explaining the Rise of Racist and Extreme Right Violence in Western Europe', *European Journal of Political Research*, vol. 30(1), pp. 185–216.

Koslowski, R. (1998) 'EU Migration Regimes', in C. Joppke (ed.), *Challenge to the Nation-State*. Oxford: Oxford University Press, pp. 153–88.

Kriesi, H. (1995) 'Bewegungen auf der Linken, Bewegungen auf der Rechten: Die Mobilisierung von zwei neuen Typen von sozialen Bewegungen in ihrem politischen Kontext', *Swiss Political Science Review*, vol. 1(1), pp. 9–52.

Kriesi, H. (2000) 'Reflections on the Swiss case'. Paper presented at the workshop on 'The Impact of Europeanization and Globalization on National Patterns of Interest Intermediation'. Florence: European University Institute (1–3 June).

Kyle, D. (1998) 'Transparent Economies and Invisible Workers: Human Smuggling under Global Economic Liberalism'. Paper presented to the conference 'Dilemmas of Immigration Control in a Globalizing World'. Florence: European University Institute (11–12 June).

Laakso, M. and P. Taagepera (1979) 'Effective Number of Parties: A Measure with Application to Western Europe', *Comparative Political Studies*, vol. 12(1), pp. 3–27.

Labrousse, A. and L. Laniel (eds) (2001) 'The World Geopolitics of Drugs, 1998/1999', special issue of *Crime, Law and Social Change*, vol. 36(1–2).

Lafferty, W., and J. Meadowcroft (eds) (2000) *Implementing Sustainable Development*. Oxford: Oxford University Press.

Lane, J.E. and S.O. Ersson (1999) *Politics and Society in Western Europe*. London: Sage Publications.

LaPalombara, J. and M. Weiner (eds) (1966) *Political Parties and Political Development*. Princeton: Princeton University Press.

Lavenex, S. (1999a) *Safe Third Countries*. Budapest: Central European University Press.

Lavenex, S. (1999b) 'The Europeanisation of Refugee Policies'. Dissertation. Florence: European University Institute.

Laver, M. (1998) 'Party Policy in Britain 1997: Results from an Expert Survey', *Political Studies*, vol. 46(2), pp. 336–47.

Laver, M., and K.A. Shepsle (1995) *Making and Breaking Governments: Cabinets and Legislatures in Parliamentary Democracies*. Cambridge: Cambridge University Press.

Laver, M. and N. Schofield (1990) *Multiparty Government: The Politics of Coalition in Western Europe*. Oxford: Oxford University Press.

Le Gloannec, A.-M. (1997) 'Europe by Other Means', *International Affairs*, vol. 73(1), pp. 83–98.

Lebor, A. (1997) *A Heart Turned East: Among the Muslims of Europe and America*. London: Little, Brown & Company.

Lees, C. (2001) *The Red-Green Coalition in Germany: Politics, Personalities and Power*. Manchester: Manchester University Press.

Leibfried, S. and P. Pierson (2000) 'Social Policy: Left to Courts and Markets?', in H. Wallace and W. Wallace (eds), *Policy-Making in the European Union, 4th Edition*. Oxford: Oxford University Press, pp. 267–92.

Lent, A. (2001) *Sex, Colour, Peace and Power: Social Movements in Britain Since 1945*. Basingstoke: Palgrave.

Leonardi, R. (1995) *Convergence, Cohesion, and Integration in the European Union*. London: Macmillan.

Lethier, P. (2001) *Argent secret: l'espion de l'affaire elf parle*. Paris: Albin Michel.

Levi, M. and D. Nelken (eds) (1996) *The Corruption of Politics and the Politics of Corruption*. Oxford: Blackwell.

Levy, D.A.L. (1997) 'Regulating Digital Broadcasting in Europe: The Limits of Policy Convergence', *West European Politics*, vol. 20(4), pp. 24–42.

Levy, D.A.L. (2001) *Europe's Digital Revolution: Broadcasting Regulation, the EU and the Nation State*. London: Routledge.

Liebert, U. and M. Cotta (eds) (1990). *Parliament and Democratic Consolidation in Southern Europe: Greece, Italy, Portugal, Spain and Turkey*. London: Pinter.

Lijphart, A. (1997) 'Unequal Participation: Democracy's Unresolved Dilemma', *American Political Science Review*, vol. 91(1), pp. 1–14.

Lijphart, A. (1999) *Patterns of Democracy: Government Forms and Performance in Thirty-Six Countries*. New Haven: Yale University Press.

LIMES (2000) 'Gli Stati-mafia: The Mafia-States', *Rivista Limes* 2.

Lindblom, C.E. (1977) *Politics and Markets: The World's Political Economic System*. New York: Basic Books.

Lipset, S.M. (1960) *Political Man: The Social Bases of Politics*. New York: Doubleday & Company.

Lipset, S.M. and S. Rokkan (1967) 'Cleavage Structures, Party Systems and Voter Alignments: An Introduction', in S.M. Lipset and S. Rokkan (eds), *Party Systems and Voter Alignments: Cross National Perspectives*. New York: Free Press, pp. 1–64.

Little, W. and E. Posada-Carbó (eds) (1996) *Political Corruption in Europe and Latin America*. London: Macmillan.

Lovecy, J. (1999) 'Governance Transformation in the Professional Services Sector: a Case of Market Integration "by the Back Door"?', in B. Kohler-Koch and R. Eising (eds), *The Transformation of Governance in the European Union*. London: Routledge, pp. 135–52.

Lovering, John (1999) 'Theory Led by Policy: The Inadequacies of the "New Regionalism" ', *International Journal of Urban and Regional Research*, vol. 23(2) (June) pp. 379–90.

Ludlow, P., R. Barre and N. Ersbøll (1995) 'Preparing for 1996 and a Larger Europe: Principles and Priorities', *CEPS Special Report No. 6.* Brussels: Centre for European Policy Studies.

Luebbert, G. (1986) *Comparative Democracy: Policy Making and Governing Coalitions in Europe and Israel.* New York: Columbia University Press.

Luther, K.R. (1999) 'Austria: from moderate to polarised pluralism?', in D. Broughton and M. Donovan (eds), *Changing Party Systems in Western Europe.* London: Routledge, pp. 118–42.

Lyrintzis, C. (1984) 'Political Parties in Post-Junta Greece: A Case of "Bureaucratic Clientelism"?', *West European Politics*, vol. 7(2), pp. 99–118.

Mahnke, D. (2001) 'Reform of the CFSP: From Maastricht to Amsterdam', in J. Monar and W. Wessels (eds), *The European Union after the Treaty of Amsterdam.* London: Continuum, pp. 227–48.

Mair, P. (ed) (1990) *The West European Party System.* Oxford: Oxford University Press.

Mair, P. (2000) 'The Limited Impact of Europe on National Party Systems', *West European Politics*, vol. 23(4), pp. 27–51.

Majone, G. (1997) 'Independent Agencies and the Delegation Problem', in B. Steunenberg and F. van Vught (eds), *Political Institutions and Public Policy: Perspectives on European Decision Making.* Dordrecht: Kluwer Academic Publishers, pp. 139–56.

March, J.G. and J.P. Olsen (1989) *Rediscovering Institutions: The Organisational Basis of Politics.* New York: Free Press.

Marcussen, M., T. Risse, D. Engelmann-Martin, H.-J. Knopf and K. Roscher (1999) 'Constructing Europe: The Evolution of French, British, and German Nation-State Identities', *Journal of European Public Policy*, vol. 6(4), pp. 614–33.

Marks, G. (1993) 'Structural Policy and Multilevel Governance in the European Union', in A. Cafruny and G. Rosenthal (eds), *The State of the European Community. The Maastricht Debates and Beyond.* Boulder: Lynne Rienner, pp. 391–410.

Marks, G. (1998) 'Territorial Identities in the European Union', in J.J. Anderson (ed), *Regional Integration and Democracy: Expanding on the European Experience.* Lanham: Rowman & Littlefield, pp. 69–91.

Marks, G. (1999) 'The Past in the Present: A Cleavage Theory of Party Response to European Integration'. Paper presented to conference on 'Multilevel Party Systems: Europeanisation and the Reshaping of National Political Representation'. Florence: European University Institute, European Forum (16–18 December).

Marks, G., L. Hooghe and K. Blank (1996) 'European Integration from the 1980s: State-Centric versus Multi-Level Governance', *Journal of Common Market Studies*, vol. 34(3), pp. 342–78.

Marks, G. et al. (1996) 'Competencies, Cracks, and Conflicts: Regional Mobilization in the European Union', in G. Marks *et al., Governance in the European Union.* London: Sage, pp. 40–63.

Marsh, D. (ed.) (1998) *Comparing Policy Networks.* Philadelphia: Open University Press.

Marsh, D. and M. Smith (2000) 'Understanding Policy Networks: Towards a Dialectical Approach', *Political Studies*, vol. 48(1), pp. 4–21.

Martin, A. (1998) 'EMU and Wage Bargaining: The Americanization of the European Labor Market?' Paper presented at the 11th International Conference of Europeanists, Baltimore, MD. February 26–28.

Massey, D. (1998) 'March of Folly: US Immigration Policy After NAFTA', *American Prospect*, vol. 37, pp. 22–33.

Massey, D. et al. (1998) *World in Motion*. Oxford: Clarendon Press.

Mayntz, R. (1987) 'West Germany', in W. Plowden (ed.), *Advising the Rulers*. Oxford: Blackwell, pp. 3–18.

McKay, G. (1998) 'DiY Culture: Notes Towards an Intro', in G. McKay (ed.), *DiY Culture: Party and Protest in Nineties Britain*. London: Verso, pp. 1–53.

McNamara, K. R. (1998) *The Currency of Ideas*. Ithaca: Cornell University Press

Mény, Y. (1992) *La corruption de la République*. Paris: Fayard.

Metcalfe, L. (2000) 'Reforming the Commission: Will Organisational Effectiveness Produce Effective Governance?', *Journal of Common Market Studies*, vol. 38(5), pp. 817–41.

Middelfart-Knarvit, K.H., H. G. Overman, S.J. Redding and A.J. Venables (2000) 'The Location of European Industry', Economic Papers, No. 142. Brussels: European Commission, Directorate General for Economic and Financial Affairs.

Milliet-Einbinder, M. (2000) 'Writing off Tax Deductibility', *OECD Observer*, vol. 220, p. 38.

Misztal, B. and A. Shupe (1992) 'Making Sense of the Global Revival of Fundamentalism', in B. Misztal and A. Shupe (eds), *Religion and Politics in Comparative Perspective: Revival of Religious Fundamentalism in East and West*. Westport: Praeger, pp. 3–9.

Mol, A. and D. Sonnenfeld (eds) (2000) 'Ecological Modernisation Around the World: Perspectives and Critical Debates', special issue of *Environmental Politics*, vol. 9(1).

Monar, J. (2000) 'Justice and Home Affairs in a Wider Europe: The Dynamics of Inclusion and Exclusion', in H. Sjursen (ed), 'Redefining European Security? The Role of the European Union in European Security Structures'. *ARENA Report No. 7/2000*. Oslo: ARENA, pp. 129–47.

Monar, J. (2001) 'Justice and Home Affairs after Amsterdam: The Treaty Reforms and the Challenge of Their Implementation', in J. Monar and W. Wessels (eds), *The European Union after the Treaty of Amsterdam*. London: Continuum, pp. 267–95.

Monar, J. and W. Wessels (eds) (2001) *The European Union After the Treaty of Amsterdam*. London: Continuum.

Money, J. (1999) *Fences or Neighbours*. Ithaca: Cornell University Press.

Morawska, E. (1999) 'Transnational Migrations in the Enlarged European Union'. Paper prepared for the Reflection Group on 'The Nature of the New Border'. Florence: European University Institute.

Moreau, P. (1997) 'Linksextremismus in Europa nach dem Zerfall des kommunistischen Machtbereichs', *Texte zur Inneren Sicherheit*, 1, pp. 19–52.

Moreau, P., M. Lazar and G. Hirscher (eds) (1998) *Der Kommunismus in Westeuropa. Niedergang oder Mutation?* Landsberg am Lech: Günter Olzog.

Morgan, K. (1995) 'The Learning Region: Institutions, Innovation, and Regional Renewal', *Papers in Planning Research, no. 157.* Cardiff: Department of City and Regional Planning, University of Wales College of Cardiff.

Mosely, L. (2000) 'Room to Move: International Financial Markets and National Welfare States', *International Organization*, vol. 54(4), pp. 737–73.

Mudde, C. (2000) *The Ideology of the Extreme Right.* Manchester: Manchester University Press.

Mudde, C. and J. van Holsteyn (2000) 'The Netherlands: Explaining the Limited Success of the Extreme Right', in P. Hainsworth (ed.), *The Politics of the Extreme Right: From the Margins to the Mainstream.* London: Pinter, pp. 144–71.

Müller, W.C. and K. Strøm (1999) *Policy, Office, or Votes? How Political Parties in Western Europe Make Hard Decisions.* Cambridge: Cambridge University Press.

Mummenday, A. and M. Wenzel (1999) 'Social Discrimination and Tolerance in Intergroup Relations: Reactions to Intergroup Difference', *Personality and Social Psychology Review*, 3, pp. 224–49.

Neuman, G.L. (1997) 'Anomalous Zones', *Stanford Law Review*, 48, pp. 1197–234.

Newton, K. and P. Norris, P. (2000) 'Confidence in Public Institutions: Faith, Culture or Performance?', in S.J. Pharr and R.D. Putnam (eds), *Disaffected Democracies. What's Troubling the Trilateral Countries?* Princeton: Princeton University Press, pp. 52–73.

Nicolet, C. (1982) *L'idée républicaine en France.* Paris: Gallimard.

Nieto, A. (1997) *Corrupción en la España democrática.* Barcelona: Ariel.

Norris, P. (1999) 'Introduction: The Growth of Critical Citizens?', in P. Norris (ed.), *Critical Citizens. Global Support for Democratic Governance.* Oxford: Oxford University Press, pp. 1–27.

Norton, P. (ed.) (1996) *National Parliaments and the European Union.* London: Frank Cass.

Notermans, T. (2000) *Money, Markets, and the State: Social Democratic Economic Policies since 1918.* Cambridge: Cambridge University Press.

Nousiainen, J. (2000) 'Finland: The Consolidation of Parliamentary Governance', in K. Strøm (ed.), *Coalition Governments in Western Europe.* Oxford: Oxford University Press, pp. 264–99.

Oakes, P.J., S.A. Haslam and J.C. Turner (1994) *Stereotyping and Social Reality.* Oxford: Oxford University Press.

OECD (1997) 'Webcasting and Convergence: Policy Implications'. Paris: OECD, Committee for Information, Computer, and Communications Policy.

OFTEL (1995) 'Beyond the Telephone, the Television, and the PC'. London: OFTEL.

Ohmae, K. (1995) *The End of the Nation-State: The Rise of Regional Economies*. New York: The Free Press.

Olsen, J.P. (1997) 'European Challenges to the Nation State', in B. Steunenberg and F. van Vught (eds), *Political Institutions and Public Policy: Perspectives on European Decision Making*. Dordrecht: Kluwer Academic Publishers, pp. 157–88.

Olson, D.M. and M.L. Mezey (eds) (1991) *Legislatures in the Policy Process: The Dilemmas of Economic Policy*. Cambridge: Cambridge University Press.

Papademetriou, D. (1996) *Coming Together or Pulling Apart*. Washington, D.C.: Carnegie Endowment for International Peace.

Paterson, W.E. (1974) *The SPD and European Integration*. Glasgow: Glasgow University Press.

Pedersen, M. (1979) 'The Dynamics of European Party Systems: Changing Patterns of Electoral Volatility', *European Journal of Political Research*, 7, pp. 1–26.

Peers, S. (1998) *Mind the Gap!* London: Immigration Law Practitioners' Association.

Pestoff, V. (2000) 'Europeanization and Globalization of Business Interest Associations: Exit Provides Two or More Voices, but Implies No Loyalty'. Paper presented at the workshop on 'The Impact of Europeanization and Globalization on National Patterns of Interest Intermediation'. Florence: European University Institute (1–3 June).

Peters, B.G., R.A.W. Rhodes and V. Wright (eds) (2000) *Administering the Summit*. London: Macmillan.

Peters, J.G. and S. Welch (1978) 'Political Corruption in America: A Search for Definitions and a Theory', *American Political Science Review*, vol. 72(3), pp. 974–84.

Peterson, J. (1997) 'States, Societies, and the European Union', *West European Politics*, vol. 20(4), pp. 1–24.

Peterson, J. and E. Bomberg (1999) *Decision-making in the European Union*. London: Macmillan.

Peterson, J. and E. Bomberg (2000) 'The EU after the 1990s: Explaining Continuity and Change', in M. Green Cowles and M. Smith (eds), *The State of the European Union: Risks, Reforms, Resistance, and Revival*. Oxford: Oxford University Press, pp. 19–41.

Peterson, J. and H. Sjursen (eds) (1998) *A Common Foreign Policy for Europe? Competing Visions of the CFSP*. London: Routledge.

Pfahl-Traughber, A. (1998) 'Die Autonomen: Portrait einer linksextremistischen Subkultur', *Aus Politik und Zeitgeschichte* B9-10 (20 February) pp. 36–46.

Pharr, S.J. and R.D. Putnam (eds) (2000) *Disaffected Democracies. What's Troubling the Trilateral Countries?* Princeton: Princeton University Press.

Philp, M. (2000) 'Corruption Control and the Transfer of Regulatory Frameworks'. Paper presented at World Bank workshop on 'Anticorruption in Transition: Confronting the Challenge of State Capture'. Warsaw: World Bank (May).

Pierson, P. (2000) 'Increasing Returns, Path Dependence, and the Study of Politics', *American Political Science Review*, vol. 94(2), pp. 251–67.

Pierson, P. (ed.) (2001) *The New Politics of the Welfare State*. Oxford: Oxford University Press.

Pintarits, S. (1996) *Macht, Demokratie und Regionen in Europa: Analysen und Szenarien der Integration und Desintegration*. Marburg: Metropolis.

Poguntke, T. (1987) 'New Politics and Party Systems: The Emergence of a New Type of Party?', *West European Politics*, vol. 10(1) (January) pp. 76–88.

PRO (1998) 'Acquisition Policy Statement' at http://www.pro.gov.uk/records-management/acquisition/policy.htm.

PRO (2000) 'Operational Selection Policy on Industrial Policy 1974–1979' at http://www.pro.gov.uk/recordsmanagement/acquisition/industryosp.htm.

Prodi, R. (2000) '2000–2005: Shaping the New Europe'. Speech to the European Parliament, Strasbourg (15 February).

Pujas, V. and M. Rhodes (1999a) 'A Clash of Cultures? Corruption and the Ethics of Administration in Western Europe', *Parliamentary Affairs*, vol. 52(4), pp. 688–702.

Pujas, V. and M. Rhodes (1999b) 'Party Finance and Political Scandal in Italy, Spain, and France', *West European Politics*, vol. 22(3), pp. 41–63.

Putnam, R. D. *et al.* (1993) *Making Democracy Work: Civic Traditions in Modern Italy*. Princeton, NJ: Princeton University Press.

Reuters (2000) 'Human Slave Traders Join Money Laundering Flood' (30 March).

Rhodes, M. (2001a) 'Globalization, Welfare States and Employment: Is there a European "Third Way"?', in N. Bermeo (ed.), *Unemployment in the New Europe*. Cambridge: Cambridge University Press, pp. 87–118.

Rhodes, M. (2001b) 'Why EMU is – or may be – Good for European Welfare States', in K. Dyson (ed.), *The European State and the Euro*. Oxford: Oxford University Press 2001, pp. 305–33.

Rhodes, R.A.W. (1997a) ' "Shackling the Leader?": Coherence, Capacity, and the Hollow Crown', in P. Weller, H. Bakvis and R.A.W. Rhodes (eds), *The Hollow Crown*. London: Macmillan, pp. 198–223.

Rhodes, R.A.W. (1997b) *Understanding Governance: Policy Networks, Governments, Reflexivity, and Accountability*. Buckingham: Open University Press.

Rhodes, R.A.W. (2000) *The Governance Narrative: Key Findings and Lessons from the ESRC's Whitehall Programme*. London: Public Management and Policy Association.

Rhodes, R.A.W. and P. Dunleavy (eds) (1995) *Prime Minister, Cabinet, and Core Executive*. London: Macmillan.

Risse, T., D. Engelmann-Martin, H.-J. Knopf and K. Roscher (1999) 'To Euro or Not to Euro. The EMU and Identity Politics in the European Union', *European Journal of International Relations*, vol. 5(2), pp. 147–187.

Risse, T. (2000) 'A European Identity? Europeanisation and the Evolution of Nation-State Identities', in M. Green Cowles, J. Caporaso and T. Risse (eds), *Europeanisation and Domestic Change*. Ithaca: Cornell University Press.

Ritaine, E. (1989) 'La modernité localisée. Leçons italiennes sur le développement régional', *Revue française de science politique*, vol. 39(2), pp. 154–77.

Rogers, P. (1998) 'New Ground, Old Assumptions: Analytical Limitations in the SDR', *Disarmament Diplomacy*, 28 [http://www.acronym.org.uk/dd/dd28/index.htm].

Rohrschneider, R. (1999) *Learning Democracy. Democratic and Economic Values in Unified Germany*. Oxford: Oxford University Press.

Rokkan, S. (1980) 'Territories, Centres, and Peripheries: Toward a Geoethnic-Geoeconomic-Geopolitical Model of Differentiation within Western Europe', in J. Gottman (ed.), *Centre and Periphery: Spatial Variations in Politics*. Beverly Hills: Sage, pp. 163–204.

Rokkan, S., and D. Urwin (1982) *The Politics of Territorial Identity: Studies in European Regionalism*. London: Sage Publications.

Rose-Ackerman, S. (1999) *Corruption and Government*. Cambridge: Cambridge University Press.

Ruggiero, V. (1997) 'Trafficking in Human Beings: Slaves in Contemporary Europe', *International Journal of the Sociology of Law*, vol. 25(240), pp. 231–44.

Rummel, R. (1996) 'Germany's Role in the CFSP: "Normalitet" or "Sonderweg"?', in C. Hill (ed.), *The Actors in Europe's Foreign Policy*. London: Routledge, pp. 40–67.

Sabel, C.F. (1993) 'Studied Trust: Building New Forms of Cooperation in a Volatile Economy', in R. Swedberg (ed.), *Explorations in Economic Sociology*. New York: Russel Sage Foundation, pp. 104–44.

Saint-Etienne, C. (1992) *L'exception francaise*. Paris: A. Colin.

Sartori, G. (1976) *Parties and Party Systems: A Framework for Analysis*. Cambridge: Cambridge University Press.

Sauder, A. (1999) 'France's Security Policy Since the End of the Cold War', in C.C. Hodge (ed.), *Redefining European Security*. London and New York: Garland Publishing Company, pp. 117–43.

Scharpf, F.W. (1999) *Governing in Europe. Effective and Democratic?* Oxford: Oxford University Press.

Scharpf, F.W. (2000a) 'Interdependence and Democratic Legitimation', in S.J. Pharr and R.D Putnam (eds), *Disaffected Democracies. What's Troubling the Trilateral Countries?* Princeton: Princeton University Press, pp. 101–20.

Scharpf, F.W. (2000b) 'The Viability of Advanced Welfare States in the International Economy: Vulnerabilities and Options', *European Review*, vol. 8(3), pp. 399–425.

Scharpf, F.W. and V.A. Schmidt (eds) (2000a) *Welfare and Work in the Open Economy, Volume 1: From Vulnerability to Competitiveness*. Oxford: Oxford University Press.

Scharpf, F.W. and V.A. Schmidt (eds) (2000b) *Welfare and Work in the Open Economy, Volume 2: Diverse Responses to Common Challenges*. Oxford: Oxford University Press.

Schelling, T. (1971) 'What is the Business of Organised Crime?', *American Scholar*, vol. 40(4), 643–52.

Schmidt, M.G. (1996) 'When Parties Matter: A Review of the Possibilities and Limits of Partisan Influence on Public Policy', *European Journal of Political Research*, vol. 30(2), pp. 155–83.

Schmidt, V. (1999) 'National Patterns of Governance under Siege: the Impact of European Integration', in B. Kohler-Koch and R. Eising (eds), *The Transformation of Governance in the European Union*. London: Routledge, pp. 155–72.

Schmitter, P.C. and J.R. Grote (1997) 'The Corporatist Sisyphus: Past, Present and Future', *European University Institute Working Paper, SPS No. 97/4*. Florence: European University Institute.

Scholte, J.A (2000) *Globalization: A Critical Introduction*. New York: St Martin's Press.

Schulten, T. and A. Stueckler (2000) 'Wage Policy and EMU'. Wirtschafts- und Sozialwissenschaftskiches Institut in der Hans-Boeckler-Stiftung & European Foundation for the Improvement of Living and Working Conditions, July.

Sciortino, G. (1999) 'Planning in the Dark: The Evolution of Italian Immigration Control', in G. Brochmann and T. Hammar (eds), *Mechanisms of Immigration Control*. Berg: Oxford, pp. 233–59.

Scott, A.J. (1998) *Regions and the World Economy: The Coming Shape of Global Production, Competition, and Political Order*. Oxford: Oxford University Press.

Seabrook, J. (1996) *Travels in the Skin Trade*. London: Pluto Press.

Sfeir, A. (1997) *Les réseaux d'allah: les Filières islamistes en France et en Europe*. Paris: Plon.

Sharpe, L.J. (ed.) (1992) *The Rise of Meso-Government in Europe*. London: Sage.

Shearer, A. (2000) 'Britain, France and the Saint-Malo Declaration: Tactical Rapprochement or Strategic Entente?', *Cambridge Review of International Affairs*, vol. 13(2), pp. 283–98.

Sidenius, N. (1999) 'Business, Governance Structures and the EU: the Case of Denmark', in B. Kohler-Koch and R. Eising (eds), *The Transformation of Governance in the European Union*. London: Routledge, pp. 173–88.

Siedentop, L. (2000) *Democracy in Europe*. London: Penguin.

Simon, R. and J. Lynch (1999) 'A Comparative Assessment of Public Opinion Toward Immigrants and Immigration Policies', *International Migration Review*, vol. 33(2), pp. 455–67.

Sjursen, H. (2000) 'Coping – Or Not Coping – with Change: Norway in European Security Structures', *European Foreign Affairs Review*, vol. 5(4), pp. 539–59.

Smith, A.D. (1992) 'National Identity and the Idea of European Unity', *International Affairs*, vol. 68(1), pp. 55–76.

Smith, B. and W. Wallace (2001) 'Constitutional Deficits of EU Justice and Home Affairs: Transparency, Accountability, and Judicial Control', in J. Monar and W. Wessels (eds), *The European Union after the Treaty of Amsterdam*. London: Continuum, pp. 125–49.

Spruyt, H. (1994) *The Sovereign State and Its Competitors*. Princeton: Princeton University Press.

St. meld nr. 38 (1998–99) 'Tilpasning av Forsvaret til deltakelse i internasjonale operasjoner'.

Steinmo, S., K. Thelen and F. Longstreth (eds) (1992) *Structuring Politics: Historical Institutionalism in Comparative Analysis*. Cambridge: Cambridge University Press.

Steunenberg, B. and F. van Vught (eds) (1997) *Political Institutions and Public Policy: Perspectives on European Decision Making*. Dordrecht: Kluwer Academic Publishers.

Stone Sweet, A. (1999) 'Judicialisation and the Construction of Governance', *Comparative Political Studies*, vol. 32(2), pp. 147–84.

Stone Sweet, A. (2000) *Governing with Judges: Constitutional Politics in Europe*. Oxford: Oxford University Press.

Storper, M. (1997) *The Regional World. Territorial Development in a Global Economy*. New York: Guildford.

Strath, B. (ed.) (2000) *Europe and the Other and Europe as the Other*. Brussels: P.I.E. Peter Lang.

Strazzari, F., and G. Dognini (2000) 'Geopolitica delle mafie jugoslave', *Rivista Limes*, 2, pp. 21–41.

Strøm, K. (2000) 'Parties at the Core of Government', in R. Dalton and M. Wattenberg (eds), *Parties Without Partisans: Political Change in Advanced Industrial Democracies*. Oxford: Oxford University Press, pp. 180–207.

Swedberg, R. (1993) 'Preface', in R. Swedberg (ed.), *Explorations in Economic Sociology*. New York: Russel Sage Foundation, pp. xiii–xxiv.

Taagepera, R. and B. Grofman (1985) 'Rethinking Duverger's Law: Predicting the Effective Number of Parties in Plurality and PR Systems – Parties Minus Issues Equals One', *European Journal of Political Research*, vol. 13(4), pp. 341–52.

Taggart, P. (1998) 'A Touchstone of Dissent: Euro Scepticism in Contemporary Western European Party Systems', *European Journal of Political Research*, vol. 33(3), pp. 363–88.

Takle, M. (2000) 'NATO and the EU's New Security Policies Require New Kinds of Legitimation: A Study of German Argumentation'. Paper presented at the ISSEI conference, Bergen (August).

Tambini, D. (2000) *Universal Internet Access: A Realistic View*. London: Institute for Public Policy Research.

Tanzi, V. (1994) 'Corruption, Governmental Activities, and Markets', *IMF Working Paper*. Washington, DC: International Monetary Fund, WP/94/99.

Tanzi, V. (1998) 'Corruption Around the World', *IMF Staff Papers*, vol. 45(4), pp. 559–94.

Teague, P. (2001) 'Deliberative Governance and EU Social Policy', *European Journal of Industrial Relations*, vol. 7(1), pp. 7–26.

Ten Napel, H.-M. (1999) 'The Netherlands: Resilience Amidst Change', in D. Broughton and M. Donovan (eds), *Changing Party Systems in Western Europe*. London: Pinter, pp. 163–82.

Thompson, D. F. (1993) 'Mediated Corruption: The Case of the Keating Five', *American Political Science Review*, vol. 87(2), pp. 369–81.

Thompson, J. B. (2000) *Political Scandal: Power and Visibility in the Media Age*. Cambridge: Polity.

Tibi, Bassam (1998) *The Challenge of Fundamentalism: Political Islam and the New World Disorder*. Berkeley: University of California Press.

Tilly, C. (1990) *Coercion, Capital, and European States: AD 990–1990.* Oxford: Blackwell.

Topf, R. (1995a) 'Beyond Electoral Participation', in H.-D. Klingemann and D. Fuchs (eds), *Citizens and the State.* Oxford: Oxford University Press, pp. 52–91.

Topf, R. (1995b) 'Electoral Participation', in H.-D. Klingemann and D. Fuchs (eds), *Citizens and the State.* Oxford: Oxford University Press, pp. 27–51.

Transparency International (2000a) 'Bribes to Political Parties an Increasing Threat to Democracy', *Press Release.* Berlin: Transparency International (19 October).

Transparency International (2000b) *Annual Report 2000.* Berlin: Transparency International.

Traxler, F. (1999) 'Wage-Setting Institutions and EMU', in G. Huemer, M. Mesch and F. Traxler (eds), *The Role of Employer Associations and Trade Unions in EMU: Institutional Requirements for European Economic Policies.* Aldershot: Ashgate, pp. 115–35.

Traxler, F. and B. Woitech (2000) 'Transnational Investment and National Labour Market regimes: A Case of "Regime Shopping"?', *European Journal of Industrial Relations*, vol. 6(2), pp. 141–59.

UNCED [United Nations Conference on Environment and Development] (1992) *Agenda 21: A Programme for Action for Sustainable Development.* New York: United Nations.

United Nations Population Division (2000) *Replacement Migration.* UNO: New York.

van Outrive, L. (1998) 'The Disastrous Justice System in Belgium: A Crisis of Democracy?', in P. Gray and P.T' Hart (eds), *Public Policy Disasters in Western Europe.* London: Routledge, pp. 23–38.

Vincent, D. (2000) *The Culture of Secrecy: Britain 1832–1998.* Oxford: Oxford University Press.

Vitorino, A. (2000) Opening speech for the conference on 'Migrations: Scenarios for the 21st Century'. Manuscript (12 July).

Waever, O. (1996) 'European Security Identities', *Journal of Common Market Studies*, vol. 34(1), pp. 103–32.

Wall, D. (1999) *Earth First! and the Anti-Roads Movement: Radical Environmentalism and Comparative Social Movements.* London: Routledge.

Wallace, H. and W. Wallace (eds) (2000) *Policy-Making in the European Union, Fourth Edition.* Oxford: Oxford University Press.

Wanna, J. (1997) 'Managing Budgets', in P. Weller, H. Bakvis and R.A.W. Rhodes (eds), *The Hollow Crown.* London: Macmillan, pp. 148–75.

Ware, A. (1996) *Political Parties and Party Systems.* Oxford: Oxford University Press.

Ware, A. (1998) 'Conclusion', in P. Burnell and A. Ware (eds), *Funding Democratisation.* Manchester: Manchester University Press, pp. 229–43.

Warwick, P. (1994) *Government Survival in Parliamentary Democracies.* Cambridge: Cambridge University Press.

Wattenberg, M.P. (2000) 'The Decline of Party Mobilisation', in R.J. Dalton and M.P. Wattenberg (eds), *Parties Without Partisans: Political Change in*

Advanced Industrial Democracies. Oxford: Oxford University Press, pp. 64–76.

WCED [World Commission on the Environment and Development] (1987) *Our Common Future*. Oxford: Oxford University Press.

Weale, A. (1992) *The New Politics of Pollution*. Manchester University Press.

Weaver, R. K. and B.A. Rockman (eds) (1993) *Do Institutions Matter? Government Capabilities in the United States and Abroad*. Washington, DC: The Brookings Institution.

Webb, P.D. (2000) *The Modern British Party System*. London: Sage Publications.

Webb, P.D., D.M. Farrell and I. Holliday (forthcoming) *Political Parties in Advanced Industrial Democracies*. Oxford: Oxford University Press.

Weller, P. (1997) 'Political Parties and the Core Executive', in P. Weller, H. Bakvis and R.A.W. Rhodes (eds), *The Hollow Crown*. London: Macmillan, pp. 148–75.

Weller, P., H. Bakvis and R.A.W. Rhodes (eds) (1997) *The Hollow Crown*. London: Macmillan.

West European Union (WEU, 1992) 'Western European Union Council of Ministers Petersberg Declaration'. Bonn, 19 June.

West European Union (WEU, 1998) 'Franco-British Summit: Joint Declaration on European Defence'. Saint-Malo, 4 December.

Whine, M. (1999) 'United Kingdom', in J.-Y. Camus (ed.), *Extremism in Europe: 1998 Survey*. Paris: Éditions de l'aube/CERA, pp. 371–84.

Williams, P. (ed.) (1999) *Illegal Immigration and Commercial Sex: The New Slave Trade*. London: Frank Cass.

Williams, R., J. Moran and R. Flanary (eds) (2000) *Corruption in the Developed World*. London: Edward Elgar.

Wilks, S. and M.W. Wright (eds) (1987) *Comparative Government–Industry Relations: Western Europe, the United States and Japan*. Oxford: Clarendon Press.

Wolfers, A. (1952) ' "National Security" as an Ambiguous Symbol', *Political Science Quarterly*, vol. 67(4), pp. 481–502.

Wright, V. and J. Hayward (2000) 'Governing from the Centre: Policy Co-ordination in Six European Core Executives', in R.A.W. Rhodes (ed.), *Transforming British Government, Vol. 2: Changing Roles and Relationships*. London: Macmillan Press in association with Economic and Social Research Council, pp. 27–46.

Ziegler, J. (1998) *Les Seigneurs du crime: Les nouvelles mafias contre la démocratie*. Paris, Seuil.

Zito, A. (2000) *Creating Environmental Policy in the European Union*. London: Macmillan.

Zolberg, A. et al. (1989) *Escape from Violence*. Oxford: Oxford University Press.

Zürn, M. (2000) 'Democratic Governance Beyond the Nation-State: The EU and Other International Institutions', *European Journal of International Relations*, vol. 6(2), pp. 183–221.

Index